CHRISTI GREEN

FRETBOARD THEORY
A
CHORDAL APPROACH

PICK-IT PUBLISHING
1204 N BARLINE CT
NAMPA, ID 83687

http://christigreenstudios.com

PHOTOGRAPHY BY:

AUTHOR, GRANT GREEN, JOSH HUFF, JOHN SINCLAIR

ILLUSTRATIONS AND

COVER DESIGN BY AUTHOR

1204 N BARLINE CT

NAMPA, ID 83687

ISBN: 978-0-9652999-1-6

ISBN: 978-0-9652999-0-9

BIOGRAPHICAL SKETCH

Christi Green is a performing guitarist whose training includes a M.M. degree in classical guitar performance and B.M. degree in jazz guitar performance from Boise State University. Christi has performed in jazz bands, duos, and trios in the Seattle and Nashville areas and currently appears in the Boise Valley as a chord melody soloist, classical guitarist, and instrumentalist/vocalist performing many musical styles.

In addition to performing, Christi teaches guitar and music theory at the college level as she has done since 1983. She composes music for the film and television market and has created the ***Learning for Life*** guitar lesson series at http://christigreenstudios.com.

This book is dedicated to my parents Ron and Shirley, and to my husband Grant for their limitless support of my musical career.

CONTENTS

PART II CHORDS IN FIRST POSITION

PART III MUSIC THEORY

PART IV PLAYING UP THE NECK

PREFACE

Throughout my years as a guitarist I have met many students of guitar, beginners and advanced alike, that have reached a point of frustration with the instrument because of their lack of knowledge in music theory and how it applies to the guitar. This is due in part to the fact that many chord books for the beginner are simply encyclopedias of chord diagrams or take a simple strum and play approach with little or no mention of chord relationships or music theory. On the other hand, books presenting theoretical concepts are often times too advanced for the student's current level. The relative ease of playing simple chords on the instrument can give the illusion that the instrument is simple by nature and in turn, can lead to a misunderstanding of the instrument's complexity and capabilities. The result is a disorganized approach leaving the student with bits and pieces of information rather than a clear concept of how music functions.

The purpose of this book is to provide an organized step by step approach to fretboard theory that will lead to an understanding of how music works from a harmonic (chordal) standpoint. This knowledge will alleviate the guesswork when learning songs by ear, aid in rapid memorization of chord progressions, and will lay the groundwork for chord melody playing and improvisation.

The book approaches the fretboard from a chordal standpoint only; therefore, it is hoped that students using this book will supplement their musical knowledge through note-reading, and technical studies such as scales and arpeggios. Examples are given in both notation and non notation forms when applicable, to accommodate the reader and non reader alike.

The songs and progressions used in this book are to be used as starting points for the basic concepts presented. The student should seek out musical selections of his or her choice to further develop these concepts and give adequate time to the fundamental steps presented. Many concepts are easy to understand; however, to use them effectively requires patience, repetition, and time on the instrument. The exercises that require written work should not be overlooked or taken lightly.

The aid of a good teacher can help in the explanation of more difficult concepts and can help the student pace himself/herself in a reasonable manner. You can find additional help at http://christigreenstudios.com.

1 Preparing To Learn

Choosing A Teacher

A good teacher can save countless hours of practice time by helping the student achieve proper technique and a good working knowledge of music and the guitar. Unfortunately, many who teach guitar are relatively untrained musicians and guitarists themselves and may not give enough attention to areas such as technique, note reading, and music theory. This lack of attention can leave the student ill-equipped to accomplish the goals he has set for himself or provide the tools that allow *learning for life*.

Although there are instructors who are untrained, there are a number of good instructors available. The following steps are pointers to help you find a qualified instructor:

l) Find out who the guitar instructors are in your area. This can be done by calling your local music stores, colleges, and universities.

2) Contact the instructors. Ask them questions about their background, such as: who they've studied with, how long they've been teaching, what styles of music they teach, what is their method or approach to the guitar, music, etc.

3) Find an instructor who teaches technique, music theory, and note reading. These are the essentials for ensuring limitless learning and enjoyment on the guitar.

4) Find out what the instructor charges and how you will be billed. Prices may vary significantly from instructor to instructor. Many instructors who have a higher fee may be well trained, and to the serious guitarist, this may be worth the extra money in the long run. Some instructors charge by the lesson, while others charge monthly. Most instructors will bill you for "no show" lessons.

5) Choose an instructor with a positive personality. Good instructors are positive in their approach to learning and will give criticism in a constructive manner.

6) Choose an instructor who is reliable. Most reliable instructors will have a predesignated time for your lesson each week and should be consistent in keeping their appointment with you. This is important for your progress because it helps you maintain a daily practice routine and ensures that mistakes will be caught early before they become a permanent part of your playing. Many instructors are also "gigging musicians" and may need to miss or reschedule from time to time. Find out up front what you can expect in terms of a consistent schedule.

7) For more information visit http://christigreenstudios.com

Practice Tips

Many professionals make guitar playing look easy, but in reality, it takes a lot of hard work and dedication. The following steps are pointers to help you with your practice sessions.

1) Set up a designated practice area and if possible, leave your guitar out of its case. Valuable time is often wasted by rounding up books, instruments, picks, chairs, etc. You will be more apt to practice if all your belongings are easily accessible, and you will pick up your instrument more often if it is left out of the case.

2) Find a minimum of 30 -45 minutes a day to dedicate to lesson materials. Nothing can replace quality time on the instrument. This time can be divided into two sessions if needed.

3) Schedule daily practice times. Having a set time to practice every day turns good intentions into a dedicated daily routine. In other words, if you do not make time for it, you will not have time for it. You don't need to practice at the same time every day; however, you need to allow time to practice everyday. Look at your routine for the day and block out the desired practice time. Try to practice when you are most alert.

4) Have a plan. Deciding what to do first every time you sit down also wastes time. You will get more out of your time and you will be more likely to practice if you have an agenda for each practice session. Plan what you will do the following day at the end of each practice session.

5) Put it in writing. If you are not willing to commit on paper to practice times and agendas, you will most likely have minimal success achieving your goals.

"If you do not make time for it, you will not have time for it!"

Your weekly practice schedule may look something like this. You can write down the general time you spent doing each item. When you are finished with your day total up your time for the day. When you are finished for the week total up your time spent on each item. That way you can quickly see where your time was spent.

Practice times for the week:

Monday	6:00 - 6:30	Friday	6:00 - 6:30
Tuesday	8:00 - 8:45	Saturday	10:00 - 11:00
Wednesday	6:00 - 6:45	Sunday	3:30 - 4:00
Thursday	off		

	Mon.	Tues.	Wed.	Thurs.	Fri.	Sat.	Sun.	total
warm-ups *scales*								
review *primary chord groups*								
new *rh picking patterns*								
memorize *bass notes*								
New Song								
total								

Notes:

Useful Tools For The Practice Room

Whether you have a dedicated corner or an entire room, there are items you may want to acquire to make your practice time more successful and fun!

Guitar Stand. As mentioned under practice tips, I strongly encourage you to keep your guitar out of it's case. To keep your guitar safe from bumps and falls a guitar stand is a must. There are several kinds and brands available. Most stands will fold up for easy transportation and storage. Or, you may prefer a wall mount hanger. This is somewhat permanent but it can be a great alternative to the floor stand if you need to keep it away from little hands!

guitar stand

music stand

Music Stand. A music stand is invaluable. In addition to positioning the music in the optimal position, it can store your books, pencil, and practice schedules keeping everything you need handy.

If you will be sitting, an **armless chair** and a **foot stool** will help you obtain a good sitting position (see page 10). These have adjustable heights and collapse for easy storage and transportation.

All of the items mentioned above come in many different styles and materials. The most readily available are made of metal. If you are going to be transporting your items often or are concerned about durability, I would recommend this material. If you prefer a more organic look, these items are also available in many types of wood and finishes.

A **metronome** and a **guitar tuner** are handy gadgets to have on hand too. (These are discussed in the next chapter.)

For maintaining your guitar you may want to have **guitar polish**, a **polish cloth, extra strings,** and a **string winder** on hand.

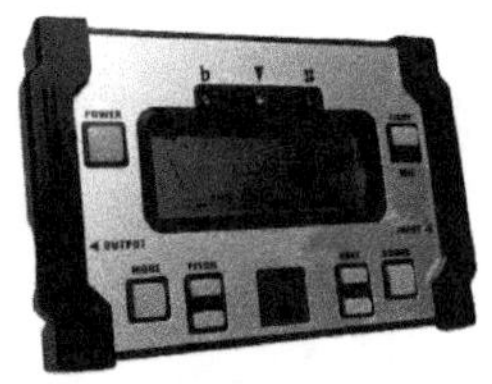

guitar tuner

hint: If it's near your birthday or Christmas you might want keep this book open to this page and strategically place it where it could be read by others - *wink, wink!*

2 Guitar Basics

There are several types of guitars to choose from in today's market. The classical, acoustic, and solid-body electric guitars are among the most popular types .

While the basics of guitar playing can be achieved on most any guitar, the type of music you desire to play will determine what type of guitar will best suit your needs. Eventually, you may end up owning several guitars to accommodate the various styles of music you play.

The ***classical guitar*** uses nylon strings and is mainly used for finger-style playing. Classical music, jazz and pop arrangements are often played on this instrument. Traditionally, this instrument is used for finger-style playing only. This instrument is often a good choice for beginners because its body style allows the guitar to be easily positioned and the nylon strings are easily depressed without causing too much soreness to the left-hand fingers.

The ***acoustic guitar*** uses steel strings and is also referred to as the steel-string guitar. The ***pick (flat-pick or plectrum),*** is used as well as the finger-style approach. Country, folk, and folk-rock music are often played on this instrument. This instrument is very popular because of its versatility and availability; however, some body-styles such as the dreadnought shape are large and make proper positioning of the instrument and hands awkward for the beginning player. The steel strings are harder for the left-hand fingers to depress and often cause soreness at first. With time and careful attention given to technique and instrument position, these problems can be overcome.

The ***solid-body electric guitar*** is made out of a solid piece of wood and needs amplification for sound. The pick is used primarily on this instrument. Country, rock, and heavy metal music are often played on this instrument. The body shape and narrow neck can make proper positioning of the instrument and hands awkward for the beginning player. Because the tone and volume are produced electronically, the student may develop a weak right-hand approach in plucking the strings. With proper attention given to these areas these problems can be overcome.

The following pictures show the three basic types of guitars described above. The parts of the guitar, or the anatomy of the guitar, are labeled to help you to use this book more effectively as well as to communicate with other guitarists, repairmen, etc.

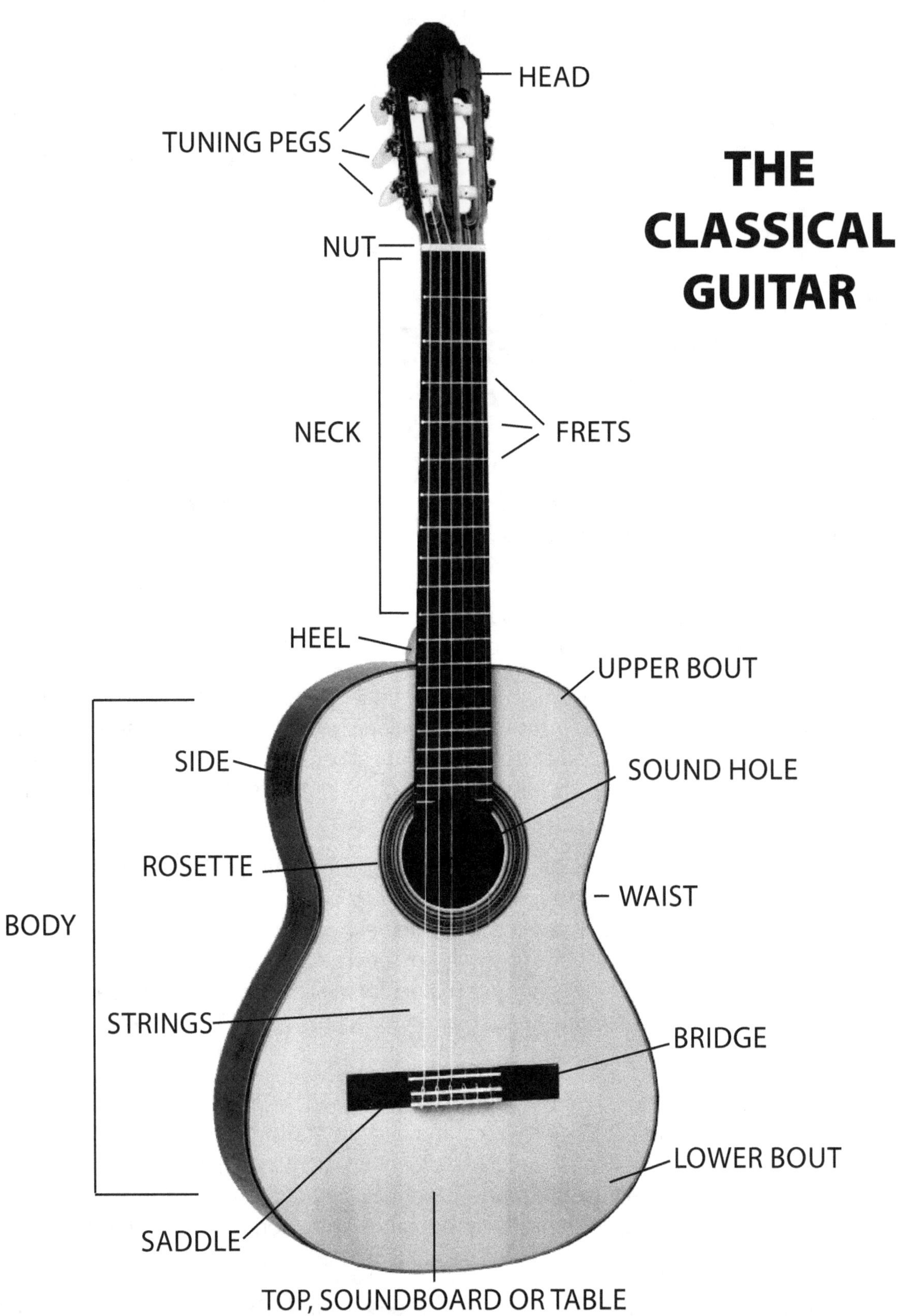
HEAD
TUNING PEGS
THE CLASSICAL GUITAR
NUT
NECK
FRETS
HEEL
UPPER BOUT
SIDE
SOUND HOLE
ROSETTE
WAIST
BODY
STRINGS
BRIDGE
LOWER BOUT
SADDLE
TOP, SOUNDBOARD OR TABLE

THE ACOUSTIC GUITAR

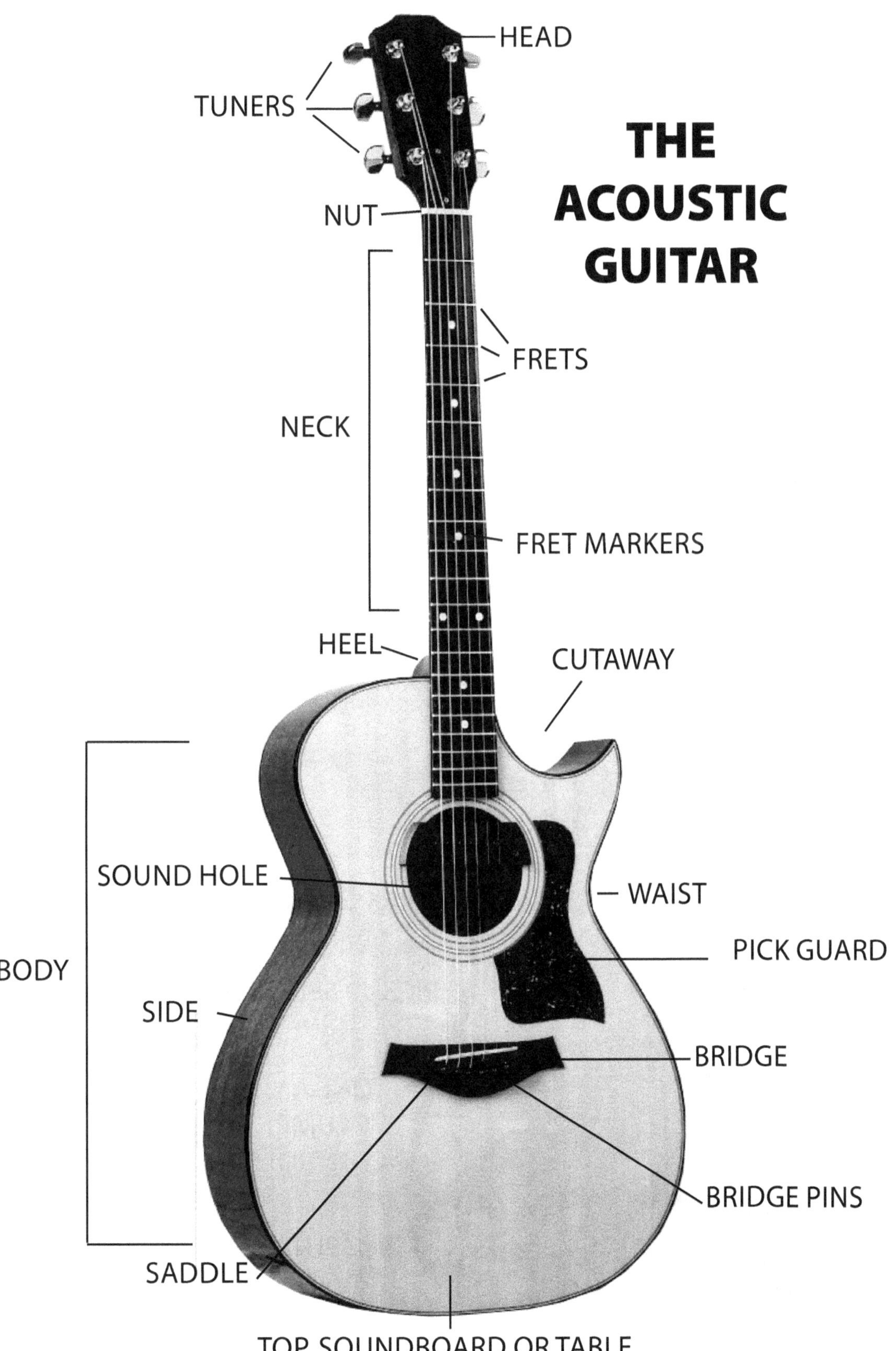

THE SOLID-BODY ELECTRIC GUITAR

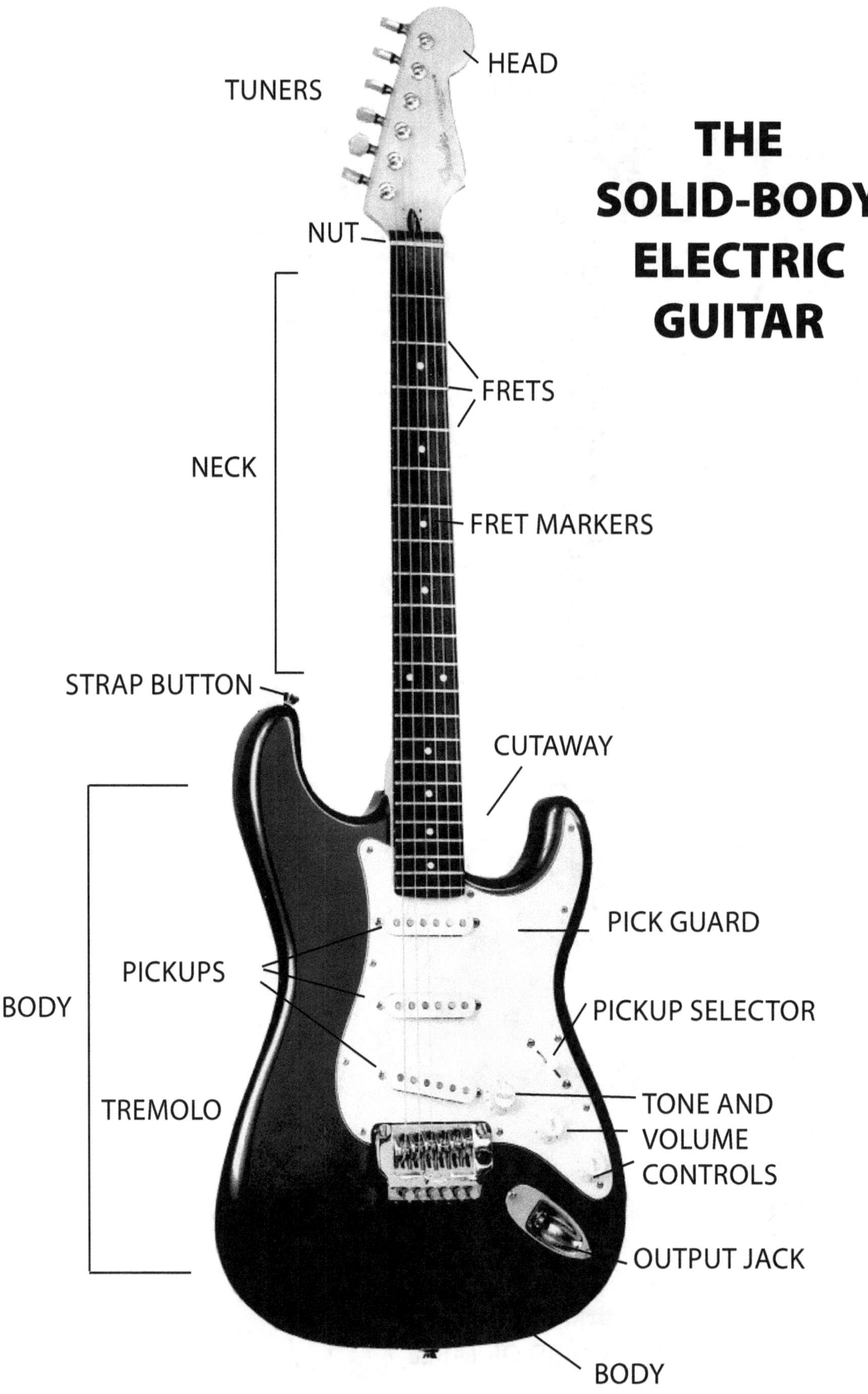

TECHNIQUE

Whether playing classical, heavy metal, jazz, rock, or country music, good technique is essential or the promotion of clean and efficient playing and the prevention of physical side effects such as tendinitis or carpal tunnel. In the paragraphs that follow, some basic points in achieving proper technique will be discussed; however, it is a good idea to seek out a good teacher who can help you spot problem areas. This will foster many good habits right from the start. (If you are a subscriber to http://christigreenstudios.com you will find many helpful videos on technique.)

YOUR INSTRUMENT

A properly functioning instrument will do wonders for your technique. To make sure the instrument is playable:

1) Check the ***action*** that is, make sure the strings are elevated properly off the neck. Generally they should be the same distance off the neck from the first fret to the last; however, some ***luthiers*** will intentionally build the guitar so the strings gradually rise off the neck with the highest point being at the highest fret. The strings should press down easily at any point on the neck. If they do not, it may be worth it to have a qualified repairman or luthier look at your instrument and make some adjustments.

2) If you play an acoustic or electric guitar, a light gauge string can make playing easier. Light gauge strings are a little easier to press down and don't tire the left hand as quickly as heavy gauge strings. If you are changing string gauges, make sure your action is adjusted properly so the guitar plays well and the strings don't buzz when any of the strings are depressed.

SITTING POSITION

Proper sitting position aids in the relaxation of the hands and fingers. If sitting properly, the body holds the guitar in place, freeing the hands to play. The ideal sitting position is the one used by classical guitarists and is easiest to achieve with a classical guitar. To accomplish this, find a comfortable armless chair and a ***foot-stool***, then do the following steps.

1) Sit on the edge of the chair and place the footstool under the left foot.

2) Place the waist of the guitar on the left thigh.

3) Make sure the instrument is parallel with the body and not leaning up against the chest in a slanted position.

4) Place the upper bout against the chest and the lower bout toward the right knee.

5) Place the right forearm on the side of the guitar making sure your right shoulder is relaxed. This will position the right hand over the sound hole and will keep the guitar from slipping out of place.

6) Angle the guitar so the head is shoulder height or higher. Your body size and the length of your arms will help to determine the exact angle for the guitar.

sitting position, classical style

STANDING POSITION

Electric players and some acoustic players may find standing more comfortable than sitting due to the wide variety of shapes and sizes found with these types of guitars. To achieve a good standing position, use a guitar strap and follow these steps:

standing position

1) Make sure your guitar has a strap button located at the heel of the guitar or on the bout for electrics. (Do not tie the strap onto the head of the instrument. Doing so interferes with the position of the guitar and gets in the way of the left hand.)

2) Adjust the strap so your left hand can reach easily around the neck without straining. The body of the guitar should be around the abdomen area or higher.

3) Make sure the head of the guitar is positioned shoulder height or higher.

RIGHT-HAND

The choice to play with a ***plectrum*** (pick) or fingers depends on your own individual needs. You should make a choice and stick with it for a while. Eventually, both skills should be developed.

The Pick

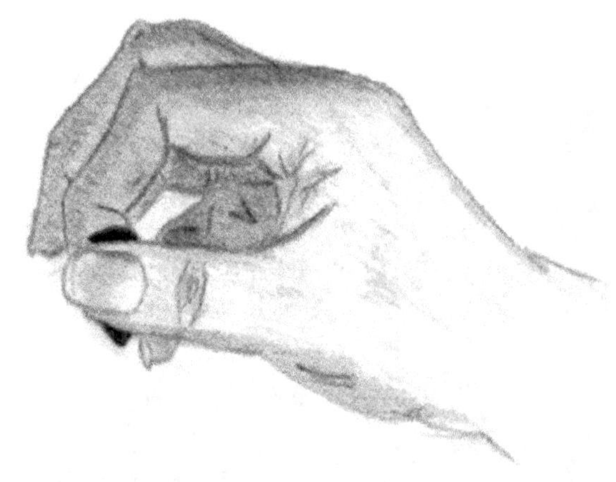

the pick

The pick is held between the thumb and index finger in the right hand.

1) Curl the index finger so it forms a three-sided box.

2) Place the pick on the last joint of the index finger and cover it with the thumb. Most of the pick should remain between the thumb and index finger with just enough of the pick showing to get the job done.

3) Angle the pick toward the floor and strike all of the strings beginning with the sixth. This movement should come from the wrist, not the arm. This will allow more control over the pick.

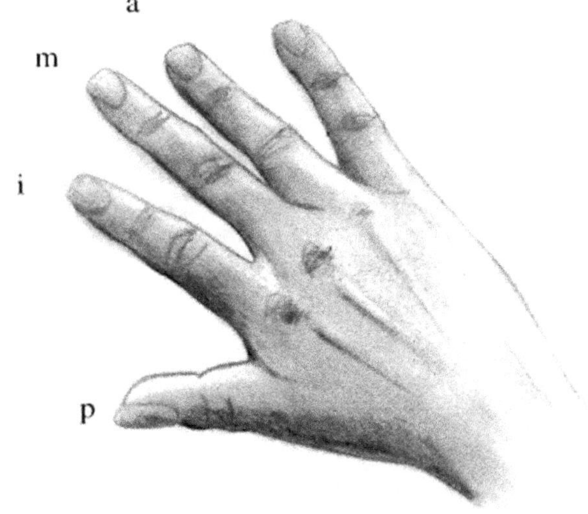

right-hand fingers

Finger-style

Finger-style utilizes the thumb, index, middle, and ring fingers in the right hand. In this book the classical names will be given to the right hand fingers. The letters are taken from the latin names for the fingers as follows: **thumb (pollex) = p, index = i, middle (medius) = m,** and **ring (annularis) = a.** In general, **p** usually plays strings *four, five, and six;* and the fingers play *strings one, two, and three.*

When striking all the strings with **p**, the thumb should remain straight. The movement should come from the wrist, not the arm.

When striking a single note with the **p, p** should move from the large muscle. It should start on the string, stay straight, and come to rest on the side of the index finger.

In either application, the string should be struck by the left side of **p.**

When striking the string with the fingers, the left side of the fingertip should be used and the finger should move freely toward the palm of the hand. (This is called the ***free stroke.***)

Placing the fingers on the strings just before it is time to play will improve tone and accuracy. (This placement is often referred to as the ***planted*** or ***prepared stroke*** among classical guitarists.)

LEFT-HAND

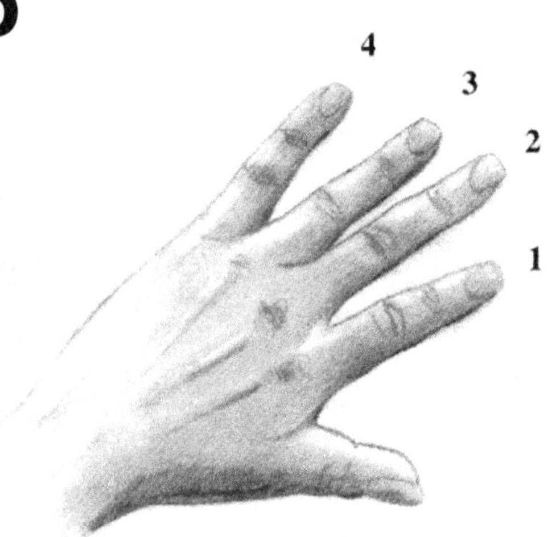

The fingers in the left hand are numbered as follows:

index =1, middle =2, ring =3, and pinky =4.

Positioning the left hand correctly is important in the production of clear notes, rhythm, and speed. The following steps will ensure a good left hand position.

1) Relax the left hand and observe that the fingers are curled and the thumb is straight. This is how your hand should look and feel when you play.

2) Reach the hand to the neck keeping the elbow close to your body.

3) Place the thumb behind the neck so it is parallel with the frets. If you are learning on a classical guitar you will want the thumb about 3/4 of the way up the neck. For acoustic and electric guitars the thumb is almost to the top but never bent over the top. The thumb should remain straight (not bending from the joint), and should be resting on the thumb print.

4) Place all the fingertips on the sixth string, (the string that is the thickest). The finger span does not need to cover all four frets, but should rest comfortably on the string.

5) Align fingers 2 and 3 across from the thumb. This will place the thumb in the center of the fingers, giving each finger equal leverage against the thumb.

6) Squeeze your thumb and fingertips together lightly. Each fingertip should balance equally against the thumb.

7) Do not move your thumb down toward the floor, but keep it in place as you move your fingers to the fifth string, then to four, three, etc. Now work your way back to the sixth string, beginning with the first string, then to two, three, etc. When working back, make sure your wrist remains under the neck of the guitar, not lifted outward beyond the neck. On each string the fingers should feel balanced against the thumb just as they did in the exercise above.

Proper left-hand position.

Notice the knuckles are parallel with the neck.

TUNING

Learning to tune your instrument is an essential part of playing. At first tuning your instrument may seem impossible, but because hearing and matching pitches are *learned processes*, with practice and patience you will become proficient at tuning. Two different tuning methods will be introduced: open tuning and harmonic tuning. Open tuning is easier or the left hand to finger but harder for the ear to hear. The opposite is true for harmonic tuning.

Tuning Tools

There are many types of devices on the market used for tuning stringed instruments. Pitch pipes and tuning forks are helpful to ensure an accurate starting pitch. Battery-operated tuners are also available and provide very precise tuning. It is suggested that if a tuner is used, it be used for checking the tuning you have done by ear. This will allow you to develop an ear for tuning and still benefit from an accurately tuned instrument.

Open String Tuning

*Open string tuning is probably the easiest to finger but not necessarily the easiest for the ear to hear because of the lower pitches involved. Open string tuning requires that the sixth string be tuned to the pitch E. A tuning fork, pitch pipe, or low E note on the piano will work. Once this string is in tune do the following steps:

1) Depress the sixth string at the fifth fret.

2) Play the sixth string then the open fifth string. Compare the pitches of the two strings.

3) Adjust the open fifth string until it matches the pitch of the sixth string.

4) Once the fifth string is in tune, depress the fifth fret of the fifth string and compare it to the open fourth string.

5) Adjust the open fourth string until its pitch matches that of the fifth string.

6) Continue this fretted string to open string relationship for the remaining strings.

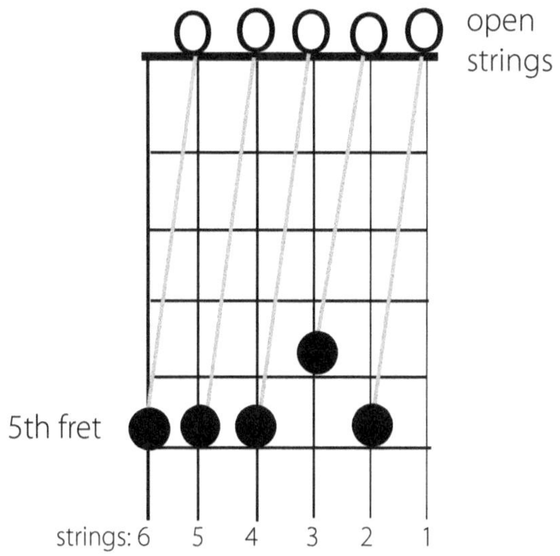

open strings

5th fret

strings: 6 5 4 3 2 1

7) The fifth fret is always used except when tuning the second string. When tuning the second string, the fourth fret of the third string must be used.

*Open string means no lrft-hand fingers are used.

HARMONIC TUNING

Another method of tuning is by harmonics. This type of tuning is a little more difficult for the left hand to achieve, but because of the high pitches it is much easier to hear. There are several different approaches that can be used; however, just one will be discussed here. A tuning fork at the pitch **A = 440 hz** is recommended for this method of tuning.

The first step is to produce a ***harmonic.*** A harmonic is created when the string is touched (but not depressed) over a fret. The harmonics used for this tuning method are found at the fifth and seventh frets. To produce a harmonic go to the fourth string, seventh fret. Touch directly over the seventh fret while plucking near the bridge with the right hand. As soon as you have plucked the string, move your left hand finger out of the way. You should hear a high, bell-like tone. It may take you a few tries to produce a good clean harmonic, but keep working at it until it becomes easy. Once you can produce harmonics, use the following method for tuning:

1) Tune the fourth string, seventh fret to A =440 Hz.

2) Compare the fifth string, fifth fret, to the fourth string, seventh fret. Adjust the fifth string until it is in tune with the fourth string.

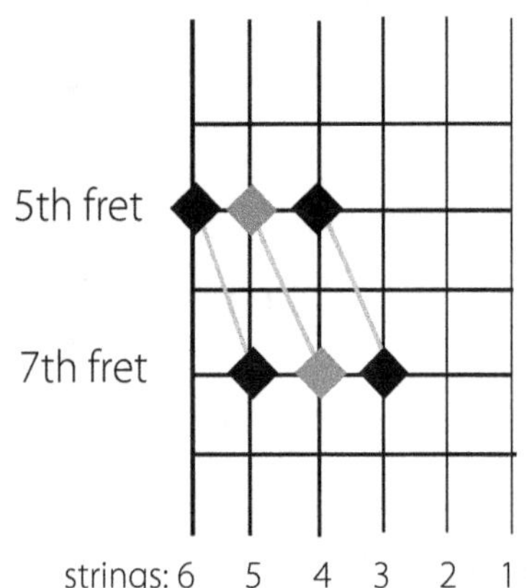

3) Compare the sixth string, fifth fret, to the fifth string, seventh fret. Adjust the sixth string until it is in tune with the fifth string.

4) Compare the fourth string, fifth fret, to the third string, seventh fret. Adjust the third string until it is in tune with the fourth string.

5) To tune the second string, play the harmonic at the seventh fret of the sixth string and compare it to the open second string. Adjust the second string until it is in tune with the sixth string.

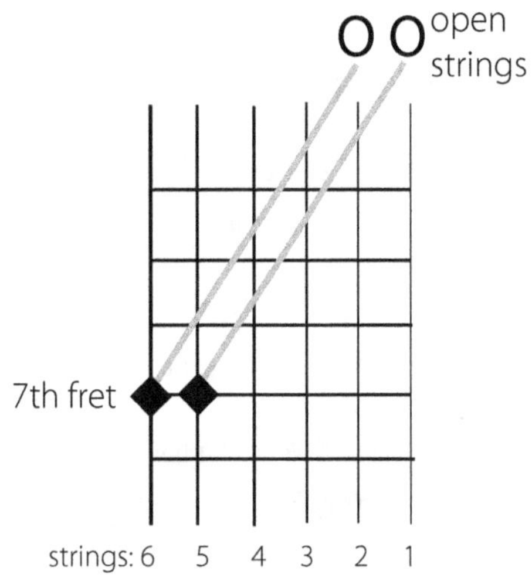

6) To tune the first string, play the harmonic at the seventh fret of the fifth string and compare it to the open first string. Adjust the first string until it is in tune with the fifth string.

7) The first and second strings can be fine tuned by comparing the second string, fifth fret, to the first string, seventh fret.

3 Music Basics

Rudiments Of Music

The rudiments of music can be divided into two parts: ***pitch*** and ***value***.

Pitch

Pitches are indicated by symbols called ***notes***. Every note has a head and some have stems and flags.

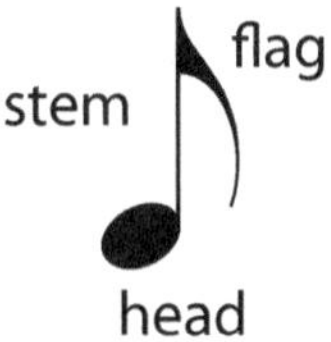

Each note is given an alphabetical name of **A, B, C, D, E, F, or G.**

The notes are placed on a ***staff.*** The staff consists of five lines and four spaces.

staff

Note heads placed on the line are called line notes.

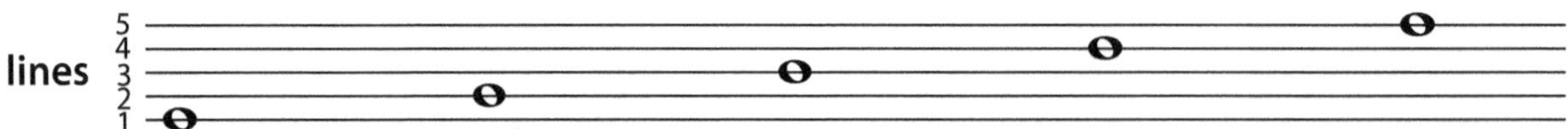

Note heads placed in the spaces are called space notes.

Ledger lines *(leger lines)* extend the range of the staff. They can be added above the staff to accommodate higher notes or below the staff to accommodate lower notes. Just like the staff, ledger lines create both line and space notes.

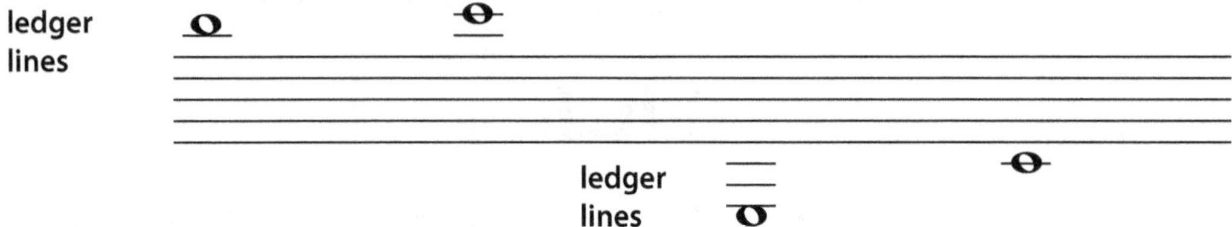

The ***G or Treble Clef sign*** is located at the beginning of the staff. This sign tells us which lines and spaces get which alphabetical names. The treble clef circles or scrolls around the second line. The second line is always named **G** hence the name the ***G clef.*** The space above the second line is called **A**. The line above a is **B**, the next space is **C** and so on forward through the alphabet.

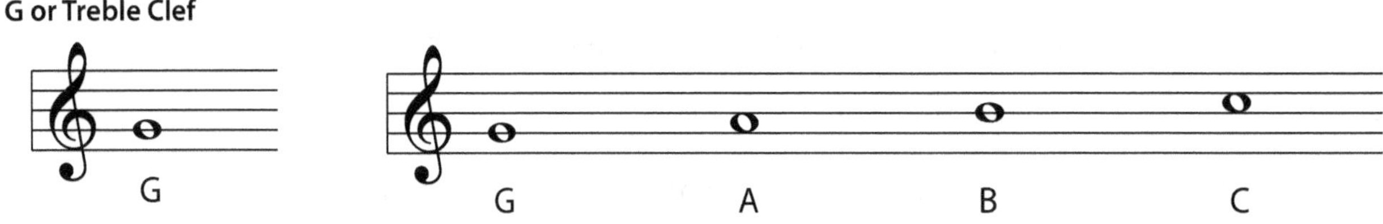

As we descend, the space below G is F the line below F is E the space below E is D and so on backward through the alphabet.

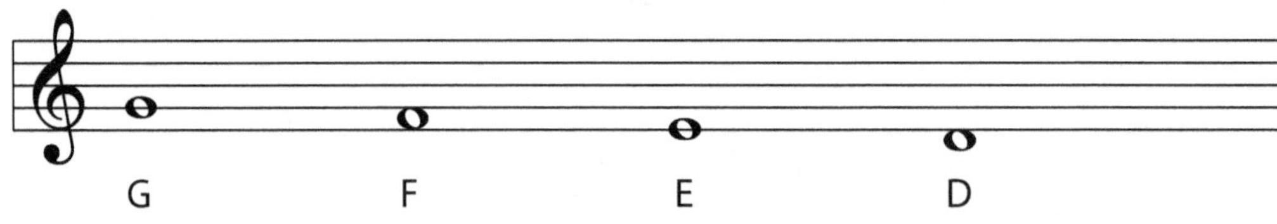

So we can conclude that when ascending on the staff the notes move line, space, line, space *forward* through the alphabet and when descending the notes move line, space, line, space *backward* through the alphabet.

Value

Values indicate how long a note or ***rest*** should be held. Notes represent sounds and rests represent silence. The most common values are as follows:

Note	Rest
whole note	whole rest
half note	half rest
quarter note	quarter rest
eighth note	eighth rest
sixteenth note	sixteenth rest

The chart below is an easy way to see how the note values compare. The arabic numeral listed with each note represents that note in number form. This will become important when we discuss time signatures.

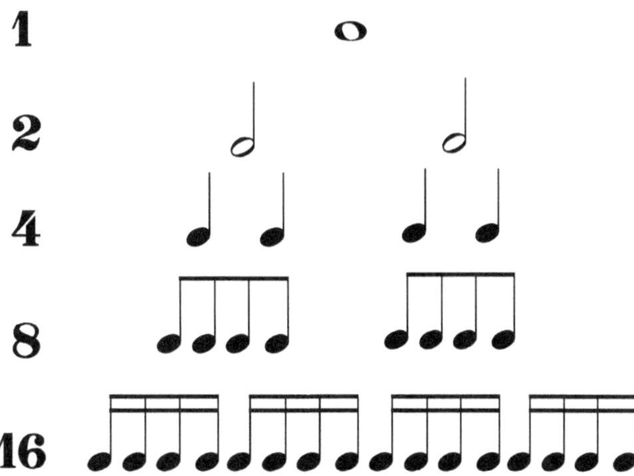

Notes are grouped together by using ***measures***. Measures are created by ***bar lines*** which intersect the staff vertically.

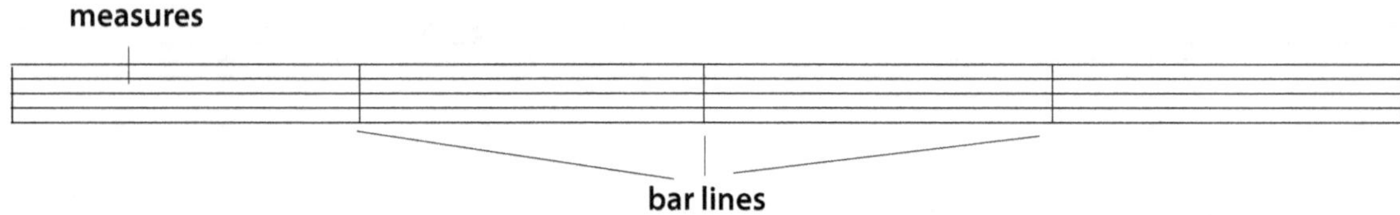

To mark the end of a section and the beginning of a new one within the music, two thin ***double bar lines*** are used. To mark the end of a piece of music, an ***ending bar line*** consisting of one thin line and one thick line is used.

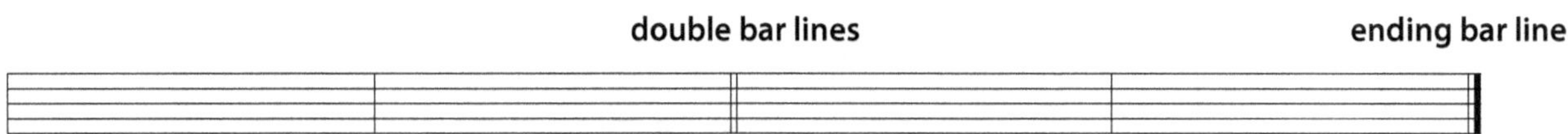

Repeat signs look like ending bar lines but they include two dots as shown. If there is a reverse repeat sign it directs us to repeat what is in between the two repeat signs.

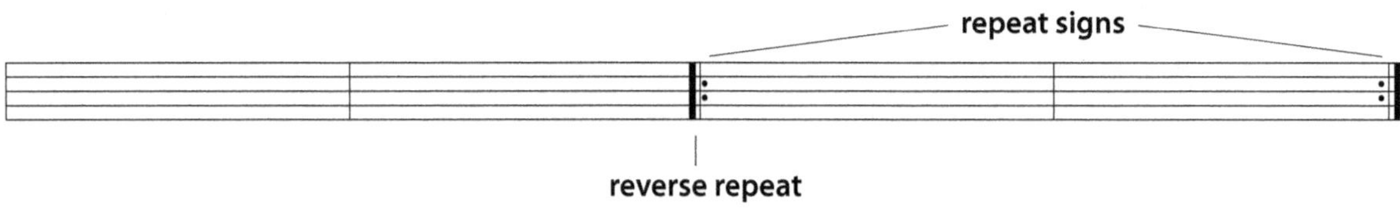

If there is only one repeat sign, it turns us back to the beginning.

beginning

Time Signatures

A ***time signature*** or ***meter signature*** consists of two numbers and is found after the treble clef sign.

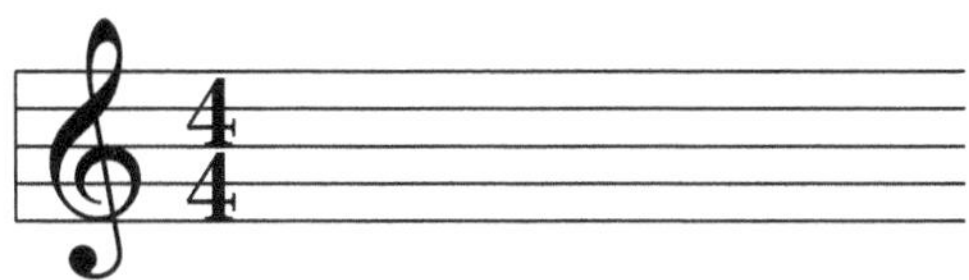

The top number shows how many beats or counts there will be before starting over with a new measure. For example, if the top number is four, count to four then start over with one again:

4 1 2 3 4-1 2 3 4 - etc.
4

The bottom number indicates the value of each beat. If the bottom number is four, then the value of each beat is equal to a quarter-note. (See the number and note chart on page 19.)

4
4 = ♩

The time signature 4/4 means that there will be four quarter-notes in every measure or, notes or rests that equal the **value** of four quarter-notes.

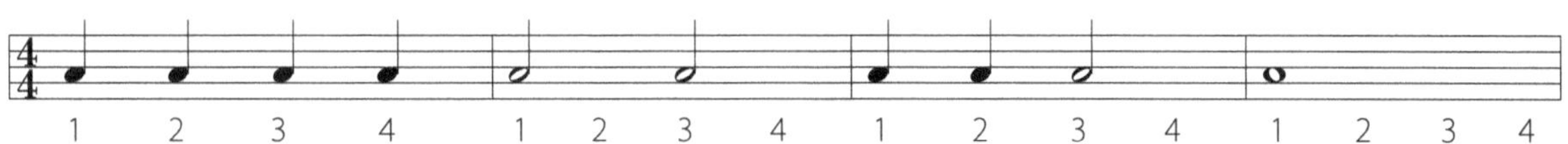

The time signature 4/4 is also known as ***common time*** and is expressed like this:

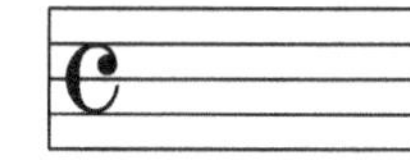

Other time signatures with the bottom number of 4 often used are 3/4 and 2/4.

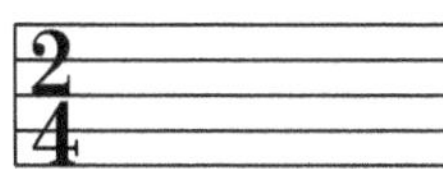

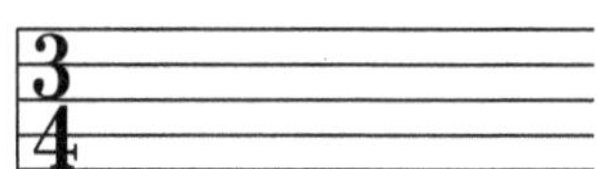

Dotted Notes

A dot to the right of the note-head increases the value of that note by half. For example, a half-note in 3/4 or 4/4 time is equal to two counts or beats. A dot would increase the note by one more count for a total of three counts.

In 3/4 time a dotted half note would take up an entire measure.

2 counts + 1 count = 3 counts

dotted half = 3 counts

We can dot any note value; however, dotting smaller note values like the quarter note can be a little trickier to count at first. This is because adding half the value of a quarter note creates a value that includes a *partial beat. Let's look at this closer.

1 & + 1 = 1 & 2

dotted quarter-note = 1 1/2 counts

What is missing to complete beat two is the '&'. Usually a dotted quarter will be followed by an eighth note to complete the beat.

*The process of dividing the beat into smaller units is called subdividing. If you are unfamiliar with this process you can learn more by logging in to http://christigreenstudios.com

PART 2
Chords In First Position

4 Playing Chords

READING A CHORD DIAGRAM

A chord diagram is a diagram of the guitar neck. The lines running horizontal across the page represent the frets. The uppermost line is the nut.

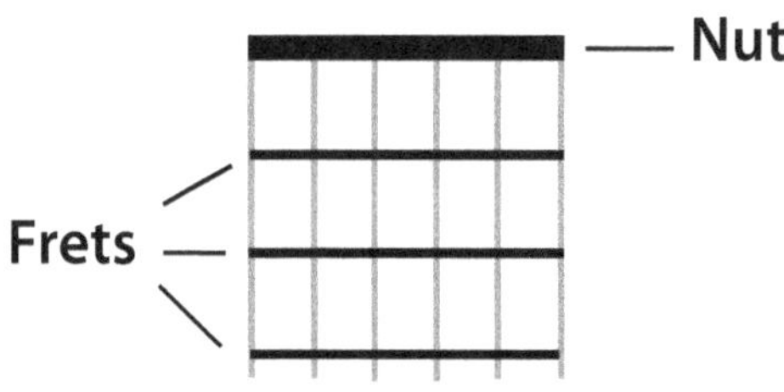

The lines running vertically represent the strings. The sixth string is on the left side; the first, on the right.

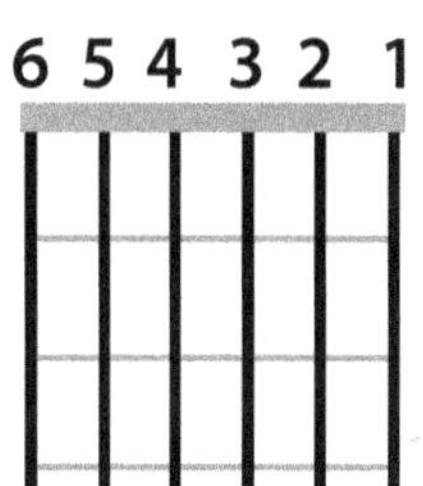

The dots indicate where the left hand fingers go. The numbers represent the left-hand fingers. The '**o**' tells us that string will be played **open** meaning there are no left-hand fingers needed.

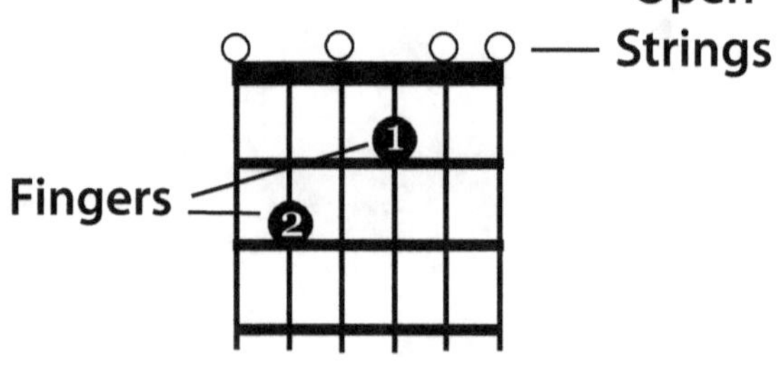

o = open string

1 = first (index) finger

2 = second (middle) finger

3 = third (ring) finger

4 = fourth (pinky) finger

Some chords do not use all the strings. The strings we want to avoid playing are marked with an 'X'.

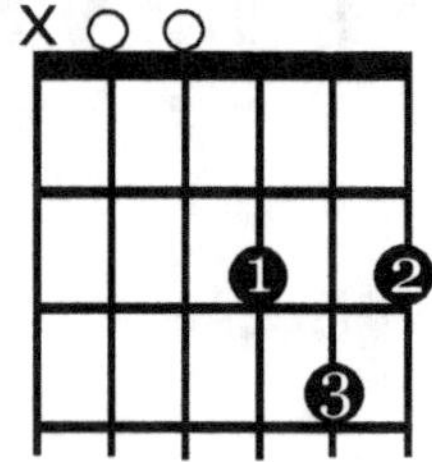

Playing the E7 Chord

Exercise 4.1

The following chord is an E7 chord. To play this, place your first finger on the third string first fret and your second finger on the fifth string second fret.

With your right-hand thumb (p) or pick, strum all the strings. You've just played your first chord!

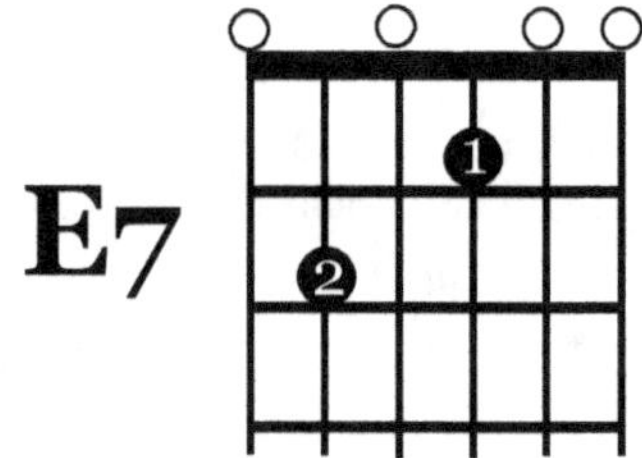

Exercise 4.2

1) Strum all the strings.

2) Pluck each string one at a time starting with the sixth. Listen for squeaks, buzzes or strings that are not sounding.

3) Adjust your left-hand fingers so they are out of the way of the other strings and are close to the frets. (You don't need to squeeze excessively, just enough to get the job done.)

4) Strive for a good clean sound. It may not happen immediately, but with enough persistence and practice you will achieve your goal!

5 Primary Chords

A piece of music will use a variety of chords, usually three or more. These chords will sound good when played together in the same piece or song. This is because the chords belong to a group or family. In other words they come from a common tonal center or key. We will learn more about why chords belong together in later chapters.

The chord groupings in this chapter are referred to as the ***Primary Chords***. Primary chords are found in many styles of music like Folk, Rock, Country, Blues, Hymns, and Carols. Because these chords are found in so many musical styles it is beneficial to learn them in groups. By learning chords in this way, you will be able to:

1) move your fingers more efficiently from one chord to another.

2) learn and memorize songs faster.

3) pick up songs by ear.

The A Group

Primary chord groups are named after the first chord in the group. As you can see 'A' is the first chord in the group so we refer to this chord grouping as the **A group**. We could also say we are playing in the key of A, meaning the tonal center starts with the **A** pitch.

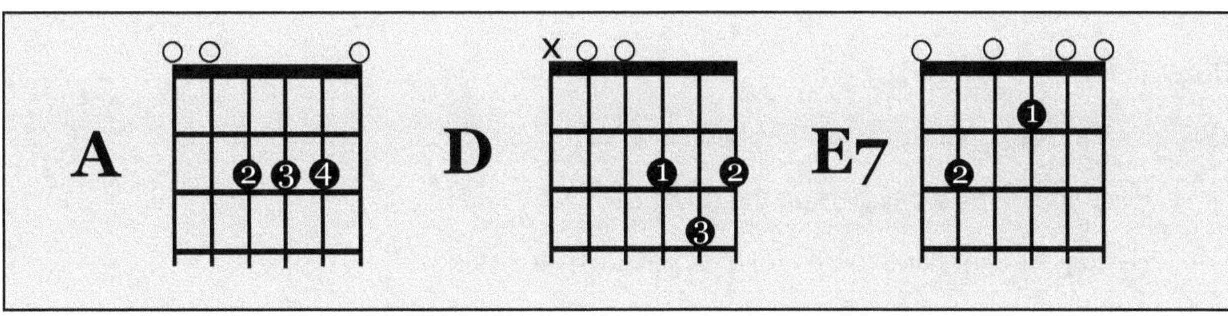

Remember the **X** in the D chord diagram means to avoid playing the sixth string.

Learning Chord Shapes

Exercise 5.1

In order to achieve success you must practice in a way that will give you good results. This is where proper sitting and hand positions really come into play. Here are a few technique tips to get you started.

- Make sure you are sitting or standing properly. (Refer to chapter 2.)
- Place the left-hand thumb so it is straight up and down like a fret. It should be centered in between the first and second fret area.
- Place your fingers on the neck as shown in the chord diagram. DO NOT let them collapse or buckle from the last finger joint. DO keep them curled with the fingertips contacting the string. This will keep them up and out of the way of other strings.
- With your right-hand pluck each string individually listening for a good clear sound.
- If you hear a squeak or buzzing sound you may not have your fingers close enough to the frets or you may not be applying enough pressure to the string. (Be careful not to squeeze in excess as this can lead to a very tired hand and really sore fingers). Experiment with your finger placement strategies until you get a good clean sound.

Exercise 5.2

The next step is to practice picking up the left-hand fingers then replacing them on the strings using the same chord shape. This will help you to grab chords easily because your fingers will start to function as a unit. Follow the steps below for each chord.

- Start by memorizing the chord. If you've worked out Exercise 5.1 you probably already have this done!
- Release your finger pressure and lift your fingers slightly away from the strings while maintaining the same chord shape.
- Set your fingers back on the strings.
- Try this process over and over for each chord until your fingers can easily be placed as a group. You can also increase the distance you lift your fingers from the strings.

Exercise 5.3

Once Exercise 5.2 is going well get the right-hand involved:

- Place your left-hand fingers on the strings.
- Using your right-hand thumb (p) or a pick, strum the strings.
- Lift the left-hand fingers.
- Repeat!

You will want to apply these exercises to every chord you learn. At first this may be difficult and time consuming but as your fingers learn to coordinate and work as a unit, new chord shapes will come quickly and easily.

Be patient. If you start to get frustrated set your instrument aside and try again later. The "I'm going to sit here until I get this" approach usually causes a great deal of frustration with the least results.

Be persistent. You will have greater success faster if you dedicate a few minutes each day to chord playing rather than to try to learn everything in one sitting. Have your guitar out of it's case and pick it up several times a day for just a few minutes at a time.

Moving From Chord To Chord

The Metronome

Now that you are having success with the A group chords it's time to practice moving from one chord to another. This is best achieved by maintaining steady beat.

There is a device called a ***metronome*** that will help you keep time. There are a few different kinds of metronomes available. The old swing arm type, the quartz metronome, and the digital to name a few. There are even metronome apps. available for smart phones.

What a metronome does is provide a steady click or beat. We can set the metronome to maintain a slow pace, medium pace or fast pace. In music we call this pace the ***tempo.*** The lower the number the slower the pace or tempo.

swing arm metronome

Moving the weight up and down on the arm changes the tempo. The higher the weight the slower the tempo.

These metronomes have to be wound to work and can slow down when it gets near the end of the wind.

Changing tempo is easy on a quartz metronome. Just turn the dial clockwise for a faster tempo. They also display a light along with the beat.

Some metronomes also show a different color and sound for beat one, which I find extremely useful.

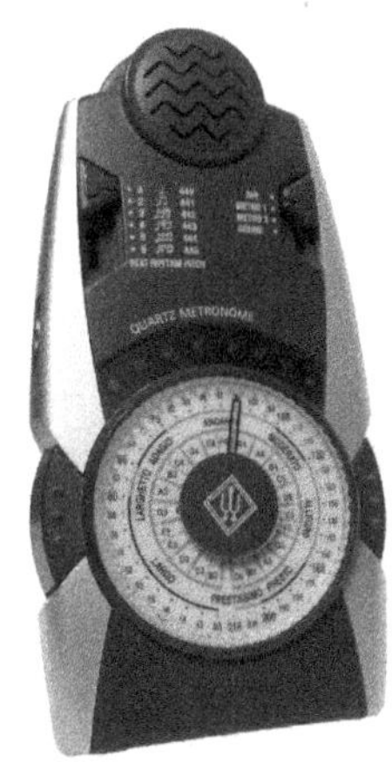

quartz metronome

Using a metronome brings consistency to practice.

- It allows you to practice at the same pace over and over.
- You don't have to guess at how fast you practiced the day before.
- It easily points out when you have fallen behind or are going too fast. (The very thing we need to know yet at the same time can be the most annoying.)
- It helps measure improvement. If you write down your starting tempo and date, later you can compare it to your new faster tempo.

Exercise 5.4

We want to use the metronome as we practice switching from chord to chord. Our first goal is to switch back and fourth between the A and E7 chords. We are going to do this by counting eight counts in between the chords. The slash mark at the beginning of each measure indicates a strum on beat one.

- Set your metronome to a slow pace, between 60 and 70 b.p.m. (beats per minute).
- Finger the A chord.
- Begin counting to eight saying the number with the click of the metronome.
- When you reach beat one again strum the A chord.
- Keep counting and move your fingers to the E7 chord and strum on beat one.
- Keep counting and move your fingers back to A strumming once again on beat one.
- Repeat this process until this becomes easy to do!

Ex. 5.4 a

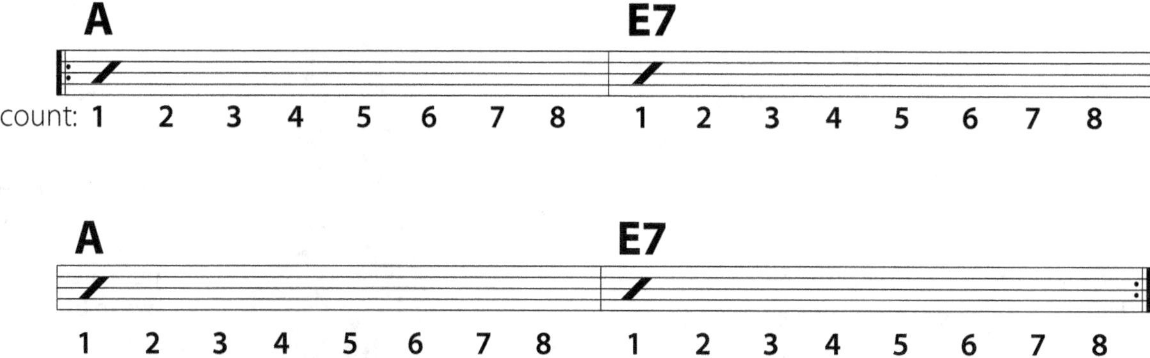

Using the same method you did for A and E7 above, try switching between the A and the D chords.

Ex. 5.4 b

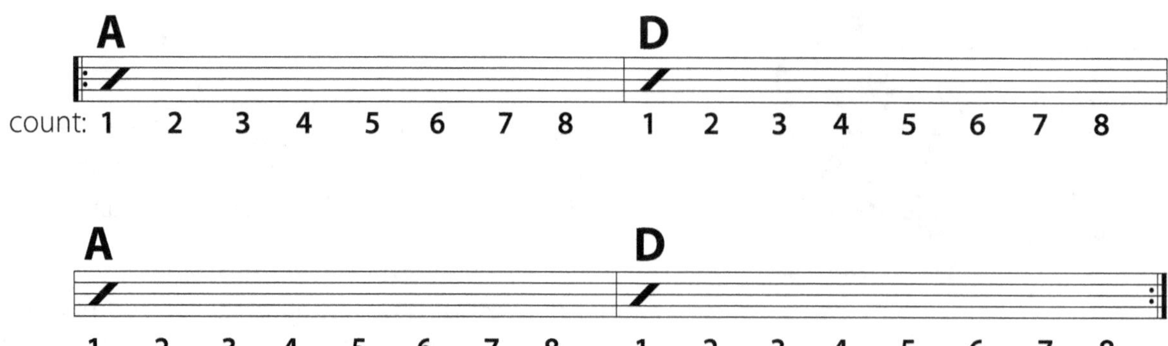

Now try switching between the D and the E7 chords.

Ex. 5.4 c

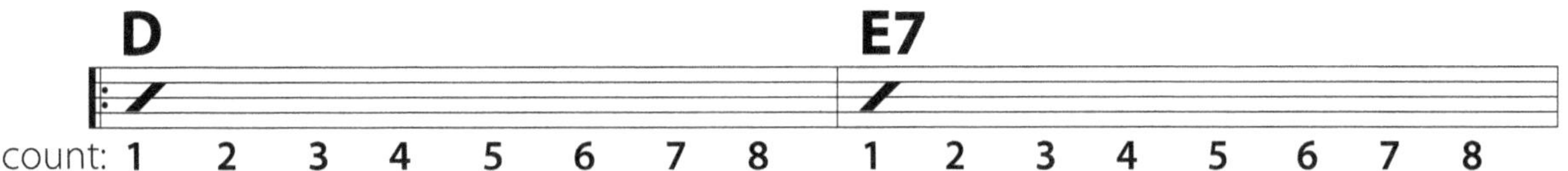

Exercise 5.5

In this exercise we will use the same 8 count approach. This time we will switch between all three chords!

Ex. 5.5 a

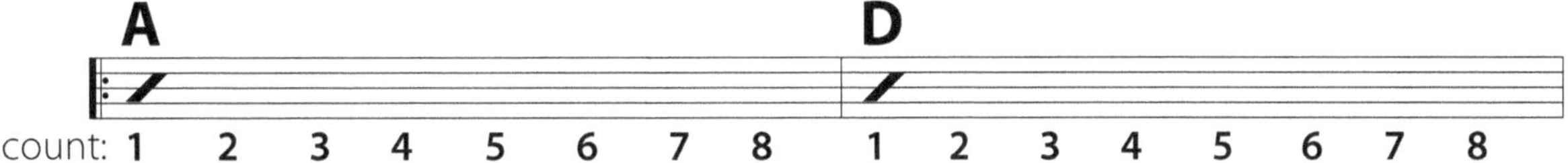

Ex. 5. 5 b

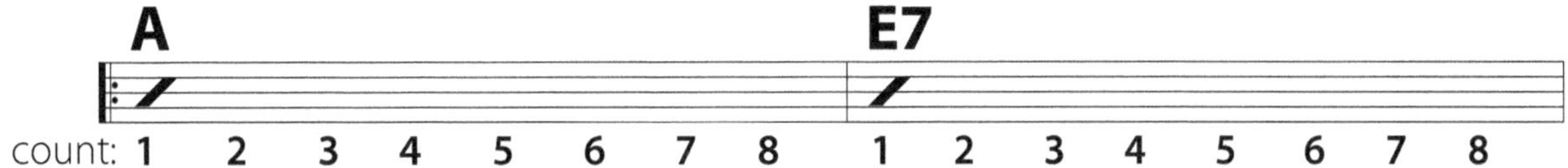

Exercise 5. 6

Once the previous exercises become easy play them again but reduce the counts in between the chords. Continue to play the chords on beat one while counting to six, four, or three.

Exercise 5. 7

In this exercise we will strum on all eight counts. Go slow so you can change smoothly and on time between beats eight and one. Notice we have a slash (/) for every number indicating we should be strumming every time we count.

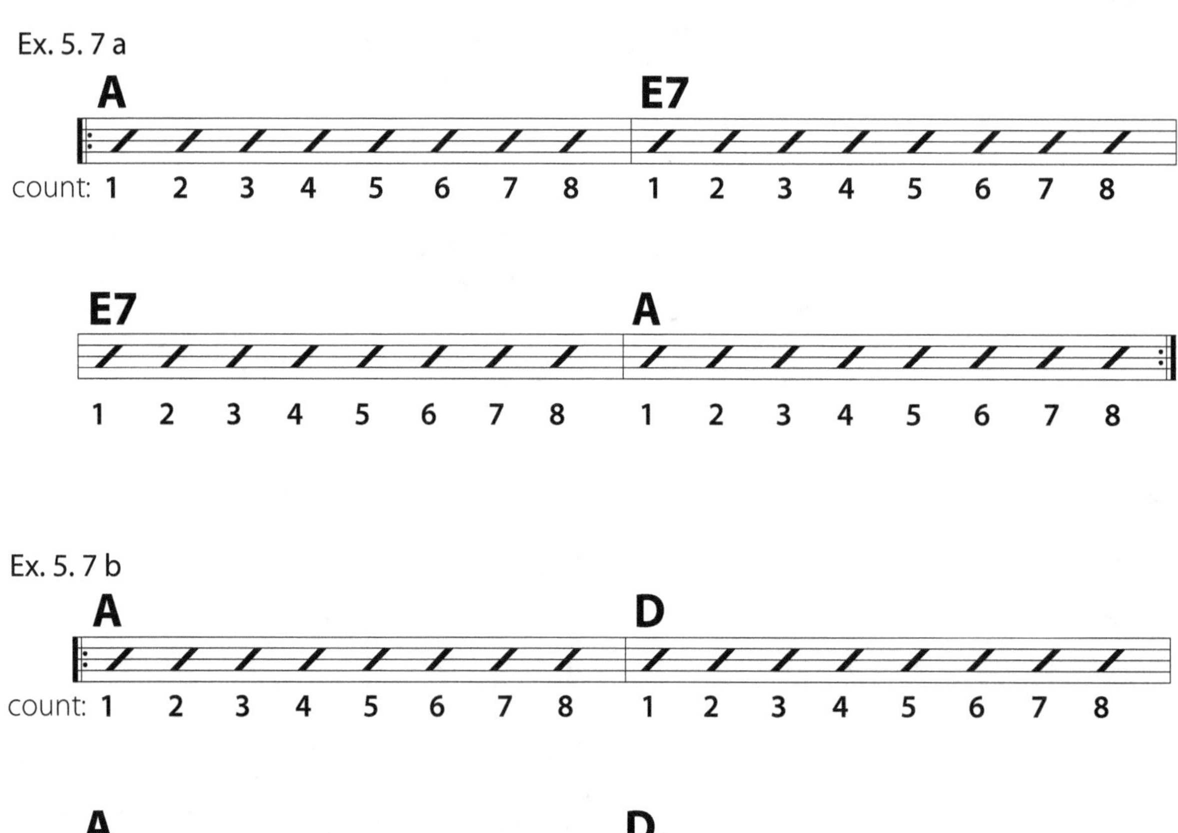

Ex. 5. 7 c

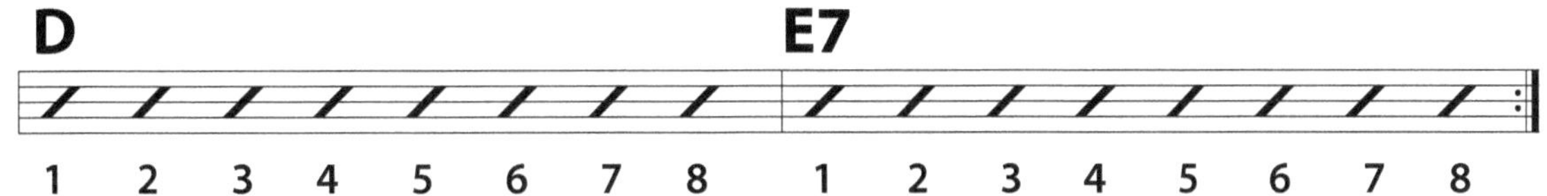

Ex. 5. 7 d

Ex. 5. 7 e

Exercise 5. 8

Try the chord progressions in exercise 7 again but reduce the counts to six, four or three.

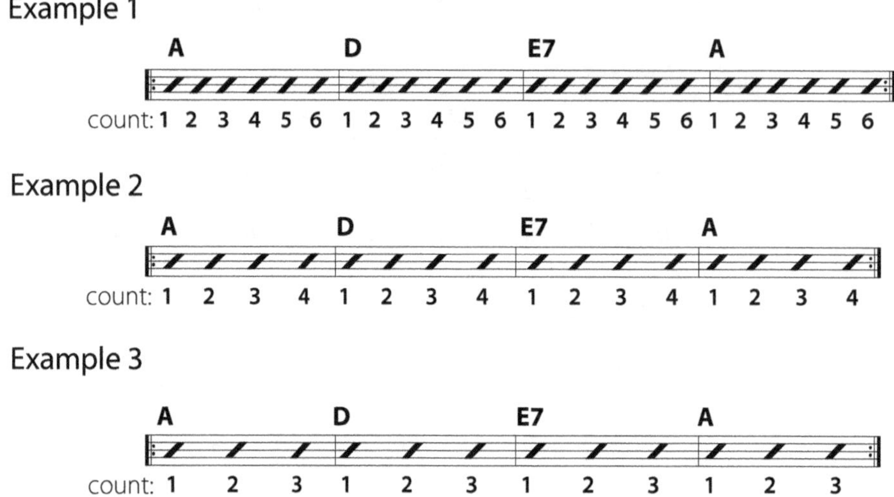

Songs Using The A Group

Once you can switch from one chord to another fairly easily you can begin to play songs. The first song is a simple folk song called ***Down In The Valley*** which uses the A and E7 chords. This is written in the form of a ***lead sheet***; that is, a single staff of music which contains the melody with the chord symbols written above.

The time signature for this piece is 3/4 which tells us that there are three beats or 3 strums per measure. Always strum 3 beats per measure *regardless of what the melodic rhythm is doing at the time*!

Although the lead sheet does not indicate an ***introduction,*** it would be helpful to play a couple of measures before you actually start to sing. To do this simply begin strumming the A chord for six beats (two measures). Then begin the song as written. After you can play through the chords smoothly without pausing try singing the melody while strumming or get a friend to play or sing the melody. (If you are subscribed to http://christigreenstudios.com you can follow along with the video.)

Down In The Valley

Nine Pound Hammer is in 4/4 or common time. This means there are four strums per measure. The beginning measure only has three beats; therefore, this song starts on beat two. Beat one is found at the end of the song. The first three notes of this piece are called ***pickup notes*** because the song does not begin on beat one. (Another term for pickup notes is ***anacrusis***.) To play ***Nine Pound Hammer***, strum four beats per measure regardless of what the melodic rhythm is doing at the time. To add an introduction, play eight beats (two measures) plus one strum for beat one in the pickup measure. Begin singing the melody on beat two.

Nine Pound Hammer

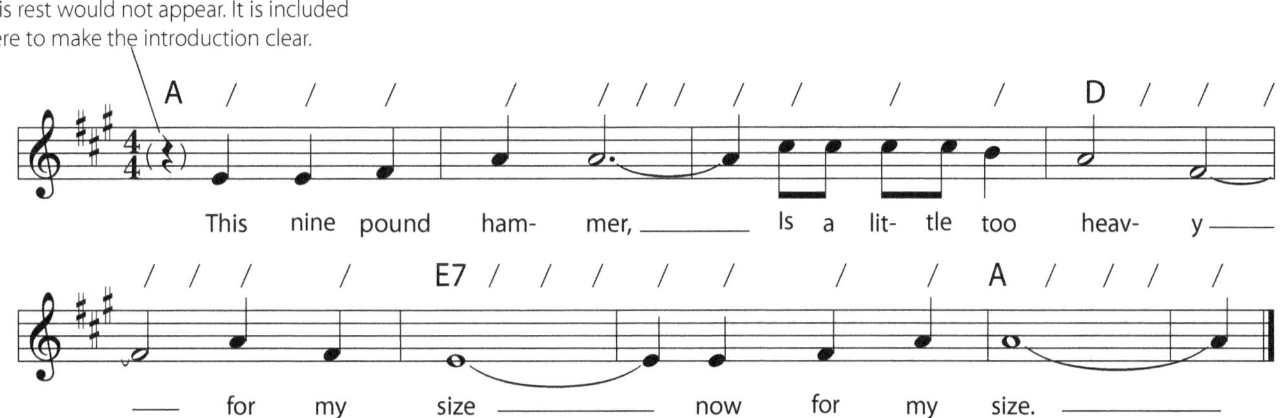

The E Group

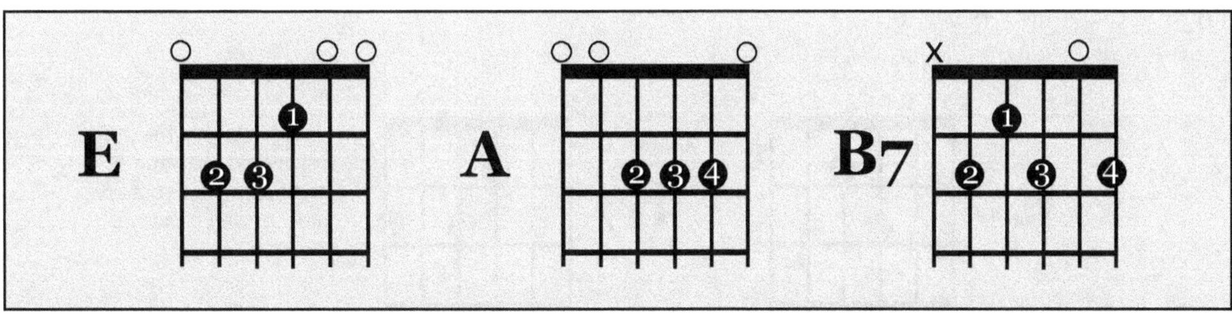

Exercise 5. 9

Practice each individual chord just as you did in the A group (exercises 1-3). Notice that A is the same in this group as in the previous group. Also observe the similarity between the E and E7 chord from the previous group. There is only one finger difference between these two chords.

Common Move, Common Finger

While switching chords in the E group, there are two basic movements the left hand fingers are making that should be observed; the ***common move*** and the ***common finger***. A common move can be found when moving the left-hand fingers from the E to the A chord. Notice that fingers two and three remain in the second fret when moving from the E chord to the A chord, but they finger different strings. Because fingers two and three stay in the same fret when changing chords a common move has occurred.

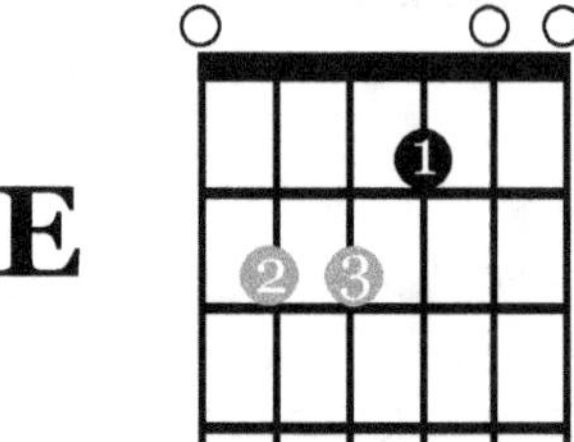

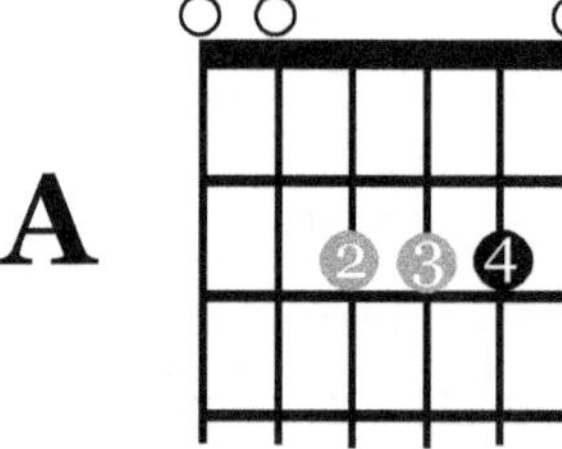

Fingers 2 and 3 stay in the same fret but move to a different string set creating a *common move* between the two chords.

When moving from the A to the B7 chord, the third finger remains on the *same* string and in the *same* fret, creating a **common finger** between the two chords. Be sure to keep the common finger on the string while changing the other fingers around it.

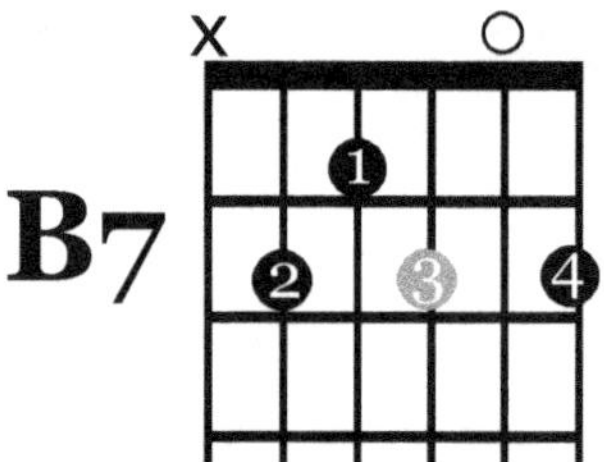

Finger 3 stays in the same fret and on the same string creating a *common finger* between the two chords.

When moving from the E to the B7 chord, the second finger remains on the *same* string and in the *same* fret, creating a common finger between the two chords. Be sure to keep the common finger on the string while changing the other fingers around it.

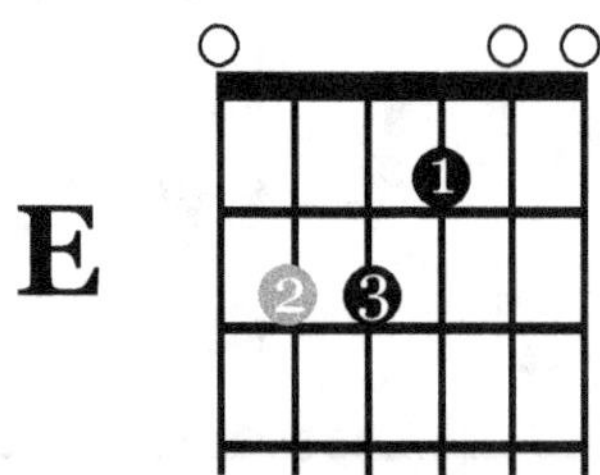

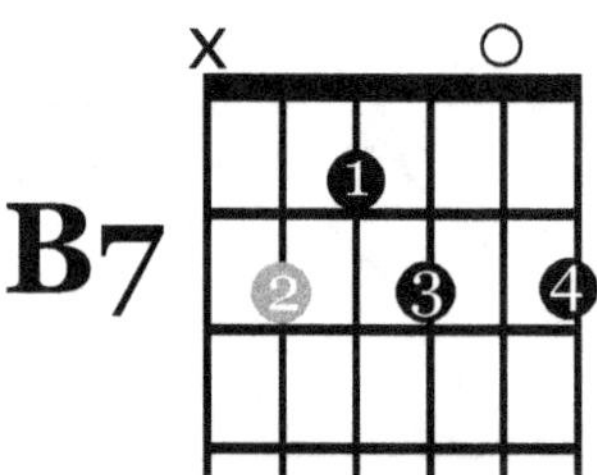

Finger 2 stays in the same fret and on the same string creating a *common finger* between the two chords.

Look for common movements in all chords you play. Not all chord changes have such clear movements; however, observing these movements whenever possible can decrease your learning time and help you to play smoother and faster.

Exercise 5.10

We want to use the metronome as we practice switching from chord to chord. Our first goal is to switch back and fourth between the E and B7 chords. We are going to do this by counting eight counts in between the chords. The slash mark at the beginning of each measure indicates a strum on beat one.

- Set your metronome to a slow pace, between 60 and 70 b.p.m. (beats per minute).
- Finger the E chord.
- Begin counting to eight saying the number with the click of the metronome.
- When you reach beat one again strum the E chord.
- Keep counting and move your fingers to the B7 chord and strum on beat one.
- Keep counting and move your fingers back to E strumming once again on beat one.
- Repeat this process until this becomes easy to do!

Ex. 5.10 a

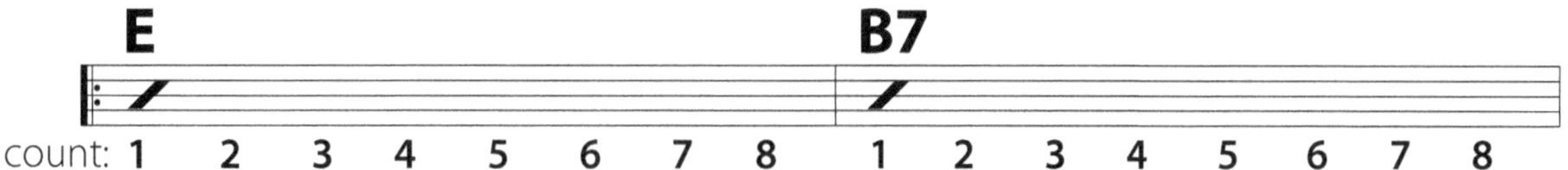

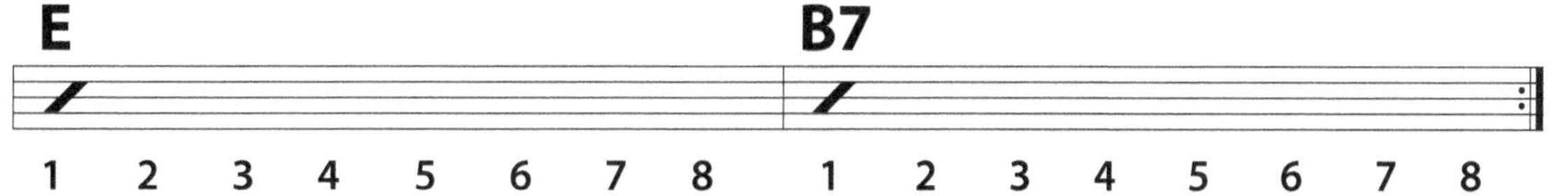

Using the same method you did for E and B7 above, try switching between the E and the A chords.

Ex. 5.10 b

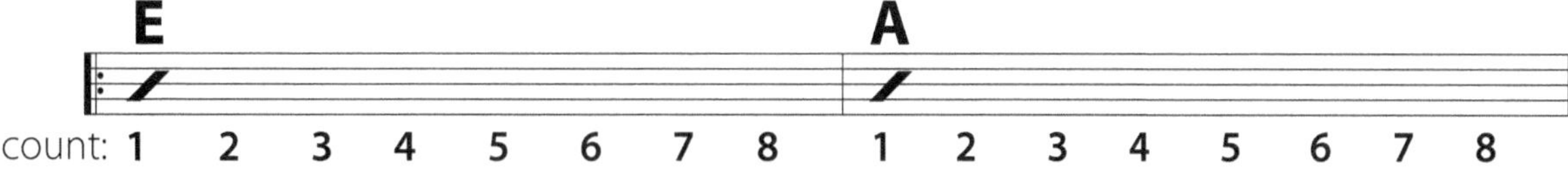

Now try switching between the A and the B7 chords.

Ex. 5.10 c

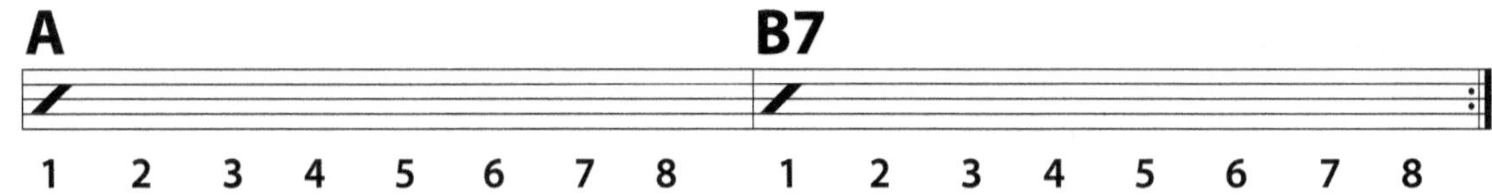

Exercise 5.11

In this exercise we will use the same 8 count approach. This time we will switch between all three chords!

Ex. 5.11 a

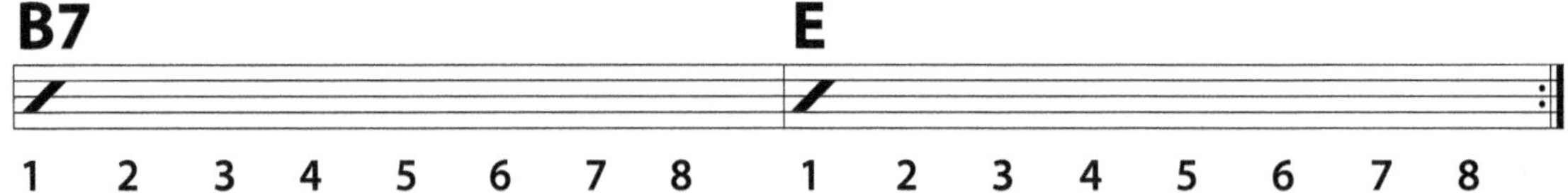

Ex. 5.11 b

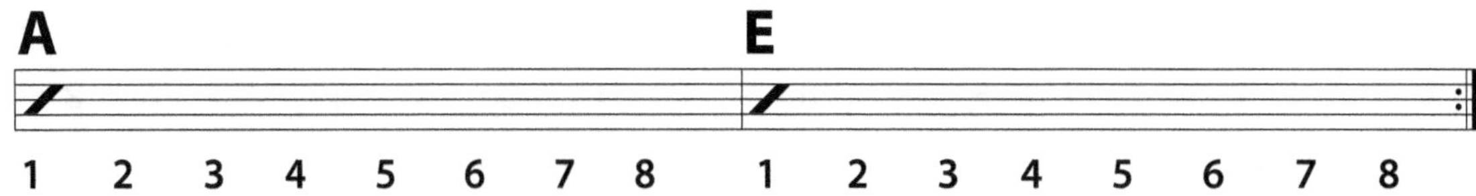

Exercise 5.12

Once the previous exercises become easy play them again but reduce the counts in between the chords. Continue to play the chords on beat one while counting to six, four, or three.

Exercise 5.13

In this exercise we will strum on all eight counts. Go slow so you can change smoothly and on time between beats eight and one. Notice we have a slash for every number indicating we should be strumming every time we count.

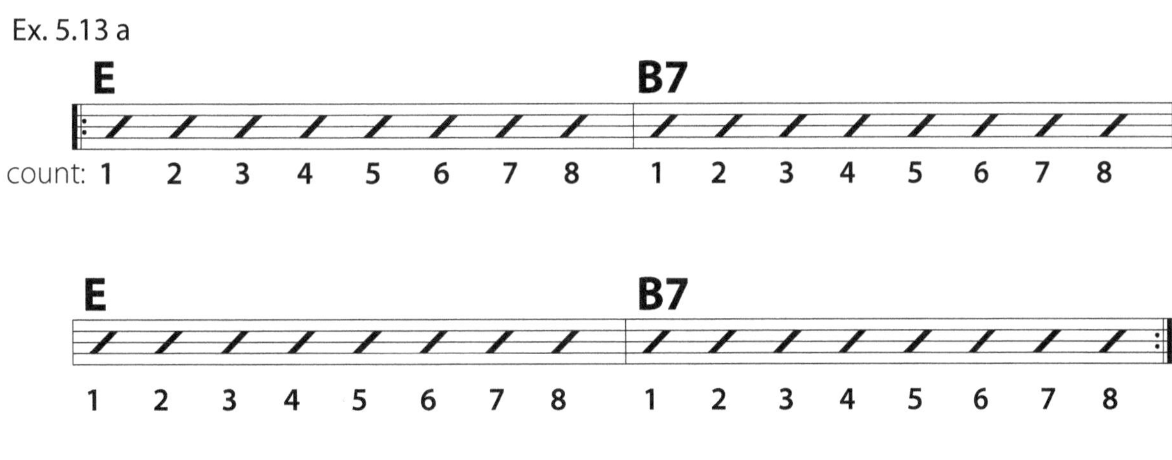

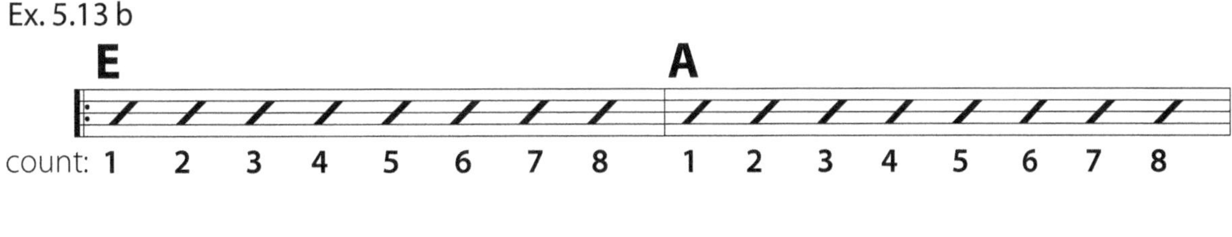

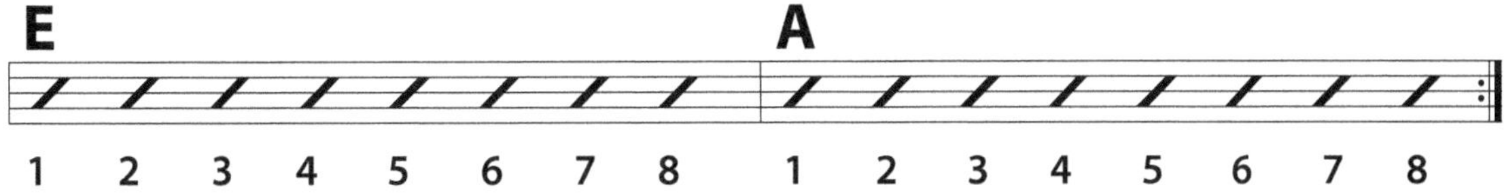

Ex. 5.13 c

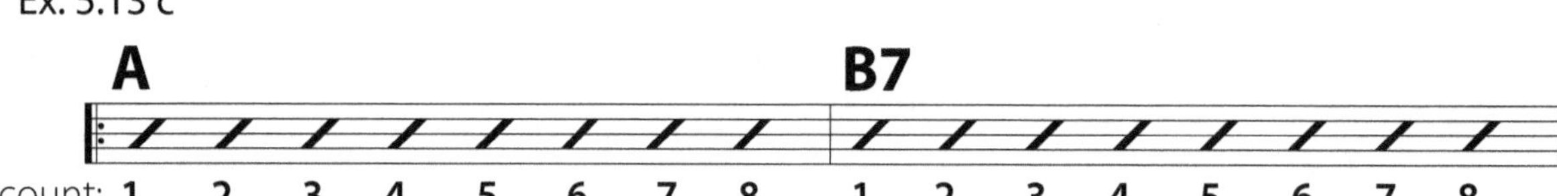

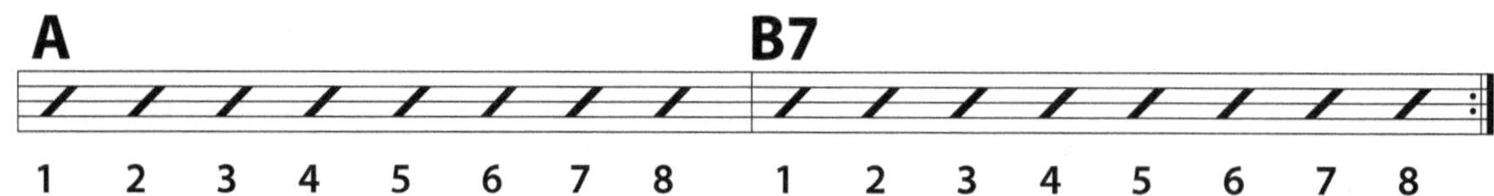

Ex. 5.13 d

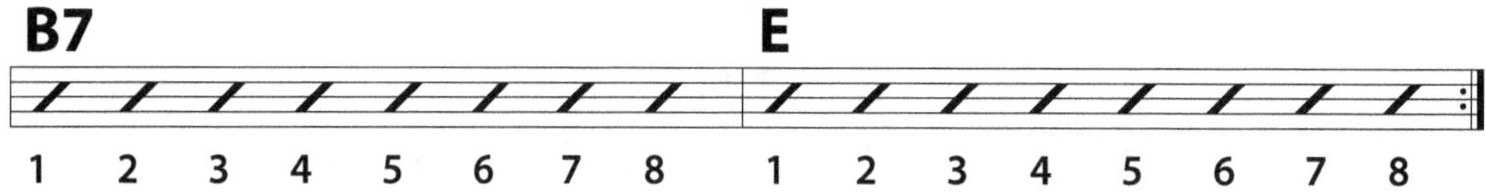

Ex. 5.13 e

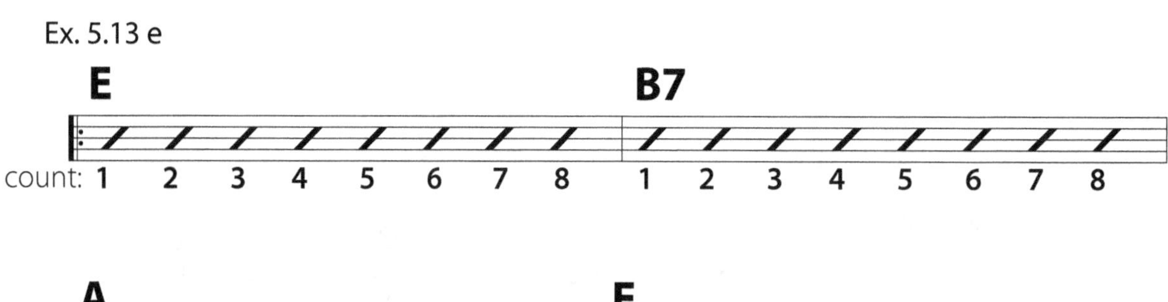

Exercise 5.14

Try the chord progressions in exercise 7 again but reduce the counts to six, four or three.

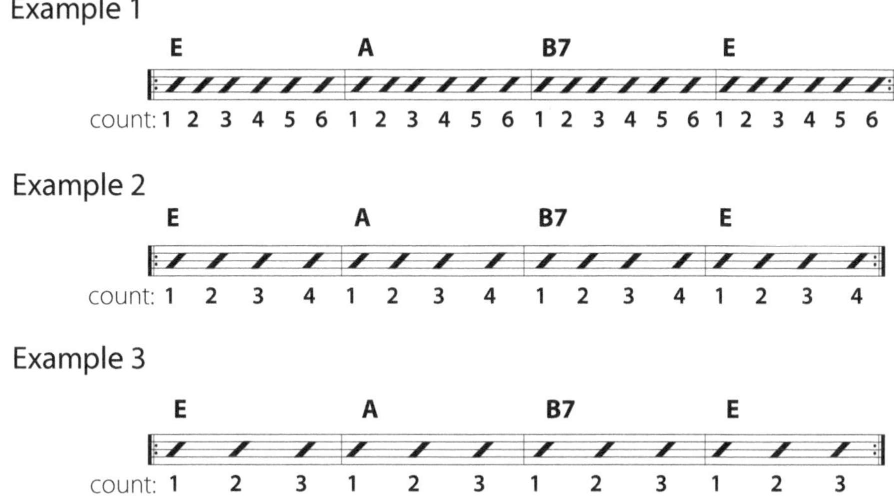

Songs Using The E Group

Amazing Grace uses the chords from the E group. It is in 3/4 time, meaning there will be three strums per measure. This song also has a pickup note on beat three. To add an introduction, strum six beats (two measures) plus two strums for beats one and two in the pickup measure. Begin singing on beat three.

Amazing Grace

Michael Row is in 4/4 time, meaning there will be four strums per measure. This song also has pickup notes beginning on beat three. To add an introduction, strum eight beats (two measures) plus two strums for beats one and two in the pickup measure. Begin singing on beat three.

Michael Row

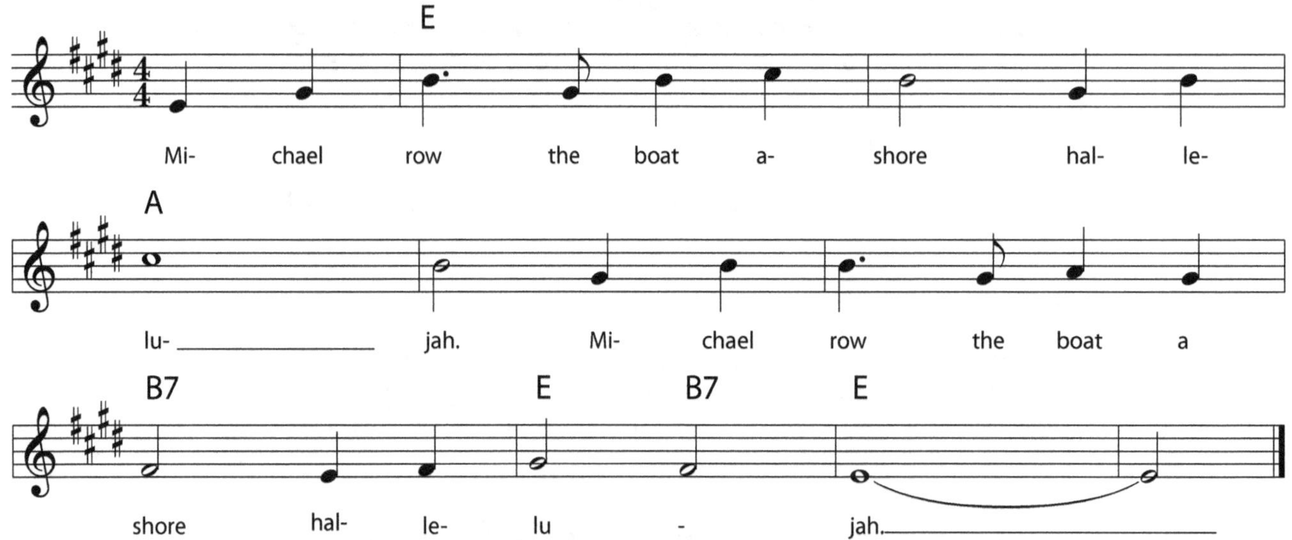

The D Group

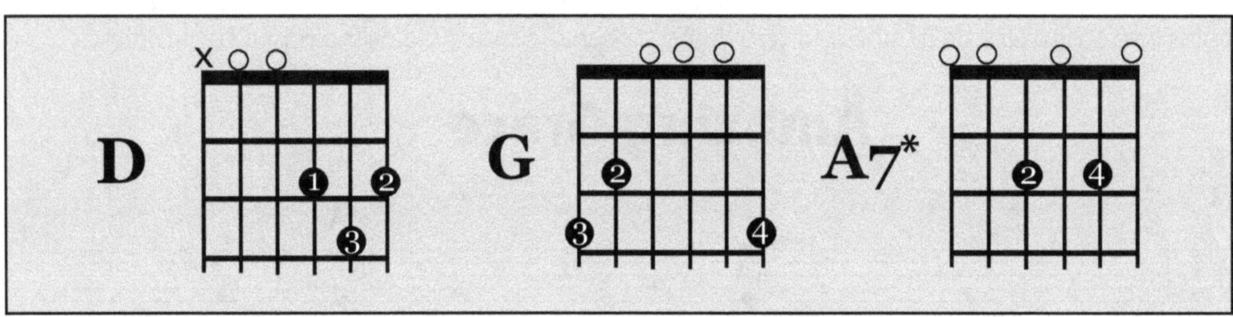

The fingering for the G chord is 2, 3, and 4. To make fingering this chord easier, begin by placing fingers 2 and 3 on the strings then reach down and place the 4th finger on the first string. Avoid the temptation to re-finger this chord. Initially, this fingering is difficult but with practice and persistence it will become easy.

Also observe the similarity between the A and A7 chords. To produce an A7 chord, finger the A chord then remove the 3rd finger from the 3rd string. You may also find fingering the A7 with the 1st and 2nd fingers easier, especially when switching from A7 back to D. This fingering produces a common move.

Just like the A chord without the third finger.

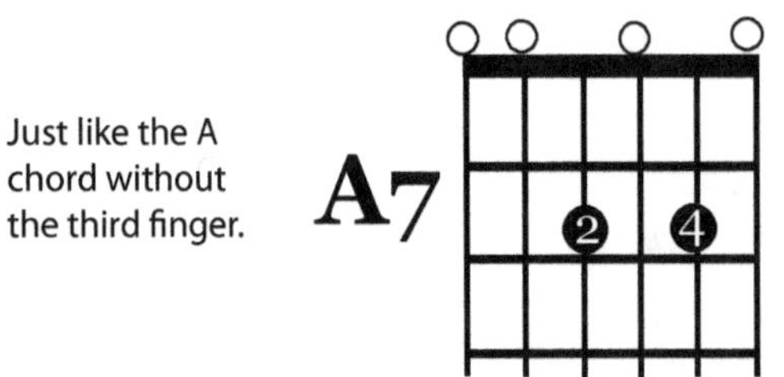

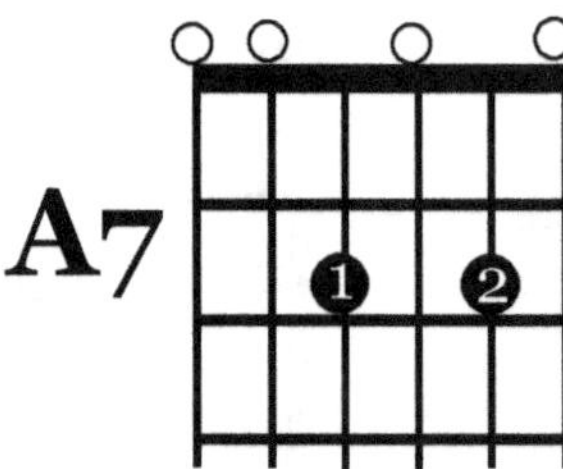

* Re-fingering this chord with 1 and 2 makes the move to D easier creating a common move between the A7 and D chords.

Exercise 5.15

We want to use the metronome as we practice switching from chord to chord. Our first goal is to switch back and fourth between the D and A7 chords. We are going to do this by counting eight counts in between the chords. The slash mark at the beginning of each measure indicates a strum on beat one.

- Set your metronome to a slow pace, between 60 and 70 b.p.m. (beats per minute).
- Finger the D chord.
- Begin counting to eight saying the number with the click of the metronome.
- When you reach beat one again strum the D chord.
- Keep counting and move your fingers to the A7 shape and strum on beat one.
- Keep counting and move your fingers back to D strumming once again on beat one.
- Repeat this process until this becomes easy to do!

Ex. 5.15 a

Using the same method you did for D and A7 above, try switching between the D and the G chords.

Ex. 5.15 b

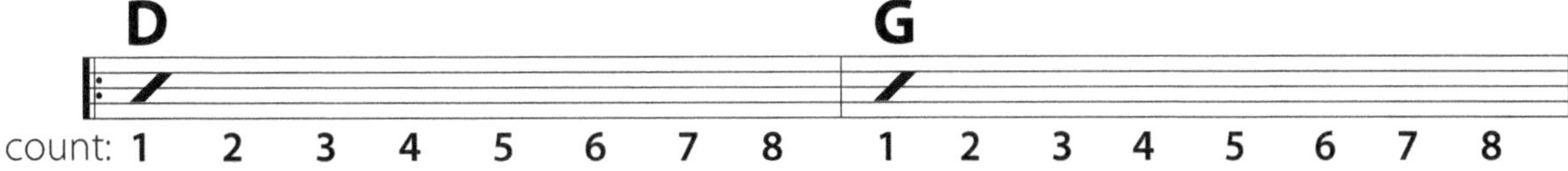

Now try switching between the G and the A7 chords.

Ex. 5.15 c

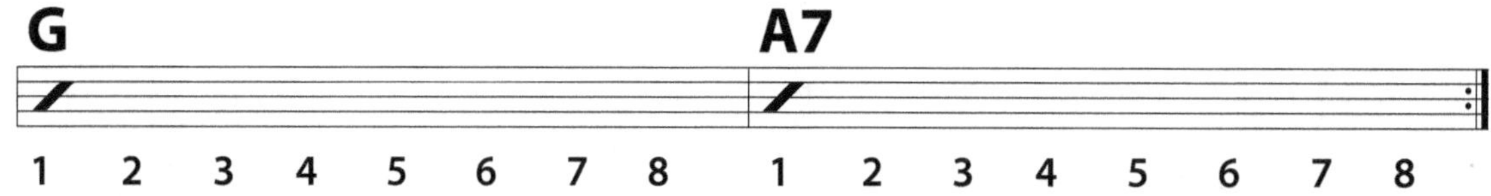

Exercise 5.16

In this exercise we will use the same 8 count approach. This time we will switch between all three chords!

Ex. 5.16 a

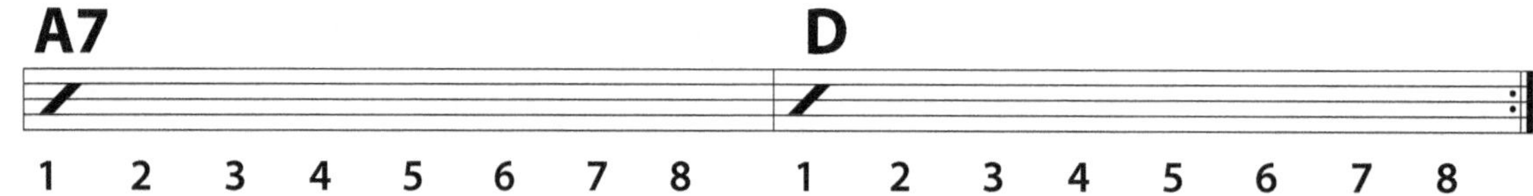

Ex. 5.16 b

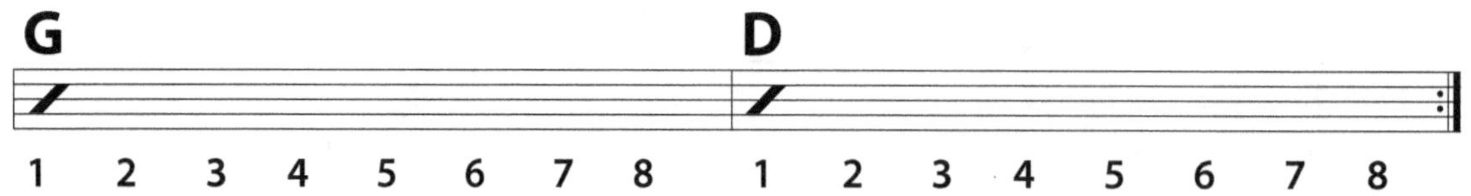

Exercise 5.17

Once the previous exercises become easy play them again but reduce the counts in between the chords. Continue to play the chords on beat one while counting to six, four, or three.

Exercise 5.18

In this exercise we will strum on all eight counts. Go slow so you can change smoothly and on time between beats eight and one. Notice we have a slash for every number indicating we should be strumming every time we count.

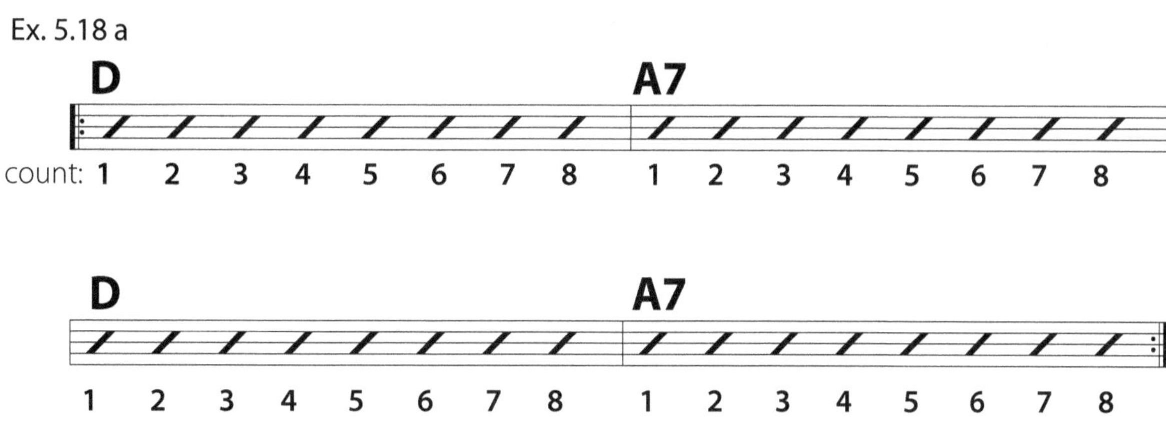

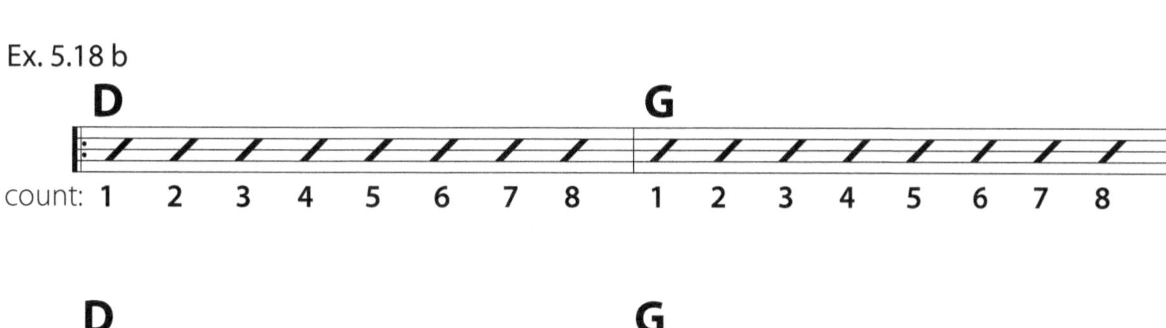

Ex. 5.18 c

Ex. 5.18 d

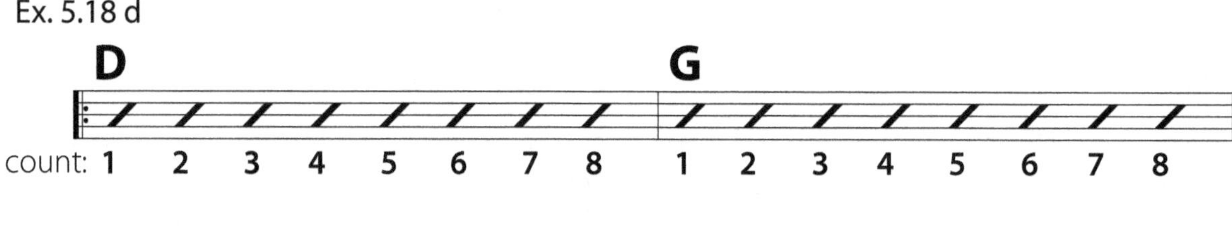

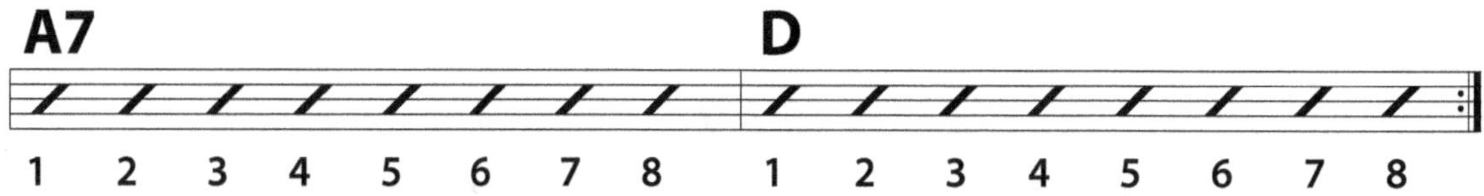

Ex. 5.18 e

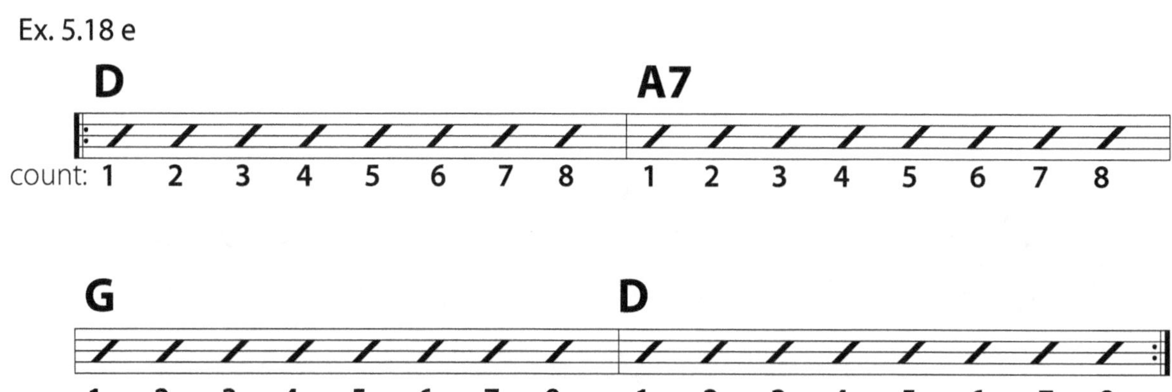

Exercise 5.19

Try the chord progressions in exercise 7 again but reduce the counts to six, four or three.

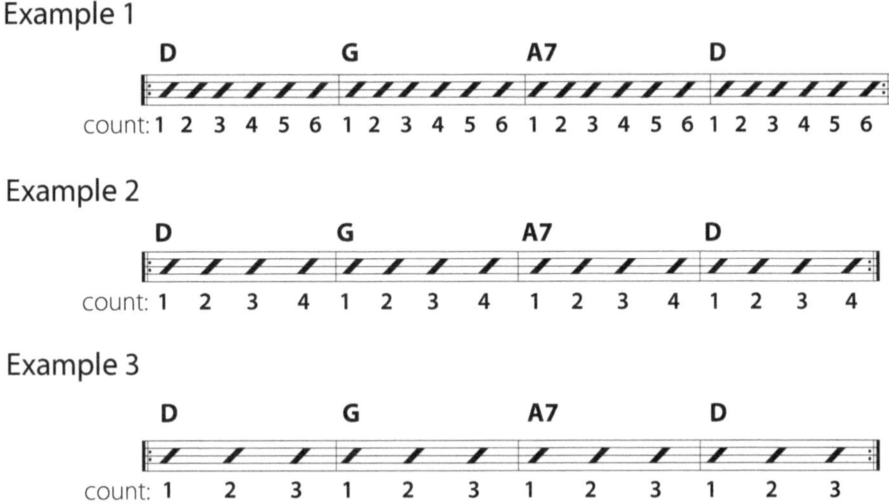

Songs Using The D Group

Streets uses the chords from the D group. It is in 3/4 time, meaning there will be three strums per measure. This song also has a pickup note on beat three. As in previous examples, to add an introduction, strum six beats (two measures) plus two strums for beats one and two in the pickup measure. Begin singing as written on beat three.

Streets

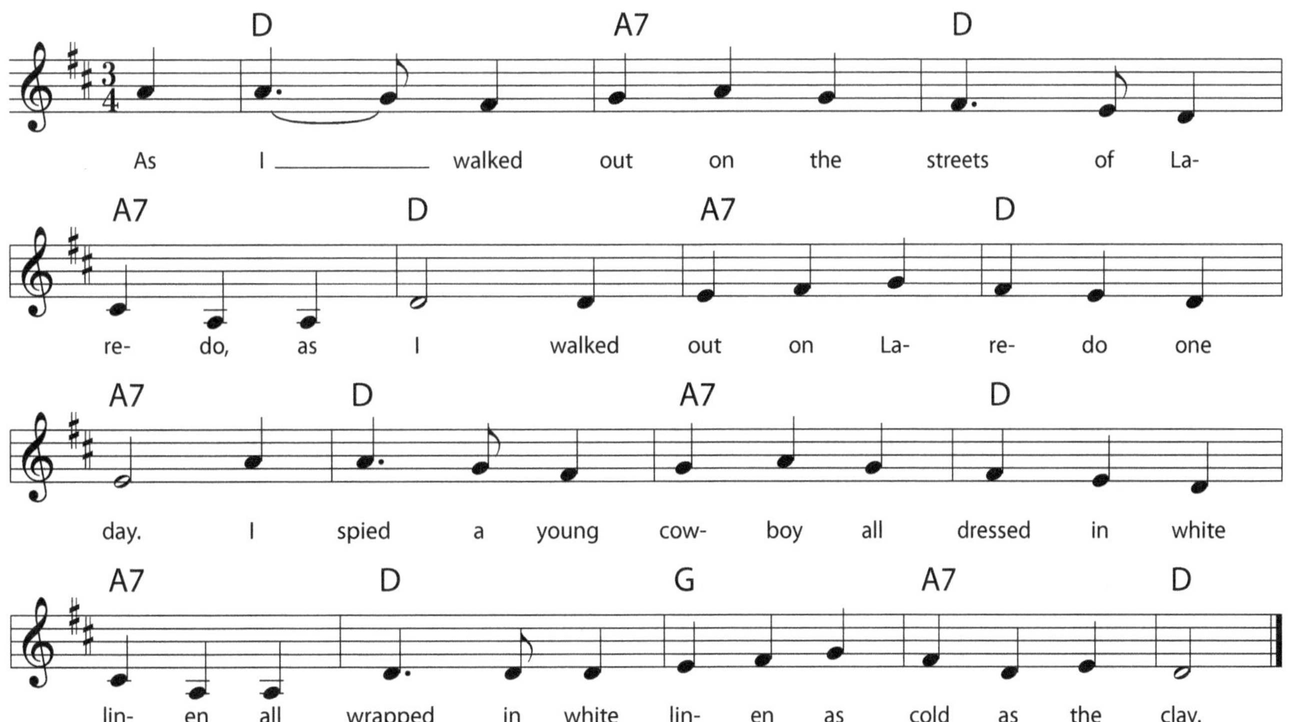

Will The Circle is in 4/4 time, meaning there will be four strums per measure. This song also has pickup notes beginning on beat three. As in previous examples, to add an introduction strum eight beats (two measures) plus two strums for beats one and two in the pickup measure. Begin singing on beat three.

Will The Circle

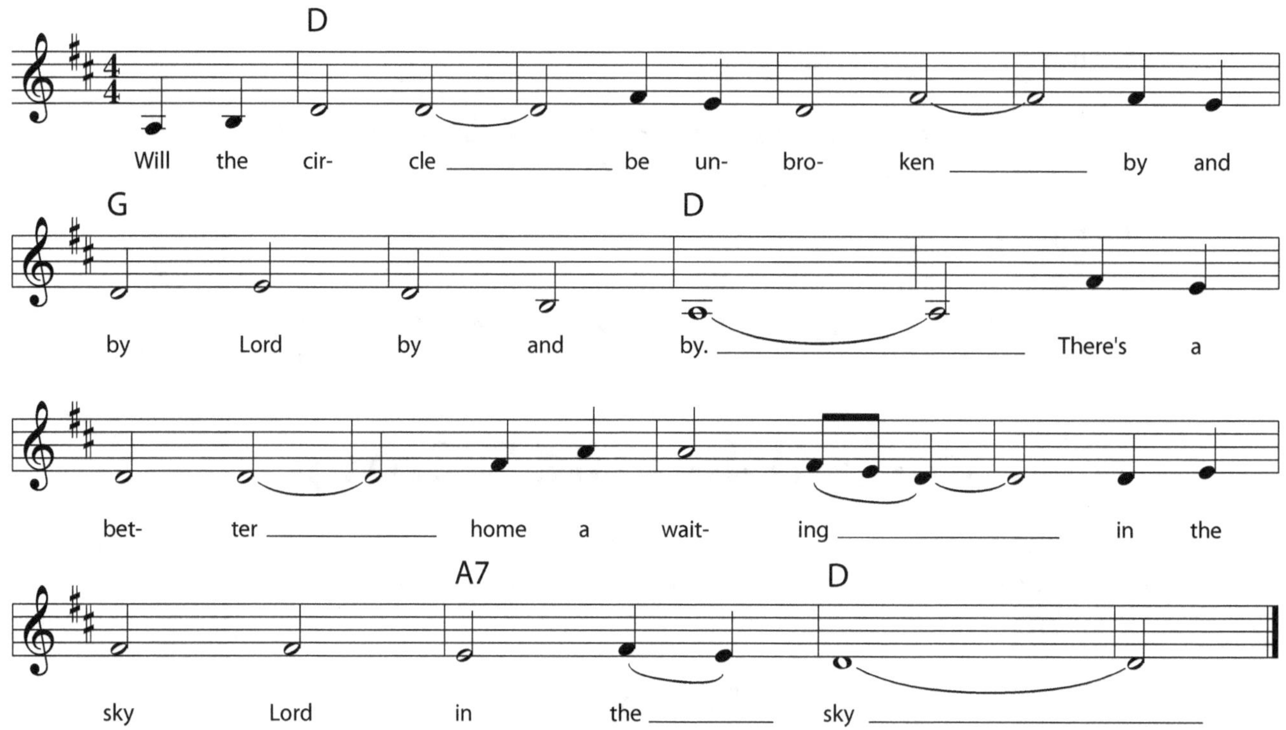

The G Group

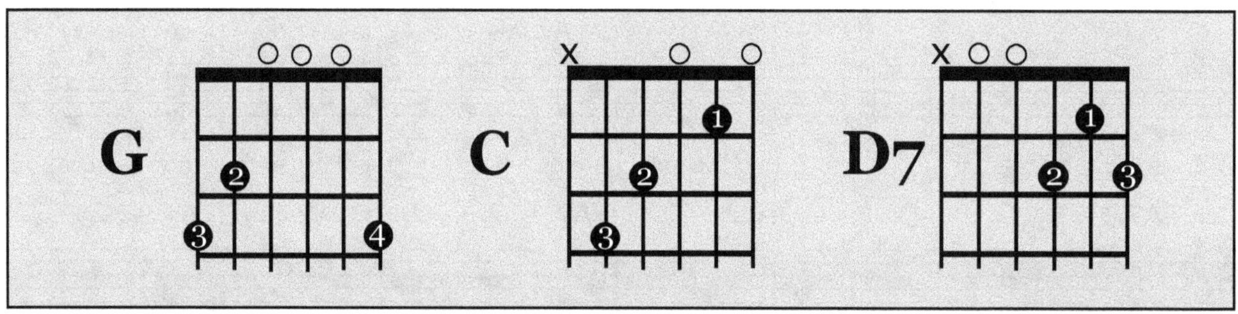

Observe the common move and common finger motions between these chords. A common move occurs between the G and C chords with fingers 2 and 3. Another common move with finger 2 occurs between the C and D7 chords making the 2nd finger a common move between all of the chords in the group. Finger 1 is a common finger to both the C and D7 chords.

Exercise 5.20

We want to use the metronome as we practice switching from chord to chord. Our first goal is to switch back and fourth between the **G** and **D7** chords. We are going to do this by counting eight counts in between the chords. The slash mark at the beginning of each measure indicates a strum on beat one.

- Set your metronome to a slow pace, between 60 and 70 b.p.m. (beats per minute).
- Finger the G chord.
- Begin counting to eight saying the number with the click of the metronome.
- When you reach beat one again strum the G chord.
- Keep counting and move your fingers to the D7 shape and strum on beat one.
- Keep counting and move your fingers back to G strumming once again on beat one.
- Repeat this process until this becomes easy to do!

Ex. 5.20 a

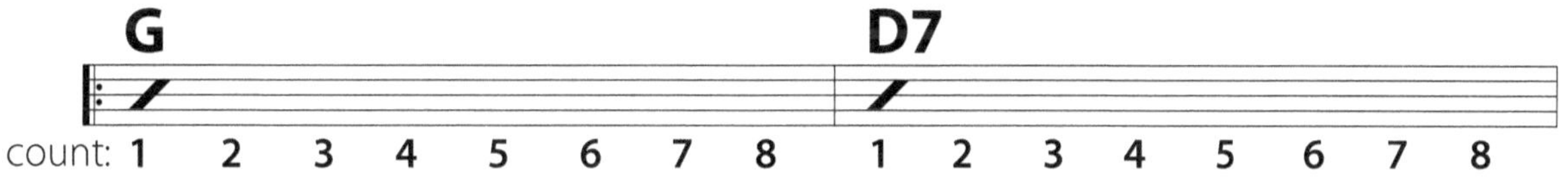

Using the same method you did for G and D7 above, try switching between the G and the C chords.

Ex. 5.20 b

Now try switching between the C and the D7 chords.

Ex. 5.20 c

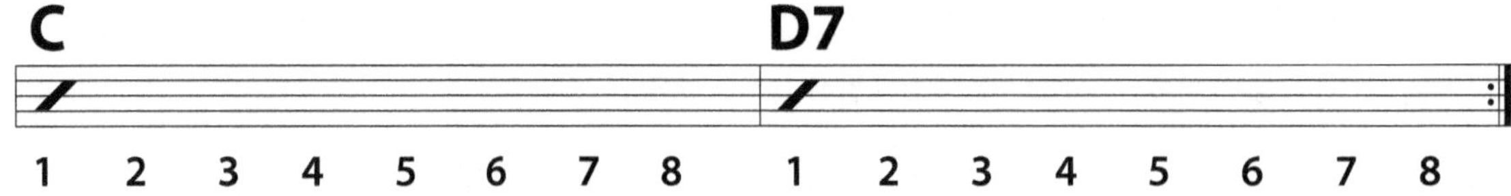

Exercise 5.21

In this exercise we will use the same 8 count approach. This time we will switch between all three chords!

Ex. 5.21 a

Ex. 5.21 b

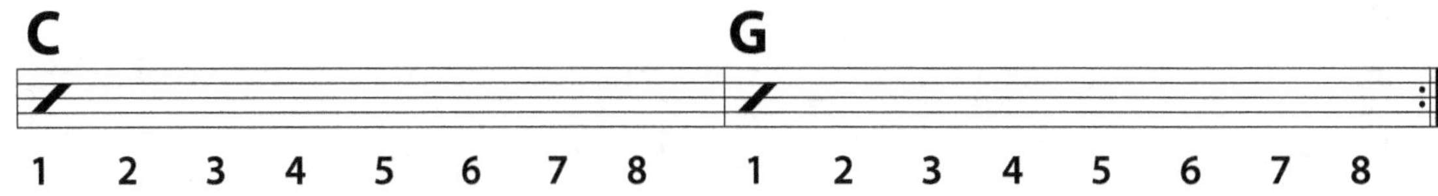

Exercise 5.22

Once the previous exercises become easy play them again but reduce the counts in between the chords. Continue to play the chords on beat one while counting to six, four, or three.

Exercise 5.23

In this exercise we will strum on all eight counts. Go slow so you can change smoothly and on time between beats eight and one. Notice we have a slash for every number indicating we should be strumming every time we count.

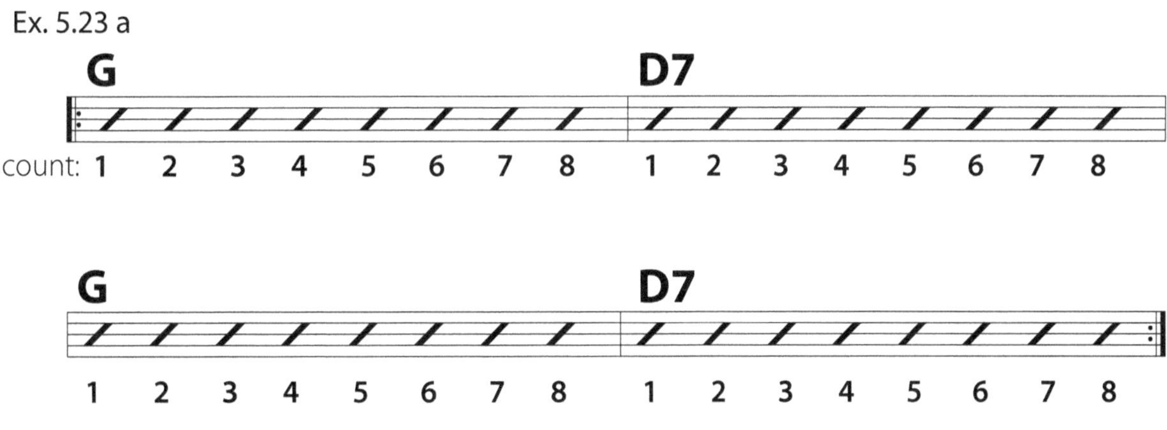

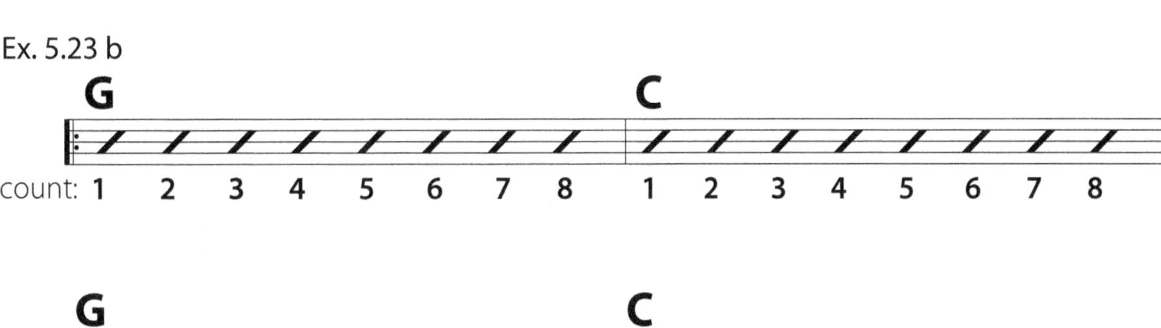

Ex. 5.23 c

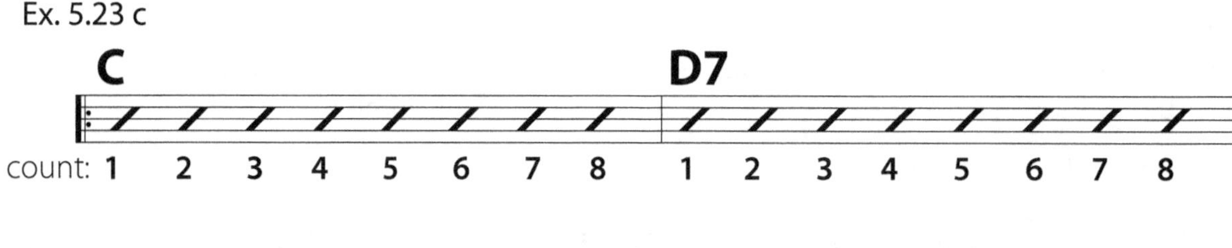

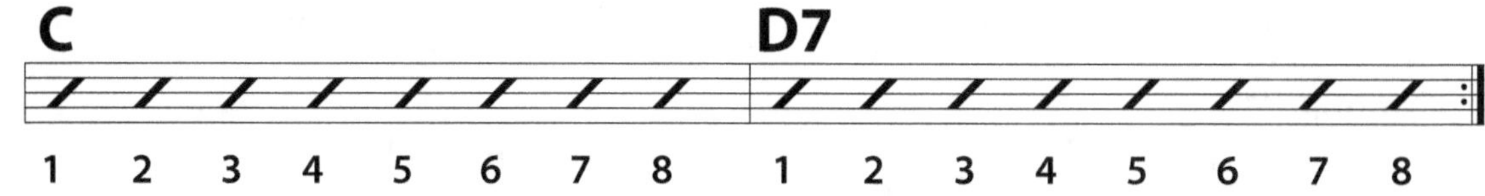

Ex. 5.23 d

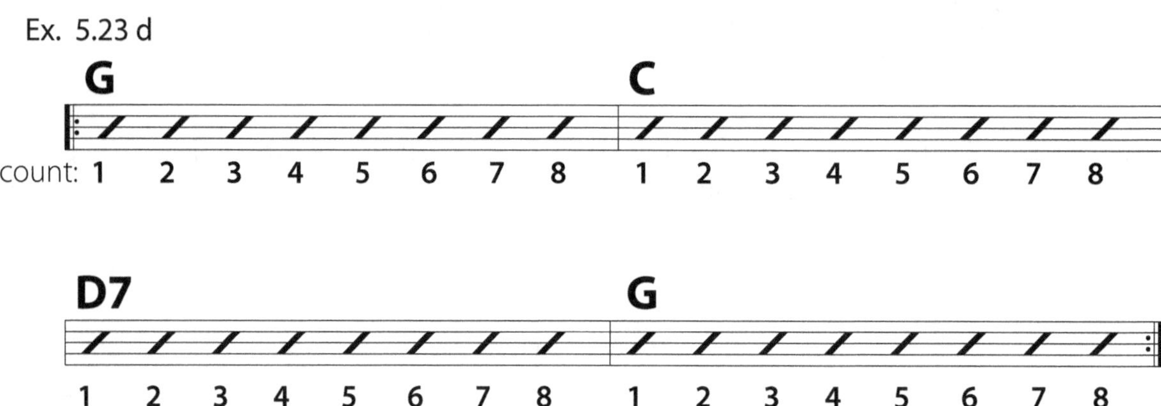

Ex. 5.23 e

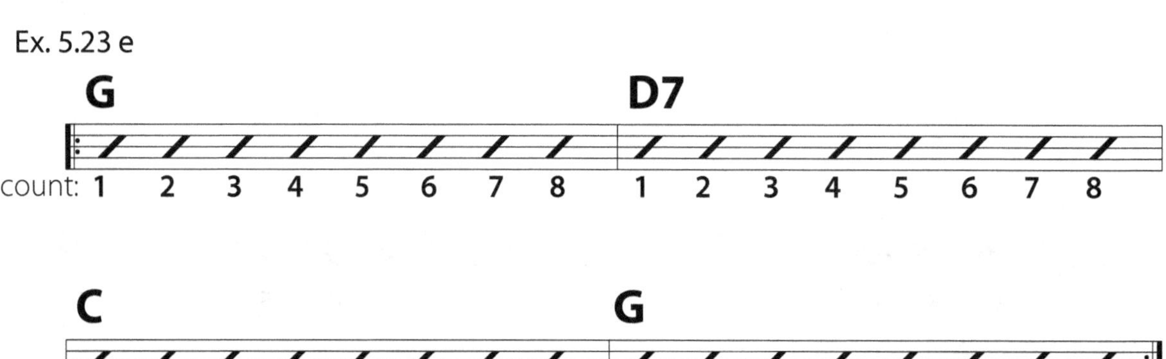

Exercise 5.24

Try the chord progressions in exercise 7 again but reduce the counts to six, four or three.

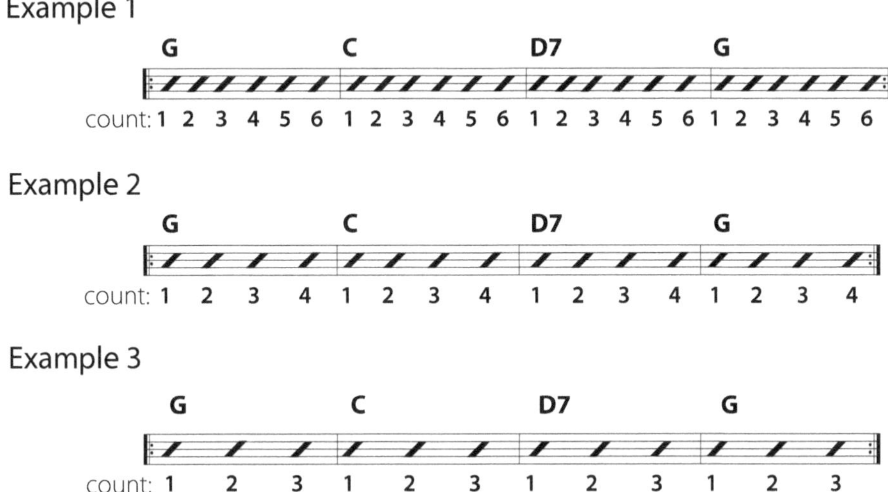

Songs Using The G Group

Yankee Doodle is in 4/4 time, meaning there will be four strums per measure. To add an introduction, strum eight beats (two measures) then begin singing on beat one.

Yankee Doodle

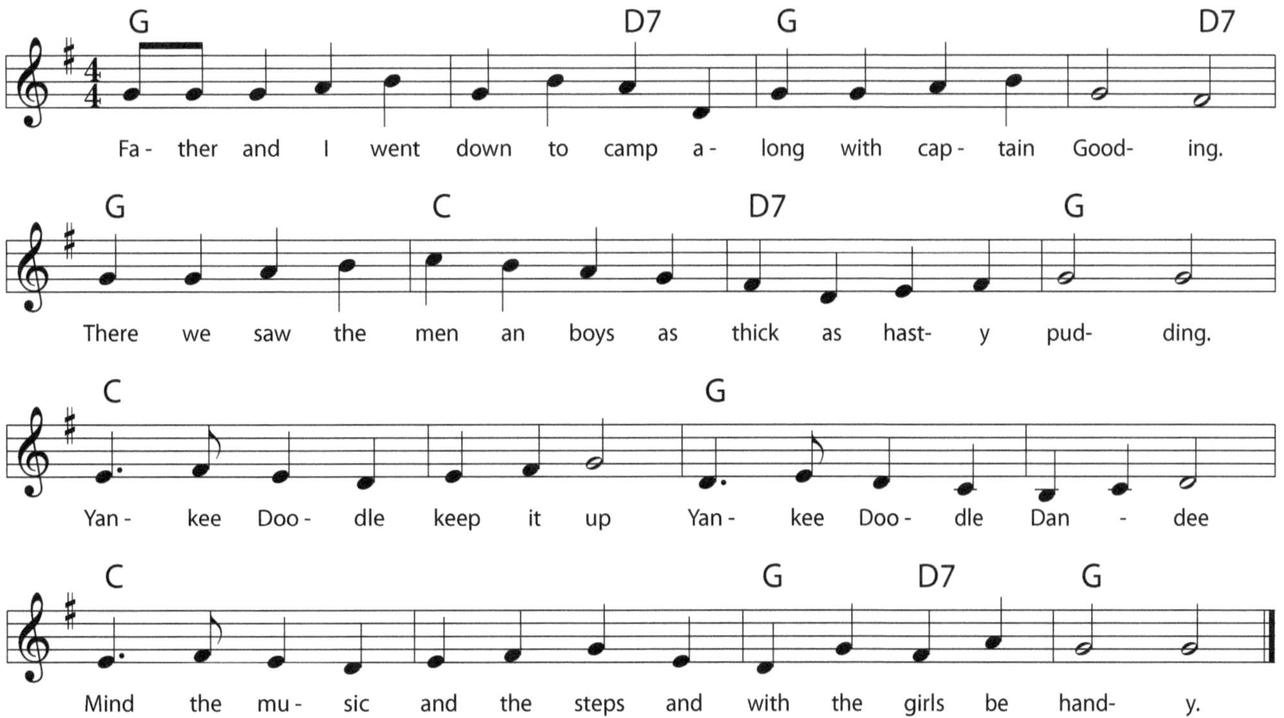

Silent Night uses the chords from the G group. It is in 3/4 time, meaning there will be three strums per measure. This song begins on beat one. To add an introduction, strum six beats (two measures)then begin singing on beat one.

Silent Night

The C Group

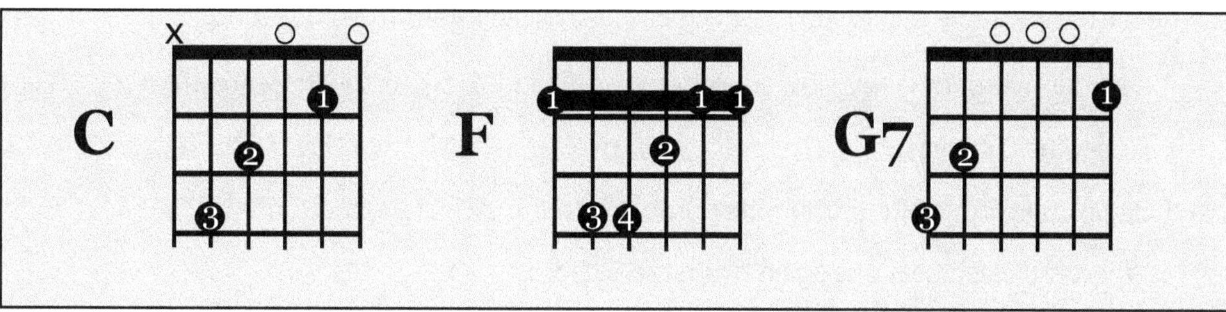

Common moves with fingers 2 and 1 occur between all of the chords. Finger 3 creates a common move between the F and G7 chords and is a common finger between the C and F chords.

The **F chord** uses *finger 1 on three of the strings*. To accomplish this we extend the *first finger* across all of the strings in the first fret creating what we call a barre (bar). ***Barre chords*** then are chords that use the first finger of the left hand to barre across one fret in order to finger several strings at one time. The barre is indicated by a solid black line joining the highest string to be barred to the lowest. Strings 6, 2, and 1 will sound from the barre finger. Strings 3, 4, and 5 will sound from their perspective fingers 2, 4, and 3 because they are placed in front of the barre finger (1).

Exercise 5.26

To play F do the following steps:

1) Extend the first finger in the left hand across the first fret so the fingertip touches the sixth string and the rest of the finger is touching strings five through one.

2) Make sure your finger is next to the fret and every part of your finger is of equal distance from the fret.

3) Use the side of the first finger rather than the palm-side. The side has more bone and will press the strings down easier.

4) Practice the barre itself by pressing all of the strings down with the first finger and strum with the right hand.

5) After you have strummed all the strings, relax the first finger in the left hand but do not remove it from the string. Relaxing the hand will prevent the hand from cramping. Later, it will help you to play more stylistically.

6) Pluck each note individually and correct the unclear notes by adjusting the first finger.

7) After you can do this fairly well add the rest of the fingers in the left hand and repeat steps 5 and 6.

Go slow, use the metronome, and don't give up. The F chord is tough at first but with enough practice and persistence it will become easy.

Exercise 5.27

We want to use the metronome as we practice switching from chord to chord. Our first goal is to switch back and fourth between the C and G7 chords. We are going to do this by counting eight counts in between the chords. The slash mark at the beginning of each measure indicates a strum on beat one.

- Set your metronome to a slow pace, between 60 and 70 b.p.m. (beats per minute).
- Finger the C chord.
- Begin counting to eight saying the number with the click of the metronome.
- When you reach beat one again strum the C chord.
- Keep counting and move your fingers to the G7 shape and strum on beat one.
- Keep counting and move your fingers back to A strumming once again on beat one.
- Repeat this process until this becomes easy to do!

Ex. 5.27 a

Using the same method you did for C and G7 above, try switching between the C and the F chords.

Ex. 5.27 b

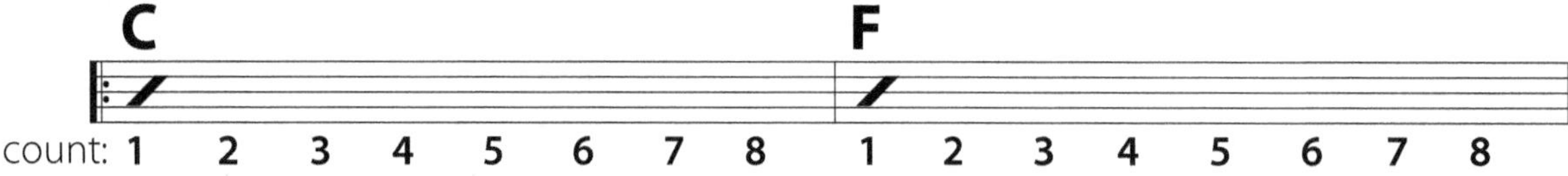

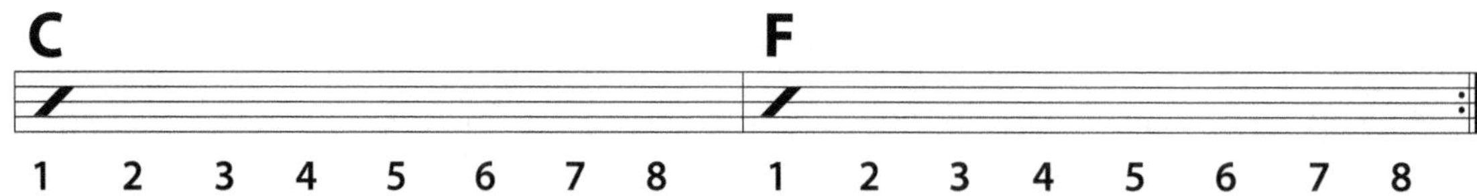

Now try switching between the F and the G7 chords.

Ex. 5.27 c

Exercise 5.28

In this exercise we will use the same 8 count approach. This time we will switch between all three chords!

Ex. 5.28 a

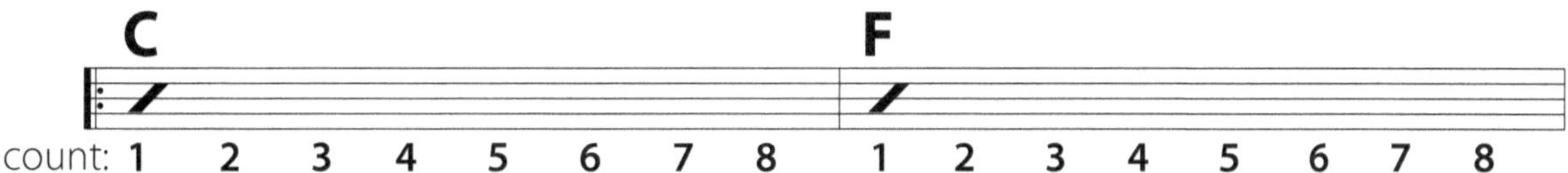

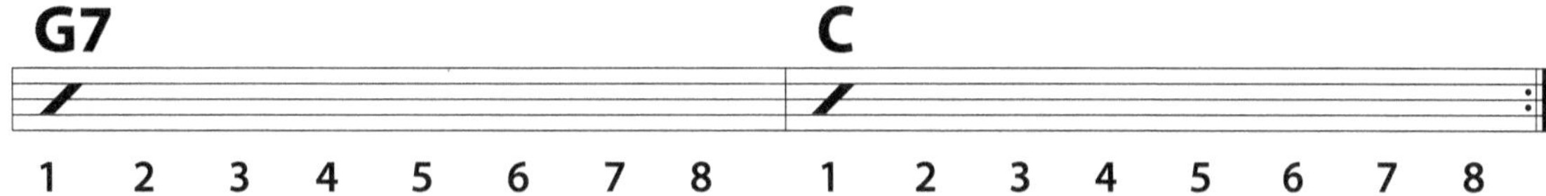

Ex. 5.28 b

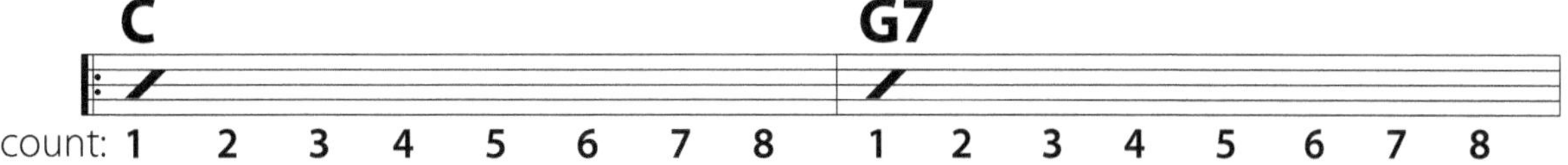

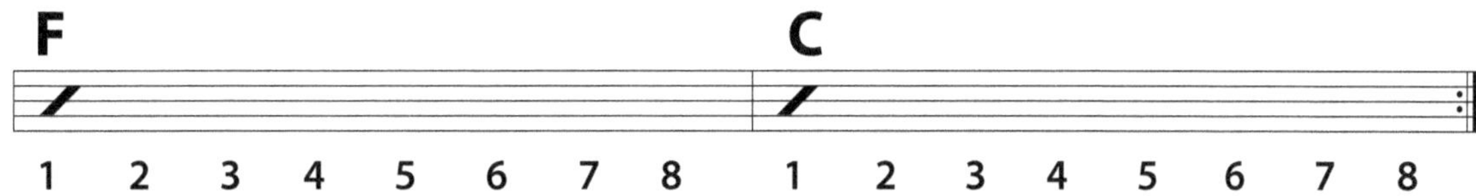

Exercise 5.29

Once the previous exercises become easy play them again but reduce the counts in between the chords. Continue to play the chords on beat one while counting to six, four, or three.

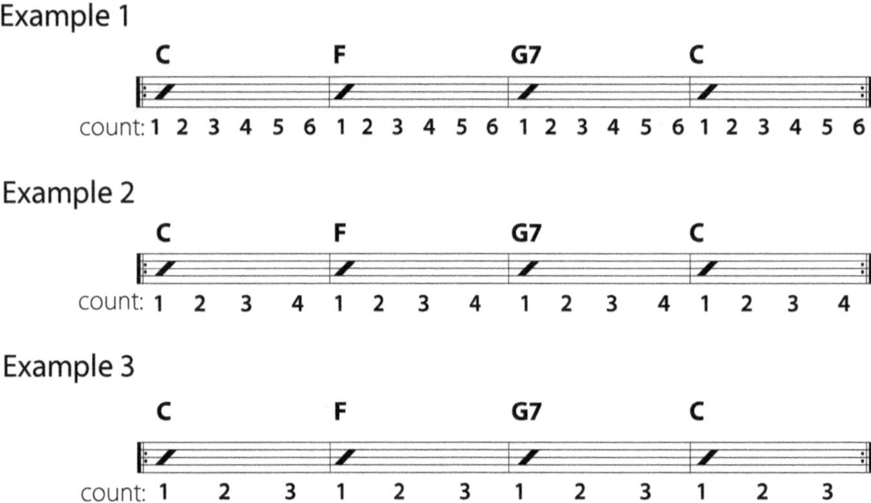

Exercise 5.30

In this exercise we will strum on all eight counts. Go slow so you can change smoothly and on time between beats eight and one. Notice we have a slash for every number indicating we should be strumming every time we count.

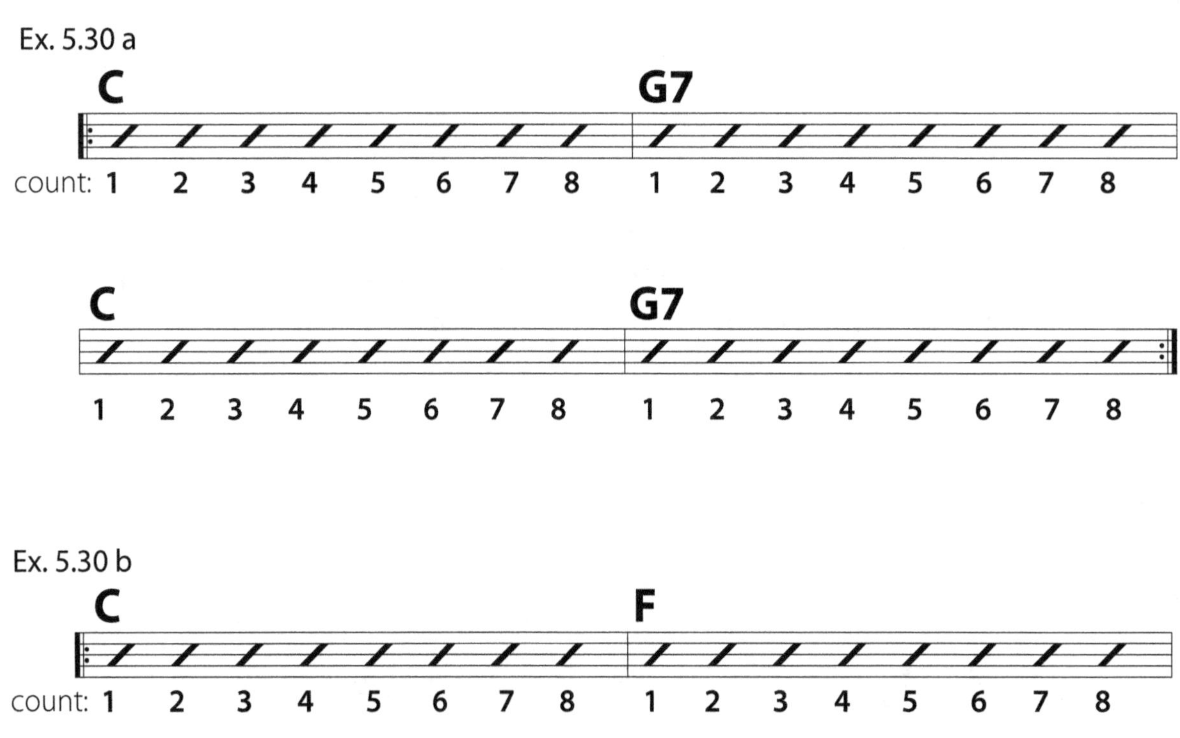

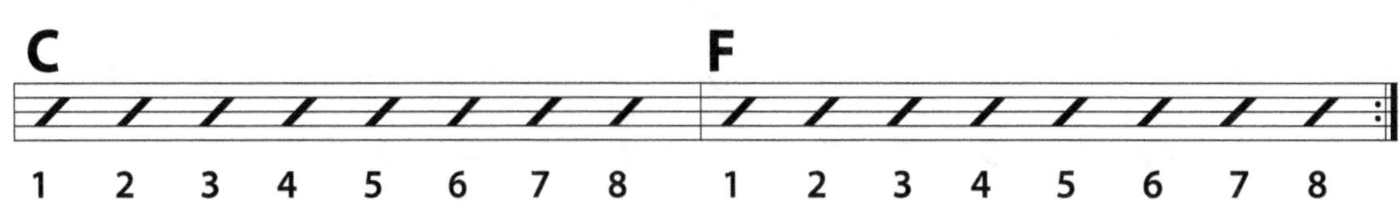

Ex. 5.30 c

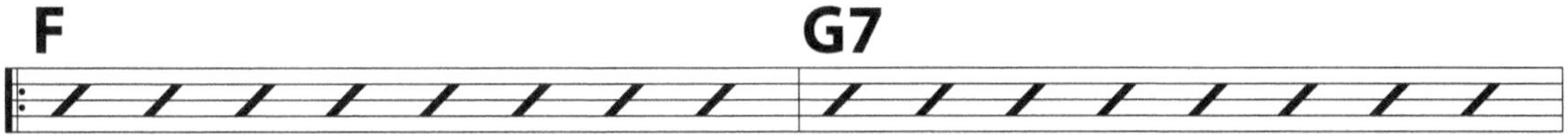

F | G7

count: 1 2 3 4 5 6 7 8 | 1 2 3 4 5 6 7 8

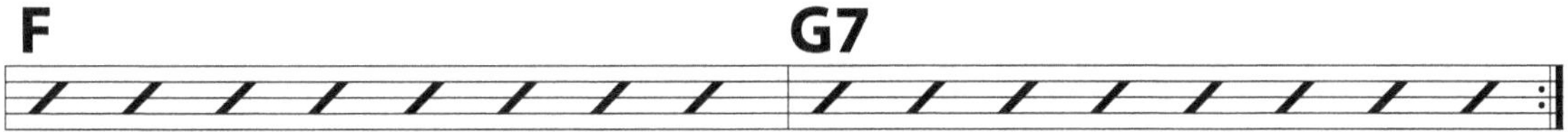

F | G7

1 2 3 4 5 6 7 8 | 1 2 3 4 5 6 7 8

Ex. 5.30 d

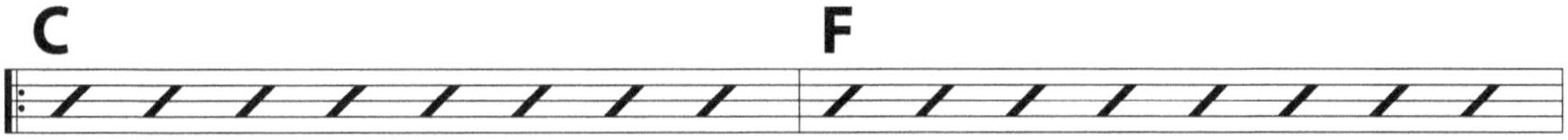

C | F

count: 1 2 3 4 5 6 7 8 | 1 2 3 4 5 6 7 8

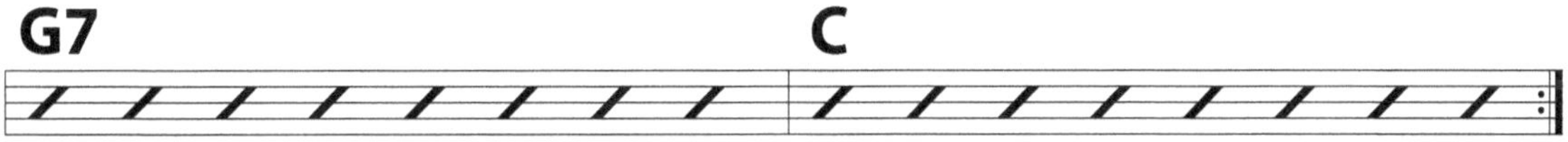

G7 | C

1 2 3 4 5 6 7 8 | 1 2 3 4 5 6 7 8

Ex. 5.30 e

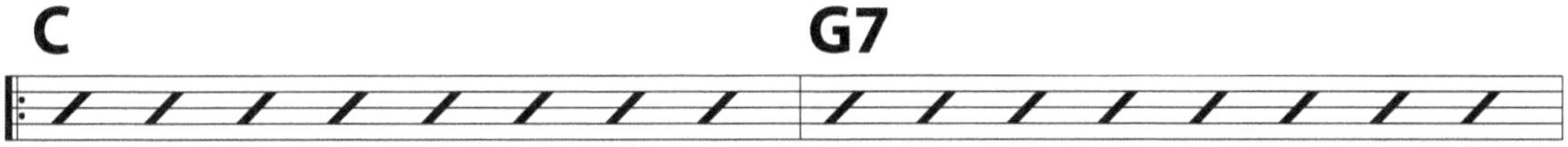

C | G7

count: 1 2 3 4 5 6 7 8 | 1 2 3 4 5 6 7 8

F | C

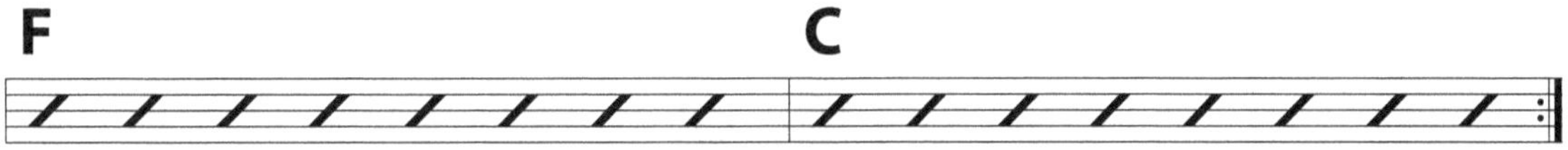

1 2 3 4 5 6 7 8 | 1 2 3 4 5 6 7 8

Exercise 5.31

Try the chord progressions in exercise 7 again but reduce the counts to six, four or three.

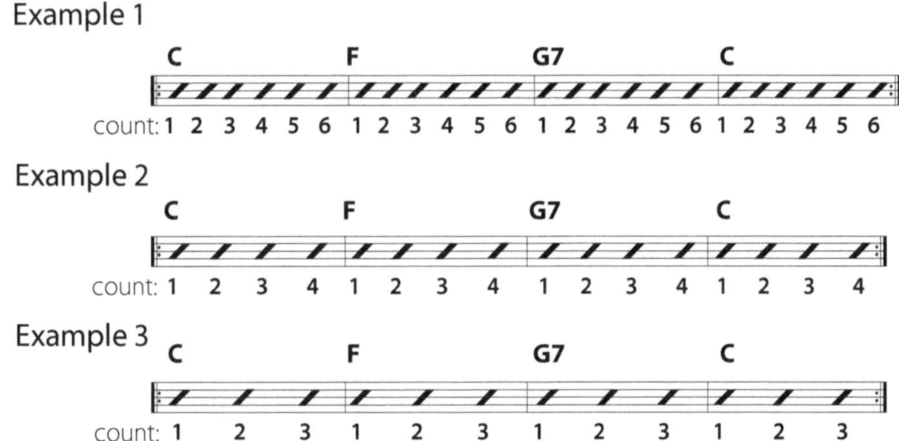

Songs Using The C Group

'Round the Mountain uses the chords from the C group. It is in 4/4 time meaning there will be four strums per measure. This song also has pickup notes beginning on beat three. As in previous examples, to add an introduction, strum eight beats (two measures) plus two strums for beats one and two in the pickup measure. Begin singing on beat three.

'Round The Mountain

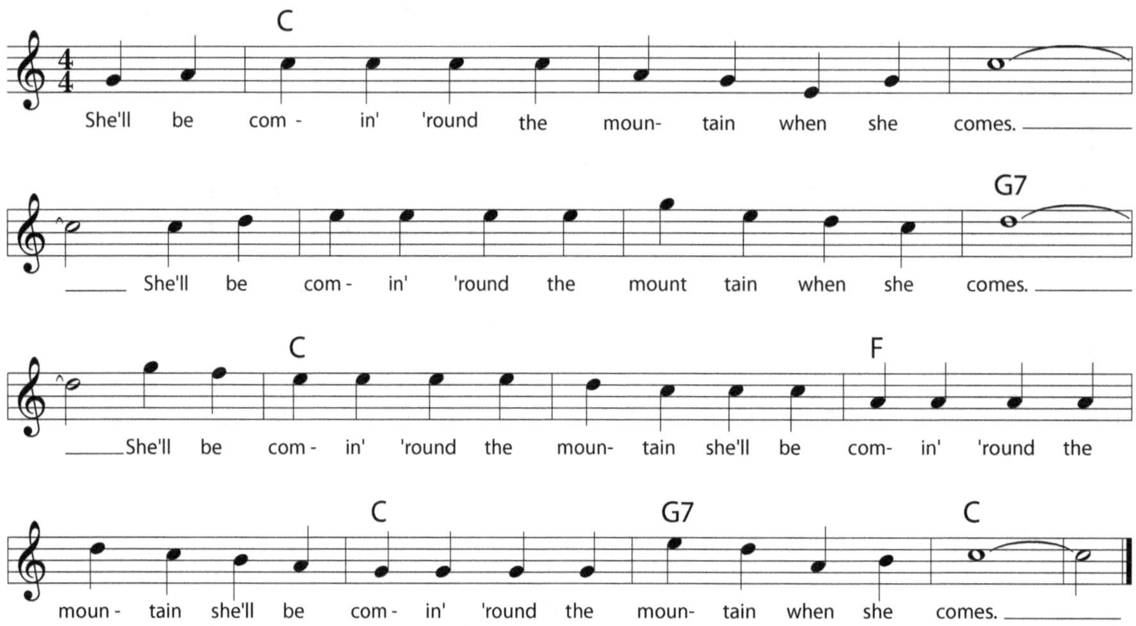

When The Saints Go Marching In is also in 4/4 time which means there will be four strums per measure. This song also has pickup notes beginning on beat two. To add an introduction strum eight beats (two measures) plus one strum for beat one in the pickup measure. Begin singing as written on beat two.

Saints

6 Right-hand Patterns

Picking Patterns

Picking patterns are rhythmic patterns created for the right hand fingers. They usually last for one measure then repeat themselves. This can add a lot of interest to accompaniments.

Right-hand patterns can be diagramed by using tablature. ***Tablature*** or ***TAB*** is a diagram of the guitar strings:

- The sixth string is the lowest line.
- The letters represent the right hand fingers- p = thumb, i = index, m = middle, a = annularis (ring).
- The notes above indicate the rhythm for the pattern.
- The time signature at the beginning of the TAB tells us there are four beats in a measure (top number) and the quarter note will get one count (bottom number).

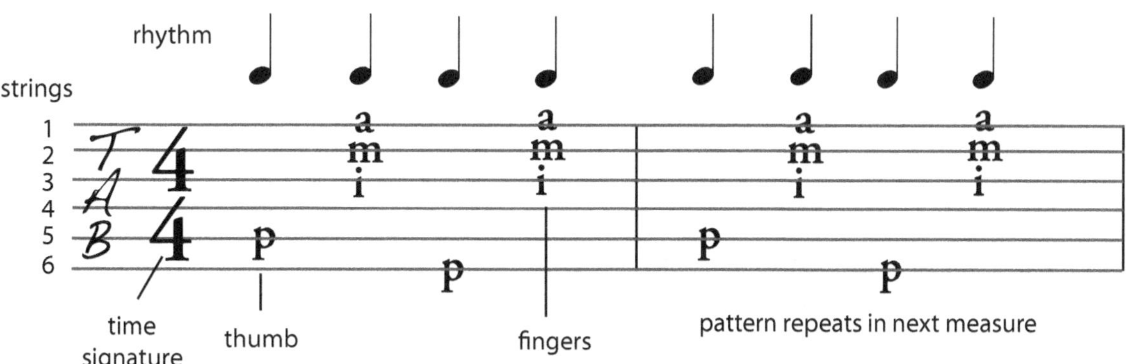

Picking Pattern In 4/4 Time

One of the easiest picking patterns is the **bass, chord, bass, chord (B C B C)** pattern in 4/4 time. The thumb (p) strikes the lower bass note by itself on beat one then fingers i, m, and a strike the upper strings on beat 2. The pattern repeats itself for beats 3 and 4 with the exception of the thumb changing strings on beat 3.

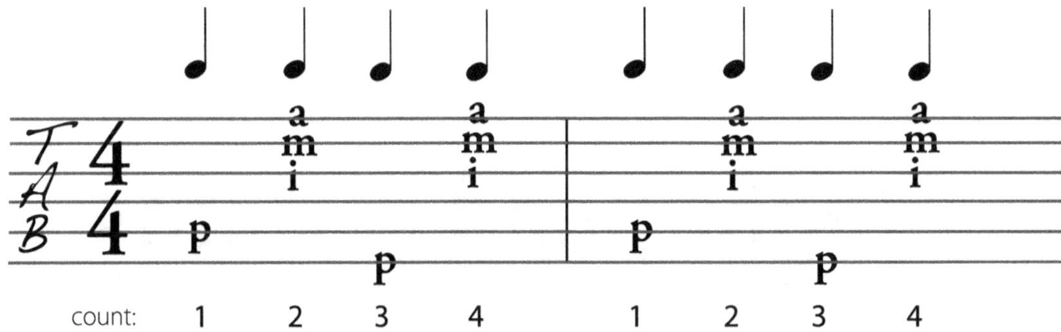

Exercise 6.1

Practice this pattern using open strings (No left-hand). Make sure fingers *i, m*, and *a* play at the same time on beats two and four.

Bass Notes

Each chord has its own set of bass notes that **p** will play. Musically, what we are doing is alternating the root and the fifth of the chord. Don't worry if that doesn't make sense to right now. It will become clear in later chapters when we talk about music theory. Below are the bass string numbers for each chord. It is important to memorize the numbers for every chord and *always* play the first number first.

Chord	Bass Strings
A	5 & 6
A7	
Am*	
C**	
B7**	
E	6 & 5
E7	
Em*	
F	
D	4 & 5
D7	
Dm*	
G	6 & 4
G7	

*These chords are found in minor keys and chord groups. (Chapter 9)

** These chords require an additional move in the left-hand.

Exercise 6.2

This pattern alternates between strings 5 and 6 in the bass (thumb part). It is the same pattern you practiced using open strings. Try it again holding down one of these chords: **A, A7, Am.**

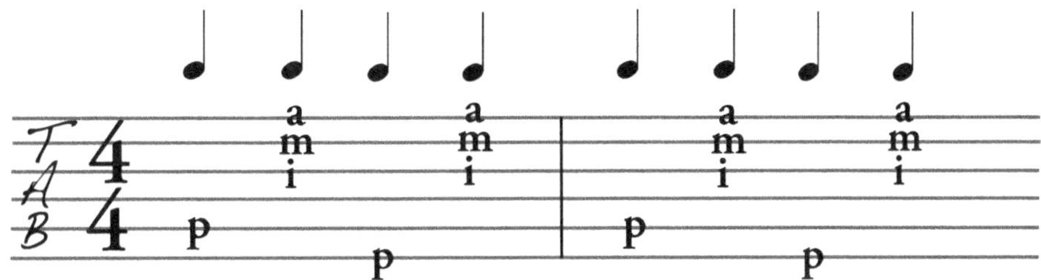

Exercise 6.3

This pattern alternates between strings 6 and 5 in the bass (thumb part). Try it again holding down one of these chords: **E, E7, Em, F.**

Exercise 6.4

This pattern alternates between strings 4 and 5 in the bass (thumb part). Try it again holding down one of these chords: **D, D7, Dm.**

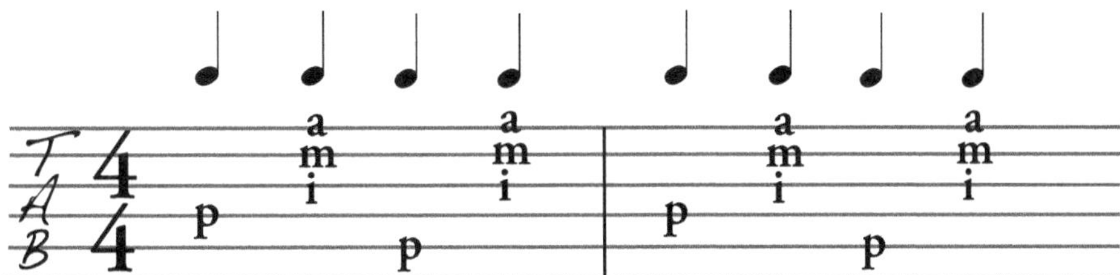

Exercise 6.5

This pattern alternates between strings 6 and 4 in the bass (thumb part). Try it again holding down one of these chords: **G, G7.**

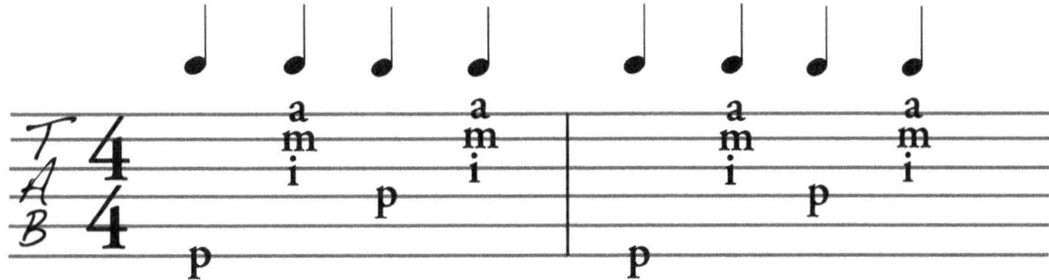

Alternating Bass Notes - C and B7 Chords

On the Bass Notes Chart the C and B7 chords show alternating bass notes between strings 5 & 6. In the diagrams below there is an X on the 6 string for both the C and B7 chords telling us to avoid this string in the right hand. As it stands, if we were to strike the 6th string it would produce a wrong note.

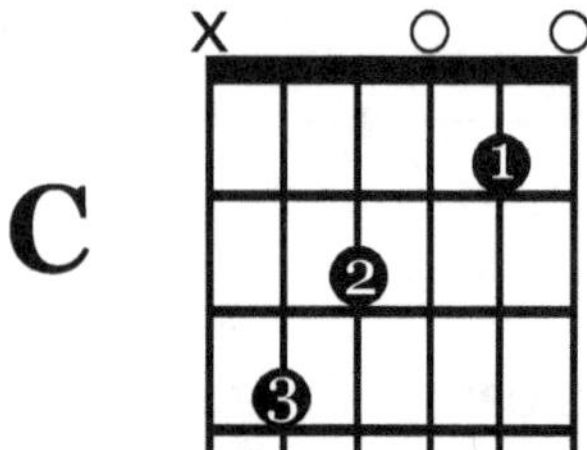

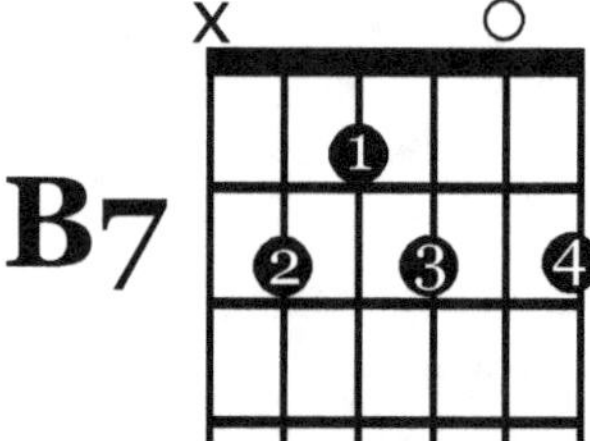

We can call upon the left hand to help us out. When it is time for the right-hand thumb to play the 6th string we can move the finger that is on the fifth string over to the sixth string as shown below. This produces the correct note when the thumb plays string six. Of course if we're going to play string 5 again we have to move it back.

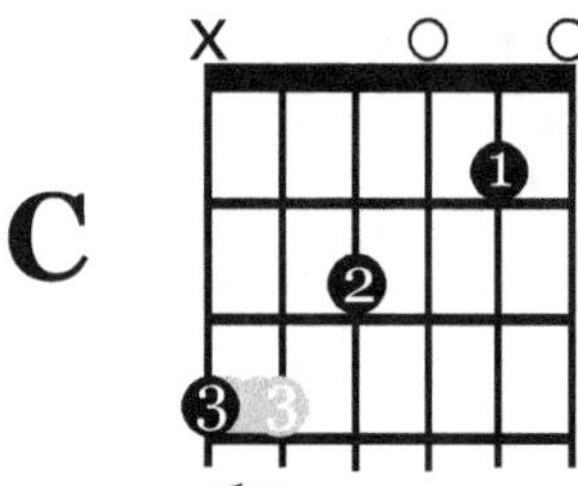

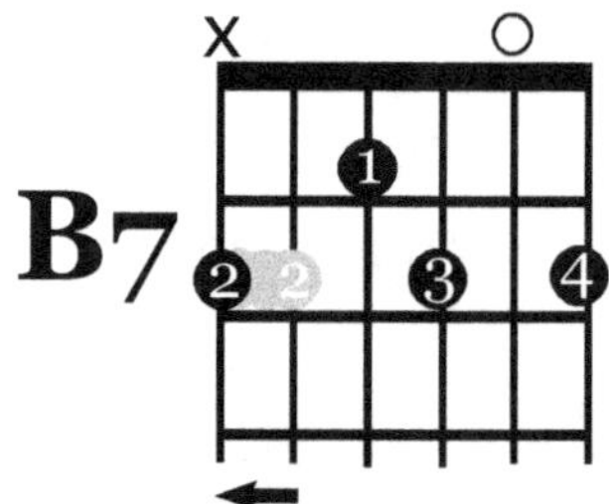

Exercise 6.6

This pattern alternates between strings 5 and 6 in the bass (thumb part). It is the same pattern you practiced using open strings and for the A, A7, and Am chords. Try it again holding down the C or B7 chord and move the left-hand fingers as needed.

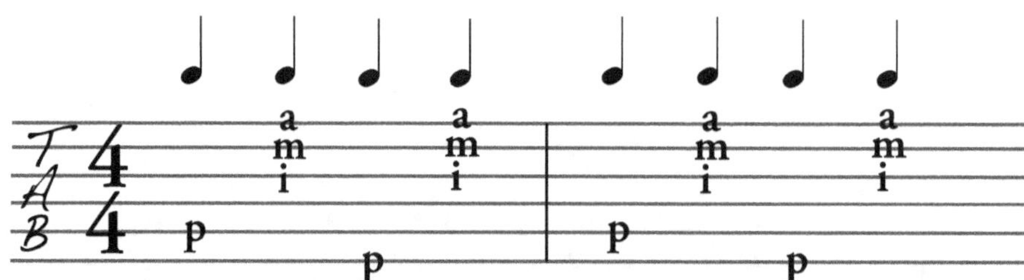

Adding 4/4 Patterns To Primary Chord Groups

Once you've had success alternating bass notes for individual chords, you can try the pattern while switching between chords in a group.

Sometimes when we change chords we may be hitting the same bass string twice in a row. For instance, when we move from an A chord measure to an E7 chord measure. The A chord bass notes are 5 then 6. The E chord bass notes are 6 then 5. This creates two sixth string bass notes in a row, one on beat 3 and one on beat 1 of the new measure. This is normal and will sound good musically. When in doubt, always stay true to the chord.

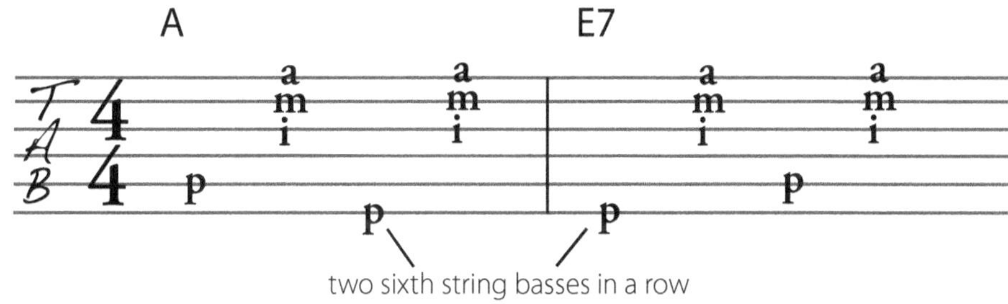

The A Group

Exercise 6.7

Practice the following chord progressions using the BCBC pattern in the right-hand:

A = 5 & 6, D = 4 & 5, and E7 = 6 & 5.

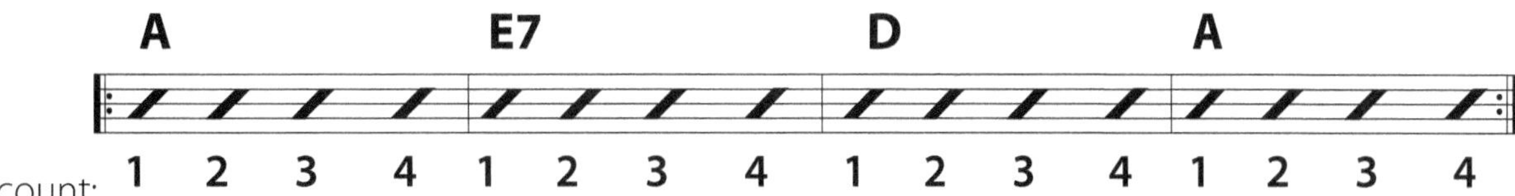

The E Group

Exercise 6.8

Practice the following chord progressions using the BCBC pattern in the right-hand:

E = 6 & 5, A = 5 & 6, and B7 = 5 & 6.

Ex. 6.8 a

Ex. 6.8 b

The D Group

Exercise 6.9

Practice the following chord progressions using the BCBC pattern in the right-hand:

D = 4 & 5, G = 6 & 4, and A7 = 5 & 6.

Ex. 6.9 a

Ex. 6.9 b

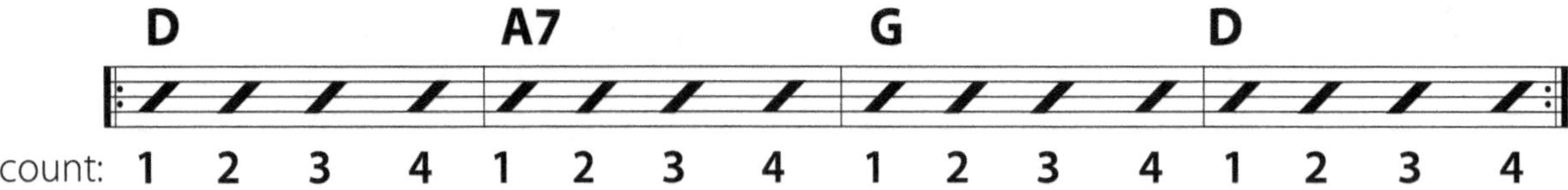

The G Group

Exercise 6.10

Practice the following chord progressions using the BCBC pattern in the right-hand:

G = 6 & 4, C = 5 & 6, and D7 = 4 & 5.

Ex. 6.10 a

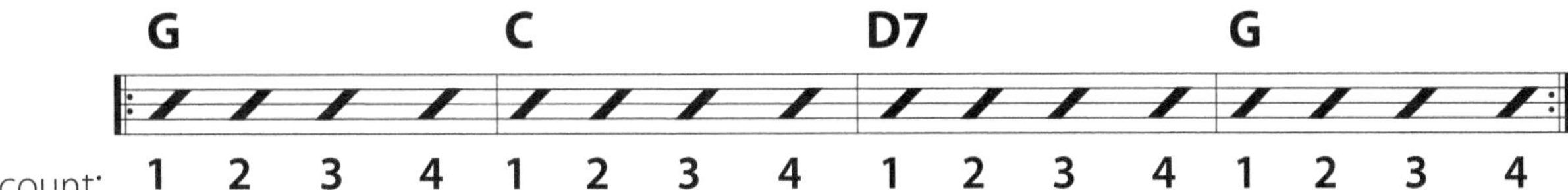

count: 1 2 3 4 1 2 3 4 1 2 3 4 1 2 3 4

Ex. 6.10 b

count: 1 2 3 4 1 2 3 4 1 2 3 4 1 2 3 4

The C Group

Exercise 6.11

Practice the following chord progressions using the BCBC pattern in the right-hand:

C = 5 & 6, F = 6 & 5, and G7 = 6 & 4.

Ex. 6.11 a

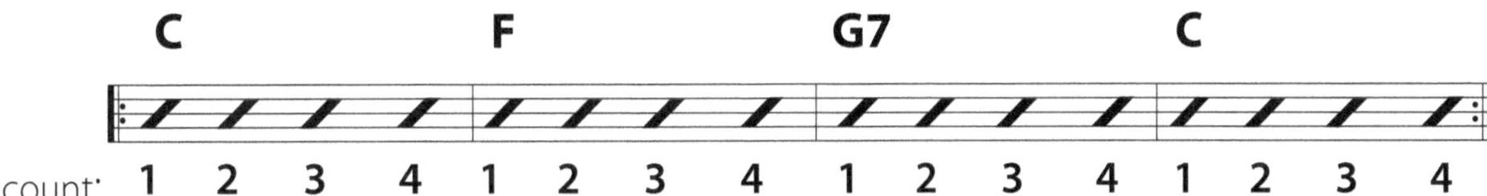

count: 1 2 3 4 1 2 3 4 1 2 3 4 1 2 3 4

Ex. 6.11 b

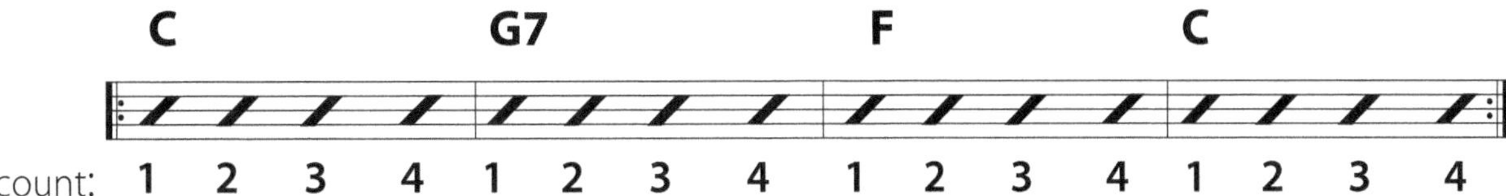

count: 1 2 3 4 1 2 3 4 1 2 3 4 1 2 3 4

Picking Pattern In 3/4 Time

The following is a **bass chord chord pattern (BCC)** in 3/4 time and is two measures in length. The thumb (p) plays the first bass note on beat one of the *first measure* and the alternate bass note on beat one of the *second measure.*

BCC pattern 1- Alternating Bass

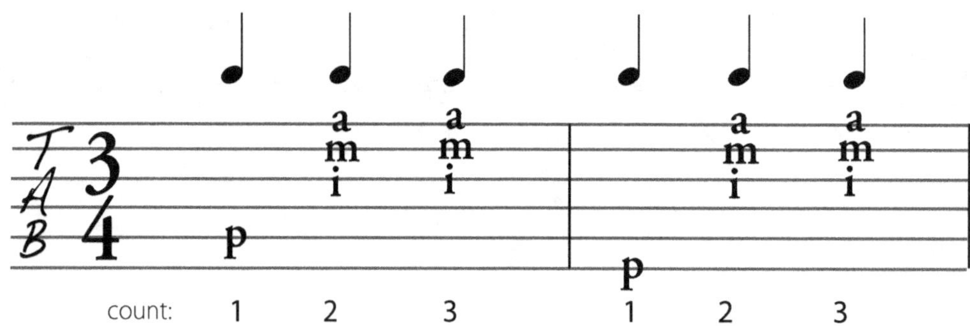

Alternating bass notes is typical for waltzes and for many pop tunes but is not always desirable for other pieces such as hymns and carols. In the latter types of music, the first bass note of a given chord may be played repeatedly avoiding alternating altogether. If you are not sure which pattern to use, play the piece both ways and let your ear be the judge.

BCC pattern 2- Non Alternating Bass

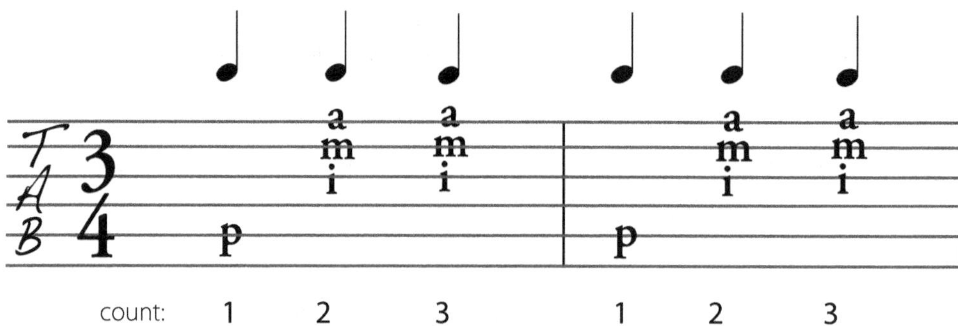

Exercise 6.12

Practice patterns 1 and 2 above using open strings (No left-hand). Make sure fingers *i, m,* and *a* play at the same time on beats two and three.

Exercise 6.13

Practice the patterns 1 and 2 above applying them to the chords you know.

Adding 3/4 Patterns To Primary Chord Groups

Once you've had success alternating bass notes for individual chords you can try the patterns while switching between chords in a group. Before you start be clear as to which pattern you will use; the alternating bass pattern or the non alternating bass pattern.

The A Group

Exercise 6.14

Practice the following chord progressions using BCC patterns 1 & 2 in the right-hand:

A = 5 & 6, D = 4 & 5, and E7 = 6 & 5.

Ex. 6.14 a

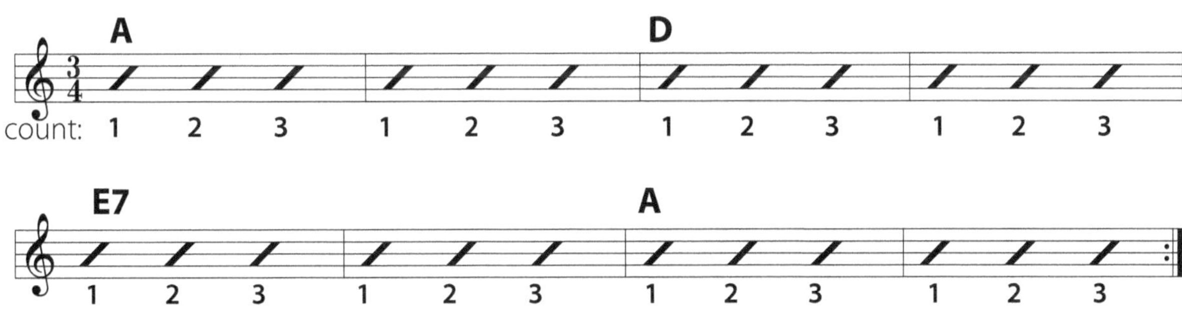

Ex. 6.14 b

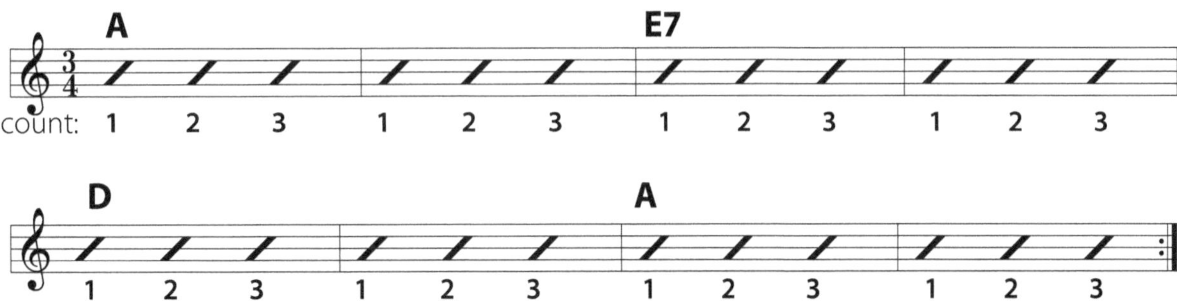

The E Group

Exercise 6.15

Practice the following chord progressions using BCC patterns 1 & 2 in the right-hand:

E = 6 & 5, A = 5 & 6, and B7 = 5 & 6.

Ex. 6.15 a

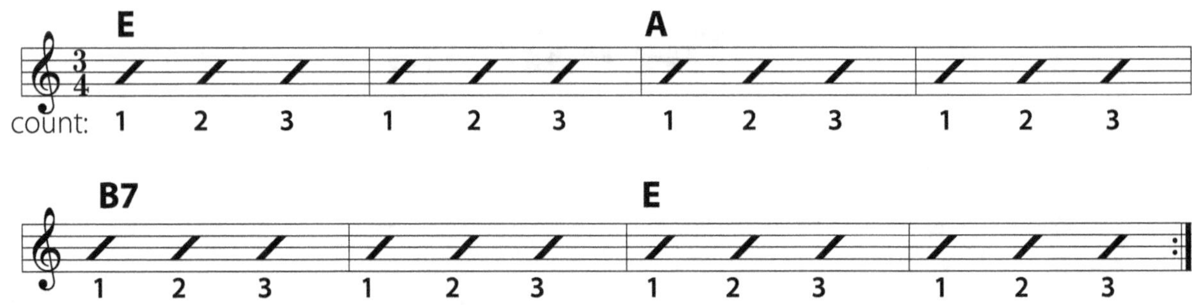

Ex. 6.15 b

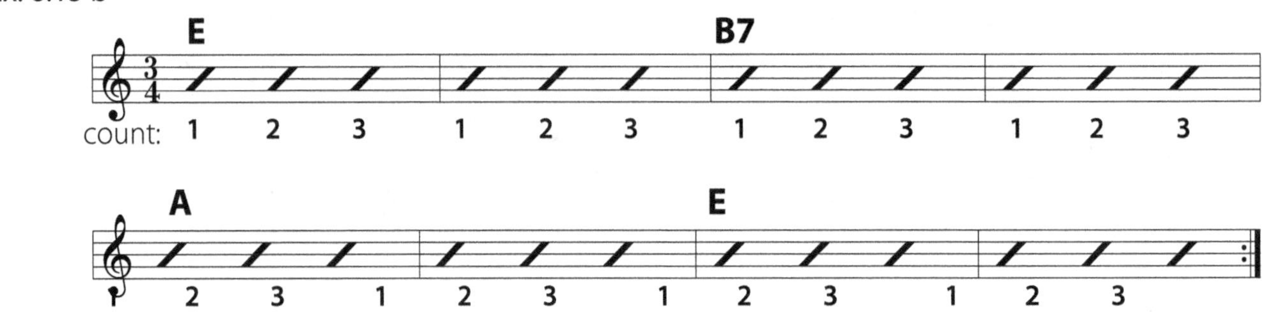

The D Group

Exercise 6.16

Practice the following chord progressions using BCC patterns 1 & 2 in the right-hand:

D = 4 & 5, G = 6 & 4, and A7 = 5 & 6.

Ex. 6.16 a

Ex. 6.16 b

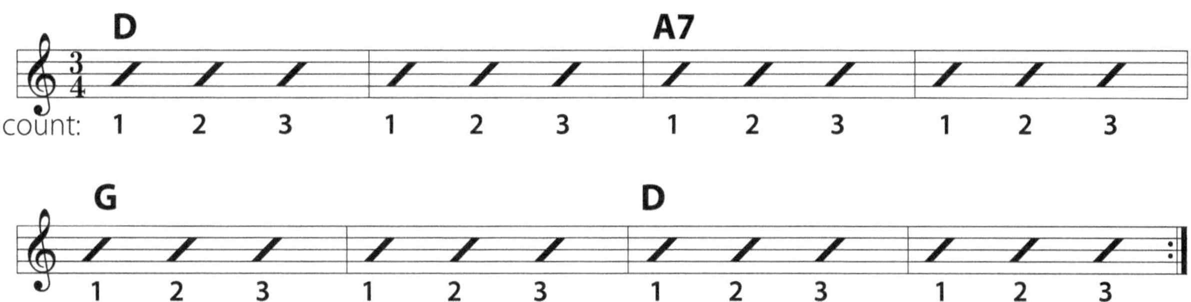

The G Group

Exercise 6.17

Practice the following chord progressions using BCC patterns 1 & 2 in the right-hand:

G = 6 & 4, C = 5 & 6, and D7 = 4 & 5.

Ex. 6.17 a

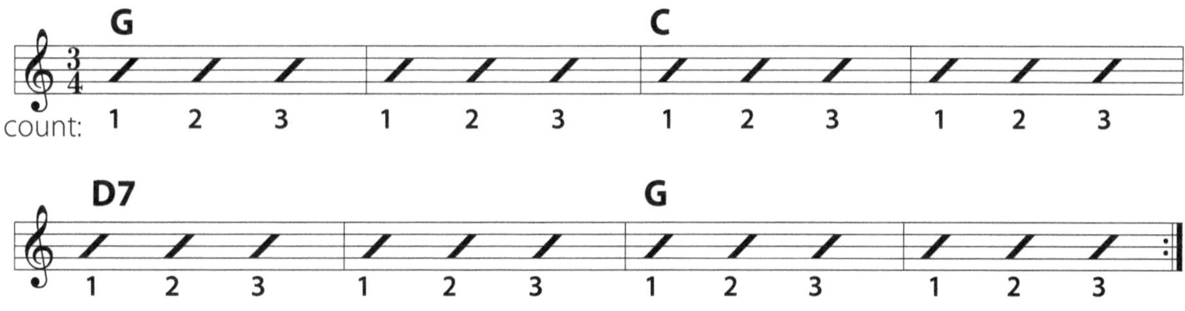

Ex. 6.17 b

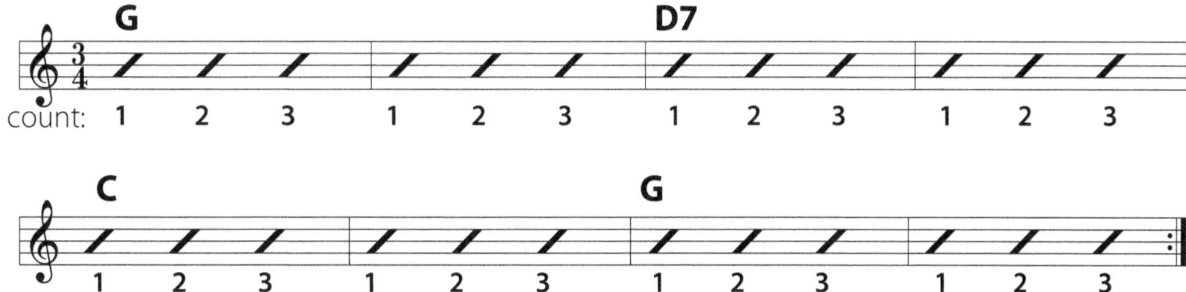

The C Group

Exercise 6.18

Practice the following chord progressions using BCC patterns 1 & 2 in the right-hand:

C = 5 & 6, F = 6 & 5, and G7 = 6 & 4.

Ex. 6.18 a

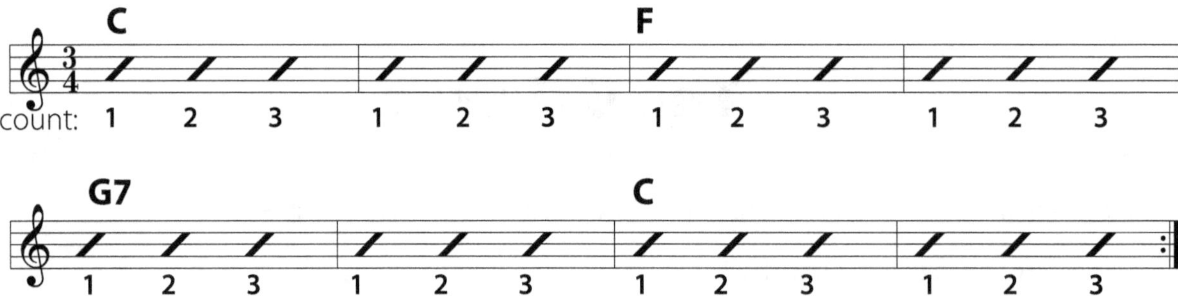

Ex. 6.18 b

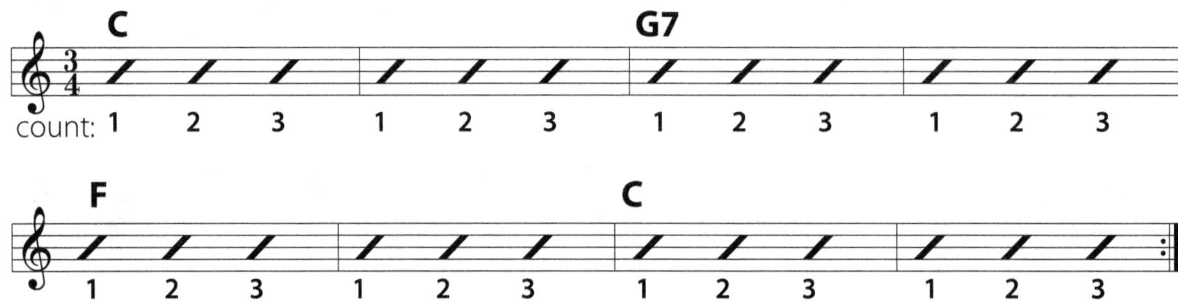

7 Scales And Key Signatures

Accidentals (Chromatic Signs)

A ***chromatic sign*** or ***accidental*** placed to the left of a note, alters the pitch of that note by one half step (one fret). A ***half step*** is the smallest distance from one pitch to the next immediate pitch, up or down. There are three accidental signs: the ***sharp***, the ***flat***, and the ***natural***.

A ***sharp*** raises the pitch by one half step. Notice that if the note is a line note the center of the sharp is also on the line. If the note is a space note the center is placed in the space.

A ***flat*** lowers the pitch by one half step. Notice that if the note is a line note the rounded part of the flat is also on the line. If the note is a space note the rounded part is placed in the space.

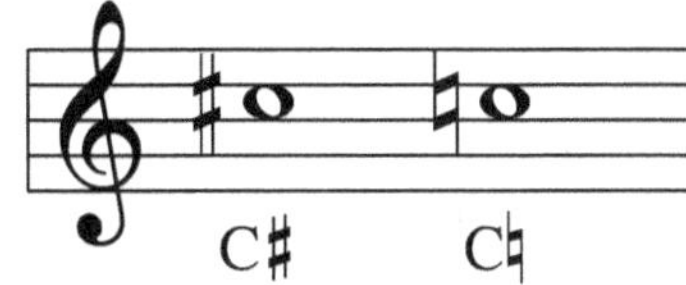

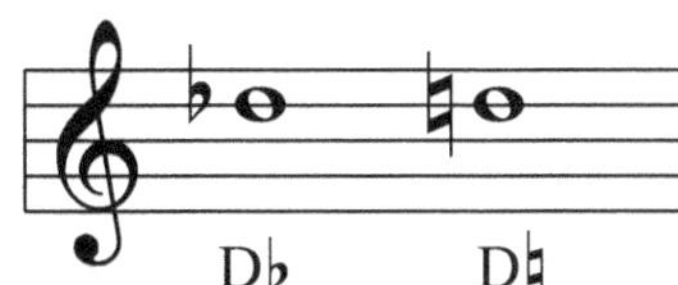

A ***natural*** cancels a sharp or flat restoring the note to its previous pitch. Notice that if the note is a line note the center of the natural is also on the line. If the note is a space note the center is placed in the space.

The Chromatic Scale

There are only twelve different pitches in western hemisphere music. These twelve pitches create the ***chromatic scale***. They are a half step apart. We can start the chromatic scale on any pitch and add half steps until the original pitch is reached an an octave higher. (An ***octave*** includes 8 notes, the first and the eighth are the same name.)

The example below shows the chromatic scale starting on the pitch C. It ascends with sharps and descends with flats. The C notes at the beginning, middle, and end of the scale represent the same pitch so they are counted as one note.

Chromatic Scale starting on C

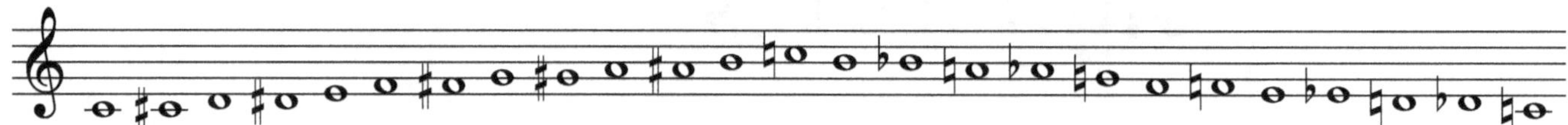

Many pitches have two different names. They are called ***enharmonic***, meaning they *sound* the same but have two *different* names. For instance **C♯** and **D♭** sound exactly alike but when written one or the other name will be chosen. This may seem confusing at first but as we study more theory the reason for this will become clear.

That is why the chromatic scale above uses only 12 pitches. The ascending and descending names are different but the pitches are the same.

C C♯/D♭ D D♯/E♭ E F F♯/G♭ G G♯/A♭ A A♯/B♭ B C

In the example below the enharmonic names are shown in gray.

Notice there is no gray box between the pitches E and F, and B and C. These are ***natural half steps***. If **E** was sharped it would sound the same as **F**. If **F** was flatted it would sound like **E**. The same would be true if we sharped **B**. **B** would sound like **C**. If **C** was flatted it would sound like **B**. **B♯**, **C♭**, **E♯**, and **F♭** are definite possibilities but they do not happen very often.

E♯ = F   F♭ = E   B♯ = C   C♭ = B

Exercise 7.1

Memorize the chromatic scale. Memorize the enharmonic spellings for each note.

The Major Scale

The major scale can be constructed from any of the twelve pitches in the chromatic scale. The major scale has seven different pitches that move alphabetically up or down. It is built using ***whole*** **(W)** and half steps **(H).** (A ***whole step*** is two half steps combined.) The major scale must follow this pattern:

W, W, H, W, W, W, H

If it does not follow the pattern exactly then it is not a major scale.

Exercise 7.2

Memorize the major scale pattern.

Scale Construction

1) To construct a **C major scale**, we must start with the pitch C and add all of the alphabetical notes in order until C is reached again.

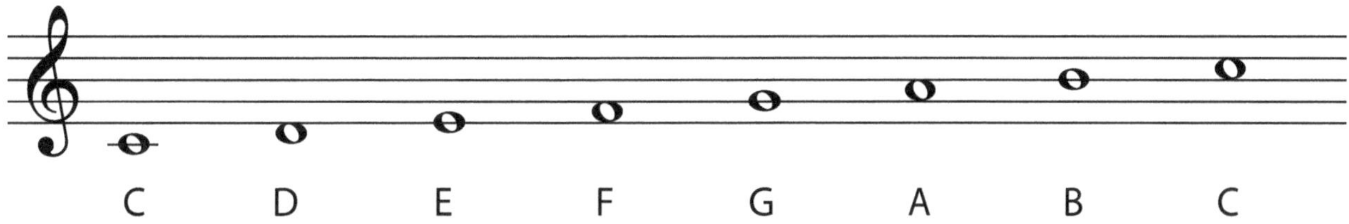

2) Next we need to measure the distance between each note. It will either be a whole step or a half step. Start at the left with C to D and work your way to the right.

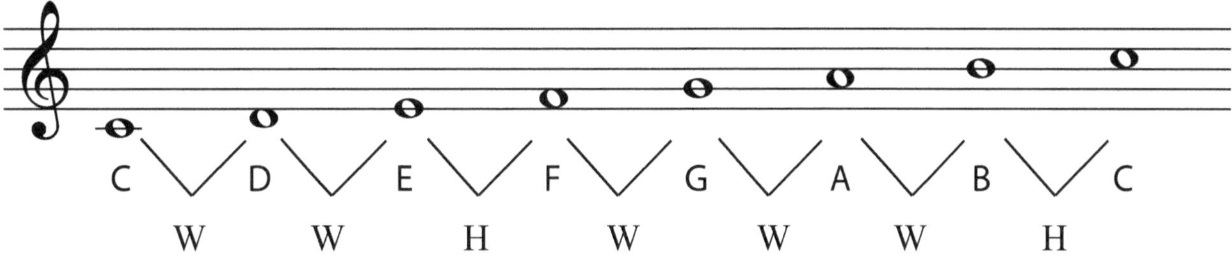

3) The whole and half step pattern matches the pattern for the major scale: W, W, H, W, W, W, H. We have created a C Major Scale!

So what's in the name? 1) It is called C because it starts on the pitch C. 2) It is a scale because the notes are moving in alphabetical order until the original pitched is reach again. 3) Finally, it is major because it follows the whole and half step pattern for a major scale.

Now let's build the **G Major Scale**.

1) To construct a G major scale, we must start with the pitch G and add all of the alphabetical notes in order until G is reached again.

2) Next we need to measure the distance between each note. It will either be a whole step or a half step. Start at the left with G to A and work your way to the right.

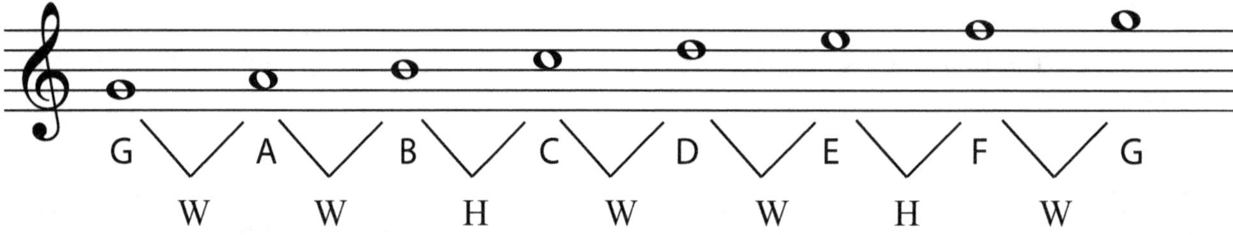

3) If the whole and half step pattern matches the pattern for the major scale: W, W, H, W, W, W, H then we have created a G Major Scale.

Unfortunately, the patterns do not match. We can see the scale pattern starts to break down between the E and the F notes and F to G isn't working either

Let's go through a couple of troubleshooting steps to see how we can fix this. First let's determine what notes are working.

- E is correct because it works with the D to E combination.
- The last G note is correct the way it is too. (Remember this note has to be the same pitch as our starting pitch.)
- That leaves the F. We can't change the fact that we need some kind of F because we need to move in alphabetical order until the original note is reached an octave higher.
- What we *can* do is *alter* the F. If we change F to F♯, the distance between E and F♯ increases by a half step and the distance between F♯ and G decreases to a half step. Now our pattern fits the major scale pattern!

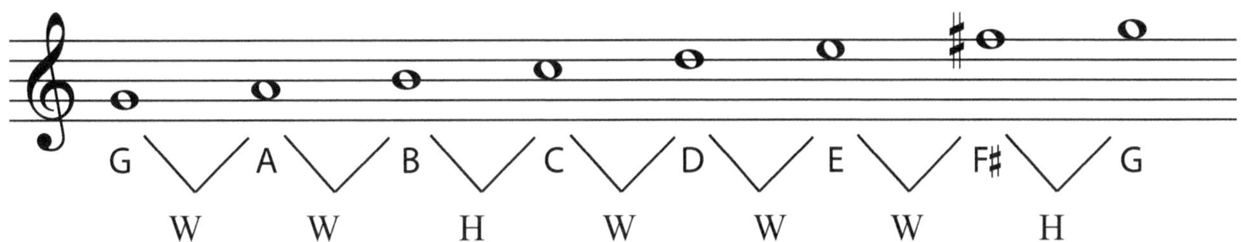

We can conclude that every time we build a G major scale we will replace F with F♯. Because this will always be true, we can place a sharp on the F line right after the treble clef. This sharp changes all the F**'s** to F♯ **'s** ***regardless of where they appear on the staff***. This is called a ***key signature***. It is called the ***key of G*** because our starting note for the scale is G.

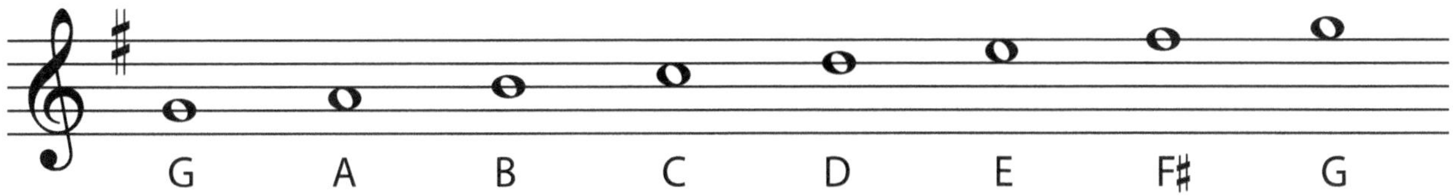

Let's try another scale, the **F Major Scale**.

1) This time we will start with F and add all of the alphabetical notes in order until F is reached again.

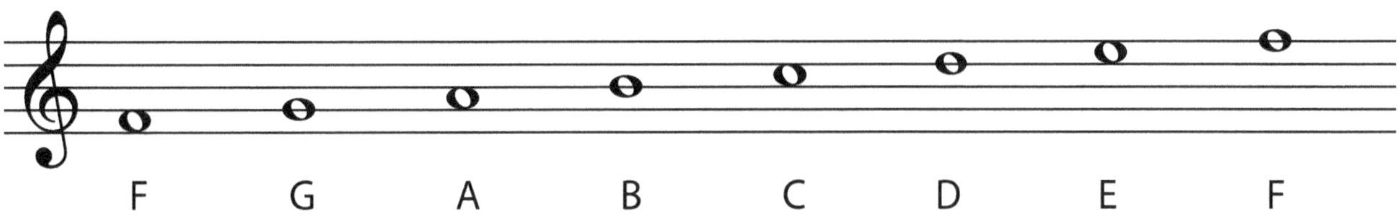

2) Next measure the whole and half step relationships starting with F to G.

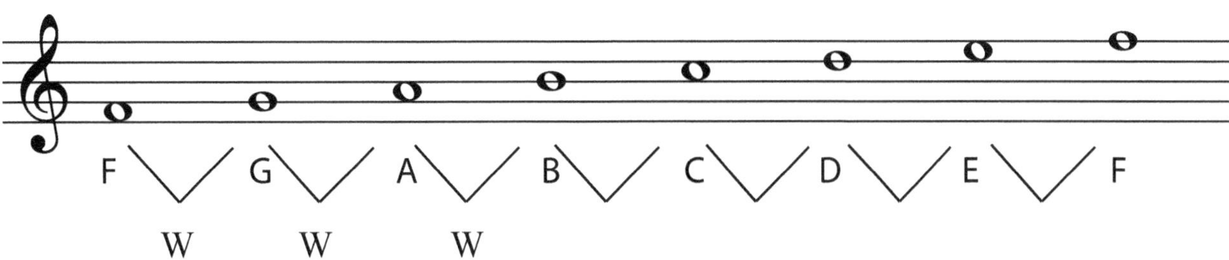

3) Almost immediately we see the pattern is broken between A and B. This needs to be fixed before we can continue. The A note works with the note before it so that points to the B note as the problem. We must reduce the distance by a half step. If we flat the **B** it gives us the half step we need. As we continue on through the rest of the scale, everything else matches our major scale pattern.

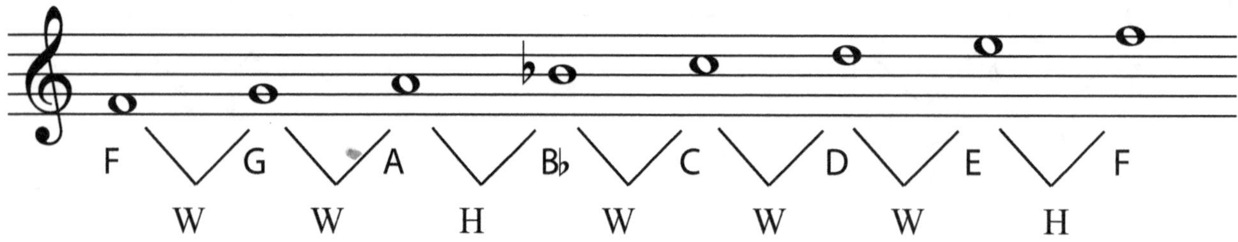

So we can conclude that every time we build a F major scale we will replace **B** with **B♭**. The flat changes all the **B's** to **B♭ 's** regardless of where they appear on the staff, giving us the key of **F**.

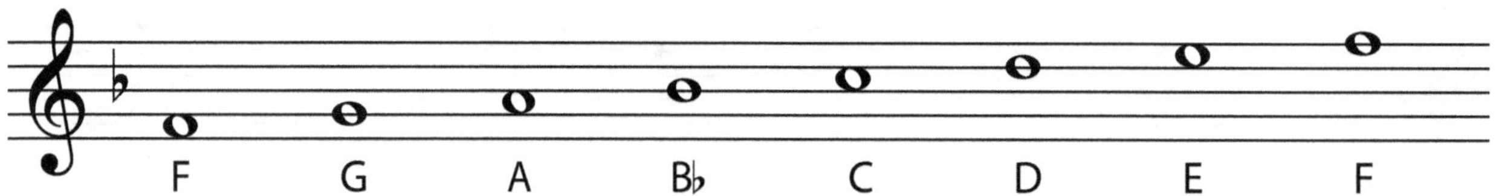

Key Signatures

Below is an example of all the key signatures notated as they would appear in a piece of music. Notice the placement of the sharps and flats for each key. The accidentals will always appear in this order regardless of where they appear on the staff. Also take note there are either sharps *or* flats in a key signature *never both.*

Sharp Keys

Flat Keys

Circle Of Fifths

It is beneficial to know and identify all twelve major tonal centers. This is easily achieved by memorizing the circle of fifths. The circle of fifths is arranged so there are five alphabetic letters between the keys. Whether moving forward or backward around the circle the key signature will increase or decrease by one sharp or flat.

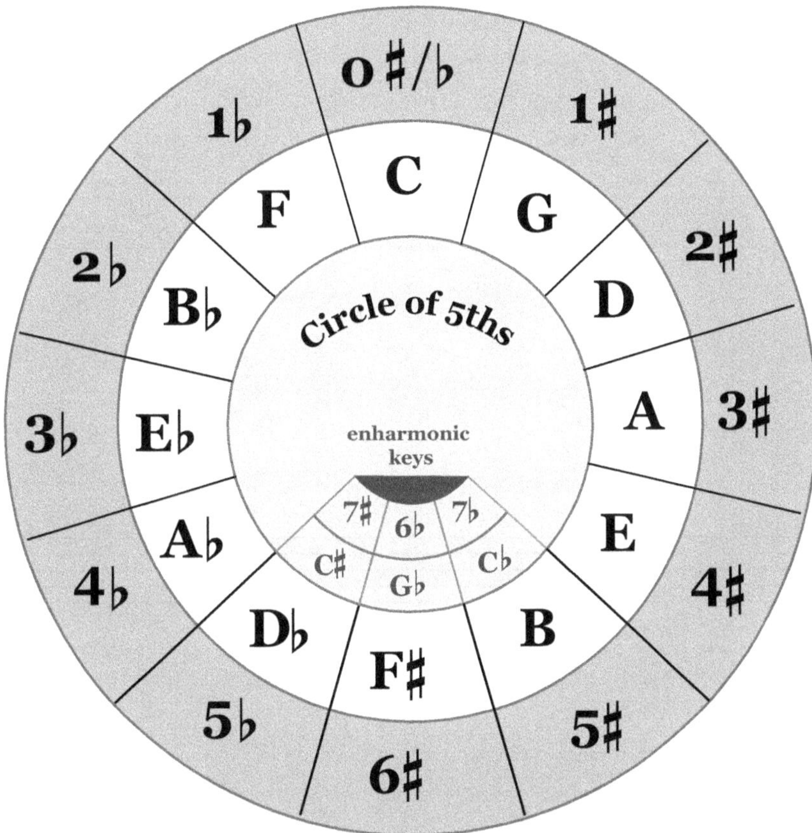

Although there are twelve tonal centers, there are actually fifteen different key signatures representing these tonal centers. Just as there are enharmonic notes, there are enharmonic keys as well. The circle above shows all keys. The enharmonic keys are as noted.

Exercise 7.3

To memorize the circle of fifths use the following steps:

1) Start with the letter C and count it as number one.

2) Count up until you reach the fifth letter from C. Your answer should be G. G is the next key from C and has one sharp.

3) Now start with G and count it as one.

4) Count up five letters. Your answer should be D. D has two sharps.

5) Keep repeating this process until you've made your way back to C again.

Notice the same process works in reverse too. (For example if you start on C and count backwards five letters your answer should be F.) Use the circle of fifths wheel above to help you with the correct answers.

Scale Degrees

Each scale member can be given a number name in addition to its letter name. These numbers are referred to as ***scale degrees***. For example, the first note in the C scale is C or one, D is two, E is three and so on. The scale degrees use upper or lower case Roman numerals as shown below.

C Major Scale

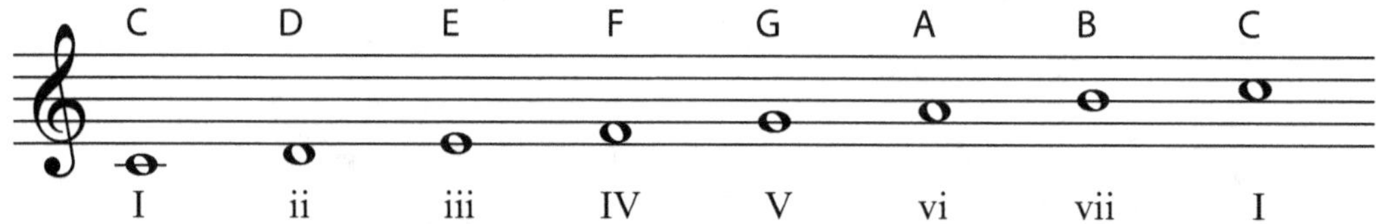

G Major Scale

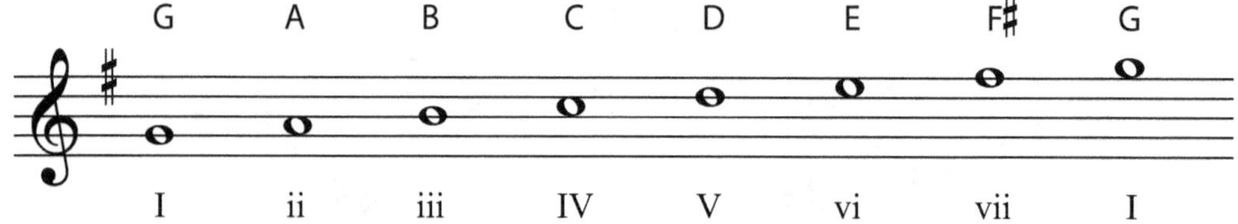

Exercise 7.4

Write out the major scale in each key using accidentals beside the appropriate notes. Show the whole/half step pattern Then rewrite the scale placing the key signature after the treble clef as shown below. Label each scale degree with the appropriate Roman numeral. Start with the key of C and follow the order of the circle of fifths.

It is important to memorize how many sharps or flats are included in each key signature and where each sharp or flat is placed on the staff. Check your accidental placement with the key signatures found on page 76 to ensure you are using the correct order.

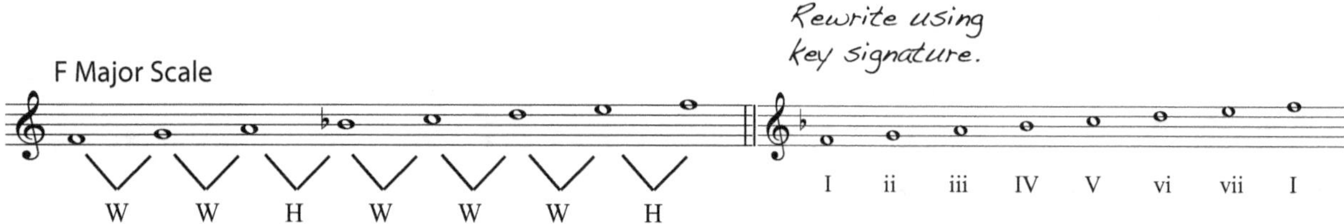

8 Chord Relationships

THE I, IV, AND V CHORD RELATIONSHIP

Chords are built from scale degrees. The chords we have been learning so far are the primary chords built on the **first (I), fourth, (IV), and fifth (V)** scale degrees of a major scale. For example, the **C group** is built from the **C major scale. C** is the first note of the scale and produces the **C** or I chord. **F** is the fourth note of the scale and produces the **F** or IV chord and **G** is the fifth note of the scale and produces the **G**(7)*or V(7) chord.

C Scale

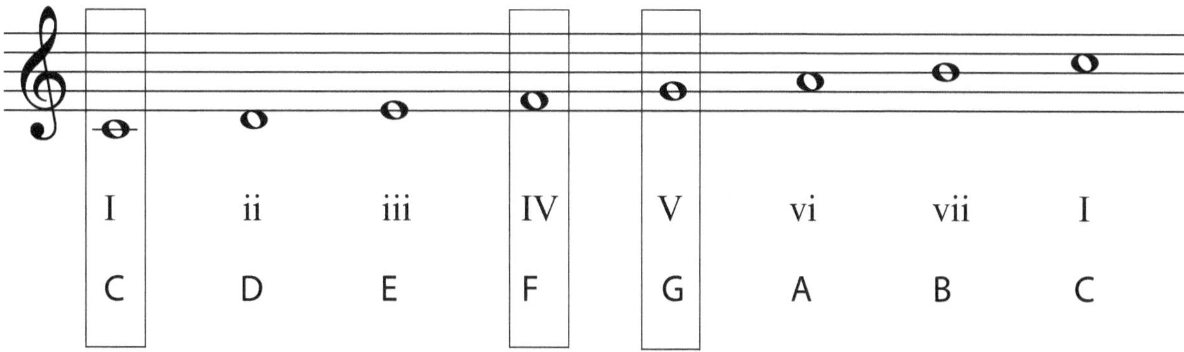

*The meaning of the '7' following the chord name will be explained in a later chapter.

In the key of G, **G** is the first note of the scale and produces the **G** or **I** chord. **C** is the fourth note of the scale and produces the **C** or **IV** chord and **D** is the fifth note of the scale and produces the **D**(7) or **V**(7) chord.

G Scale

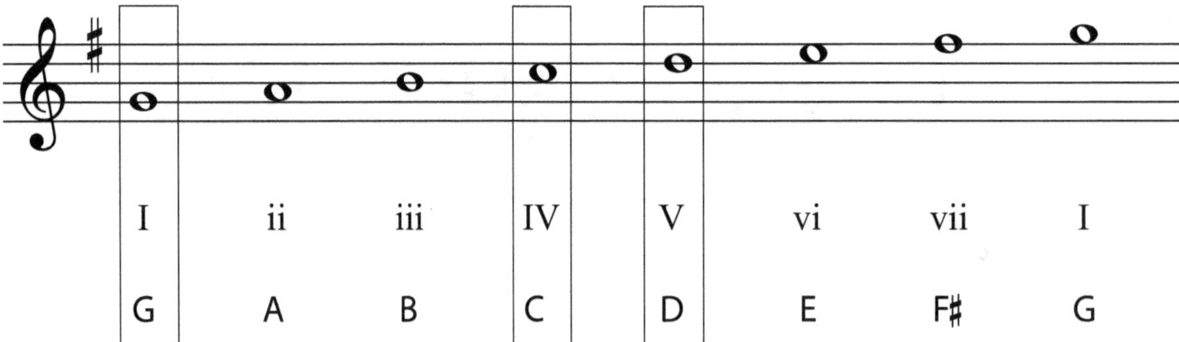

In the key of F, **F** is the first note of the scale and produces the **F** or **I** chord. **B♭** is the fourth note of the scale and produces the **B♭** or **IV** chord and **C** is the fifth note of the scale and produces the **C**(7) or **V**(7) chord.

If the scale degree uses an accidental in it's name the chord must also include the accidental in it's name. That is why the **IV** chord is given the name **B♭** instead of **B** (which would be a completely different chord).

F Scale

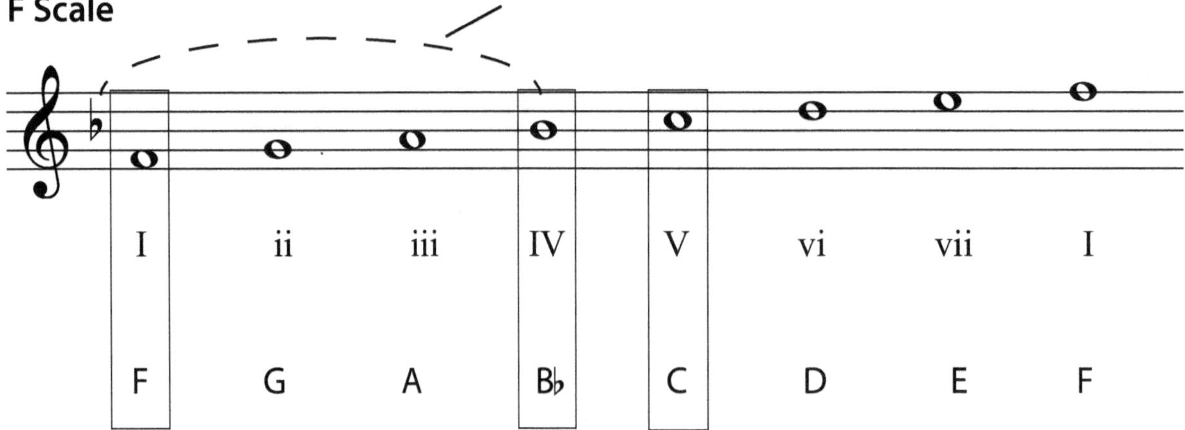

Exercise 8.1

Fill in the **I**, **IV**, and **V** Chords for every key in the chart below.

If you are subscribed to Christi Green Studios (http://christigreenstudios.com) you can log in and check your answers.

Key of:	I	IV	V(7)
C			
G			
D			
A			
E			
B			
F#			
Db			
Ab			
Eb			
Bb			
F			

Transposing

The term ***transpose*** means to rewrite a piece of music in a key that is different from the original key. By knowing the chord numbers we can easily transpose music from one key to another. For instance, *Down in the Valley* was originally written in the key of **A major** as shown below. In this key the **A** chord is **I** and the **E7** chord is **V**(7). To transpose it to a different key, we simply substitute any **I** and **V**(7) chord in the new key for **A** and **E7**. The example below shows *Down in The Valley* in the original key of **A major**. The next example of *Down in The Valley* shows it transposed to the key of **E major**. Notice that the **E chord** has been substituted for the **A chord**, the **B7 chord** for the **E7 chord.**

Down In The Valley
(key of A)

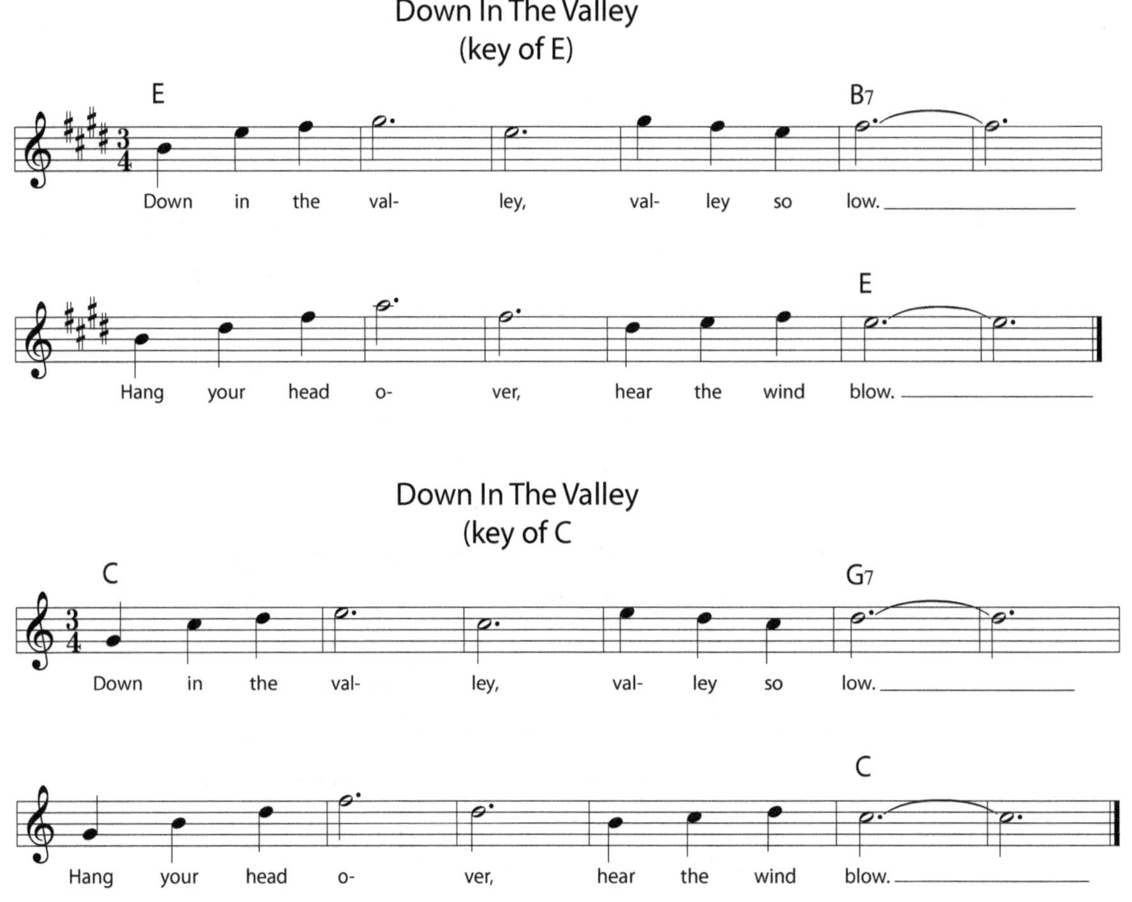

Notice that the notes and key signature change as well as the chords. We must make these changes or we would be singing and playing in two different keys! (And *THAT* would not be pretty!)

Exercise 8.2

Transpose the chords and melodies for the Songs Listed below:

Silent Night: original key - G, new key C. (pg. 52)

Amazing Grace: original key - E, new key G. (pg. 39)

Saints: original key - C, new key A. (pg. 58)

Streets: original key - D, new key E. (pg. 45)

9 Minor Keys And Chord Groups

Relative Minor Keys

For every major key there is a ***relative minor key***. Major and minor keys are relative if they share the same key signature. To find the relative minor of a major key, start with the first note of the scale and count up to the sixth note. The sixth note is the name of the relative minor key. We can then use our new note to build a new a new scale, the A minor scale.

For example, to find the relative minor key of C major, start with the C scale and count up six notes. You should land on A. A minor and C major are relatives because they share the same key signature meaning they use the same notes.

C Major Scale

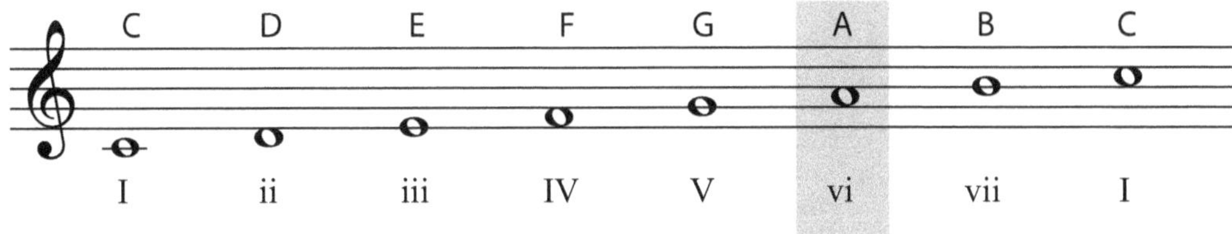

A Minor Scale - built off of the 6th scale degree of the C scale.

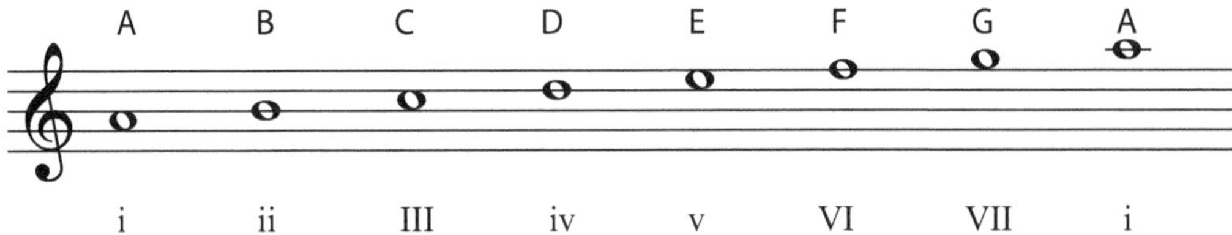

Let's find the relative minor for G major. Start with the G scale and beginning with G as one find the sixth note of the scale.

Your answer should be E. We can use our new note to build a new scale, the E minor scale.

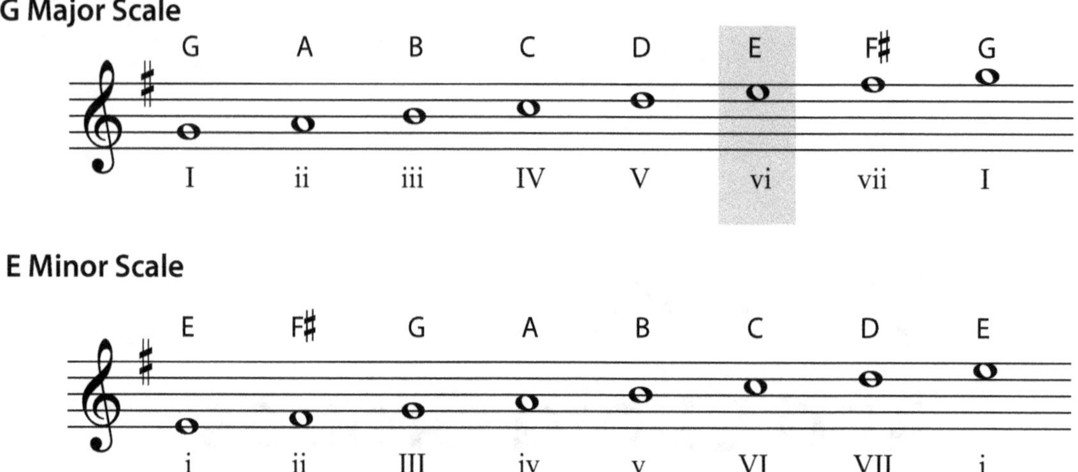

A scale built from the sixth scale degree of a major scale is always minor. As mentioned earlier they share all of the same notes. The difference then is the *sound* of the scale. Major scales sound 'brighter' or 'happier' while minor scales sound 'sad' or 'darker'. Even though we are using all of the same notes, because we changed our starting position our pattern of whole and half steps has changed.

The pattern for a minor scale is: **W, H, W, W, H, W, W.**

A Natural Minor Scale

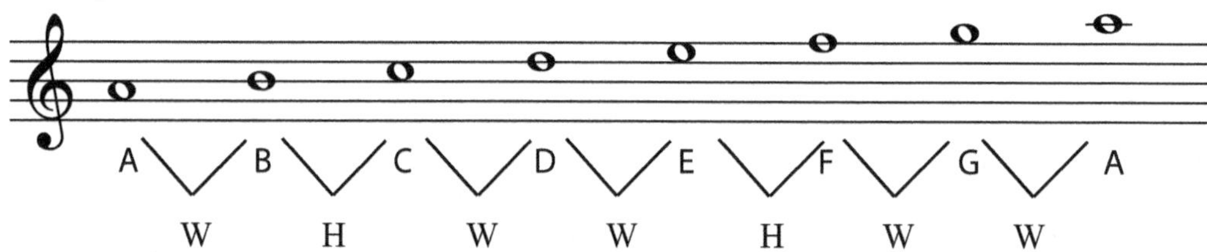

E Natural Minor Scale

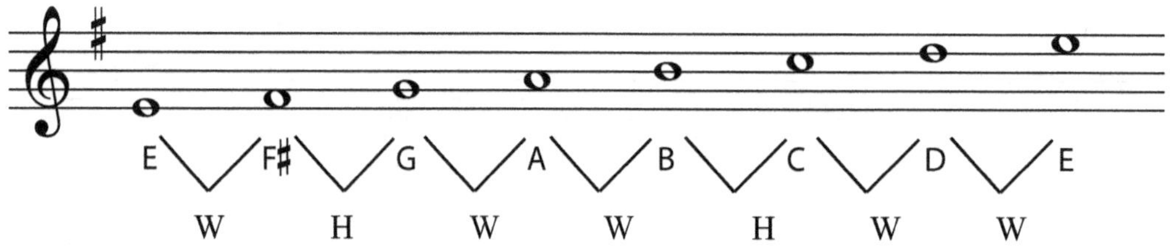

The chart below shows key signatures for the major and relative minor keys.

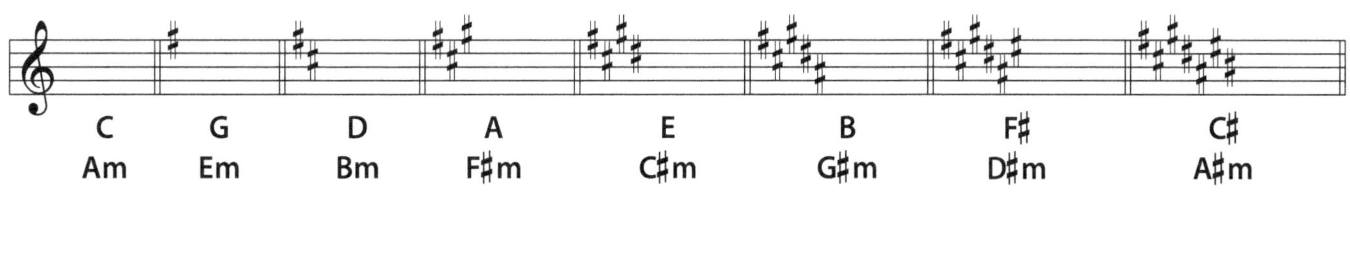

Three Kinds Of Minor

The minor scale we just learned is referred to as the ***natural minor***, meaning it uses the exact same notes as it's relative major.

We can produce a new scale from the natural minor by altering just one note. This new scale is called the ***harmonic minor scale***. The harmonic minor scale is exactly like the natural minor scale except we raise the seventh scale degree up one half step. In our example below the seventh scale degree is G. To raise G up a half step we would replace G with G♯. We treat the G♯ as an *accidental* meaning it is changed in the music but it is *never* included in the key signature.

A Natural Minor Scale

A Harmonic Minor Scale

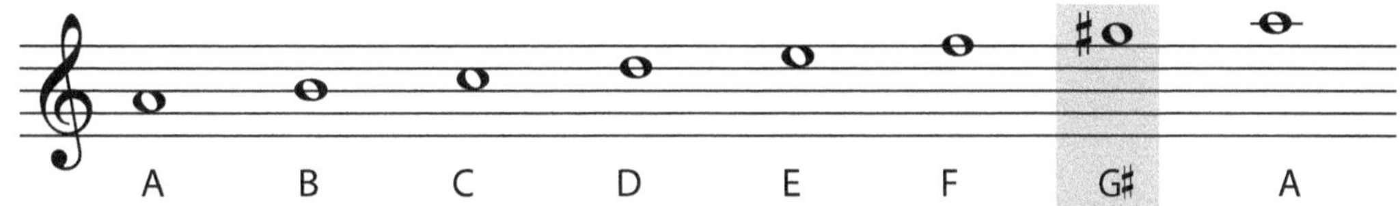

The third type minor scale is called the ***melodic minor***. It raises both the 6th and the 7th scale degree of the natural minor scale. At this point this scale is not important to our studies from a chordal standpoint so there is no need to discuss this further.

Exercise 9.1

Write out the natural minor and harmonic minor scales for each key. Start with the Key of Am and work your way through the circle of fifths. You can check your answers at http://christigreenstudios.com

Minor Chord Groups

The chord groups below are built from the harmonic minor scale. The one chord (i) is minor, the four chord (iv) is minor, and the five chord (V7) is major. These are the primary in the keys Am and Em.

Minor chord names always use a lower case 'm' that follows the chord name. Chords that do not have the lower case 'm' are major chords.

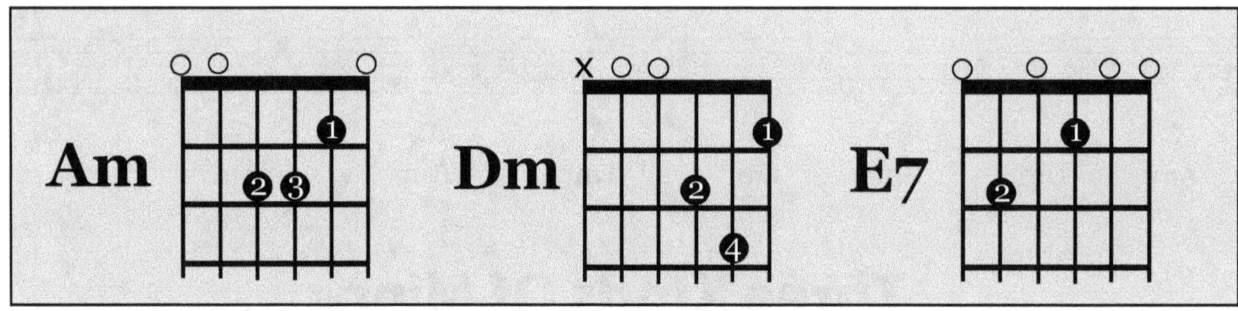

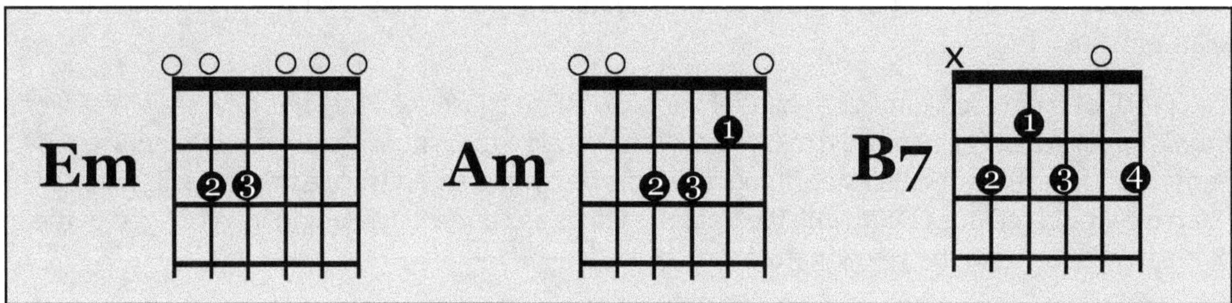

A Minor Group

Exercise 9.2

Work these chords out the same way you did for the chord groups in chapter 5. Only the eight count strum is shown in the examples below. *Be sure to practice the six, four and three counts as well.*

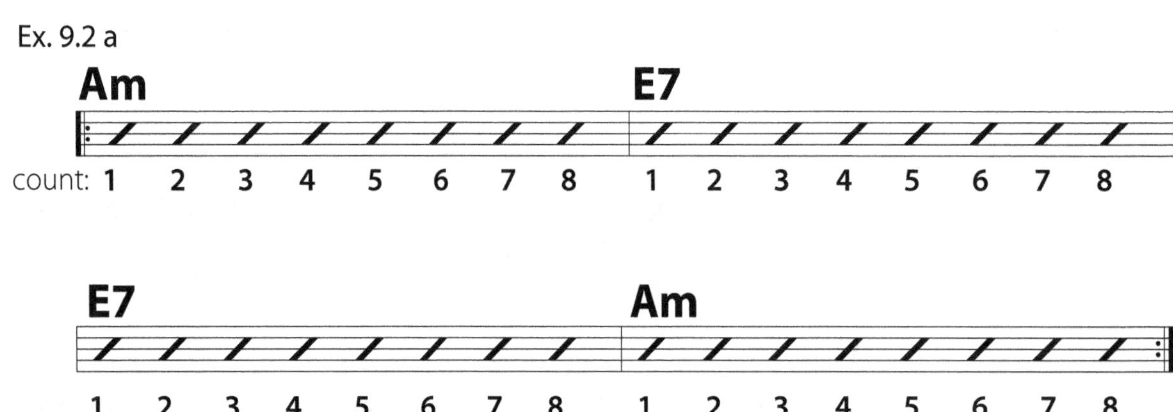

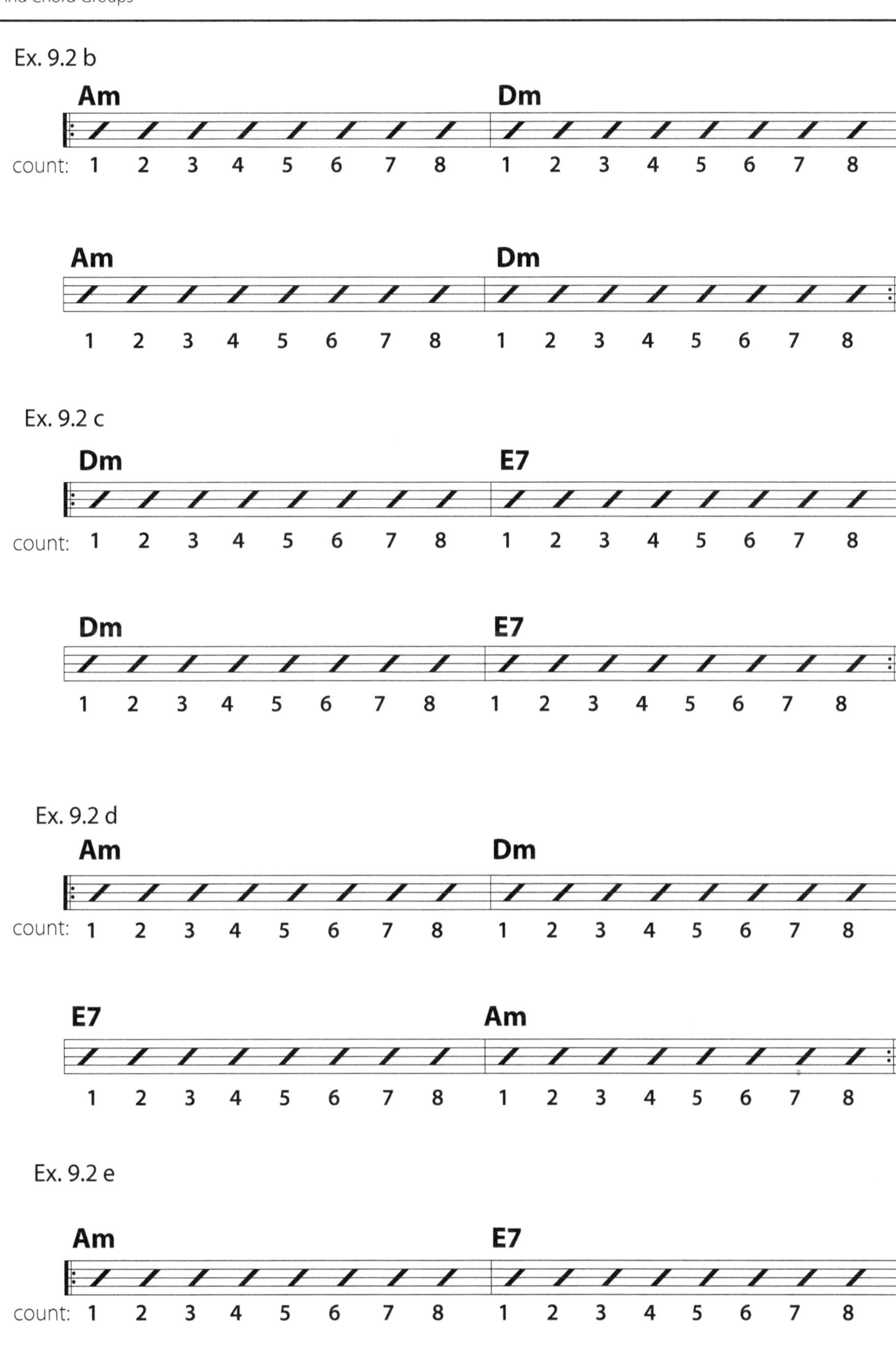
Ex. 9.2 b
Am
Dm
count: 1 2 3 4 5 6 7 8 1 2 3 4 5 6 7 8
Am
Dm
1 2 3 4 5 6 7 8 1 2 3 4 5 6 7 8
Ex. 9.2 c
Dm
E7
count: 1 2 3 4 5 6 7 8 1 2 3 4 5 6 7 8
Dm
E7
1 2 3 4 5 6 7 8 1 2 3 4 5 6 7 8
Ex. 9.2 d
Am
Dm
count: 1 2 3 4 5 6 7 8 1 2 3 4 5 6 7 8
E7
Am
1 2 3 4 5 6 7 8 1 2 3 4 5 6 7 8
Ex. 9.2 e
Am
E7
count: 1 2 3 4 5 6 7 8 1 2 3 4 5 6 7 8
Dm
Am
1 2 3 4 5 6 7 8 1 2 3 4 5 6 7 8

Exercise 9.3

Try the chord progressions in exercise 9.4 again but reduce the counts to six, four or three.

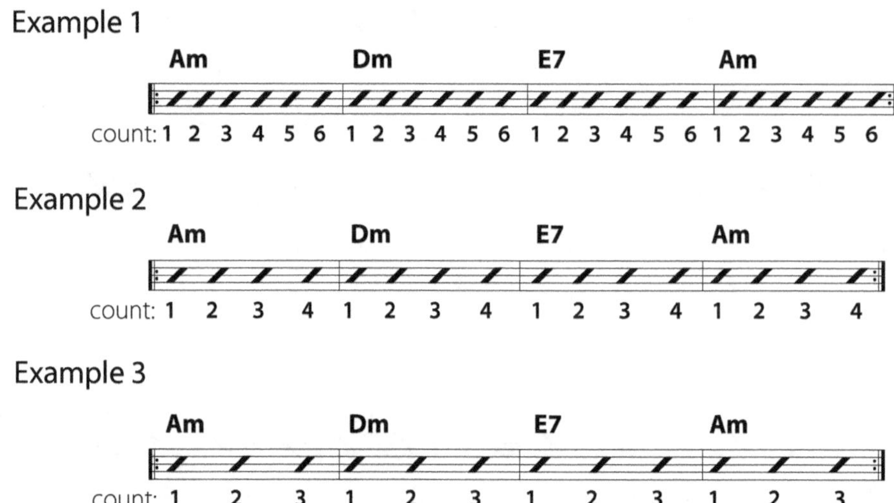

E Minor Group

Ex. 9.4 a

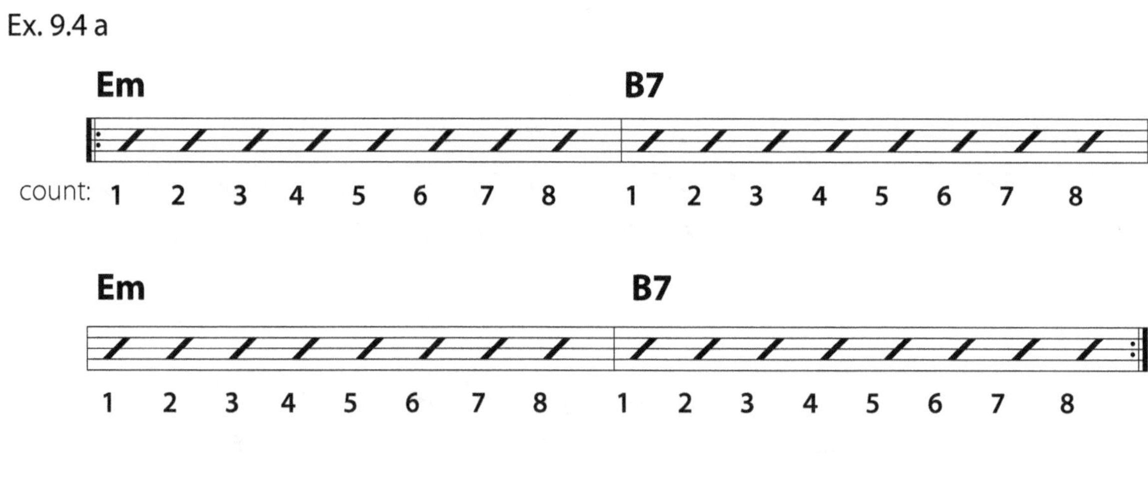

Ex. 9.4 b

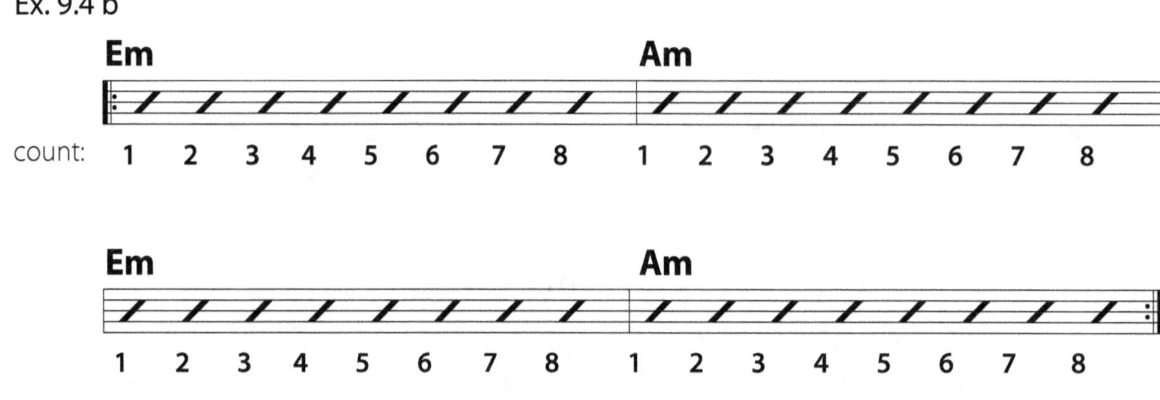

Ex. 9.4 c

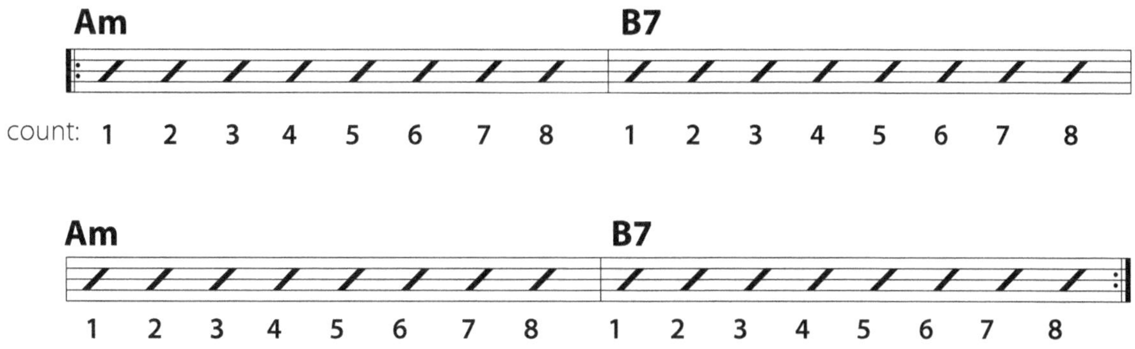

Am
B7
count: 1 2 3 4 5 6 7 8 1 2 3 4 5 6 7 8
Am
B7
1 2 3 4 5 6 7 8 1 2 3 4 5 6 7 8

Ex. 9.4 d

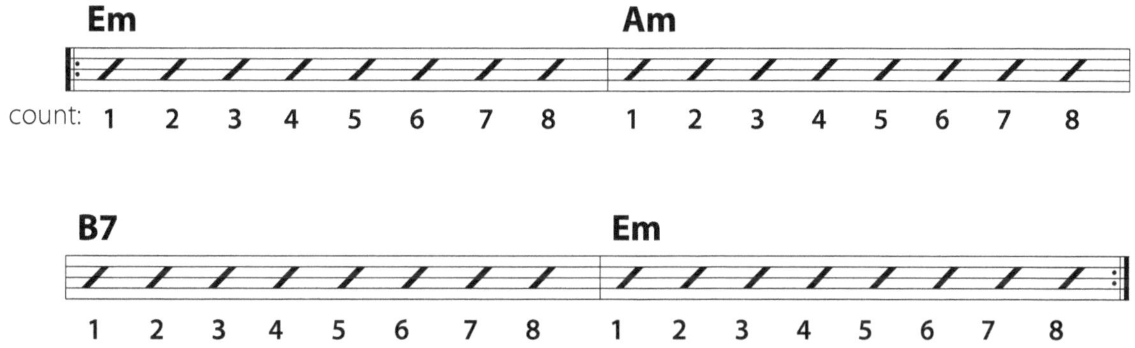

Em
Am
count: 1 2 3 4 5 6 7 8 1 2 3 4 5 6 7 8
B7
Em
1 2 3 4 5 6 7 8 1 2 3 4 5 6 7 8

Ex. 9.4 e

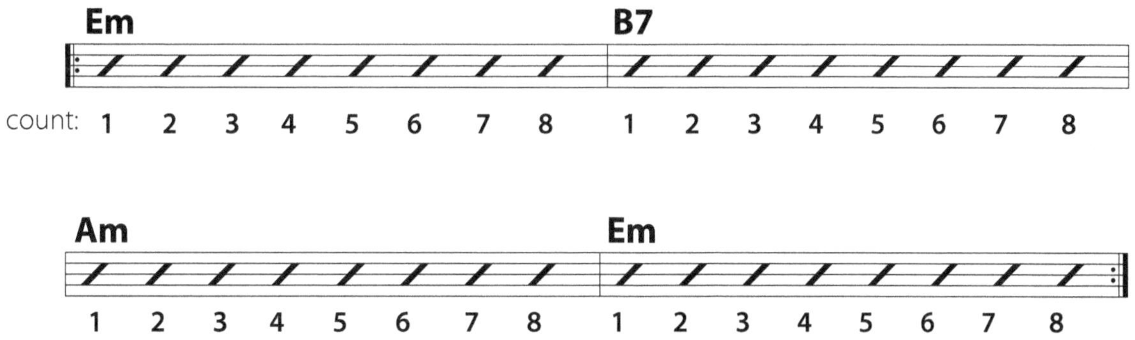

Em
B7
count: 1 2 3 4 5 6 7 8 1 2 3 4 5 6 7 8
Am
Em
1 2 3 4 5 6 7 8 1 2 3 4 5 6 7 8

Exercise 9.5

Try the chord progressions in exercise 7 again but reduce the counts to six, four or three.

Example 1

Em Am B7 Em
count: 1 2 3 4 5 6 1 2 3 4 5 6 1 2 3 4 5 6 1 2 3 4 5 6

Example 2

Em Am B7 Em
count: 1 2 3 4 1 2 3 4 1 2 3 4 1 2 3 4

Example 3

Em Am B7 Em
count: 1 2 3 1 2 3 1 2 3 1 2 3

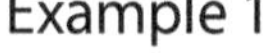

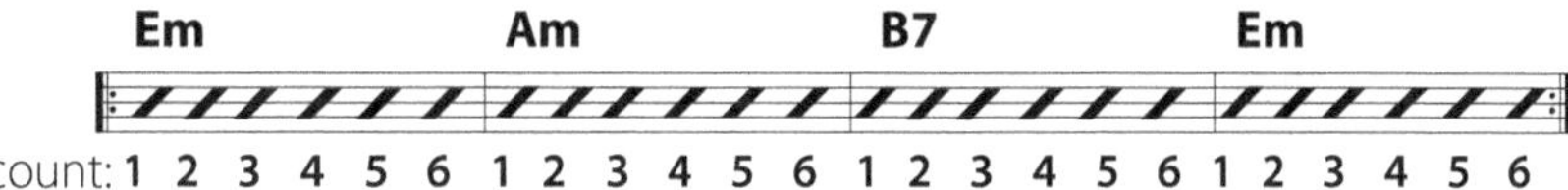

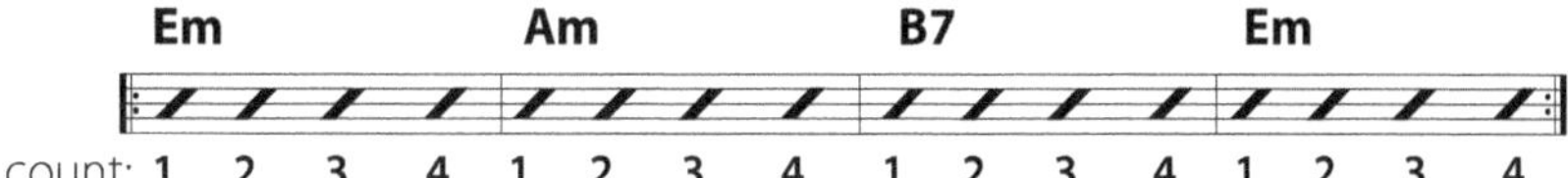

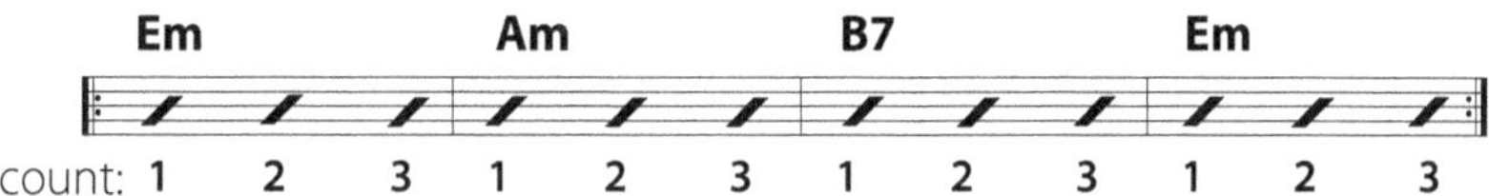

Songs For The Minor Chord Groups

Poor Wayfarin' Stranger uses the chords from the A minor group for the verse. It also uses two major chords in the chorus, F and C. It is in 4/4 time, meaning there will be four strums per measure. This song has pickup notes beginning on beat two. To add an introduction, strum eight beats (two measures), plus one strum for beat one in the pickup measure. Begin singing as written on beat two.

Poor Wayfarin' Stranger

Greensleeves uses the chords from the A minor group and C and G major. It is in 3/4 time, meaning there will be three strums per measure. This song has a pickup note beginning on beat three. To add an introduction, strum six beats (two measures) Begin singing as written on beat three.

Greensleeves

Go Down uses the chords from the E minor group plus the C major chord. It is in 4/4 time, meaning there will be four strums per measure. This song has a pickup note on beat four. To add an introduction, strum eight beats (two measures), plus three strums for beats one, two, and three in the pickup measure. Begin singing as written on beat four.

Go Down

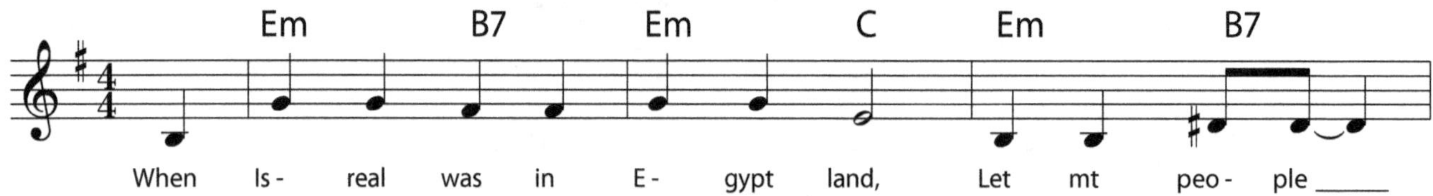

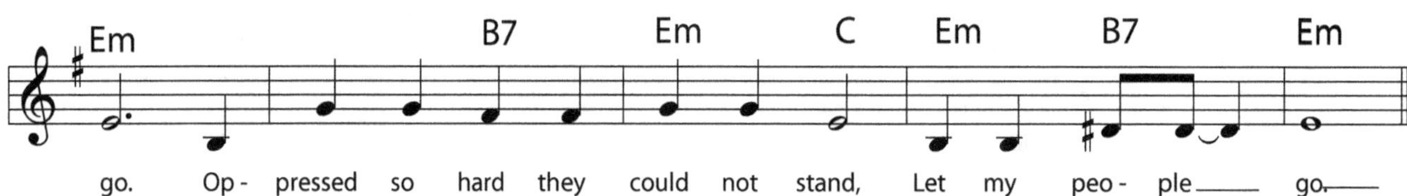

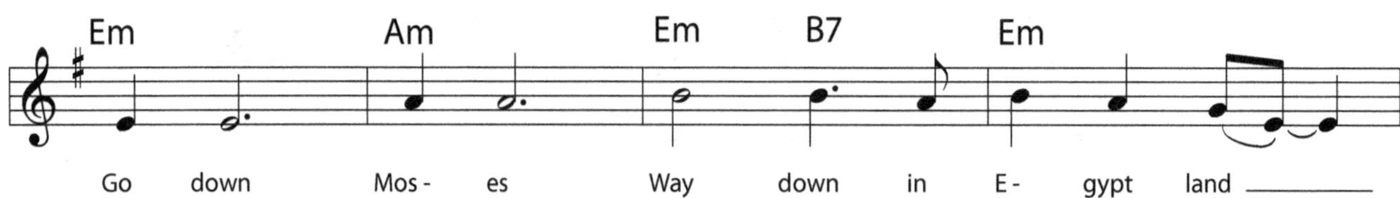

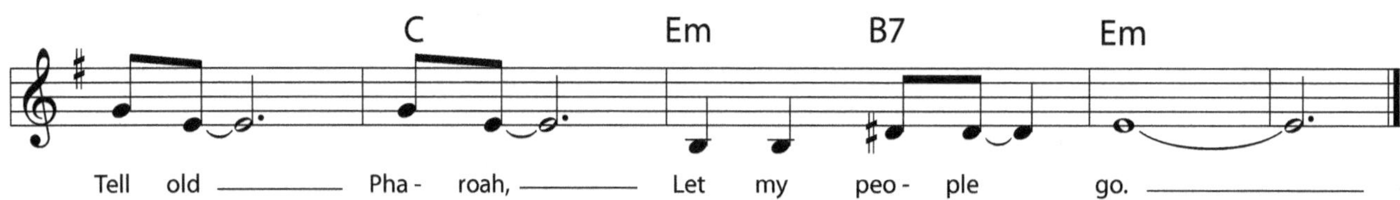

10 Intervals

An *interval* is the distance from one pitch to another either ascending or descending. Intervals are measured in whole and half steps. Intervals take the quality of major (M), minor (m), perfect (P), diminished (d or °), or augmented (a or +). The example below shows the intervals found within one octave.

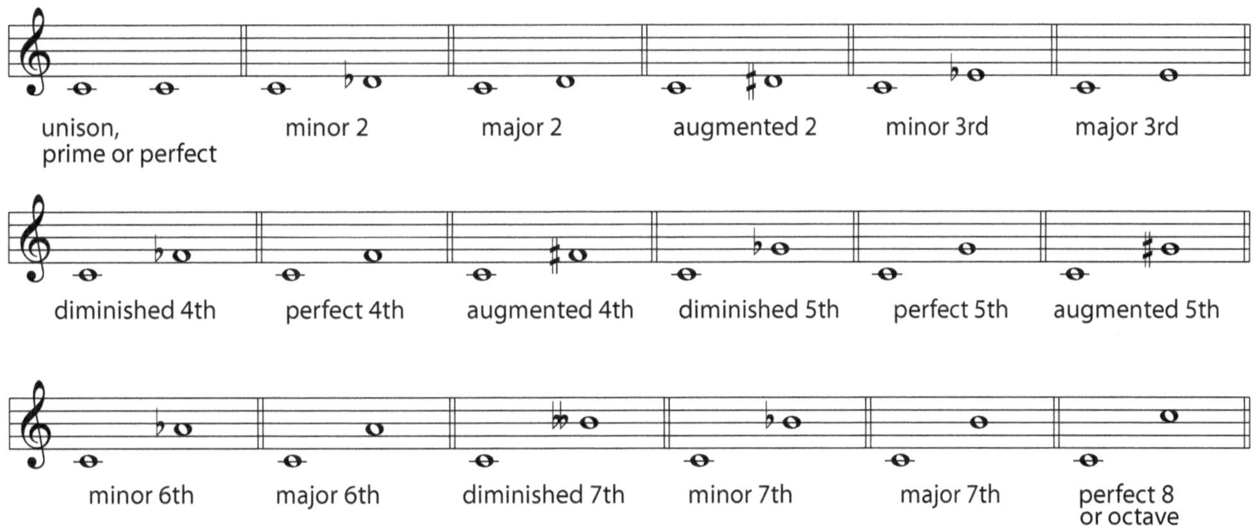

To find the interval number, count your starting note as one. Then continue to count alphabetically until the second note of the interval is reached. The interval number should always be figured out *before* attempting to determine the quality of the interval.

Example 1

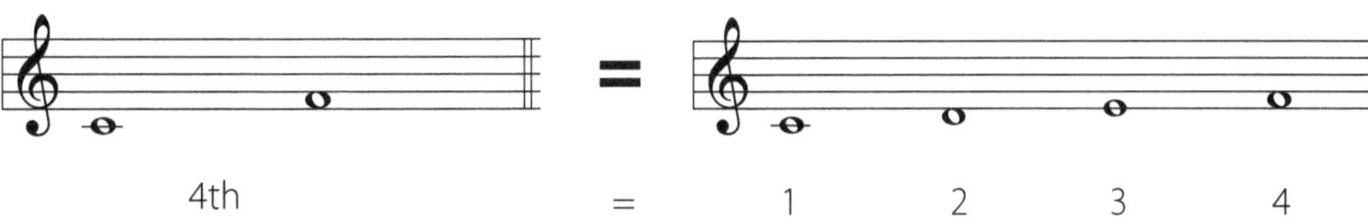

4th = 1 2 3 4

Then count the whole and half steps between two notes this gives us the interval *quality* meaning it will be major, minor, perfect, augmented, or diminished.

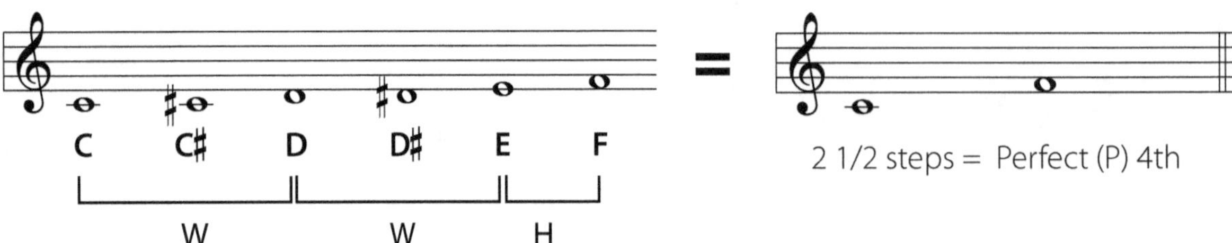

The interval from C to F is a perfect fourth. It is a fourth because four alphabetical letters are involved, and it is perfect because there are 2 ½ steps between the pitches. All interval relationships work this way.

Intervals are a very important part of music. They are used in creating melodies as well as chords. In the following chapter we will be using intervals to discover how chords are built.

Interval Name	Abbreviation	Steps
unison, prime or perfect	P1	0 steps
minor 2	m2	H step
major 2	M2	W step
augmented 2	A2	1 ½ steps
minor 3rd	m3	1 ½ steps
major 3rd	M3	2 steps
diminished 4th	d4	2 steps
perfect 4th	P4	2 ½ steps
augmented 4th	A4	3 steps
diminished 5th	d5	3 steps
perfect 5th	P5	3 ½ steps
augmented 5th	A5	4 steps
minor 6th	m6	4 steps
major 6th	M6	4 ½steps
diminished 7th	d7	4 ½steps
minor 7th	m7	5 steps
major 7th	M7	5 ½steps
perfect 8 or octave	P8	6 steps

Exercise 10.1

Study the intervals until they become very familiar.

Hint: You can practice recognizing intervals by comparing the notes that make up a melody. You can use the songs in chapter 5 to get you started.

11 Building And Naming Chords

The Triad

A ***triad*** consists of three different pitches: a **root or one (1), a third (3) , and a fifth (5)**. These three notes are the minimum number of pitches needed to create a chord. The alphabetical name of the chord is always the same as the root. For example, if the root is C, C is the the name of the chord.

To build a triad:

- Pick a starting pitch. This pitch will be the root (I).
- To find the third, start with the root and count up alphabetically to the 3rd letter (pitch) above the root. Make sure you count the root as one.
- To find the fifth, start with the root and count up alphabetically to the 5th letter (pitch) above the root. Make sure you count the root as one.

In this example, we'll choose C as our root (I). Count up 3 letters: C, D, E. E is 3 letters above C . E is the 3rd. Start with C again and count up 5 letters: C, D, E, F, G. G is five above C. G is the fifth.

Here is another example starting with F as the root.

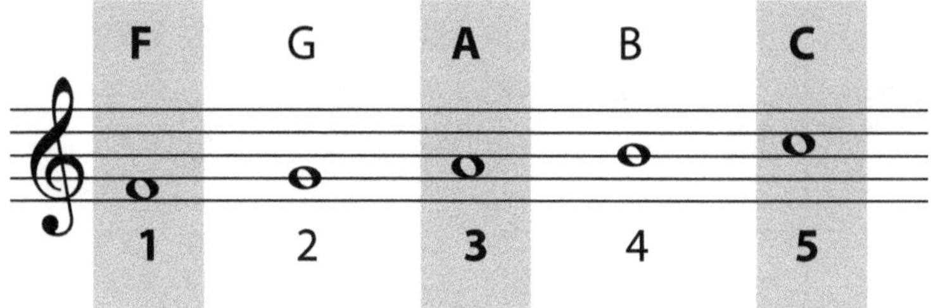

See if you can figure out the next one starting on G.

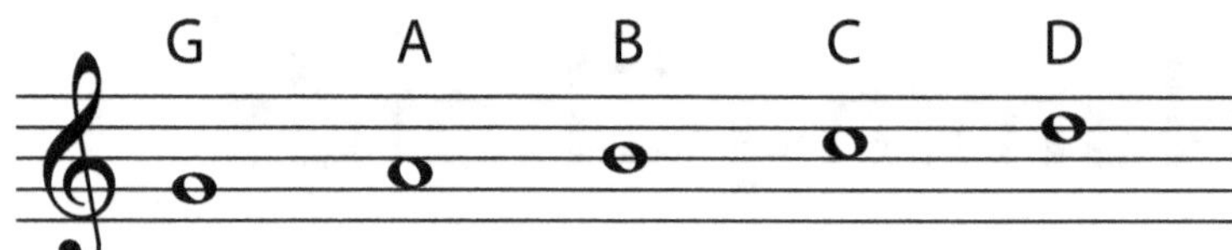

Answer = G (1), B (3), D (5).

Harmonizing The Major Scale

A triad can be built on any scale degree. We can ***harmonize*** or build triads on every pitch in the major scale. The following example is the harmonized C major scale.

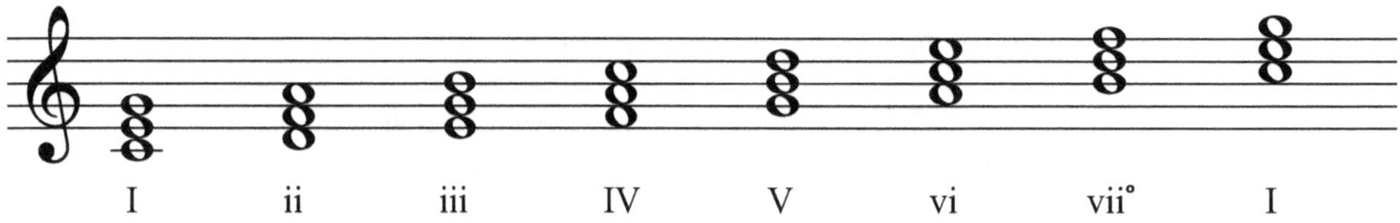

Here is the G scale with the 3rds and 5ths added. The ♯s in parenthesis are ***guide accidentals.*** Guide accidentals remind us that F is sharped throughout because of our key signature. It is very important to be mindful of the effect the key signature has on our triads as one misspelling can greatly alter the sound.

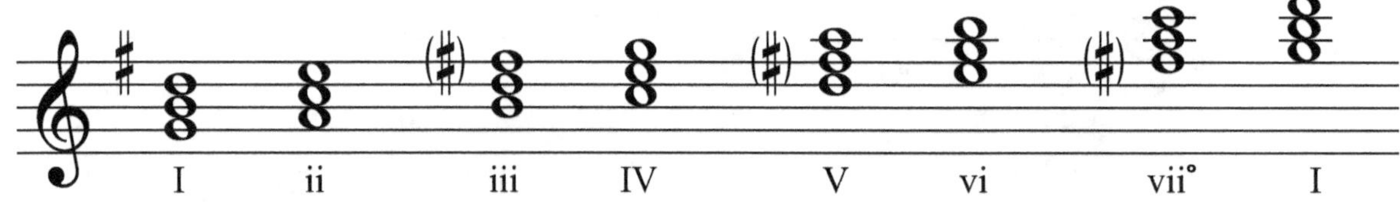

Major And Minor Triads

Both ***major*** and ***minor triads*** are produced when harmonizing the major scale. The upper case Roman numerals indicate major triads, the lower case, minor triads. This means that ***triads built on I, IV, and V will always be major. Triads built on ii, iii, and vi will always be minor.*** The triad built on vii produces a ***diminished*** **(°)** quality.

The difference between the major and minor triad is the type of *third* used. In major triads the interval formed by the root and third is a *major third (M3=2 steps)*. In minor triads a *minor third* (*m3*=1 ½ steps) is formed between the root and the third.

The distance from the 3rd to the 5th is also measured. For a **major triad** this distance is a *minor third (m3)* and for a **minor triad** it is a *major third (M3)*.

In both triads the relationship between the root and the 5th remains the same. (P5 = 3 1/2 Steps.)

So to conclude, a **major triad** must have a *major third (M3)* formed by the root and third and a *minor third (m3)* formed by the third and fifth. A **minor triad** must have a *minor third (m3)* formed by the root and third and a *major third (M3)* formed by the third and fifth.

Diminished Triads

The seventh scale degree produces a *diminished* **(°)** quality. A ***diminished triad*** is built with *minor thirds*. The distance from the root to the third is a *minor third* and the distance from the third and the fifth is also a *minor third*.

m3
m3

Commercial Chord Names

We have discussed labeling the scale degrees by numbers; however, in commercial playing (i.e The typical symbols used in lead sheets and chord charts) letter names and symbols are used. (The following description of chord symbols is based on the current standard most music publishers are using as of this writing.)

All letter names use capital letters. The letter name is the *same* as the root of the chord.

For **major chords** just the letter name is used. Major chords are found on the I, IV and V scale degrees.

C G B♭ D

For **minor chords** the letter name followed by a *lower case 'm'* is used. Minor chords are found on the ii, iii, and vi scale degrees.

Cm Gm B♭m Dm

In jazz charts you will most likely see a dash for minor instead of the small m.

C- G- B♭- D-

Diminished chords use the letter name followed by the symbol ° or the abbreviation *dim*. Diminished chords are found on the vii scale degree.

C° G° or B♭dim Ddim

Exercise 11.1

1) Write out the major scale in every key.

2) Harmonize the scales by adding a third and fifth to each scale degree.

3) Write in the Roman numerals below each scale degree.

4) Write the commercial names below each Roman numeral. Be sure to include the accidental in the name of the chord when appropriate. (For example, if the root name is F♯ then the chord name would also be F♯, not F.)

5) Use a key signature *and* include guide accidentals as demonstrated in the harmonization of the G major scale.

12 Seventh Chords

Seventh chords are built by adding the seventh note above the root to the triad. There are four pitches in a seventh chord, the root (1), third (3), fifth (5) , and seventh (7).

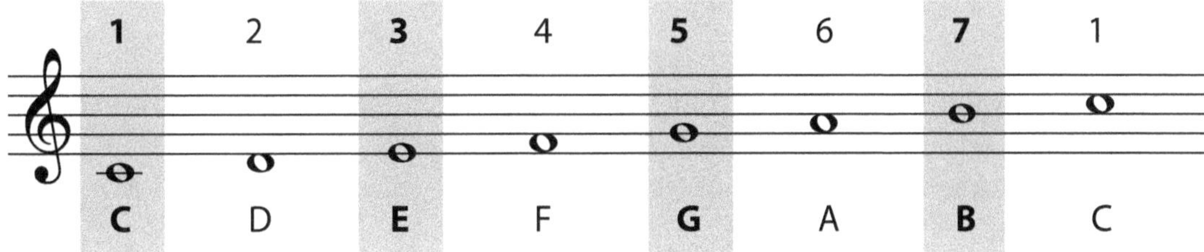

As discussed under intervals, there are three kinds of sevenths, the minor seventh (m7), the major seventh (M7), and the diminished seventh (d7 or ^{o}). The two we are going to concern ourselves with here are the major and minor sevenths. The minor seventh is five full steps from the root, the major seventh is five and a half steps from the root.

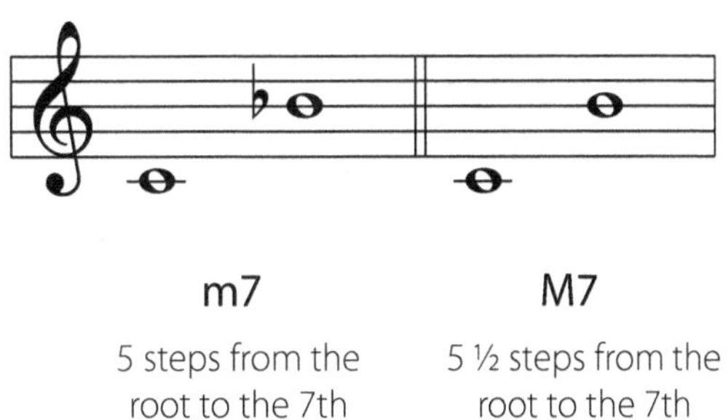

m7

5 steps from the root to the 7th

M7

5 ½ steps from the root to the 7th

Adding Sevenths To The Harmonized Major Scale

We can add the add the seventh note above the root to our harmonized C scale as shown below. Notice that if the triad is built on the staff lines then the seventh will also be included on a line. If the triad is built on the staff spaces the seventh will also be included on a space.

Harmonized C Scale including 7ths.

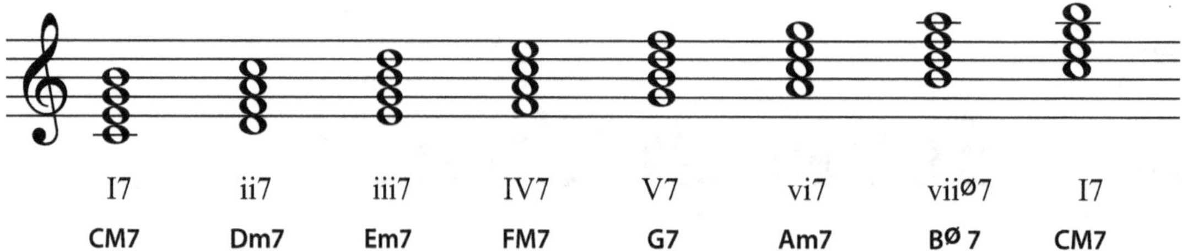

Harmonized G Scale including 7ths.

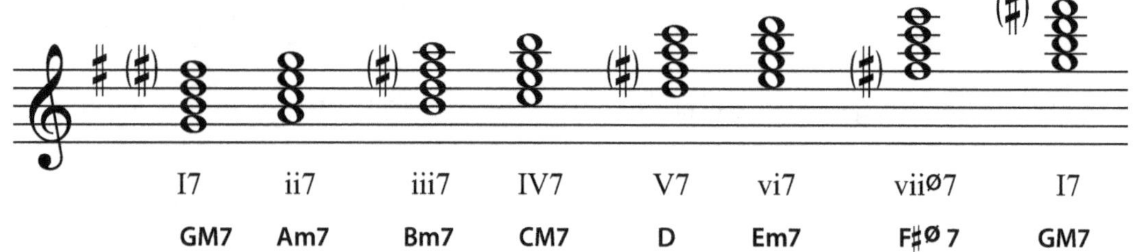

If we analyze the seventh chords created from the scale we can come to the following conclusions:

- the I7 and IV7 scale degree are major triads and take the major 7 - **M triad + M7.**

  expressed this way: **CM7, Cmaj7 or CΔ7**

- the V7 chord is a major triad and takes the minor 7 - **M triad + m7**

  expressed this way: **G7**

- ii7, iii7, and vi7 are minor triads and take the minor 7 - **m triad + m7**

  expressed this way: **Dm7, Dmin7 or D-7**

- viiø7 is a diminished triad and takes the minor 7 - **d triad + m7**

  expressed this way: **$B^{ø}7$ or $Bm7^{\flat 5}$**

Notice that when we add sevenths to the triads the triads become more defined. For instance, I, IV, and V are all major triads but when we add the sevenths, V is different from I and IV. When we begin to learn the seventh chords in the following chapters you will begin to hear how different in sound these chords really are.

Exercise 12.1

Harmonize each major scale using roots, thirds, fifths, and sevenths. Include the Roman numerals and the commercial chord names below each chord.

13 Altering First Position Chords

First (open) position major chords, can be altered to create **minor (m), minor seventh (m7), major seventh (M7), seventh (7), diminished seventh (°7) and half diminished seventh (ø7) chords.** It is important to know on which strings the **roots (R), thirds (3),** and **fifths (5)** lie, in order to alter the chords.

Since all of the chords use more than three strings, there will be more than one R, 3, or 5 in the chord. Even though some of the chord members are doubled, these chords are still considered triads because only three *different* pitches are used.

All of the chords in this chapter are shown in diagram form and in notation. A check above the diagram indicates the better choice if more than one option is possible.

In jazz the m3 and m7 chord tones can also be expressed ♭3 and ♭7 respectively. This is how they will be referred to throughout this chapter.

A Major

The **A chord** is spelled A (R), C# (3), E (5). The chord diagram shows us where these pitches are located.

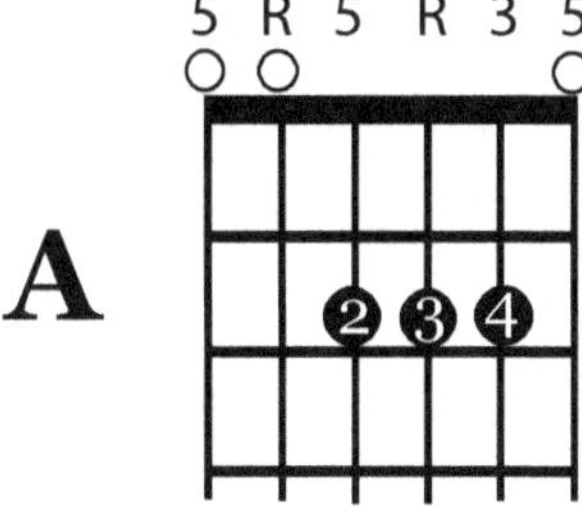

A Major 7

To create an **AM7** chord from the A chord we must first identify the pitch that creates the **M7**. In this case it is **G♯**.

Next, we need to find a string where the **G♯** can be placed. This form gives two* options. One option is to place **G♯** on the fourth fret, sixth string, eliminating the extra 5th. This could be a good choice since there are three 5ths in the chord already; however, it probably isn't the *best* choice because it is difficult to finger and it is usually best to keep R as the lowest note. Also, **G♯** and **A** are a half step apart. This creates an unpleasant ***dissonance*** when these notes are played so close together. (*dissonance* - a word used to describe sounds that create tension in music.)

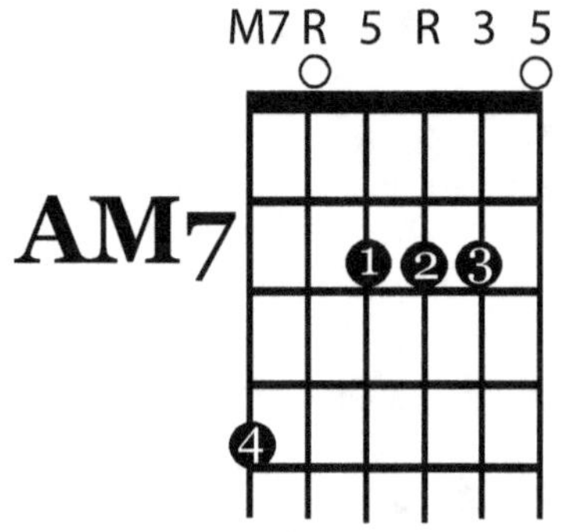

✓The second choice is to eliminate R on the third string and replace it with **G♯** on the first fret. This is a good choice because the root remains in the lowest voice, there is no dissonance created, and it is easy to finger.

✓

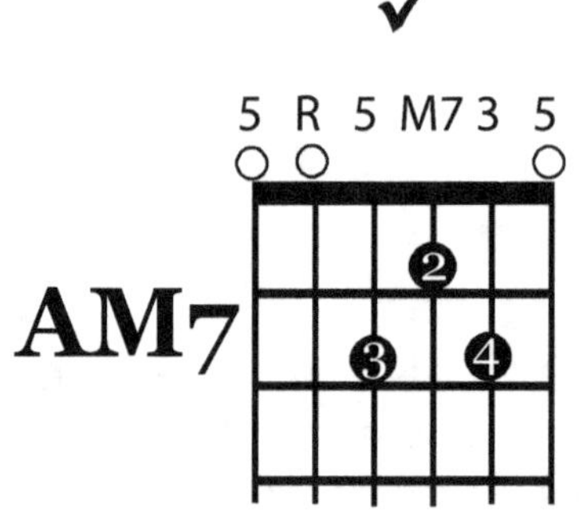

A 7

To create an **A7** chord from the A chord we must first identify the pitch that creates the minor seventh (**m7** or **♭7**). In this case it is **G**.

Next, we need to find a string where the **G** can be placed. This form gives two options. The first option is to place **G** on the fourth fret, sixth string, eliminating the extra 5th. This could be a good choice since there are three 5ths in the chord already but just like our first example, it probably isn't the *best* choice because it is difficult to finger and it is usually best to keep R as the lowest note.

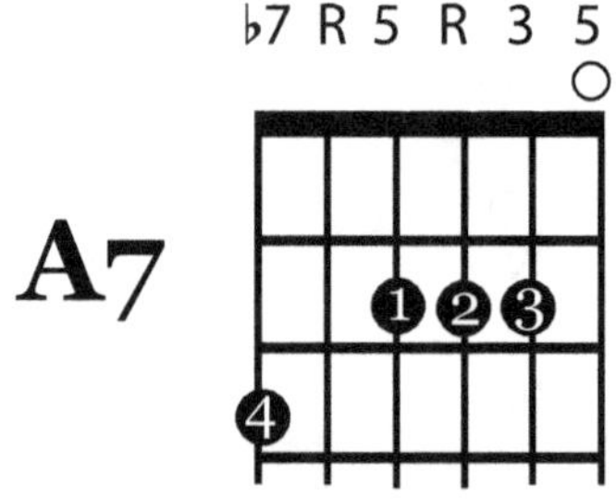

*If you've been experimenting ,you've probably discovered that the M7 could be placed on the first string as well. These options have been eliminated for this form because they are actually part of the G form.

✓The second choice is to eliminate R on the third string and replace it with the open string G. This is a good choice because the root remains in the lowest voice, and it is easy to finger.

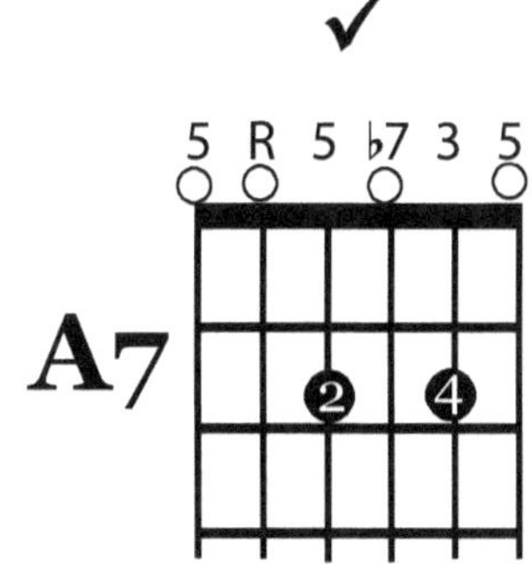

A minor

To change the A chord into an **Am** chord, first identify the pitch that creates the minor third (**m3** or **♭3**). In this case it is C. Next, find a string where the C can be placed. Since the second string is the only string with a 3rd this would be the logical choice. Replace C♯ (second fret) with C on the first fret.

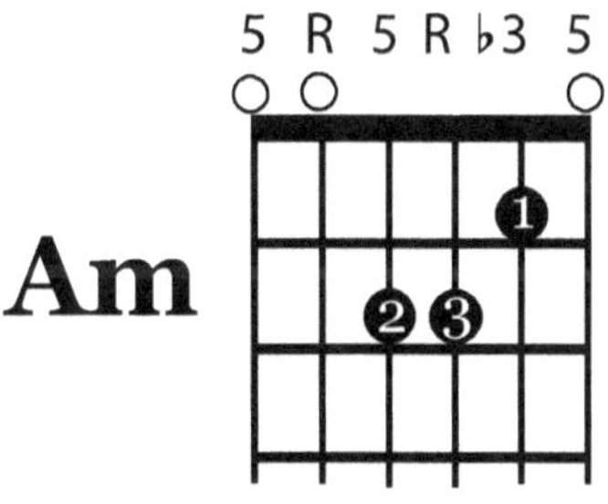

A minor 7

The choices for this chord are to *combine* the options for the **A7** chord and the **Am** chord. The best choice for the **♭7** (G) is on the third string and for the **♭3** (C), the second string.

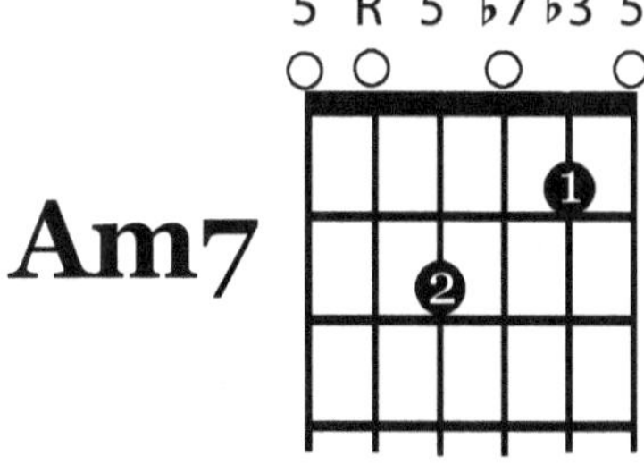

E Major

The E chord is spelled **E** (R), **G♯** (3), **B** (5).

R 5 R 3 5 R

E

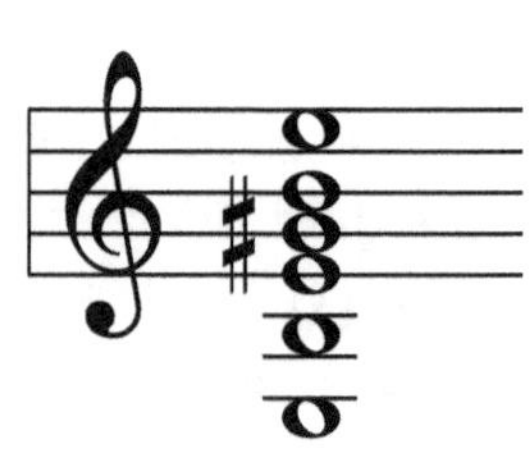

E Major 7

To alter the E chord and create an **EM7** chord, first identify the pitch that creates the **M7**. In this case it is **D♯**. Next, find a string where the **D♯** can be placed. This form gives two options. The first choice is to eliminate the 5th, B, on the second string and replace it with **D♯** at the fourth fret.

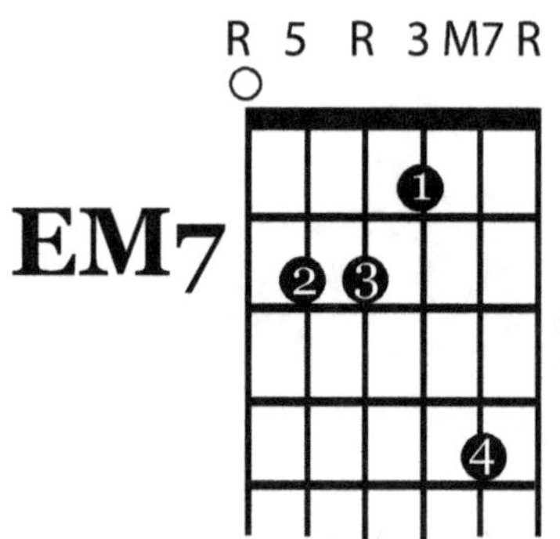

Although it is easy to finger a dissonance is created between the root **E** (first string) and **M7** **D♯** (second string). For this reason this would not be the best choice for most situations.

✓The second choice is to place **D♯** on the first fret, fourth string eliminating R. This is usually the better choice since there are three roots in the chord already and no dissonance is created.

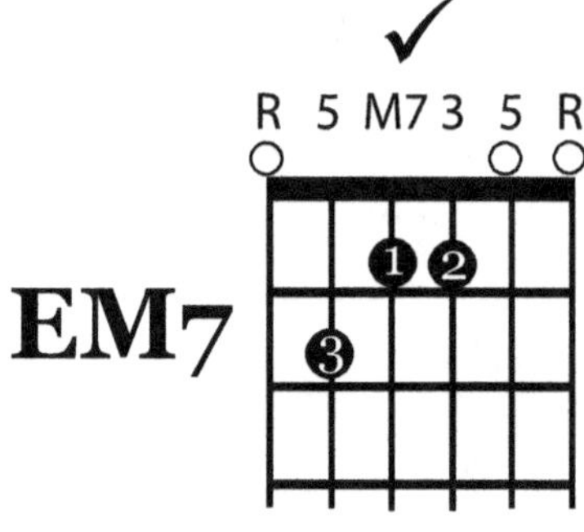

E7

✓To alter the E chord and create an **E7** chord, first identify the pitch that creates the ♭**7**. In this case it is **D**. Next, find a string where the **D** can be placed. Again, we have two options. The first choice is to eliminate the 5th on the second string and replace it with the **D** note at the third fret.

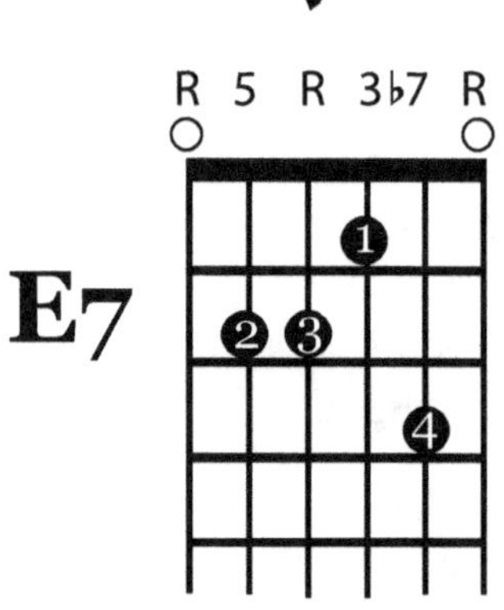

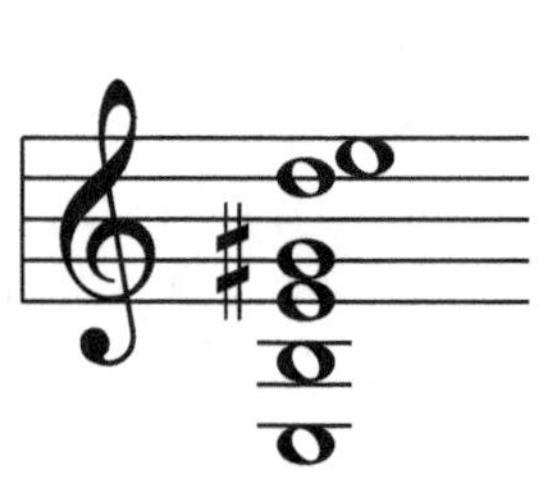

✓The second choice is to place D on the open fourth string eliminating the root.

In this case either choice is a good one. Let your ear determine which one sounds better for the piece you're playing at the time.

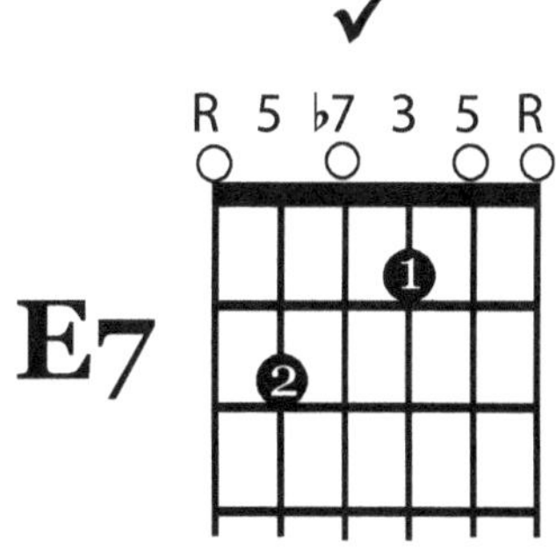

E minor

To alter the E chord into an **Em** chord, first identify the pitch that creates the **♭3**. In this case it is G. Next, find a string where the G can be placed. Since the third string is the only string with a 3rd, this would be the logical choice. Replace G# (first fret) with the open G.

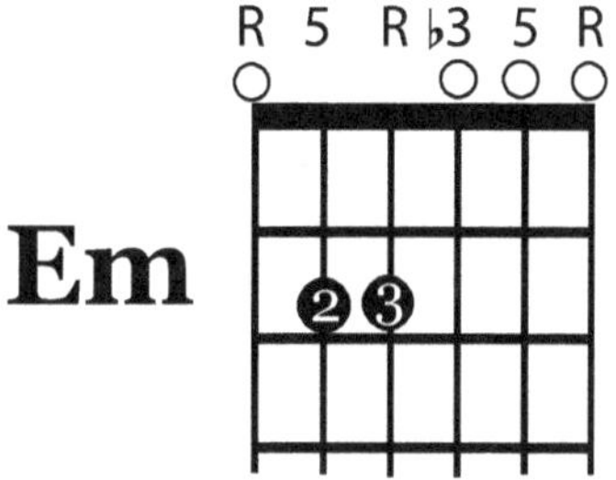

E minor 7

The choices for this chord would be to combine the options for the **E7** chord and the **Em** chord. The best choice for the **♭3** (G) is on the third string and either choice for the **♭7** will work well.

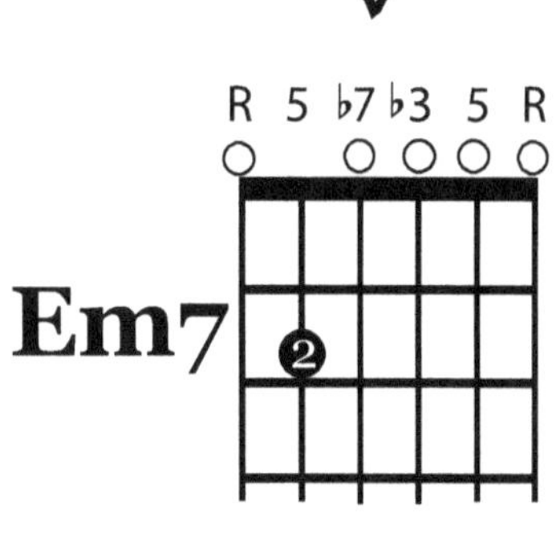

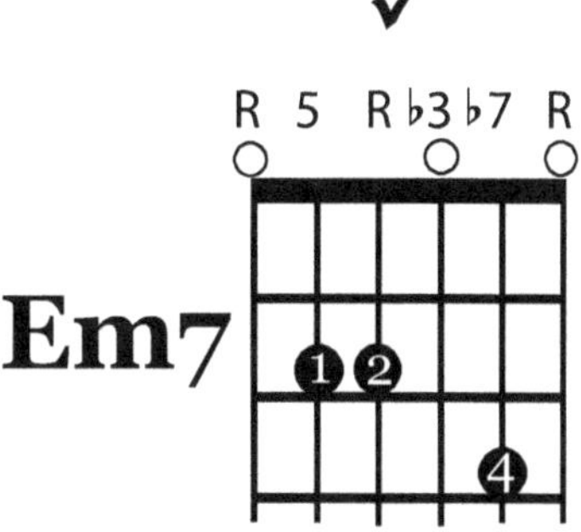

D Major

The D chord is spelled D (R), F# (3), A (5).

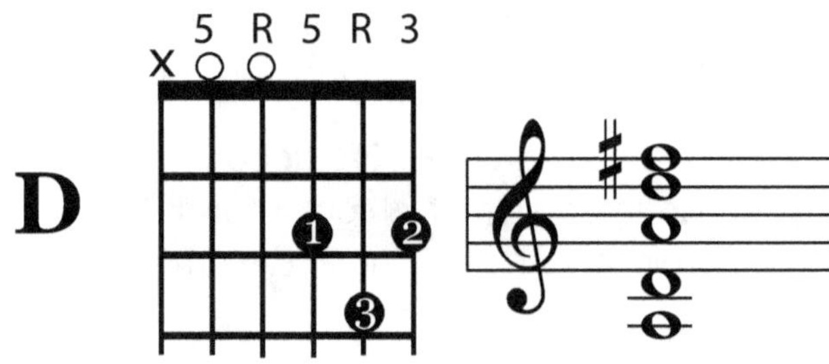

D Major 7

To alter the D chord and create a **DM7** chord, first identify the pitch that creates the **M7**. In this case it is **C♯**. Next, find a string where the **C♯** can be placed. This form gives two options. We can place **C♯** on the fourth fret, fifth string, eliminating the 5th of the chord. This could be a good choice since there are two 5ths in the chord already; however, it probably isn't the best choice because it is difficult to finger and it is usually good to keep R as the lowest note. Also **C♯** and **D** are a half step apart and create a dissonant sound when played so close together. For this reason this would not be the best choice for most situations.

✓The second choice is to eliminate R on the second string and replace it with **C♯** on the second fret. This is a good choice because the root remains in the lowest voice, there is no dissonance created, and it is easy to finger.

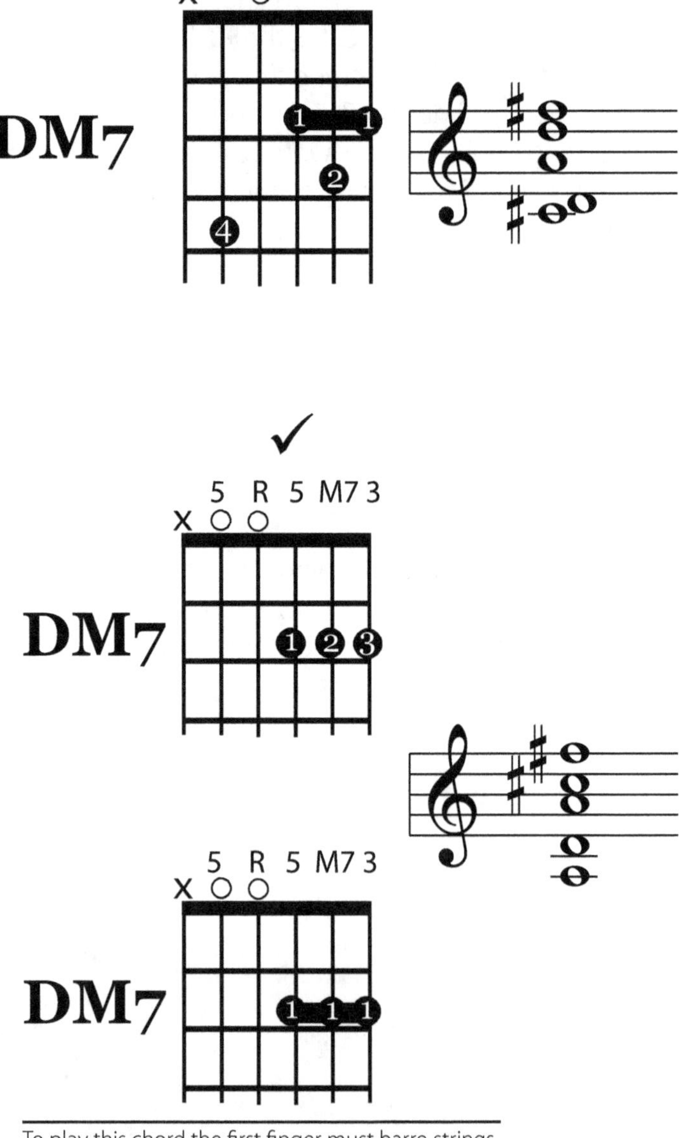

To play this chord the first finger must barre strings 1,2, and 3. See chapter 14 for an explanation.

D7

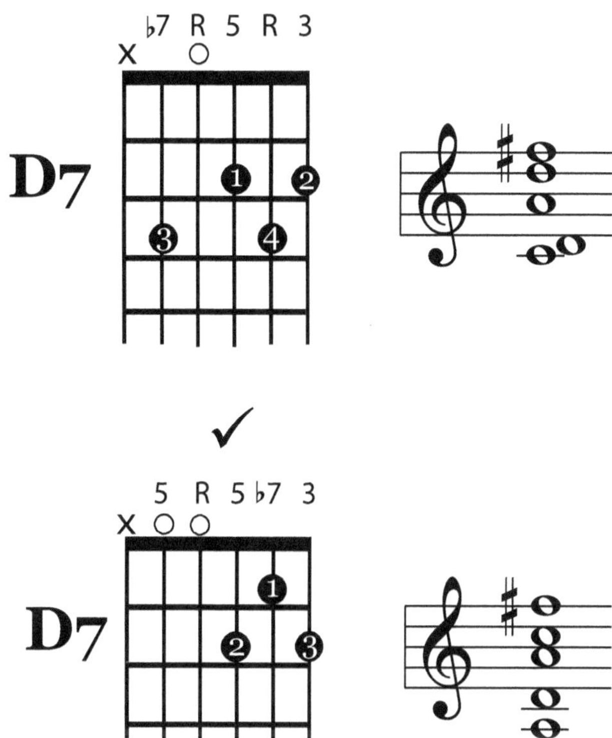

To alter the D chord and create a D7 chord, first identify the pitch that creates the ♭7. In this case it is C. Next, find a string where the C can be placed. This form also gives two options. The first choice is to place C on the fourth fret, fifth string, eliminating the 5th. This could be a good choice since there are two 5ths in the chord already; but as pointed out above, it probably isn't the best choice because it is difficult to finger and it is usually good to keep the root as the lowest note.

✓The second choice is to eliminate R on the second string and replace it with the C on the first fret. This is a good choice because the root remains in the lowest voice, there is no dissonance created, and it is easy to finger.

D minor

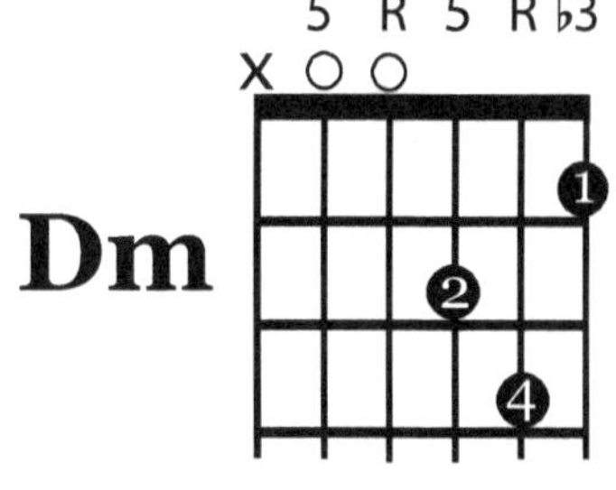

To alter the D chord to a **Dm** chord, first identify the pitch that creates the ♭3. In this case it is F. Next, find a string where the F can be placed. Since the first string is the only string with a 3rd, this would be the logical choice. Replace F♯ (second fret) with F on the first fret.

D minor 7

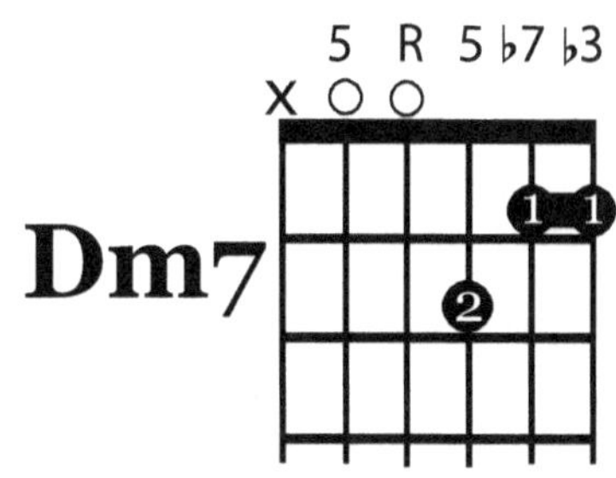

The choice for this chord is to combine the options for the **D7** chord and the **Dm** chord. The best choice for the ♭7 (C) would be on the second string and for the ♭3 (F), the first string.

C Major

The C chord is spelled C (R), E (3), G (5).

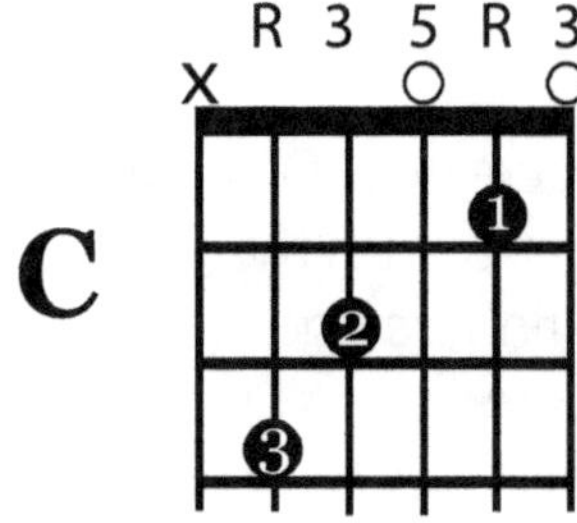

C Major 7

To alter the C chord and create a **CM7** chord, first identify the pitch that creates the **M7**. In this case it is B. Next, find a string where the B can be placed. This form offers two options. The first choice is to place B on the second fret, fifth string, eliminating R. This could be a good choice since there are two roots in the chord already; however, it probably isn't the best choice because it is usually good to keep the root as the lowest note.

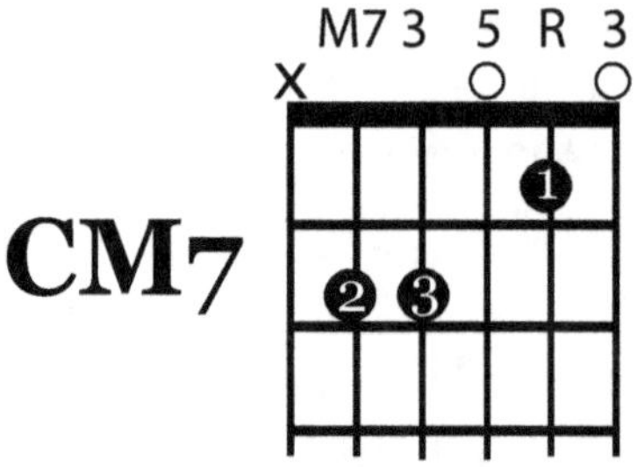

✓The second choice is to eliminate R on the second string and replace it with the open B. This is a good choice because the root remains in the lowest voice.

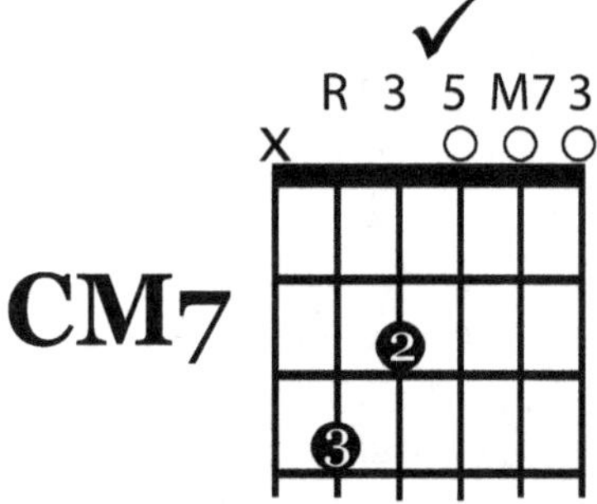

C7

To alter the C chord and create a **C7** chord, first identify the pitch that creates the ♭**7**. In this case it is B♭ Next, find a string where the B♭ can be placed. This form also gives two options. The first choice is to place B♭ on the first fret, fifth string eliminating R. This could be a good choice since there are two roots in the chord already; but as pointed out above, it probably isn't the best choice because it is usually good to keep the root as the lowest note.

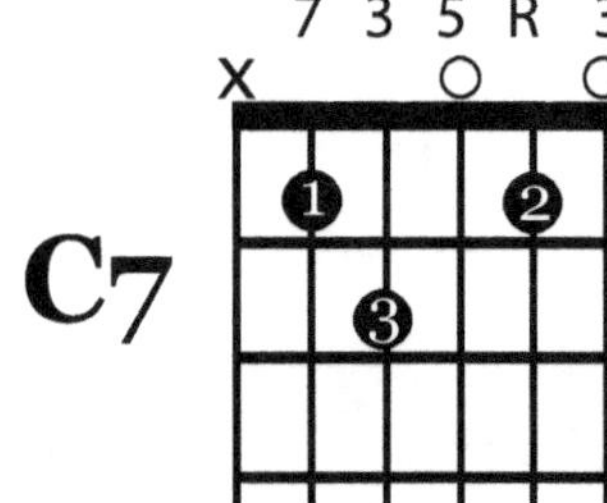

✓The second choice is to eliminate the 5th on the third string and replace it with B♭ at the third fret.

This is a good choice because the root remains in the lowest voice, and it is easy to finger. This chord has no 5th, but it still sounds good because the 5th is expendable.

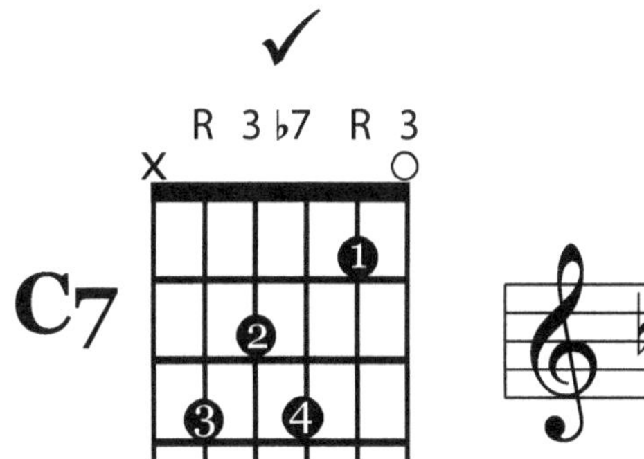

C minor

To alter the C chord to a **Cm** chord, first identify the pitch that creates the ♭3. In this case it is E♭. Next, find a string where the E♭ can be placed. This form has two 3rds, one on the fourth string and the open first string. To make this form work, one of the thirds must be eliminated. The easiest for fingering is to eliminate the 3rd on the first string. This means that the first string is avoided altogether and the ♭3 is placed on the first fret, fourth string.

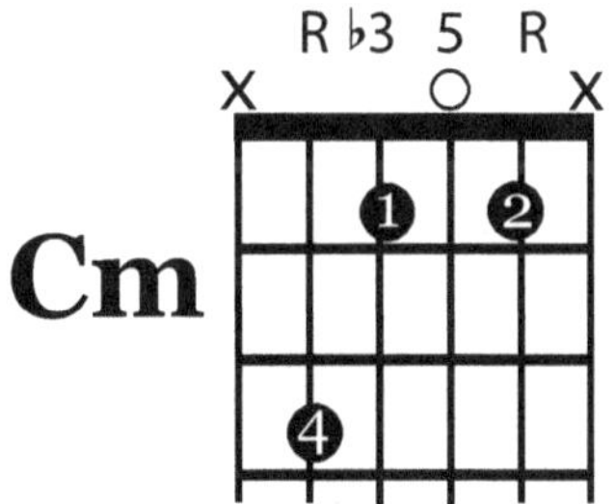

C minor 7

The choice for this chord would be to combine the options for the **C7** chord and the **Cm** chord. The best choice for the ♭7 (B♭) is on the third string and the ♭3 (E♭), the fourth string. Again, the first string would be eliminated.

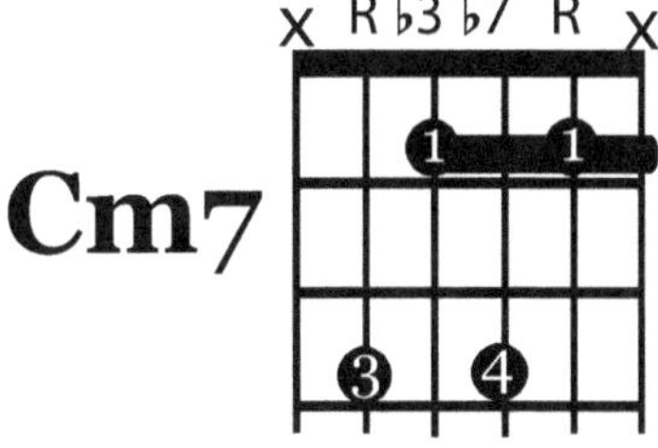

G Major

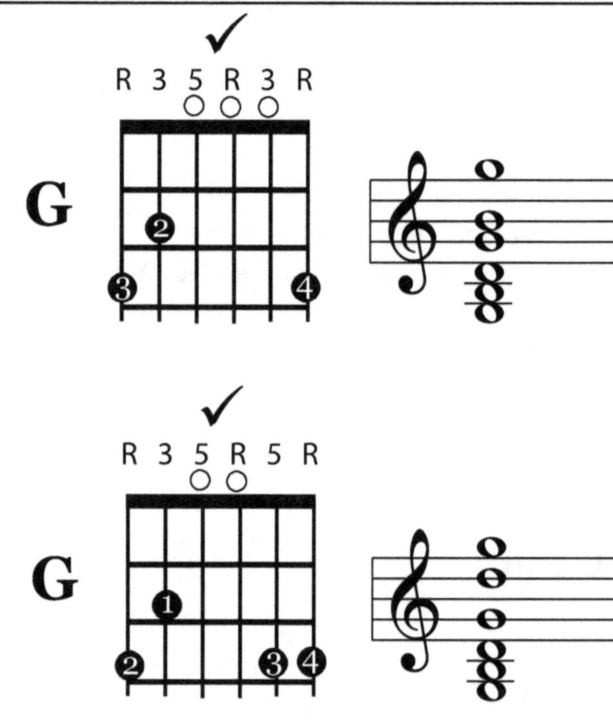

The G chord is spelled G (R), B (3), D (5).

✓There are two good finger choices for the G chord. The first one is the standard G chord voicing. Notice that the fingering is 2, 3, and 4. Make sure you follow this fingering as it will make changing chords much easier.

The second fingering eliminates the 'extra' 3rd of the chord and replaces it with the 5th. Even though there are the same notes in the chord the reordering of the notes (voicings) change the sound.

The best choice here will depend on the style of music you are playing and the desired sound you are going for.

G Major 7

M7 3 5 R 3 R

GM7

To alter the G chord and create a **GM7** chord, first identify the pitch that creates the **M7**. In this case it is F♯. Next, find a string where the F♯ can be placed. This form gives three options. The first choice is to place F♯ on the sixth string eliminating R. This could be a good choice since there are three roots; however, this probably isn't the best choice since it is usually good to keep the root as the lowest note.

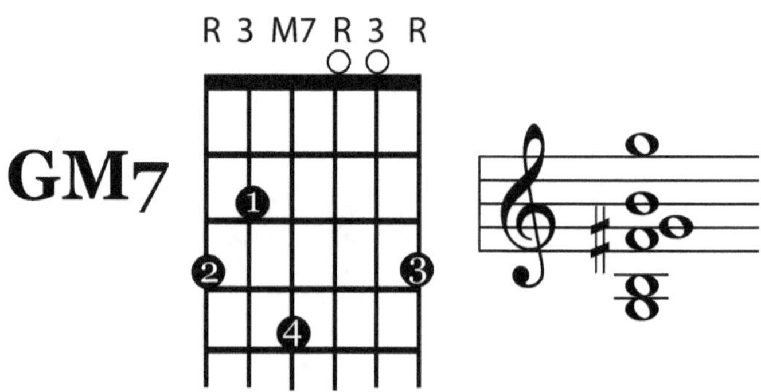

The second choice is to place F♯ on the fourth fret of the fourth string eliminating the 5th. This could be a good choice since the 5th is expendable; however, it probably isn't the best choice because F♯ (fourth string) and G (third string) are a half step apart and create a dissonance when played together.

✓The third choice is to eliminate R on the first string and replace it with F♯ on the second fret.

This is a good choice because there is no dissonance created, the fifth is included, and it is easy to finger.

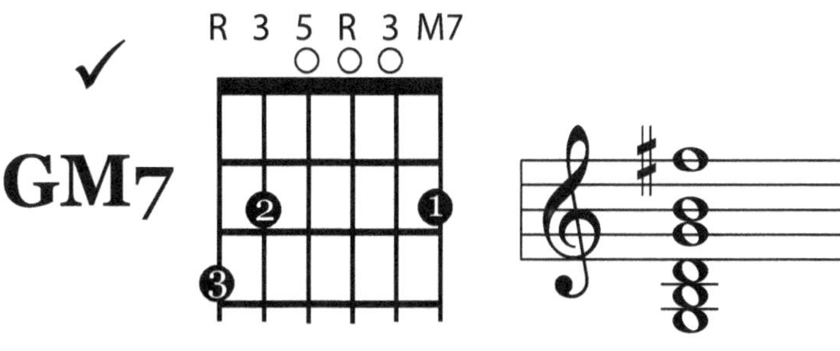

G7

To alter the G chord and create a **G7** chord, first identify the pitch that creates the ♭7. In this case it is F. Next, find a string where the F can be placed. This form also gives three options. The first choice is to place the ♭7 on the sixth string eliminating R. As stated above this could be a good choice because there are three roots in the chord already; but as pointed out above, it probably isn't the best choice because it is usually good to keep the root as the lowest note.

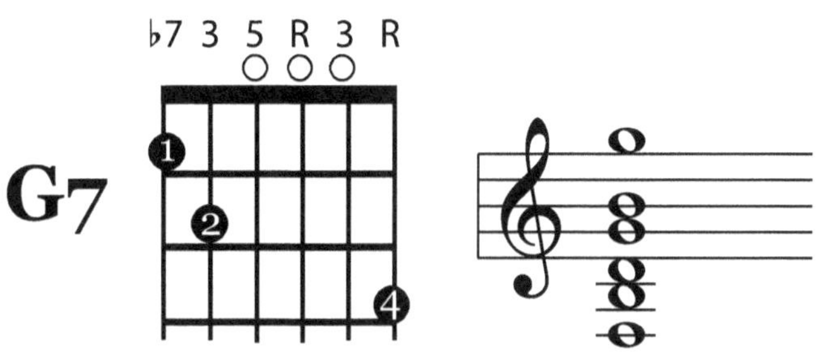

The second choice is to place F on the third fret, fourth string eliminating the 5th of the chord. It probably isn't the best choice either because it doesn't include the 5th and is more complicated to finger.

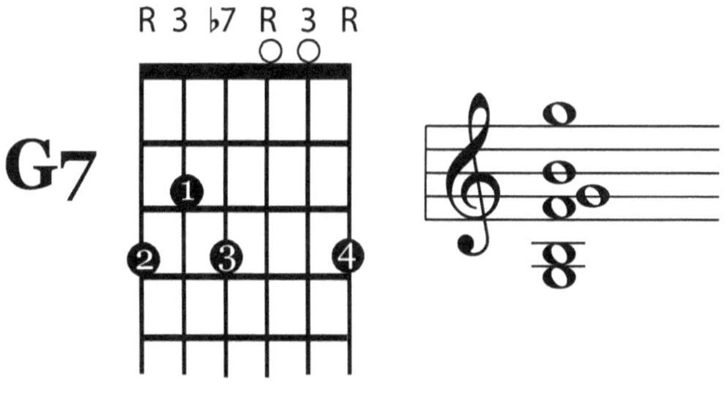

✓The third choice is to finger the F on the first string first fret. This includes all the members of the chord and is easiest to finger.

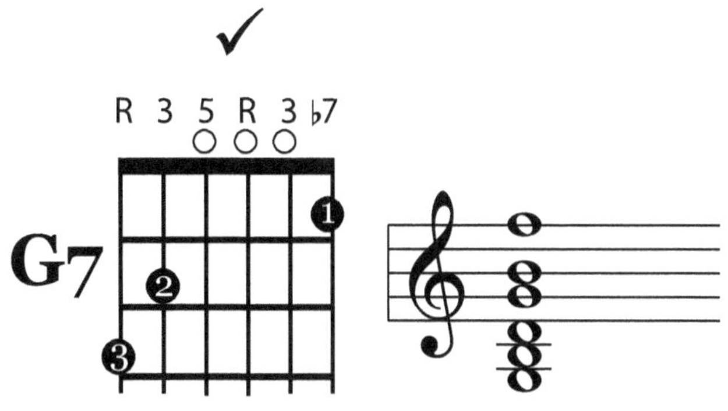

G minor

To alter the G chord into a **Gm** chord, first identify the pitch that creates the **♭3**. In this case it is **B♭**. Next, find a string where the **B♭** can be placed. This chord has two 3ds, one on the fifth string and one on the second allowing for three different options. The first two choices use strings six through three. In this case the **♭3** on the fifth string (first fret) is used and the **♭3** on the second string eliminated.

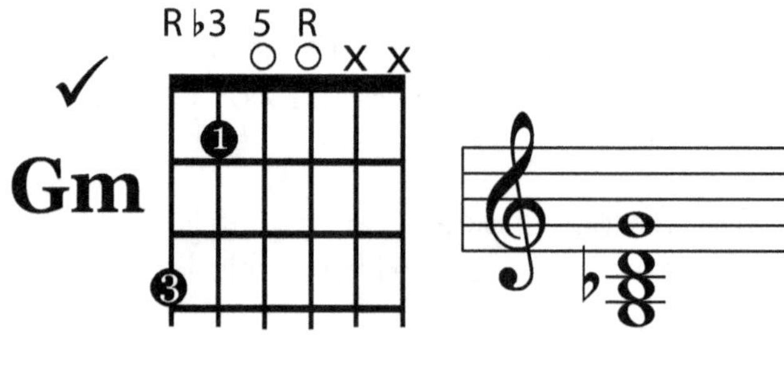

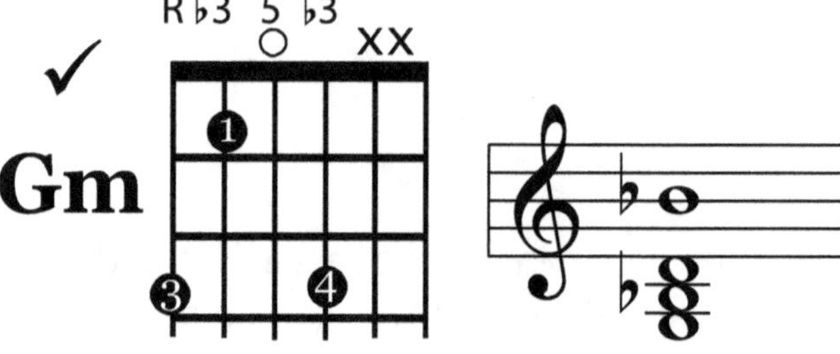

The third choice is to skip the fifth string and play strings six, four, three, two, and one. The **♭3** **B♭**, is fingered at the third fret, third string. The 5th D, is fingered at the third fret, second string.

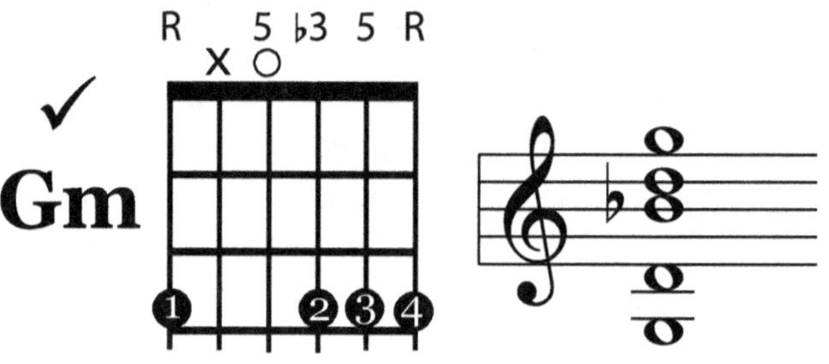

All three choices produce chords that are similar in difficulty. Which one to choose in this case will depend on the voicing that best suits your need.

G minor 7

Our choices for this chord are to combine the options for the **G7** chord and the **Gm** chord. There are several options. The first choice is to place the **♭7** (**F**) on the fourth string and the **♭3** (**B♭**) on the fifth string. This eliminates the first string.

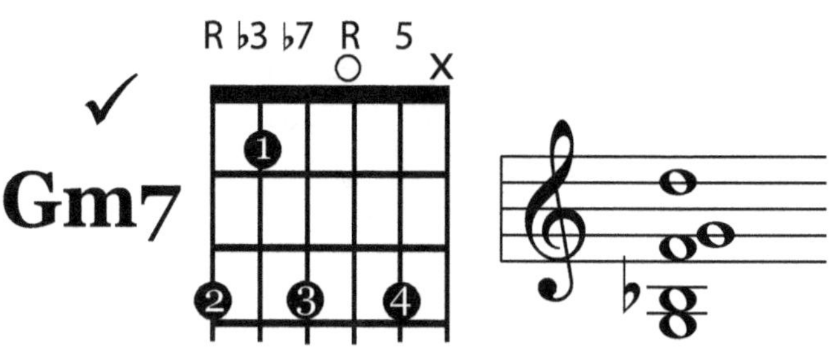

Another choice is to substitute **B♭** for R on the third string (third fret), and place the **♭7** on the first string. This would eliminate the fifth string.

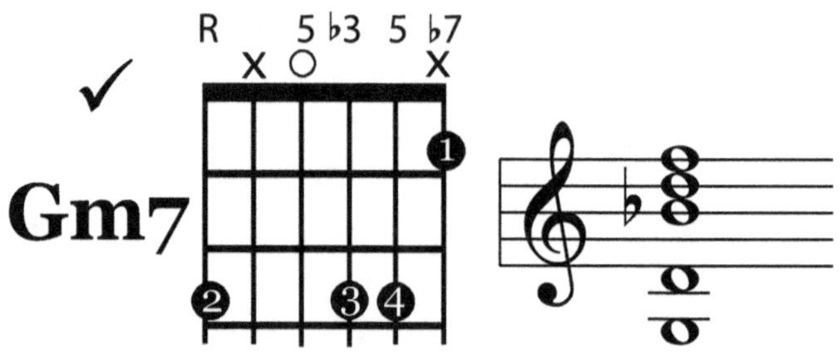

PART 4
PLAYING UP THE NECK

14 Barre Chords

Barre chords are chords that use the first finger of the left hand to 'bar' or stretch across one fret in order to play several strings at one time (just like the F chord in the C group). The barre is indicated by a solid black line joining the highest string to be barred with the lowest as shown in the diagram below.

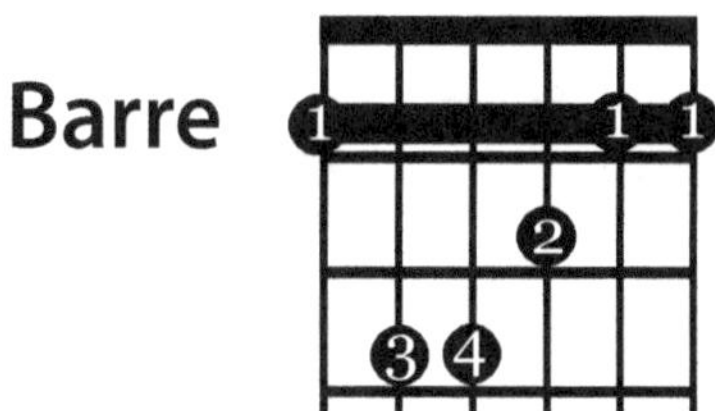

As you can see, the first finger is playing the note on the 6th string as well as the notes on the 2nd and 1st. All of the notes played in barre chords are fretted or fingered, in other words there are *no open strings.*

For this reason barre chords can be moved anywhere on the neck to form a chord. There are five ***barre forms*** in all : **C ,A, G, E,** and **D**. They spell the word **CAGED** which will be an important word to keep in mind when moving the shapes up the neck.

The ***barre forms*** are modeled after their respective open position chords as we will see in the pages that follow. When learning these be sure you can easily recognize the shape of all 5 forms.

The A Form

Compare the *A chord* to the *A form*. The two have identical fingerings except for the first finger bar in the A form. ***The lowest root (R) is ALWAYS found on the 5th string under the 1st finger.***

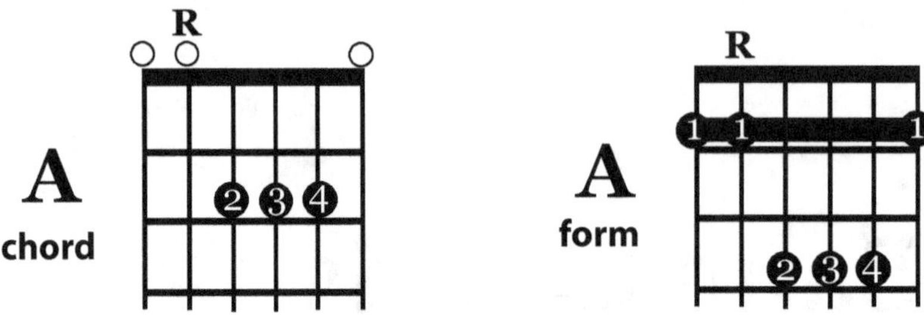

The E Form

Compare the *E chord* to the *E form*. The two have identical shapes but use different fingerings. ***The lowest root (R) is ALWAYS found on the 6th string under the 1st. finger.***

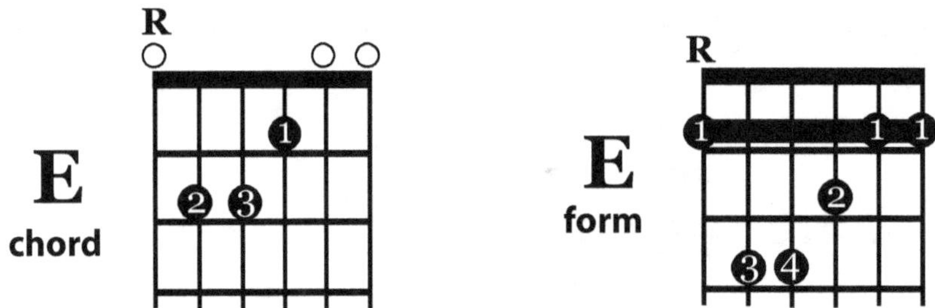

The D Form

Compare the *D chord* to the *D form*. The two have identical shapes but use different fingerings. ***The lowest root (R) is ALWAYS found on the 4th string under the 1st finger.*** (In this form the barre is not necessary unless you are also including the fifth string.)

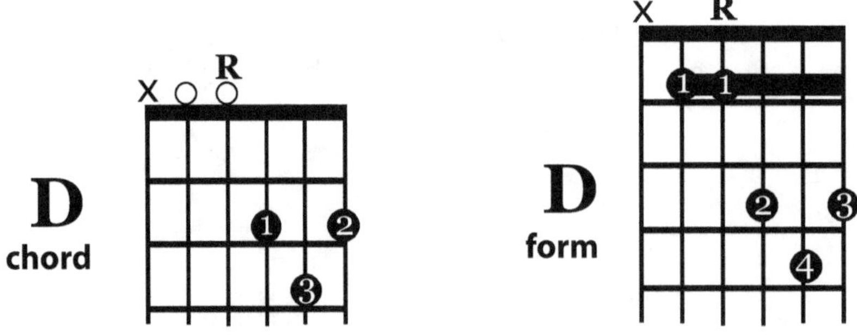

The G Form

Compare the *G chord* to the *G form*. The two have identical fingerings except for the 1st finger bar in the G form. ***The lowest root of the G form is found on the 6th string under the 3rd finger.***

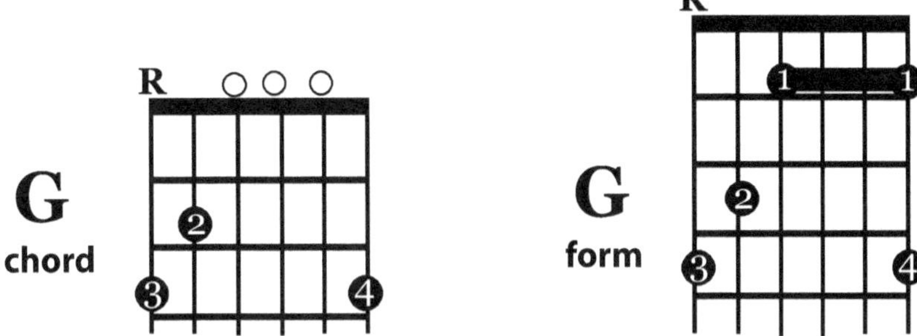

The C Form

Compare the *C chord* to the *C form*. The two have identical shapes but use different fingerings. ***The lowest root (R) of the C form is found on the 5th string under the 4th finger.***

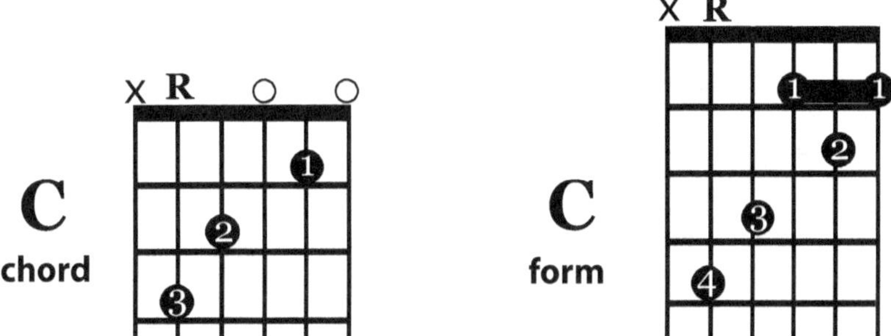

It is important to memorize which string the root lies under for each form. An easy way to remember string numbers for the roots is to remember the word **CAGED.** The C and A form roots are located on the fifth string, G and E form roots are on the sixth string, and the D form root is on the fourth string.

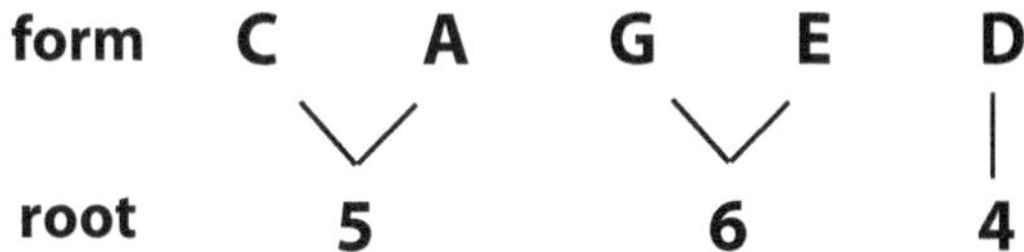

Remember barre chords use fretted strings only, no open strings. For this reason you can move any barre shape any place on the neck to create a chord.

For instance, if you are playing the A form and are barring on the first fret you will be playing a B♭ chord. The chord is B♭ because the fifth string first fret is named B♭. If you moved the form up to the second fret you would get a B chord, up one more to the third fret a C chord, etc. As you move up the neck fret by fret you will be moving *chromatically*.

All of the barre forms move chromatically up and down the neck; however, their roots are found on different strings.

Exercise 14.1

Practice moving each form up and down the neck chromatically (fret by fret). Say the name of each chord out loud as you go.

After you feel comfortable with this, try skipping around from one fret to another until you can choose any fret and any form at random and give the name of that chord.

C FORM	A FORM
root = 5 string	root = 5 string
3 = C	0 = A
4 = C♯/D♭	1 = A♯/B♭
5 = D	2 = B
6 = D♯/E♭	3 = C
7 = E	4 = C♯/D♭
8 = F	5 = D
9 = F♯/G♭	6 = D♯/E♭
10 = G	7 = E
11 = G♯/A♭	8 = F
12 = A	9 = F♯/G♭
13 = A♯/B♭	10 = G
14 = B	11 = G♯/A♭
15 = C	12 = A

G FORM	E FORM	D FORM
root = 6 string	root = 6 string	root = 4 string
3 = G	0 = E	0 = D
4 = G♯/A♭	1 = F	1 = D♯/E♭
5 = A	2 = F♯/G♭	2 = E
6 = A♯/B♭	3 = G	3 = F
7 = B	4 = G♯/A♭	4 = F♯/G♭
8 = C	5 = A	5 = G
9 = C♯/D♭	6 = A♯/B♭	6 = G♯/A♭
10 = D	7 = B	7 = A
11 = D♯/E♭	8 = C	8 = A♯/B♭
12 = E	9 = C♯/D♭	9 = B
13 = F	10 = D	10 = C
14 = F♯/G♭	11 = D♯/E♭	11 = C♯/D♭
15 = G	12 = E	12 = D

15 Chords At Five Levels

The C Chord At Five Levels

Now that moving each bar form chromatically is fairly familiar, we can begin to play the *same* chord at five different positions on the neck. This is accomplished through the five barre forms: **C A G E D**.

For instance, the C chord can be played five different ways by using the five forms.

To do this start with the C chord in first (open) position.

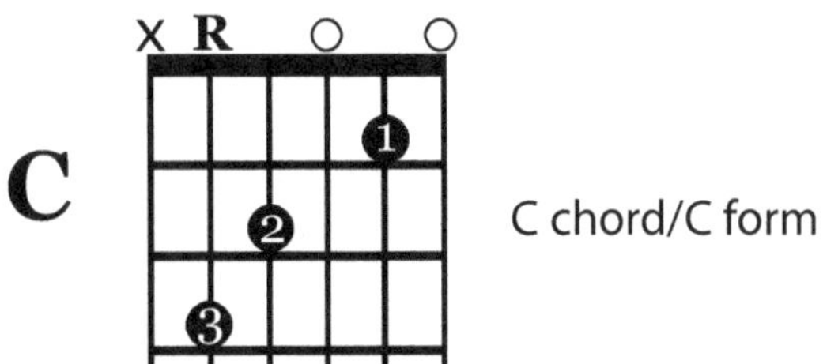

The next form is the A form. The C root is still on the fifth string. It is now played with the 1st finger. You should be barring at the third fret and fingering the A form.

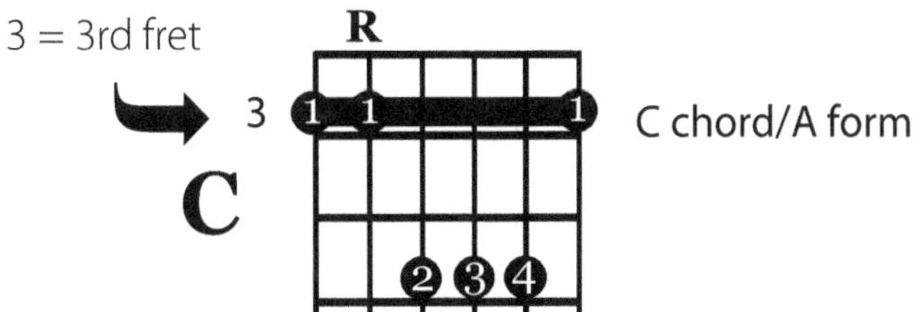

The G form follows. The C root is fingered with the 3rd finger at the 8th fret. You should be barring at the fifth fret and fingering the G form.

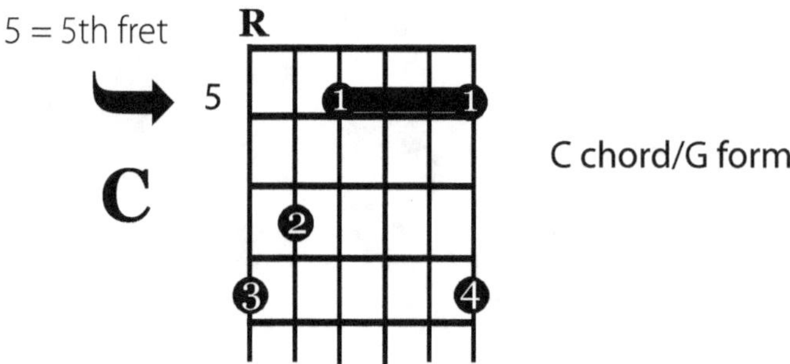

The next form is the E form. The C root is still on the sixth string. It is now played with the 1st finger. You should be barring at the eighth fret and fingering the E form.

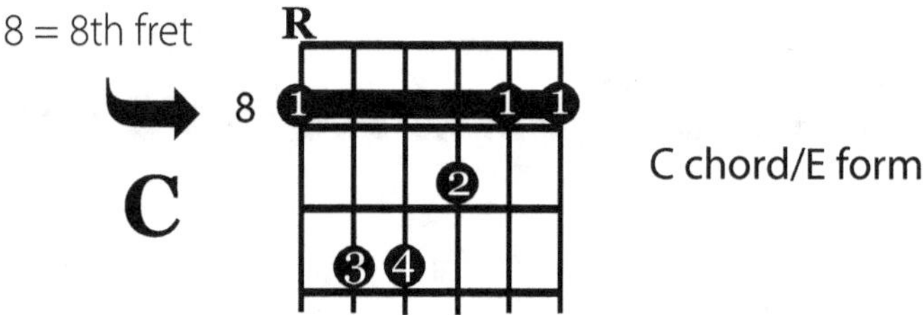

The last form is the D form. The C root is fingered with the 1st finger at the 10th fret. You should be fingering the D form.

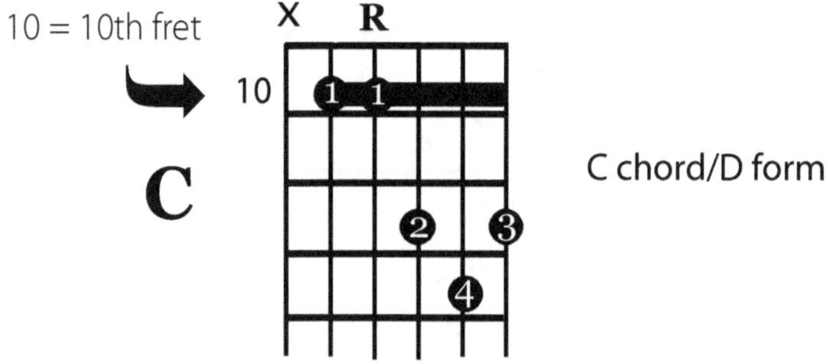

You should see that the forms overlap each other. In other words, some of the same notes are used in neighboring forms but they use different fingers.

Every chord will work the same way as our example above. The difference will be the starting form.

The G Chord At Five Levels

Let's find all of the **G chords** on the neck.

Find the G chord that is lowest on the neck (as close to the first fret as possible). You should be fingering the open position G chord. Remember this is also the G form.

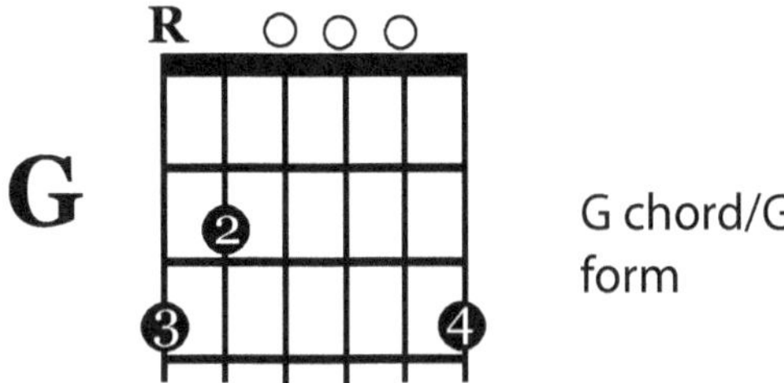

Think of the word CAGED and find the form that is next after G.

Your answer should be the **E form**.

Locate the E form on the fretboard so it produces the G chord. You should be barring at the third fret.

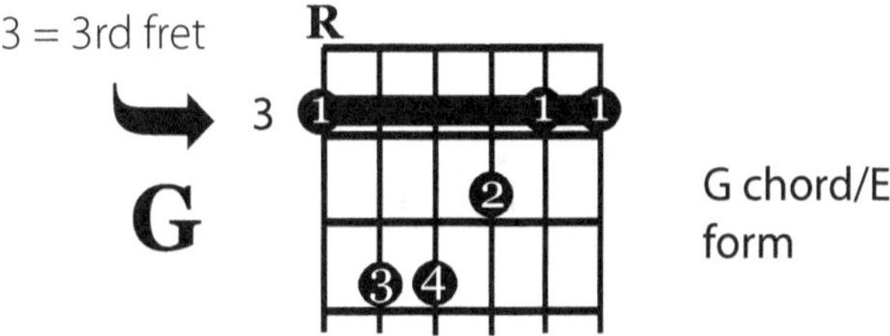

Again, think of the word CAGED and find the form that is next after E.

Your answer should be the D form.

Locate the D form on the fretboard so it produces the G chord. You should be barring at the fifth fret.

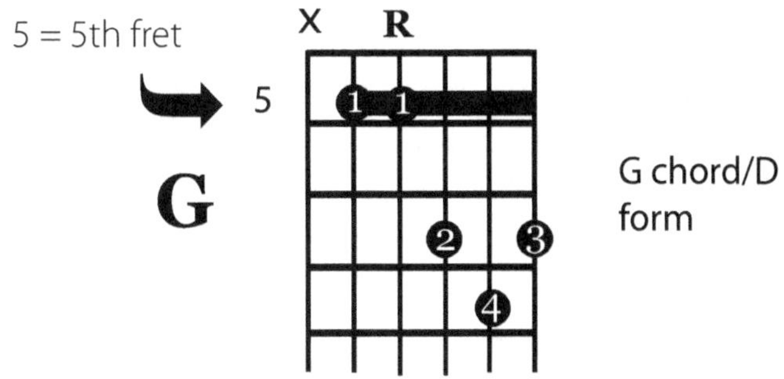

The form following D is the C form. (Since we started in the middle of the word we just circle back to the beginning of the word CAGED.)

Locate the C form on the fretboard so it produces the G chord. You should be barring at the seventh fret with the root fingered under the 4th finger at the tenth fret.

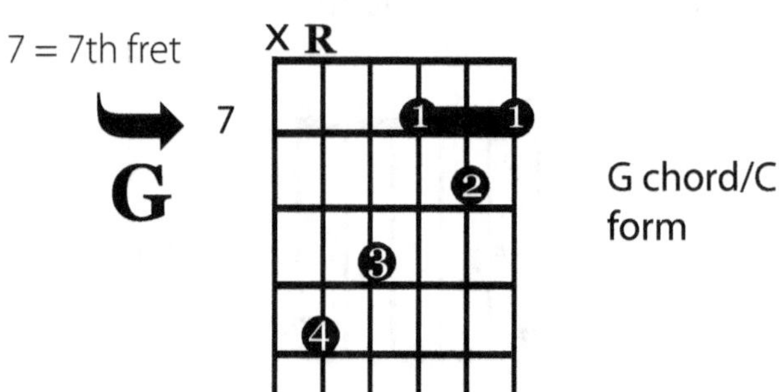

Once again, think of the word CAGED and find the form that is next after C.

Your answer should be the A form.

Locate the A form on the fretboard so it produces the G chord. You should be barring at the tenth fret.

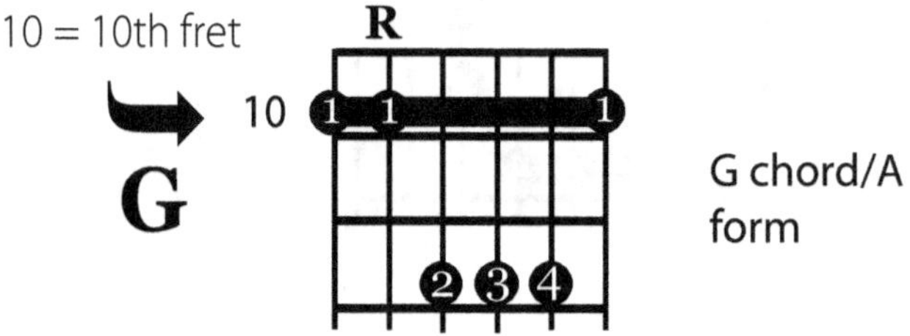

Exercise 15.1

Work through the circle of fifths until all chords have been completed. Start with the lowest form possible on the lowest part of the neck. Remember to work forward then backward through the word CAGED. (Note that not all chords begin with the C form.)

Mastering chords at five levels may be difficult to grasp at first. Don't get discouraged if it seems you're spending much time and gaining little progress. With persistence and effort you will be playing these forms up and down the neck with ease!

16 Altering Barre Forms

By now you should be very familiar with where the roots, thirds, fifths, and sevenths are found in every open chord form. Since the barre forms are modeled after the open forms, altering these forms will work the same way.

In this chapter we will take one form at a time and create the following *five chord qualities: Major, Major 7, 7, minor, m7. Our examples will show the open form on the left and the barre chord on the right. To keep things simple, all barre forms are shown for the C chord only but remember barre chords are moveable so each quality can be reproduced at every fret.

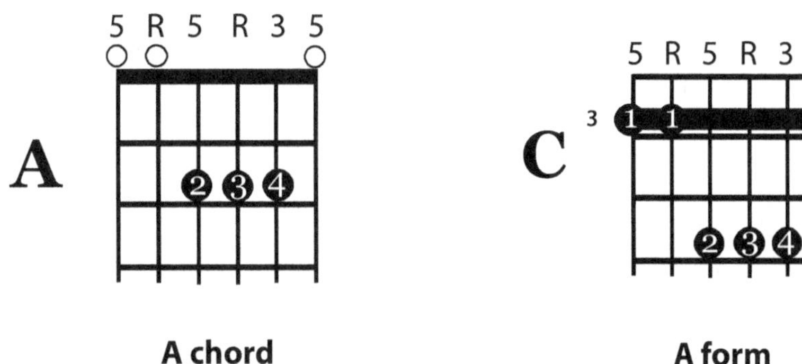

A chord **A form**

So to conclude, we are combing the chord qualities we learned in chapter 13 with the moveable barre concept discussed in chapter 14. This yields some pretty incredible results! If we take the five chord qualities and multiply that by the five forms we get twenty-five different chord types. If we multiply the twenty-five chord types by our twelve chromatic positions (frets), we end up with **three hundred chords!**

5 chord qualities x 5 barre forms = 25 chords.

25 chords x 12 chromatic positions (frets) = 300 chords.

*Half diminished (ø7 or m7♭5) forms are located in chapter 18, page 148.

THE A FORM

A chord
A form
5 R 5 R 3 5
A
C
3
5 R 5 M7 3 5
AM7
CM7
5 R 5 ♭7 3 5
A7
C7
5 R 5 R ♭3 5
Am
Cm
5 R 5 ♭7 ♭3 5
Am7
Cm7

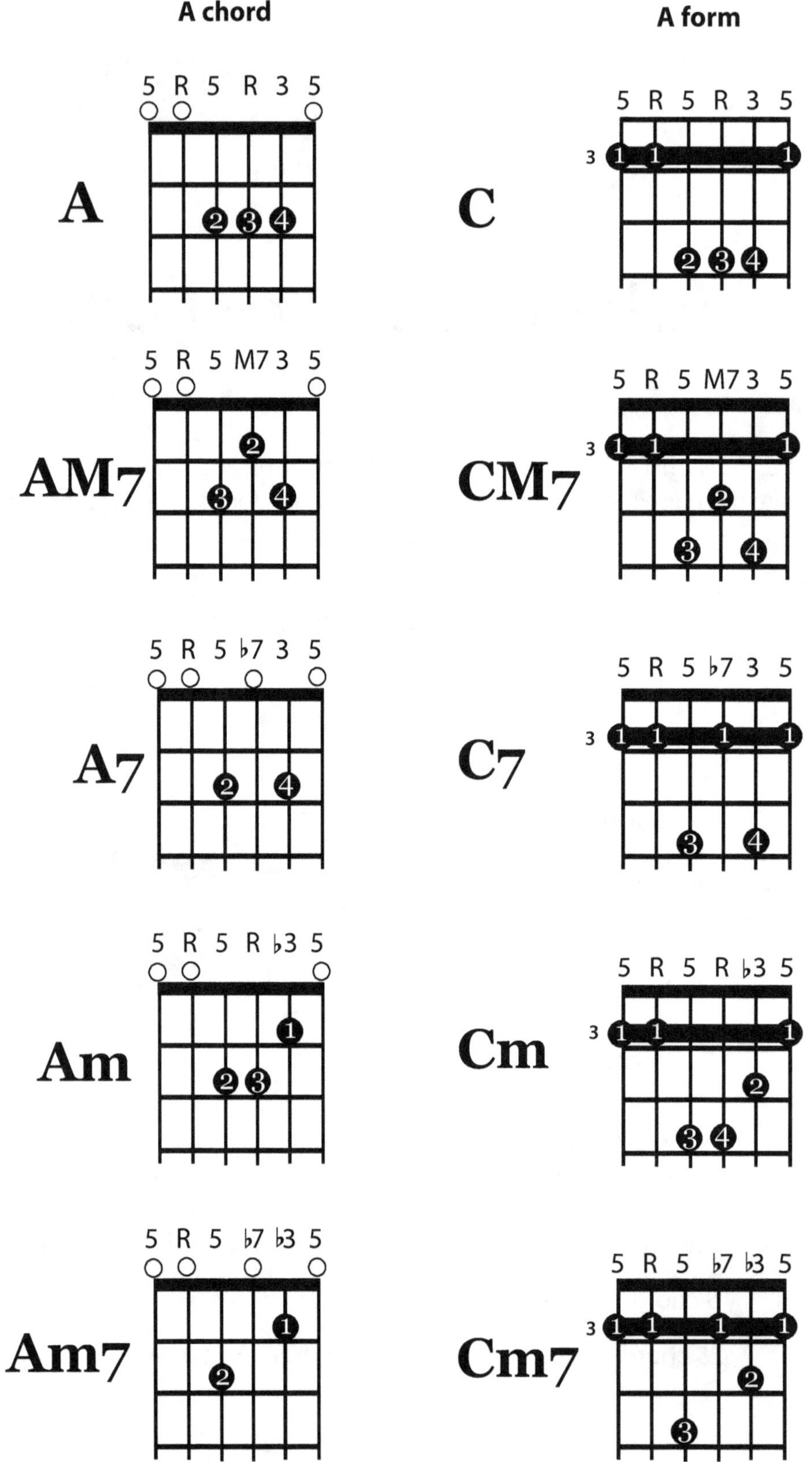

THE E FORM

E chord
E form
R 5 R 3 5 R
E
C
8
R 5 M7 3 5 R
R X M7 3 5 X
EM7
CM7
R 5 ♭7 3 5 R
E7
C7
R 5 R ♭3 5 R
Em
Cm
R 5 ♭7 ♭3 5 R
Em7
Cm7

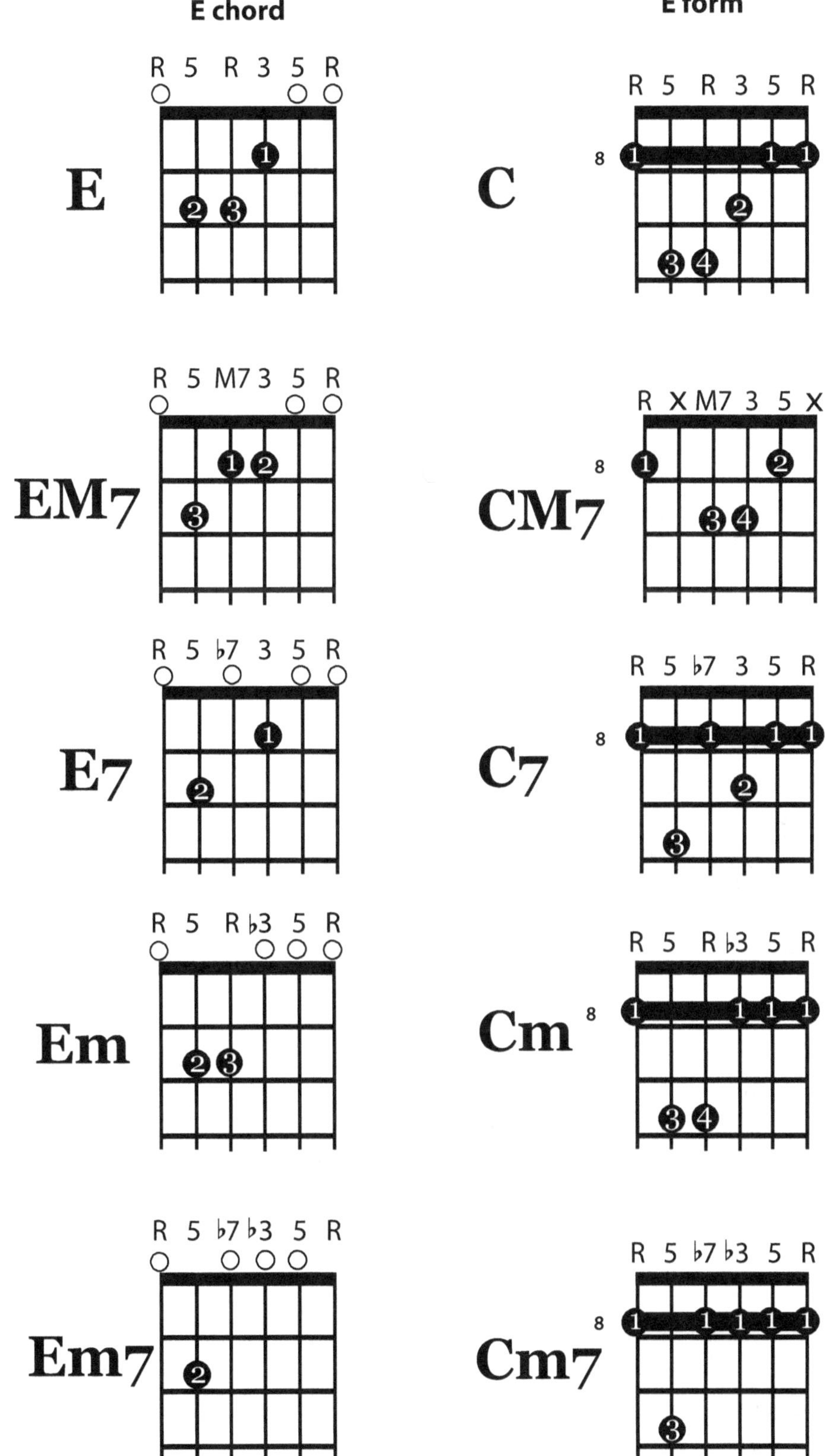

THE D FORM

D chord
D form
5 R 5 R 3
X 5 R 5 R 3
10
D
C
5 R 5 M7 3
X 5 R 5 M7 3
DM7
CM7
optional fingering
5 R 5 ♭7 3
X 5 R 5 ♭7 3
D7
C7
5 R 5 R ♭3
X 5 R 5 R ♭3
Dm
Cm
5 R 5 ♭7 ♭3
X 5 R 5 ♭7 ♭3
Dm7
Cm7

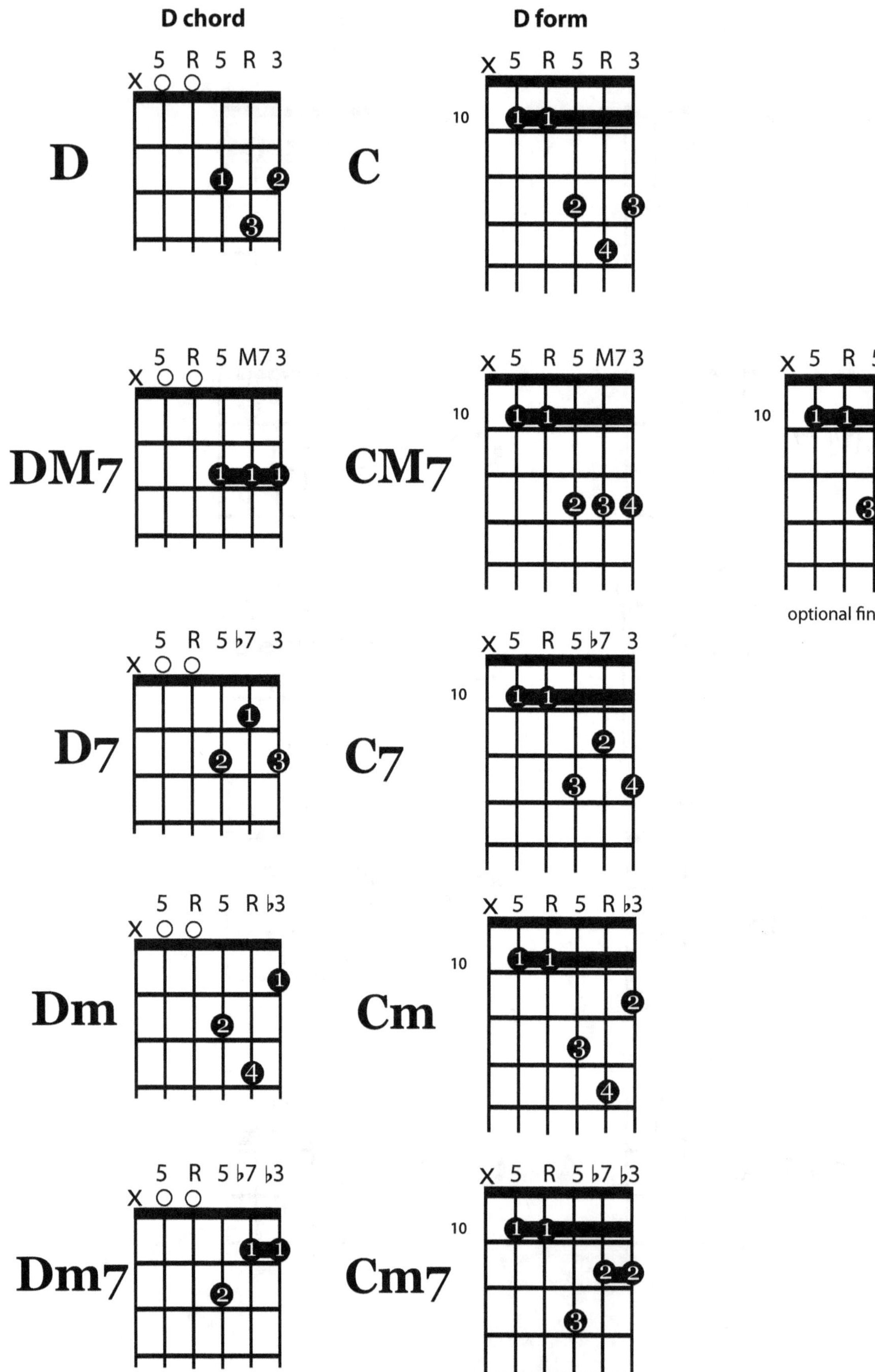

THE C FORM

C form

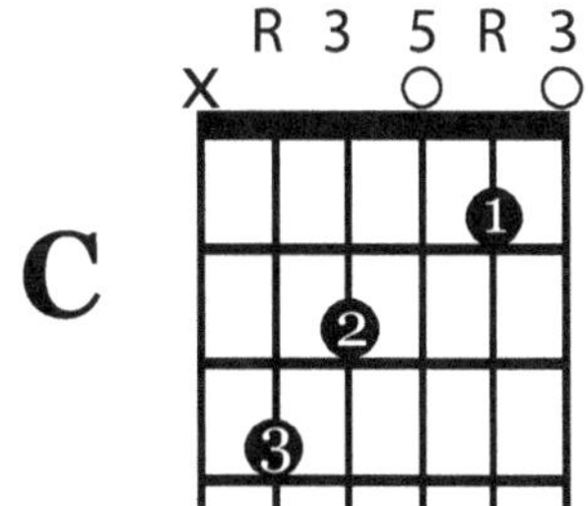

C

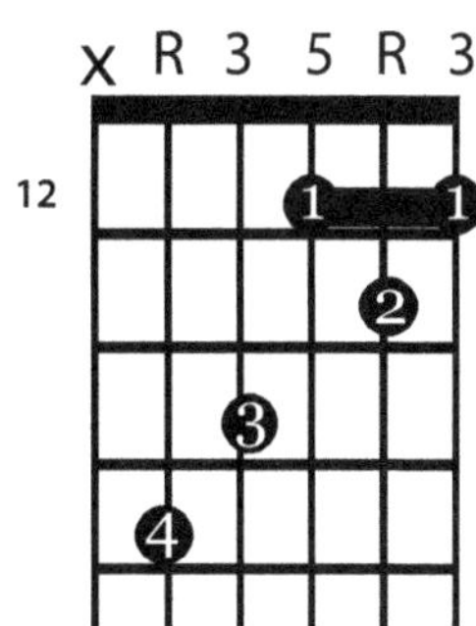

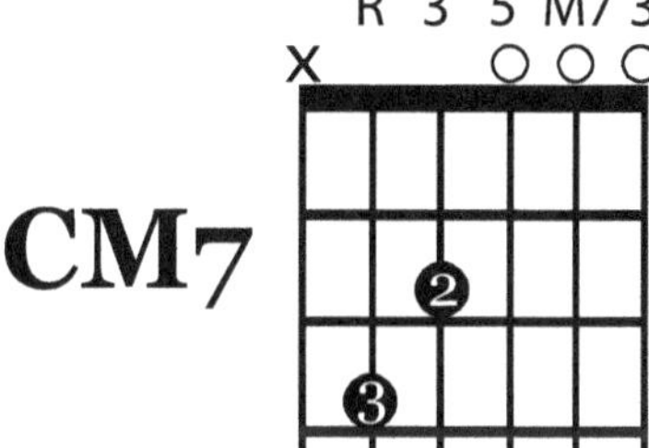

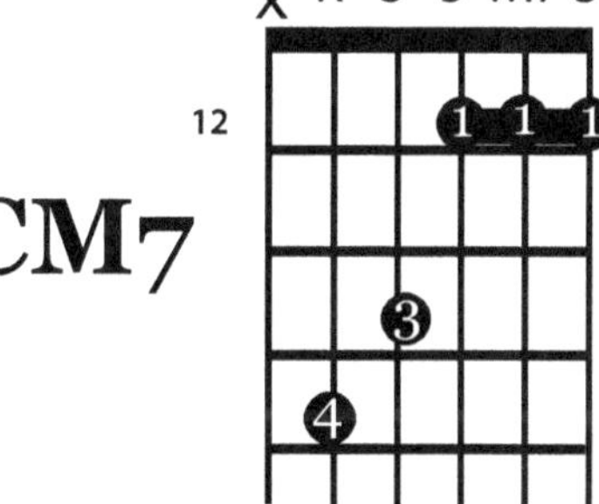

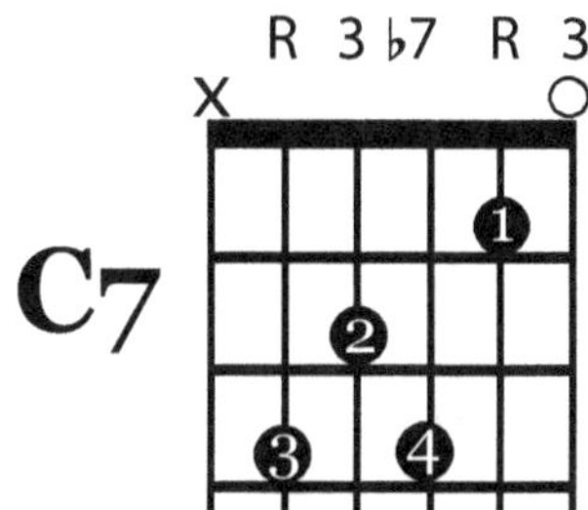

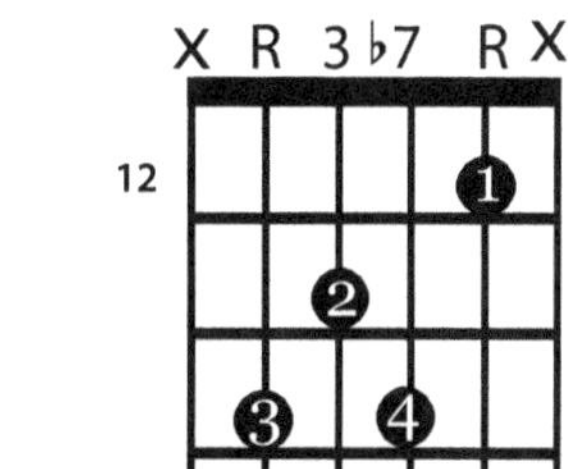

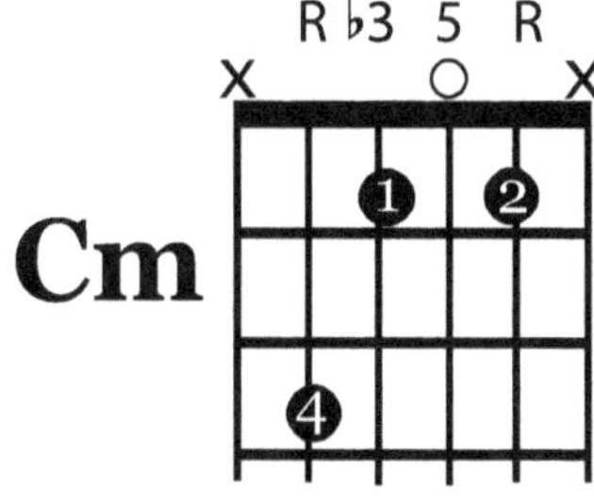

Cm

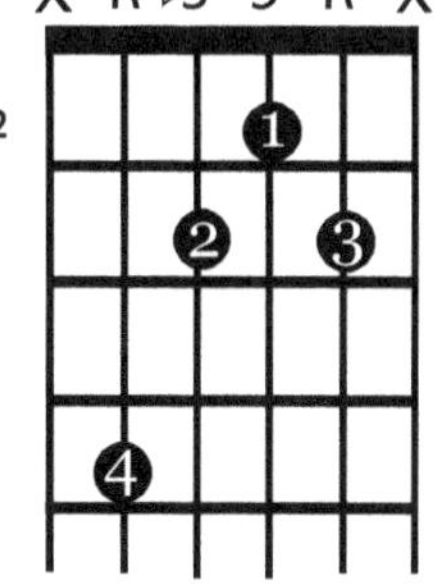

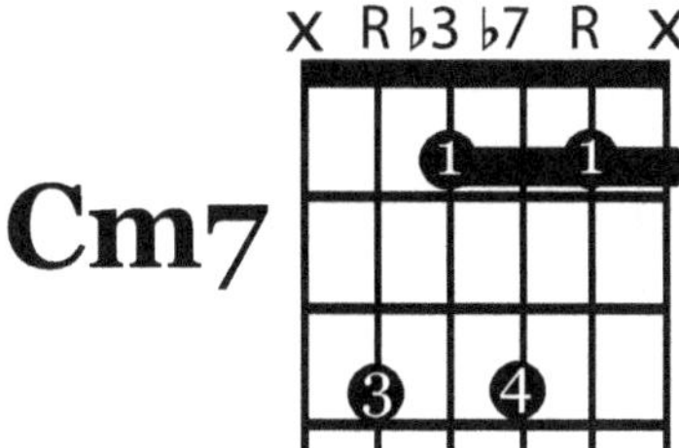

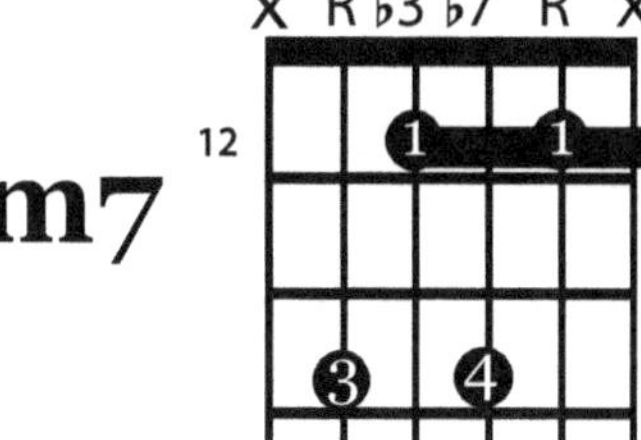

THE G FORM

G chord

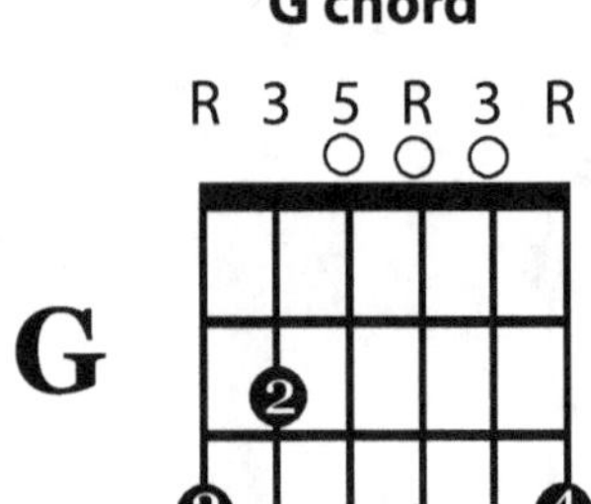

G form

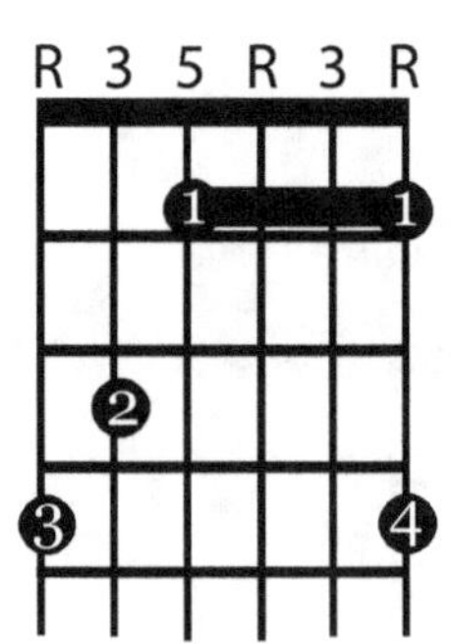

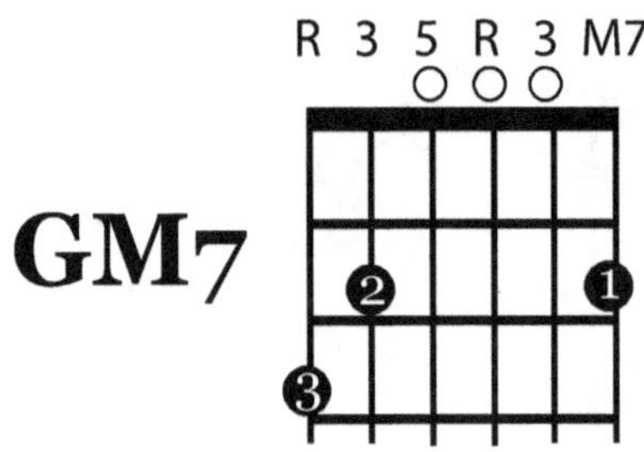

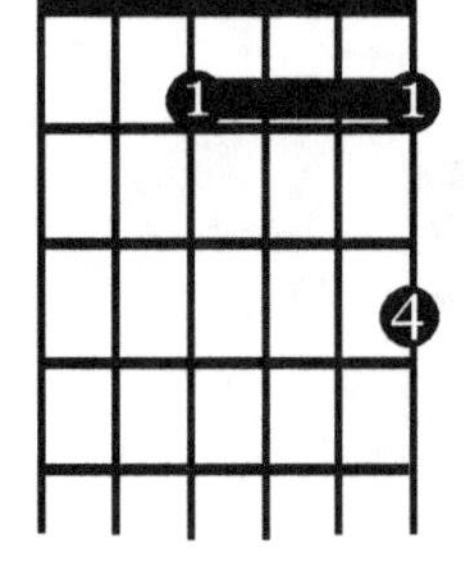

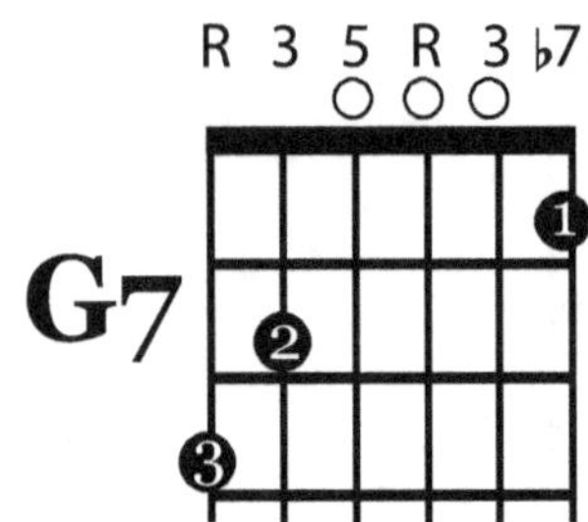

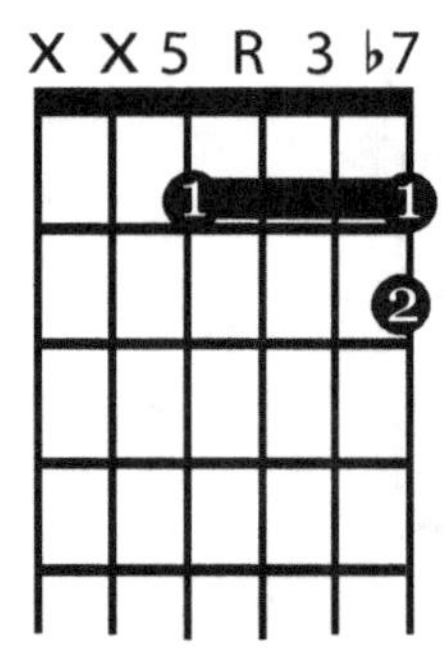

*When altering the G form, fingerings on all six strings can be difficult and impractical. It is easier to use some of the strings as shown.

Note that the forms using strings 4-1 do not have the root in the lowest voice.

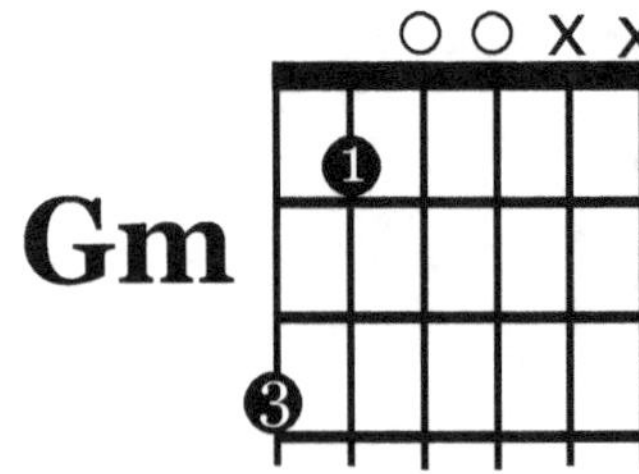

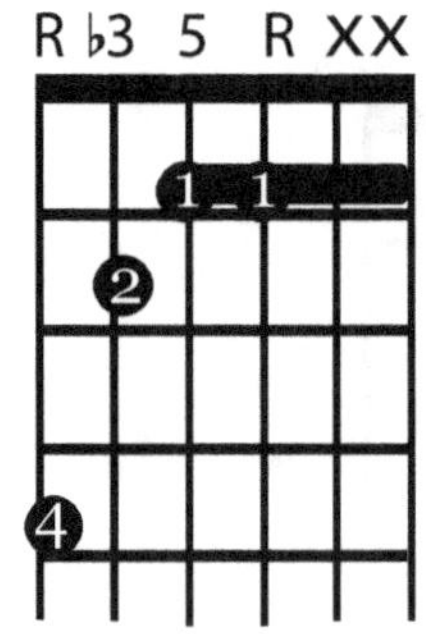

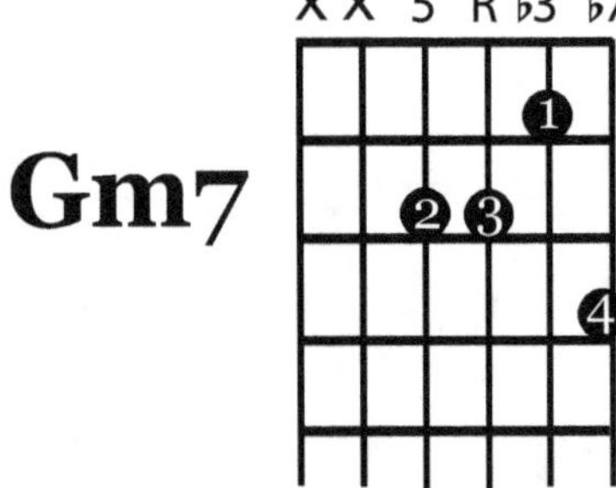

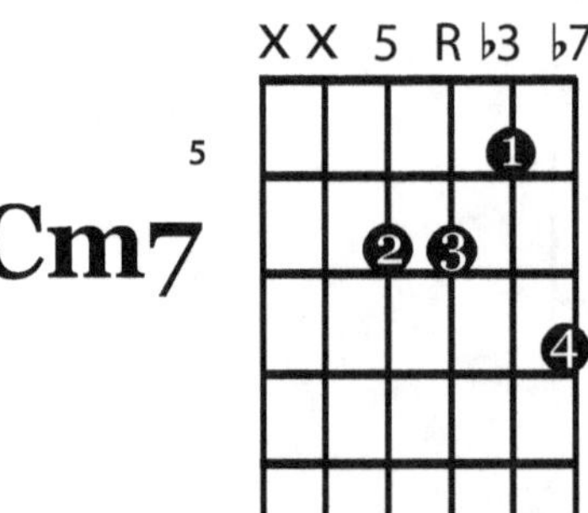

17 Chord Progressions

PRIMARY CHORDS USING BARRE FORMS

Once the major chords are working well at five levels we can begin playing the primary chords (1, IV , and V) at five levels. Because the forms are moveable, the chord groups are also moveable. Compare the open A group to the B♭ group .

A Group, Fretted B♭ Group

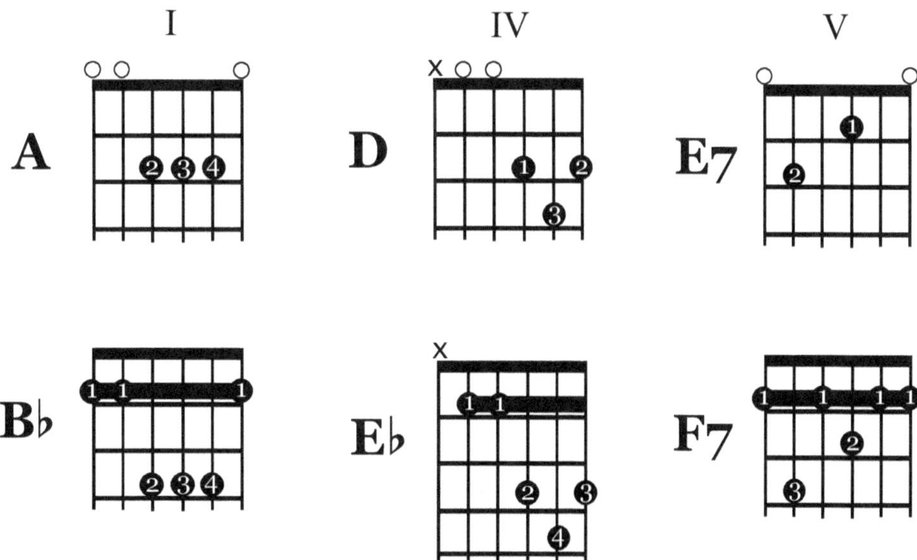

Notice how the shapes are the same but because barre chords are used, the actual chord names have changed. By moving these chord groups up and down the neck, primary chords can be played in every key using the forms found in the A group.

A Group, Fretted A Form Group

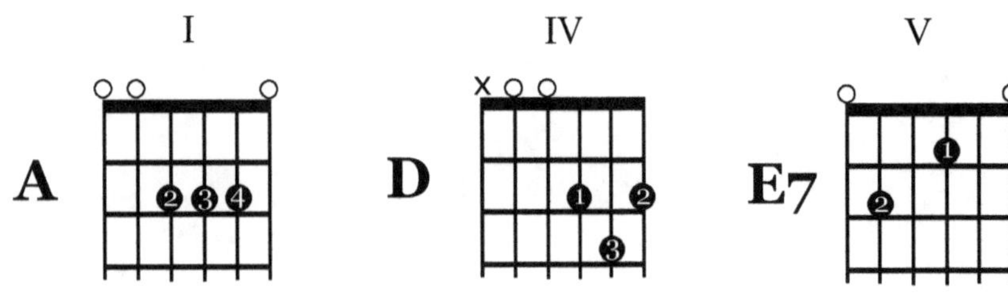

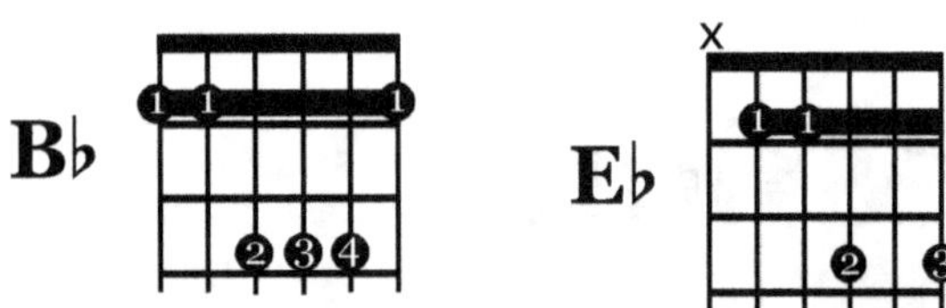

If we play the A group open, we are in the key of A. I, IV, and V7 in the key of A produces the A, D and E7 chords. These chords become our models or forms for playing in each key up the neck. The chart to the right shows all keys using the A group forms.

KEY	FRET (Root)	I	IV	V7
A	0	A	D	E7
A♯/ B♭	1	A♯ B♭	D♯ E♭	E♯7 F 7
B	2	B	E	F♯7
C	3	C	F	G7
C♯/ D♭	4	C♯ D♭	F♯ G♭	G♯7 A♭7
D	5	D	G	A7
D♯/ E♭	6	D♯ E♭	G♯ A♭	A♯7 B♭7
E	7	E	A	B 7
F	8	F	B♭	C 7
F♯/ G♭	9	F♯ G♭	B C♭	C♯7 D♭7
G	10	G	C	D 7
G♯/ A♭	11	G♯ A♭	C♯ D♭	D♯7 E♭7
A	12	A	D	E7

Exercise 17.1

Practice the A form group moving up one fret at a time. Be sure to say the chord names aloud as you play.

I (A form) IV (D form) V7 (E7 form) I (A form)

I (A form) V7 (E7 form) IV (D form) I (A form)

E Group, Fretted E Form Group

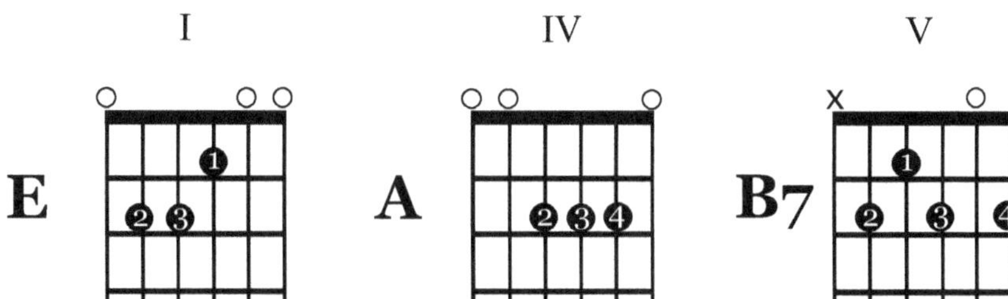

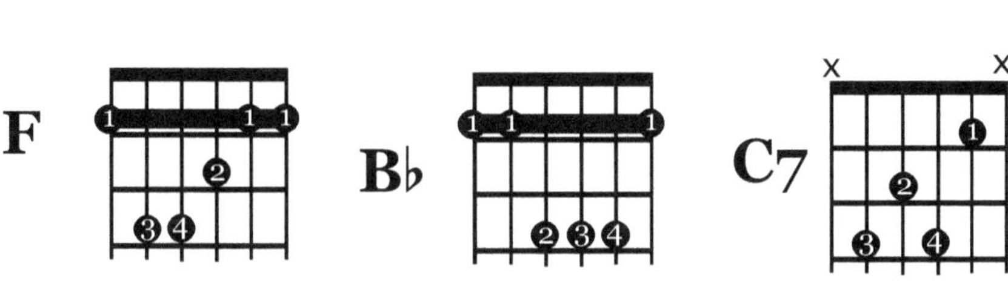

KEY	(Root) FRET	I	IV	V7
E	0	E	A	B 7
F	1	F	B♭	C 7
F♯/ G♭	2	F♯ G♭	B C♭	C♯7 D♭7
G	3	G	C	D 7
G♯/ A♭	4	G♯ A♭	C♯ D♭	D♯7 E♭7
A	5	A	D	E7
A♯/ B♭	6	A♯ B♭	D♯ E♭	E♯7 F 7
B	7	B	E	F♯7
C	8	C	F	G7
C♯/ D♭	9	C♯ D♭	F♯ G♭	G♯7 A♭7
D	10	D	G	A7
D♯/ E♭	11	D♯ E♭	G♯ A♭	A♯7 B♭7
E	12	E	A	B 7

Exercise 17.2

Practice the E form group moving up one fret at a time. Be sure to say the chord names aloud as you play.

I (E form)	IV (A form)	V7 (C7 form)	I (E form)
/ / / /	/ / / /	/ / / /	/ / / /

I (E form)	V7 (C7 form)	IV (A form)	I (E form)
/ / / /	/ / / /	/ / / /	/ / / /

D Group, Fretted D Form Group

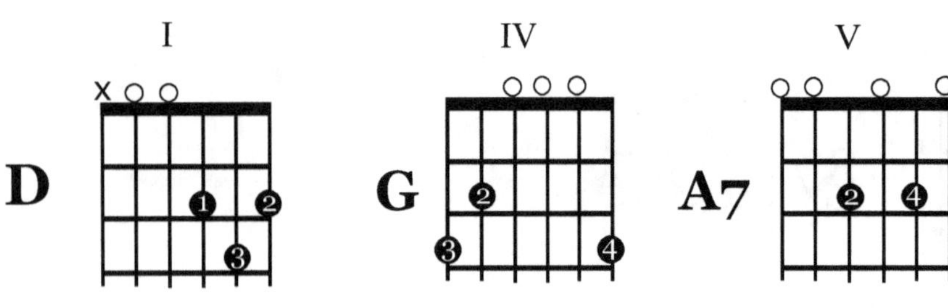

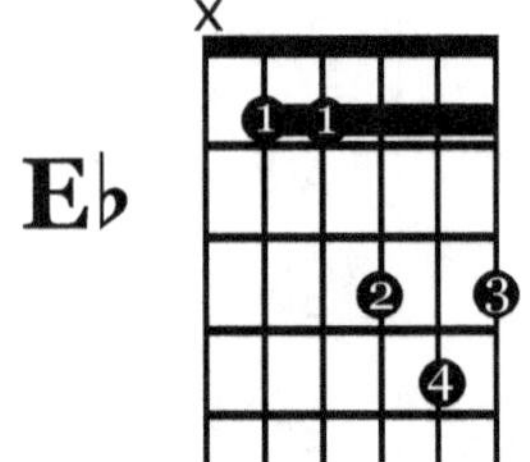

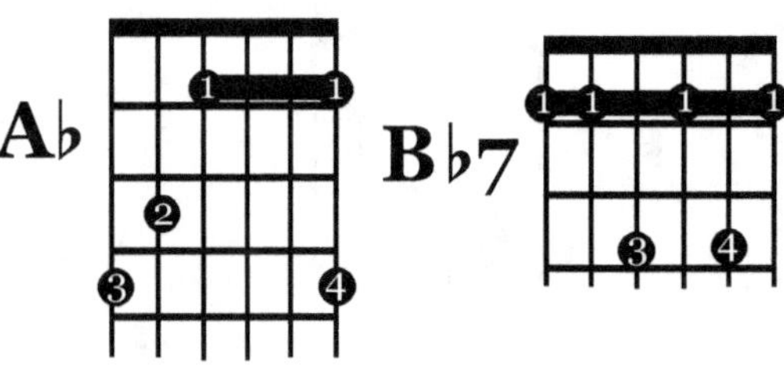

KEY	(Root) FRET	I	IV	V7
D	0	D	G	A7
D♯/ E♭	1	D♯ E♭	G♯ A♭	A♯7 B♭7
E	2	E	A	B7
F	3	F	B♭	C7
F♯/ G♭	4	F♯ G♭	B C♭	C♯7 D♭7
G	5	G	C	D7
G♯/ A♭	6	G♯ A♭	C♯ D♭	D♯7 E♭7
A	7	A	D	E7
A♯/ B♭	8	A♯ B♭	D♯ E♭	E♯7 F7
B	9	B	E	F♯7
C	10	C	F	G7
C♯/ D♭	11	C♯ D♭	F♯ G♭	G♯7 A♭7
D	12	D	G	A

Exercise 17.3

Practice the D form group moving up one fret at a time. Be sure to say the chord names aloud as you play.

I (D form) | IV (G form) | V7 (A7 form) | I (D form)

I (D form) | V7 (A7 form) | IV (G form) | I (D form)

G Group, Fretted G Form Group

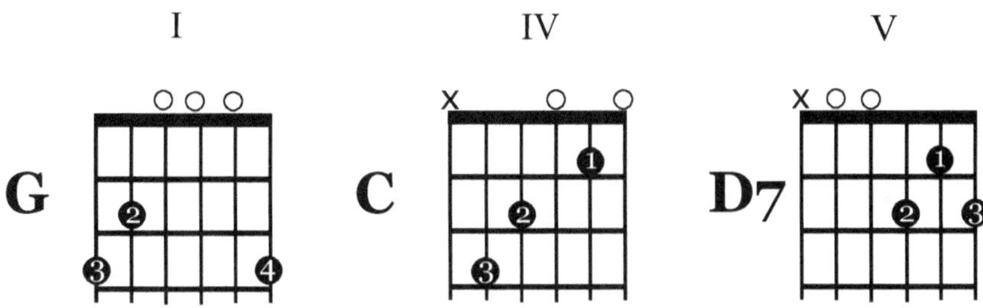

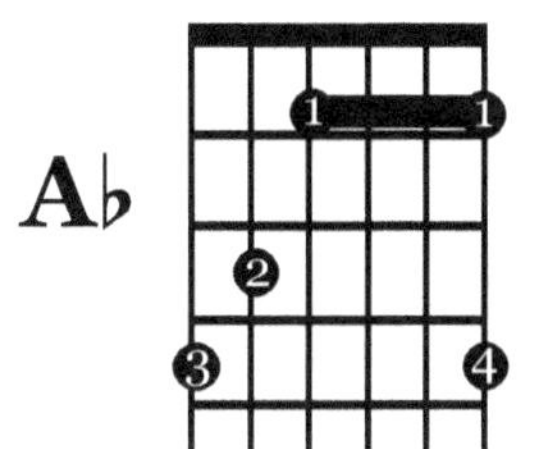

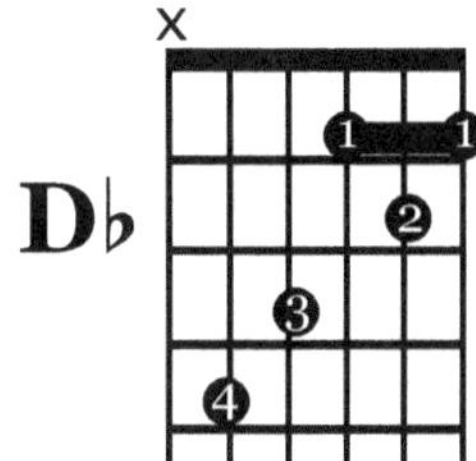

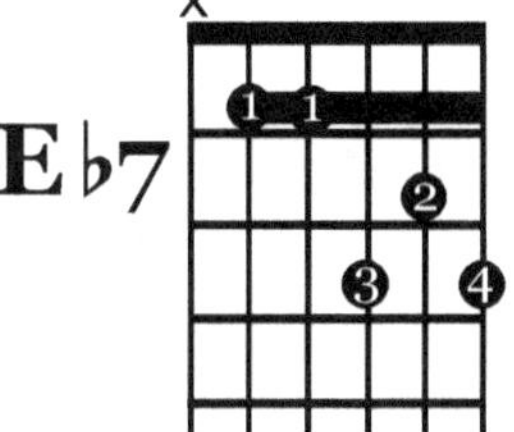

KEY	FRET (Root)	I	IV	V7
G	3	G	C	D 7
G♯/ A♭	4	G♯ A♭	C♯ D♭	D♯7 E♭7
A	5	A	D	E7
A♯/ B♭	6	A♯ B♭	D♯ E♭	E♯7 F 7
B	7	B	E	F♯7
C	8	C	F	G7
C♯/ D♭	9	C♯ D♭	F♯ G♭	G♯7 A♭7
D	10	D	G	A7
D♯/ E♭	11	D♯ E♭	G♯ A♭	A♯7 B♭7
E	12	E	A	B 7
F	13	F	B♭	C 7
F♯/ G♭	14	F♯ G♭	B C♭	C♯7 D♭7
G	15	G	C	D 7

Exercise 17.4

Practice the G form group moving up one fret at a time. Be sure to say the chord names aloud as you play.

I (G form) | IV (C form) | V7 (D7 form) | I (G form)

I (G form) | V7 (D7 form) | IV (C form) | I (G form)

C Group, Fretted C Form Group

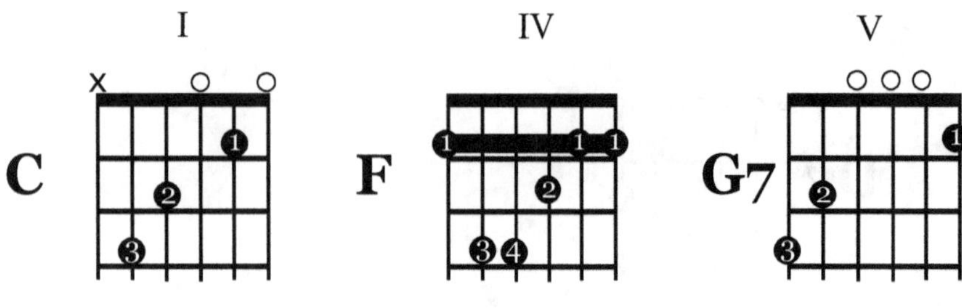

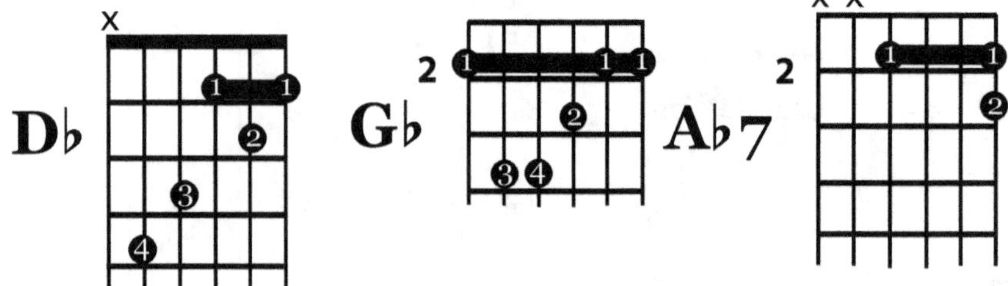

KEY	(Root) FRET	I	IV	V7
C	3	C	F	G7
C#/ Db	4	C# Db	F# Gb	G#7 Ab7
D	5	D	G	A
D#/ Eb	6	D# Eb	G# Ab	A#7 Bb7
E	7	E	A	B 7
F	8	F	Bb	C 7
F#/ Gb	9	F# Gb	B Cb	C#7 Db7
G	10	G	C	D 7
G#/ Ab	11	G# Ab	C# Db	D#7 Eb7
A	12	A	D	E7
A#/ Bb	13	A# Bb	D# Eb	E#7 F 7
B	14	B	E	F#7
C	15	C	F	G7

Exercise 17.5

Practice the C form group moving up one fret at a time. Be sure to say the chord names aloud as you play.

I (C form) IV (E form) V7 (G7 form) I (C form)

I (C form) V7 (G7 form) IV (E form) I (C form)

Am Group, Fretted Am Form Group

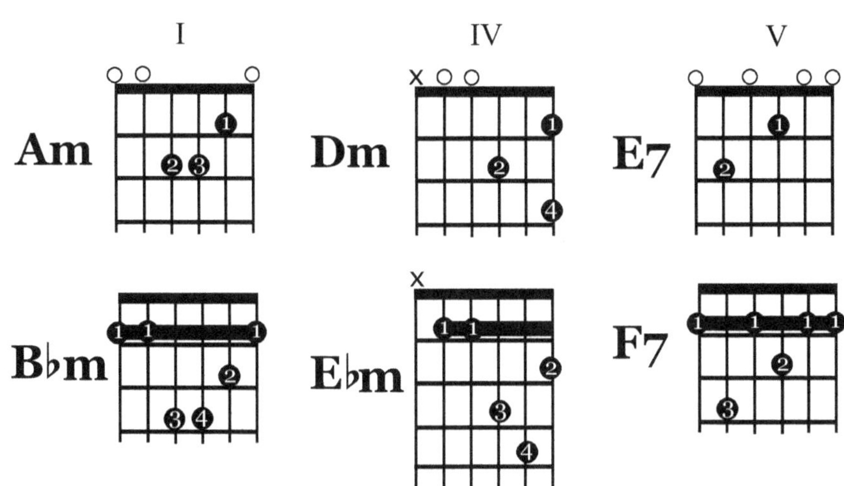

KEY	FRET (Root)	i	iv	V7
Am	0	Am	Dm	E7
A♯m/ B♭m	1	A♯m B♭m	D♯m E♭m	E♯7 F 7
Bm	2	Bm	Em	F♯7
Cm	3	Cm	Fm	G7
C♯m/ D♭m	4	C♯m D♭m	F♯m G♭m	G♯7 A♭7
Dm	5	Dm	Gm	A7
D♯m/ E♭m	6	D♯m E♭m	G♯m A♭m	A♯7 B♭7
Em	7	Em	Am	B 7
Fm	8	Fm	B♭m	C 7
F♯m/ G♭m	9	F♯m G♭m	Bm C♭m	C♯7 D♭7
Gm	10	Gm	Cm	D 7
G♯m/ A♭m	11	G♯m A♭m	C♯m D♭m	D♯7 E♭7
Am	12	Am	Dm	E7

Exercise 17.6

Practice the Am form group moving up one fret at a time. Be sure to say the chord names aloud as you play.

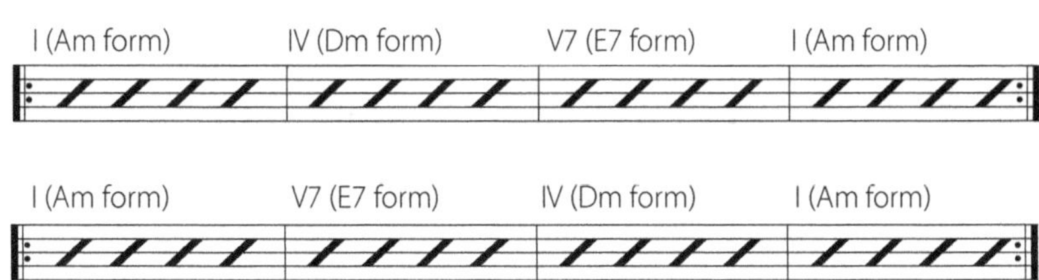

Em Group, Fretted Em Form Group

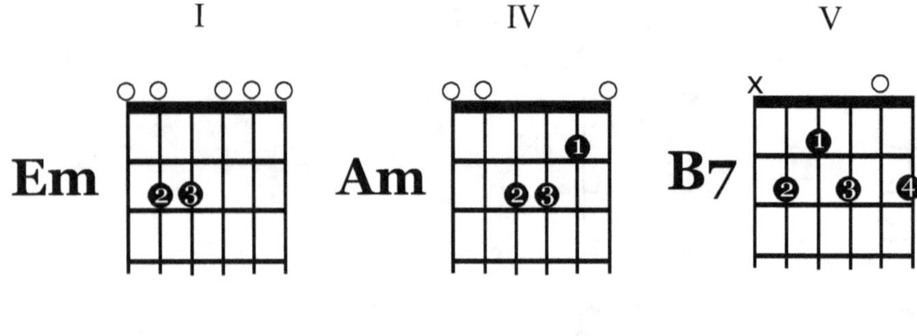

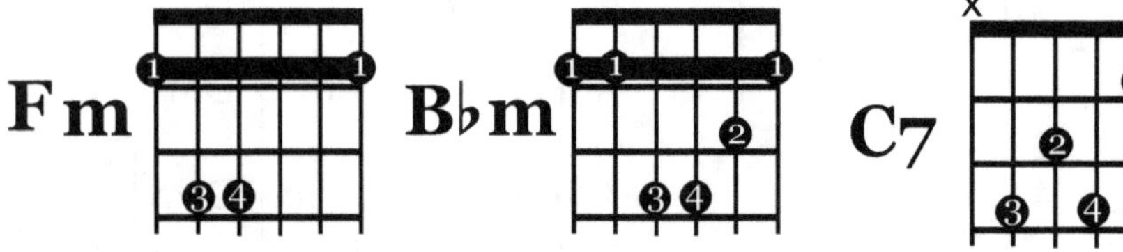

KEY	(Root) FRET	i	iv	V7
Em	0	Em	Am	B 7
Fm	1	Fm	B♭m	C 7
F♯m/ G♭m	2	F♯m G♭m	Bm C♭m	C♯7 D♭7
Gm	3	Gm	Cm	D 7
G♯m/ A♭m	4	G♯m A♭m	C♯m D♭m	D♯7 E♭7
Am	5	Am	Dm	E7
A♯m/ B♭m	6	A♯m B♭m	D♯m E♭m	E♯7 F 7
Bm	7	Bm	Em	F♯7
Cm	8	Cm	Fm	G7
C♯m/ D♭m	9	C♯m D♭m	F♯m G♭m	G♯7 A♭7
Dm	10	Dm	Gm	A7
D♯m/ E♭m	11	D♯m E♭m	G♯m A♭m	A♯7 B♭7
Em	12	Em	Am	B 7

Exercise 17.7

Practice the Em form group moving up one fret at a time.Be sure to say the chord names aloud as you play.

I (Em form) | IV (Am form) | V7 (C7 form) | I (Em form)

I (Em form) | V7 (C7 form) | IV (Am form) | I (Em form)

Twelve Bar Blues Chord Progression

One of the most widely used chord progressions in contemporary music is the twelve bar blues progression. Basic blues progressions use the primary chords, are relatively simple to play, and are easy to improvise over.

One of the easiest ways to play the blues progression is to use the E form group (E, A, and C7 forms). Begin by playing the primary chords in the key of A major (E form, fifth fret), as shown below.

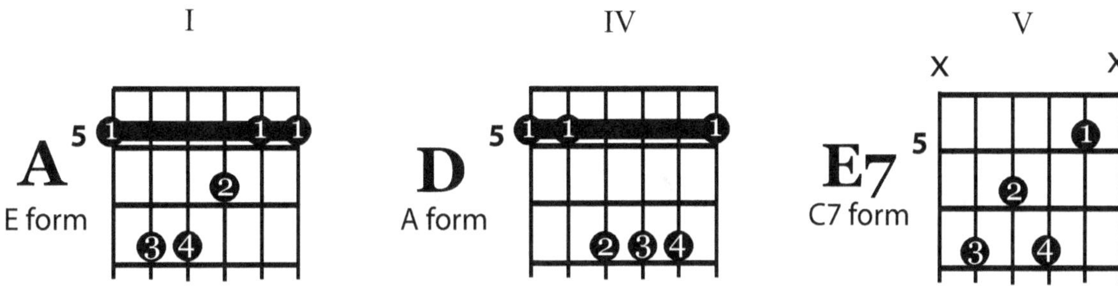

The A form is also used for the V chord. Notice that it is two frets higher (seventh fret) than the D chord (fifth fret).

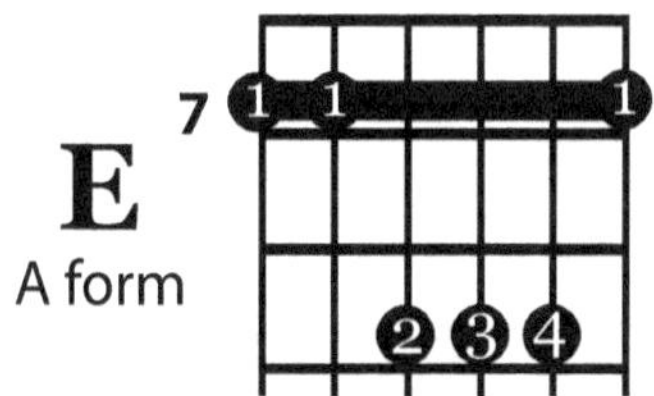

Below is a basic example of a 12 bar blues progression. Notice when we play the V chord, the A form is used in measure 9 and the C form is used in measure 12.

Also in measure 12, the E7 chord is placed over beat two. This means the A chord will continue through beat one and the E7 will be struck on beat 2.

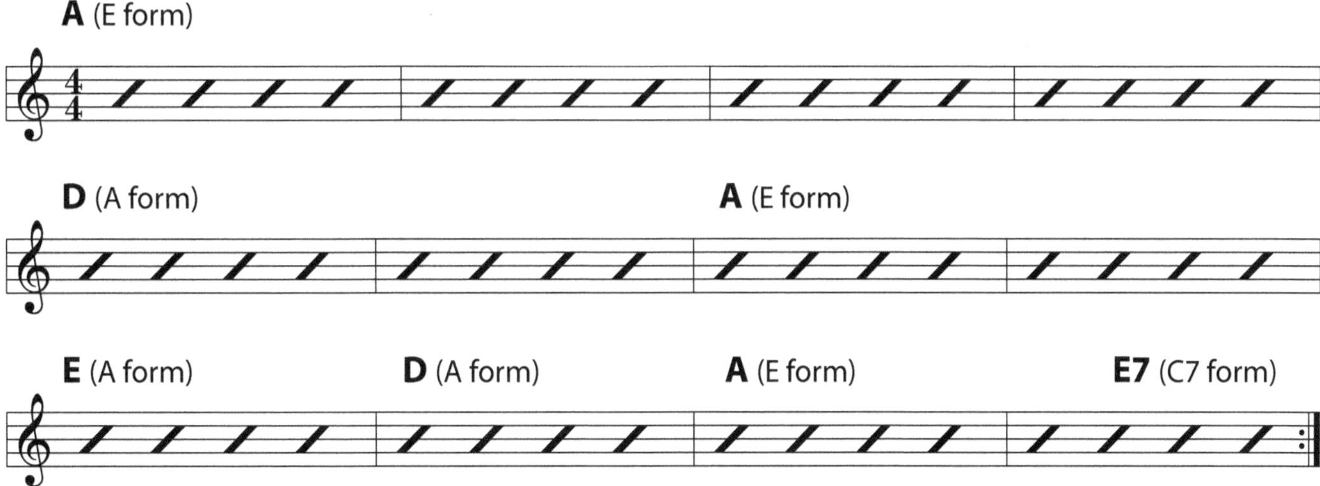

Exercise 17.8

Play and memorize this chord progression. After you have mastered it in the key of A try playing it in other keys. Be sure to know what key you are playing in and the name of each chord.

Here are few key suggestions to get you started: F, G, Bb, C, E.

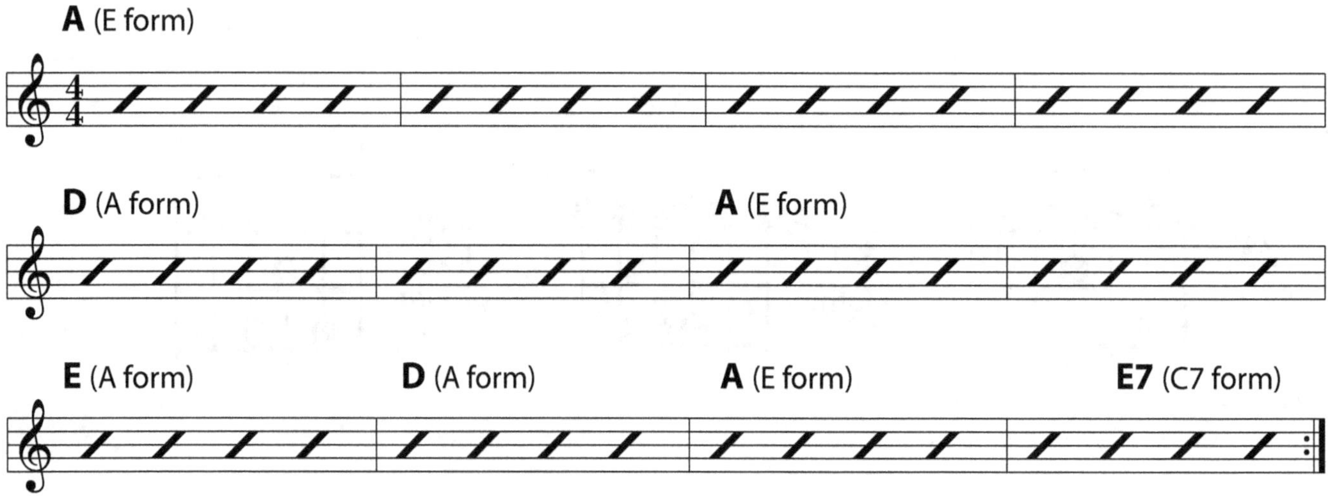

The E and A forms work well for the blues progression because both forms have a root-fifth combination (open fifth) on the lowest strings. (E form: strings 6 and 5. A form: 5 and 4 as shown below.) By striking only these strings we can create a more effective blues or rock drive.

Because the third of the chord is eliminated this string combination works well with distortion or overdrive effects.

For now finger the chord as usual but strike only the strings shown in black above.

Blues Rhythms

An eight note rhythm is usually used when playing the blues progression. This either done in ***straight eighths*** or ***swing eighths***.

A *straight* eighth pattern uses even eighths meaning both eighth notes in the beat are the exact same length.

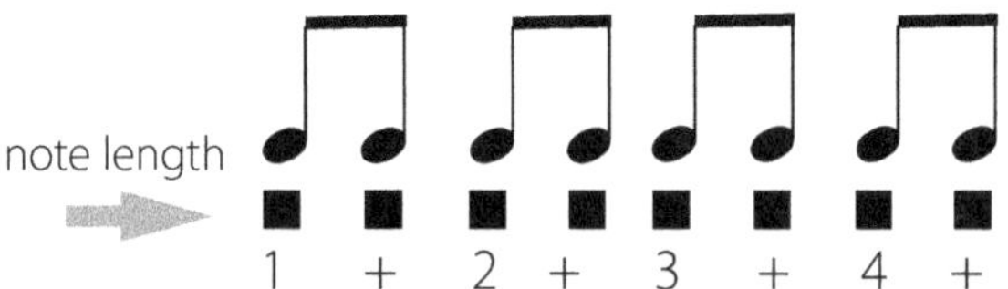

When using *swing* eighths the first eighth note is *interpreted* slightly longer than the second eighth. The exact feel is hard to express on paper. Artist interpretation, style and tempo all play a part of capturing the 'right feel'.

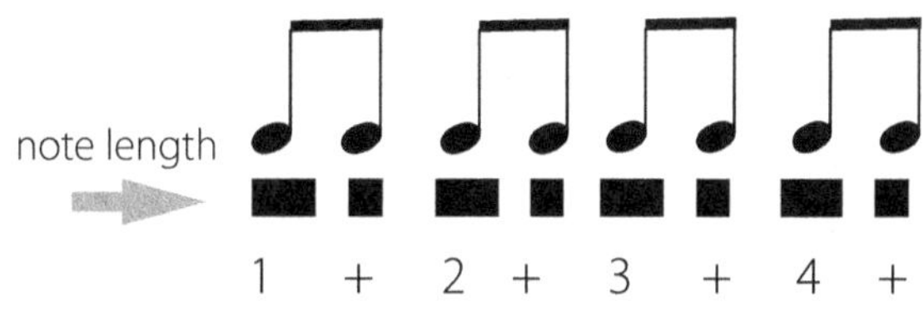

If you are subscribed to http://christigreenstudios.com be sure to listen to the interpretations of straight and swing feels to get a basic understanding of what these sound like.

You may see this rhythm at the beginning of a chart suggesting the eighth notes are to be interpreted as swing.

If it is a hard swing it may be notated with a dotted eighth and sixteenth note.

The Shuffle Pattern

Another pattern often played with the blues progression is the ***shuffle pattern.*** The shuffle pattern requires an extra step in the left hand on beats 2 and 4 of every measure. This means that we have to re-finger our chord slightly to free up the 4th finger. Even though we are re-fingering, we are still basing our pattern on the E and A forms.

E Form Shuffle

The 2nd finger is present on the diagram but it is grayed out and an X is over the string, meaning you will not strike this string. It is there for visual purposes only and it is not necessary in most cases to hold this finger down. The 3rd finger is grayed out on beats 2 and 4. This finger should remain down while finger 4 plays two frets above because you will return to it on the next beat.

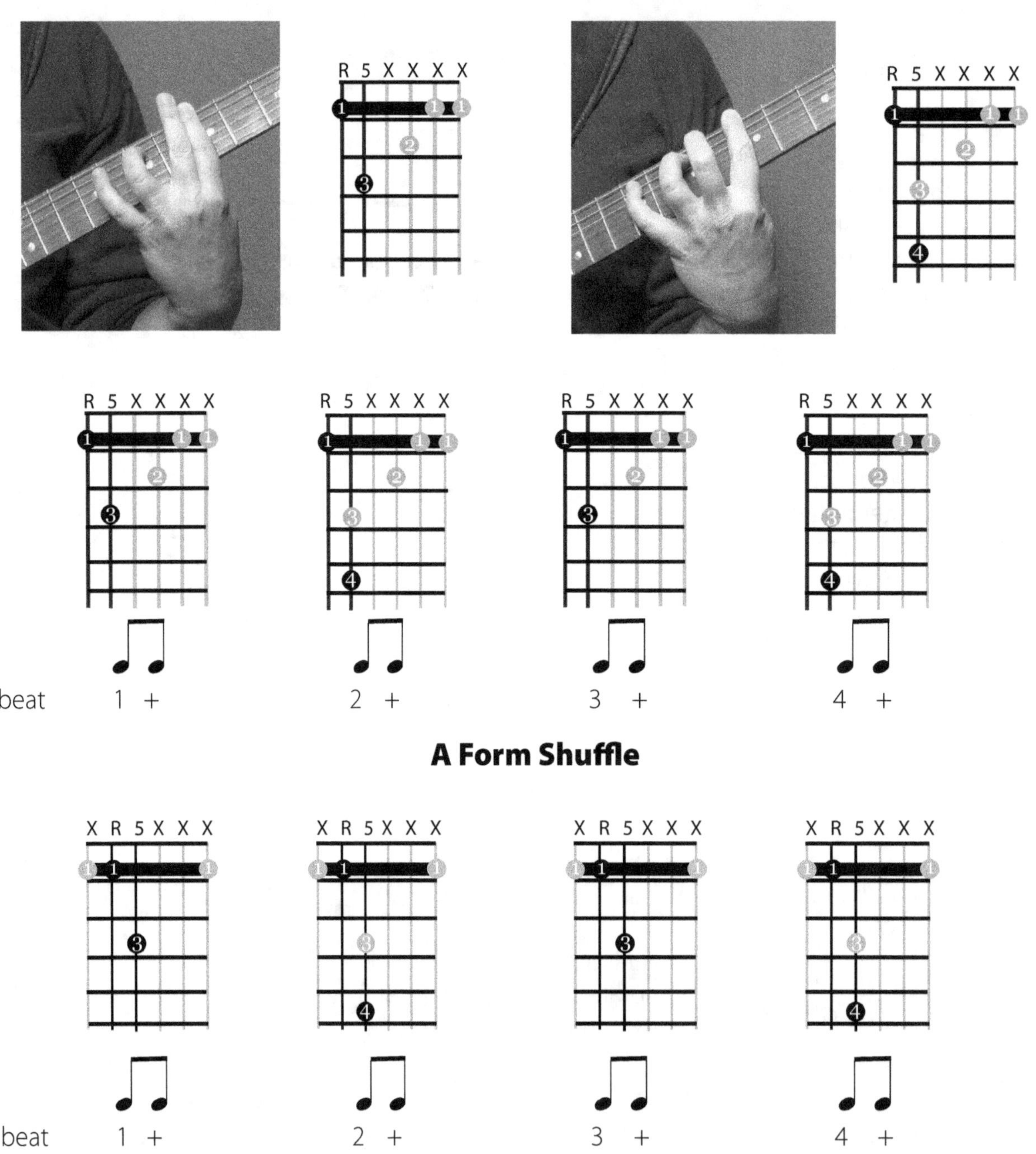

Exercise 17.9

Play the Blues progression again using the shuffle patterns above for the E and A forms. Once again work this out in several keys.

Blues Progression Using Other Forms

One of the more popular keys for the blues is the key of E. If you tried playing the previous progression in the suggested forms, you may have found this difficult to do since this is played at the 12th fret where the fret spacing is narrow.

One solution is to play the progression using open chords (E group). Since this is the open version of the progression we just learned, the shuffle will work the same way.

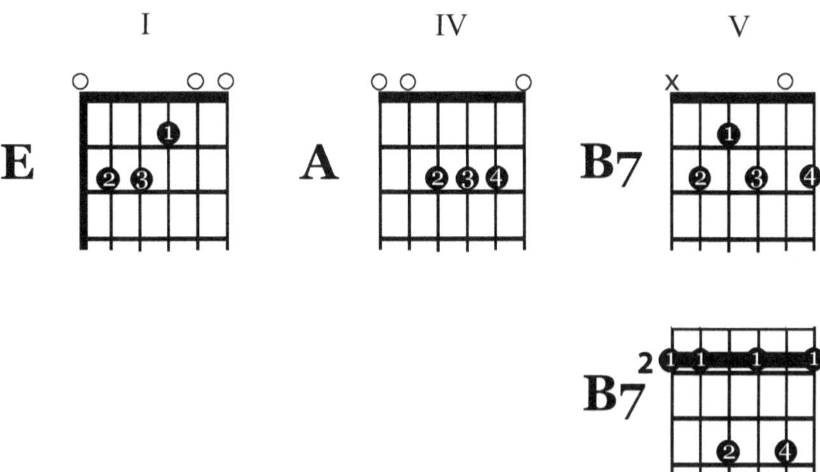

Exercise 17.10

Play the Blues progression again using open chords.

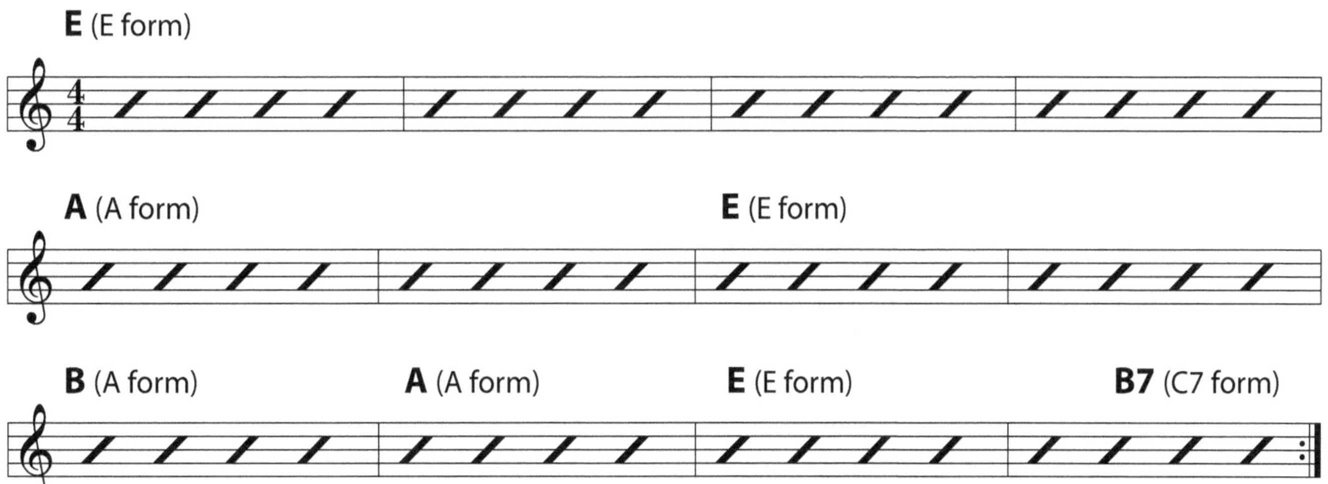

Another solution for E and other keys is to start with the A form. The I chord uses the A form and the IV and V7 chords use the E or E(7) forms. Since just the A and E forms are used, the shuffle pattern we learned earlier will still apply.

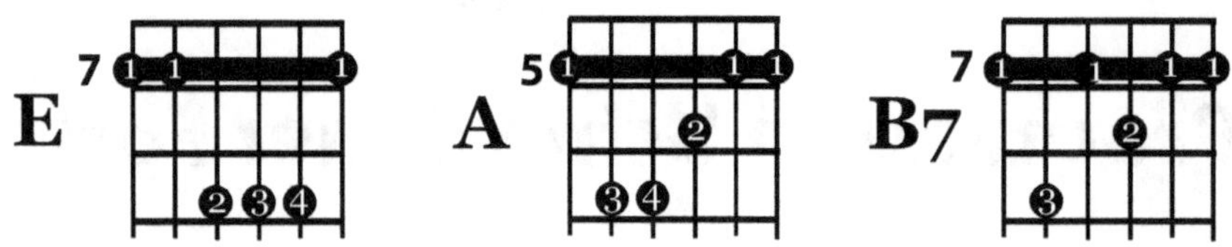

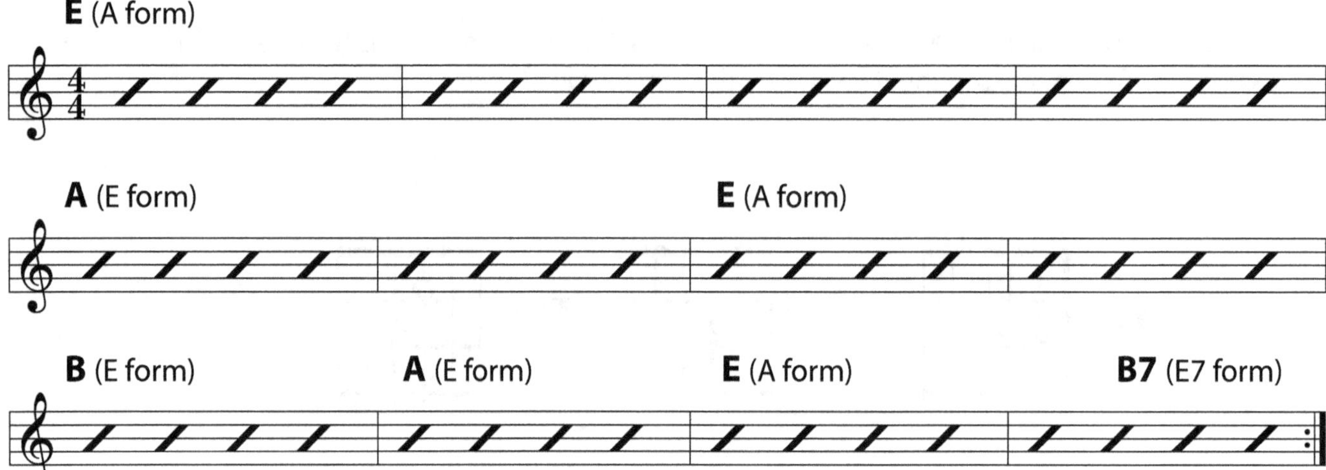

Exercise 17.11

Play the Blues progression above using the shuffle pattern for the E and A forms. Once again, work this out in several keys.

The ii, V I Chord Progression

The ii, V, I progression is very common in jazz. It is often used as a ***turnaround***, meaning it links the end of a piece to the beginning. The examples that follow use the E and A forms; however, any form combination can be used.

Key of C starting with the A(m) form.

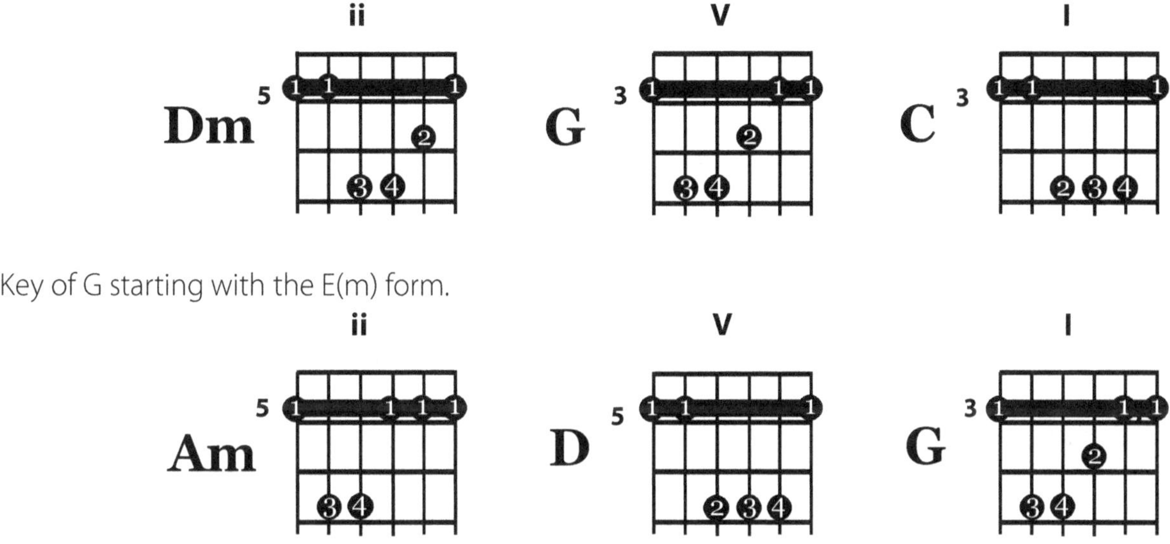

The ii7, V7 IM7 Chord Progression

Here is the ii, V, I progression with sevenths added to the chord.

Key of C starting with the A(m7) form.

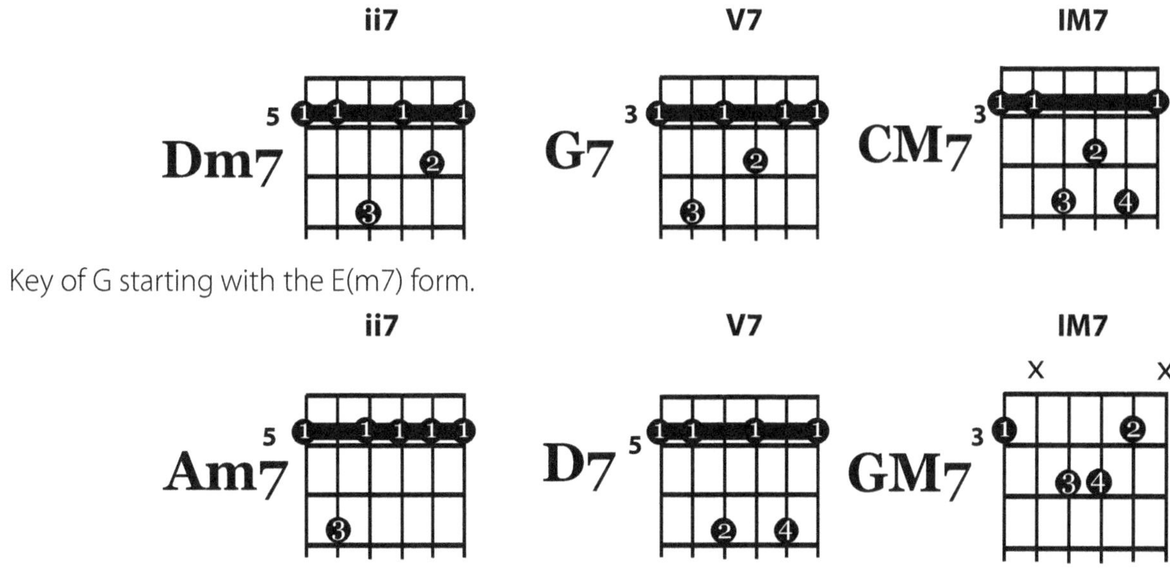

Exercise 17.12

Work out the chord progressions below using the A and E forms for the key of C. If there are two chords per measure play the first chord on beat one and the second chord on beat three.

ii, V, I Progression

ii7, V7, IM7 Progression

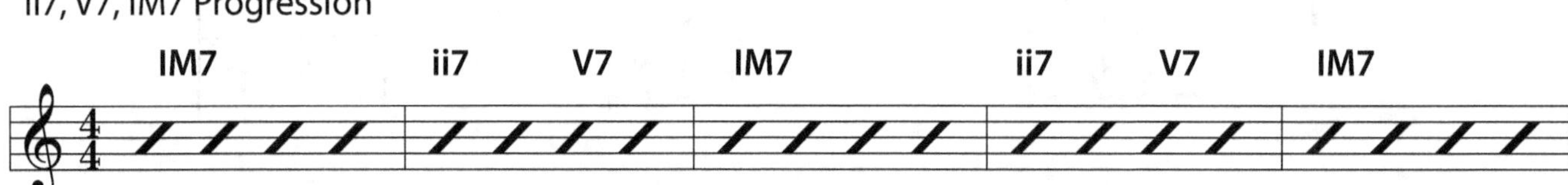

When To Use Sevenths

The sevenths added to the chord add *color*. Some chord progressions like the one below, use sevenths on some chords but not others. The sevenths color the chord but do not change the chord function; therefore, it is acceptable to play the progression with sevenths on some of the chords but not all.

The genre of music will also dictate the use of sevenths. As you study different musical styles you will get a feel for when to add or omit sevenths.

Exercise 17.13

Play the progressions above in the following keys:

key of:

D = Em, A, D or Em7, A7, DM7

A = Bm, E, A or Bm7, E7, AM7

E = F♯m, B, E or F♯m7, B7, EM7

F = Gm, C, F or Gm7, C7, FM7

B♭ = Cm, F, B♭ or Cm7, F7, B♭M7

Once you've mastered these keys use the circle of fifths to complete the progressions in all keys.

Exercise 17.14

When the E and A chord forms feel comfortable explore the same progressions using the other forms.

vi, ii, V, I Chord Progression

The vi, ii, V, I chord progression is another widely used chord progression. The famous song *All I Have To Do Is Dream* recorded by the Everly Brothers (and many others), use this progression. If you have done the ii, V, I progression all you need to do is add the vi, to the beginning and you've got it!

Here is the vi, ii(7), V(7), I chord progression in the key of C using open chords. It is a typical example of mixing seventh and non seventh chords.

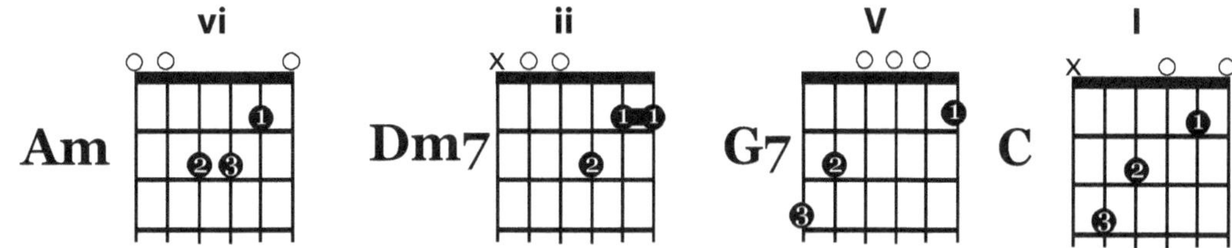

Here is the chord progression in the key of C using fretted chords.

Key of C starting with the E form.

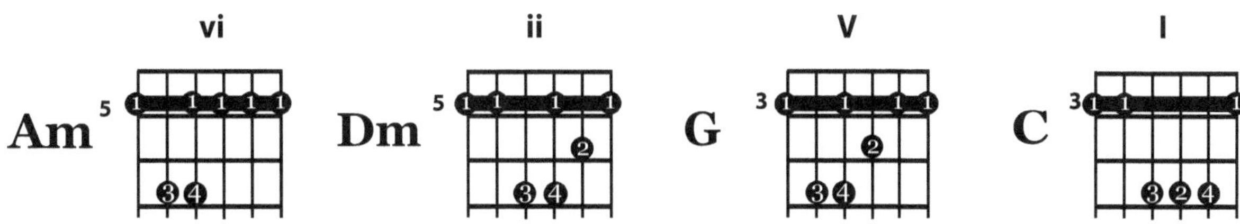

Key of G starting with the A form.

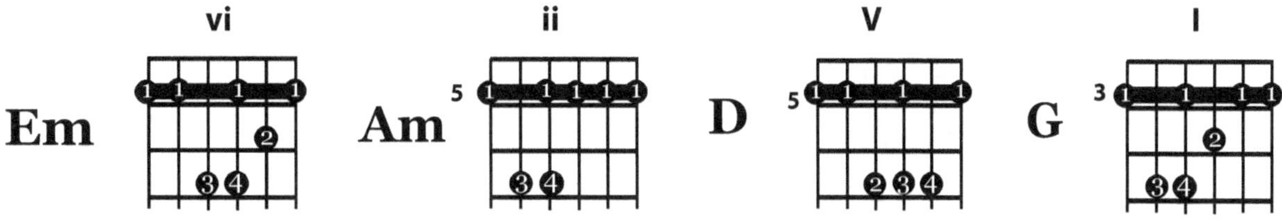

vi7, ii7, V7, IM7 Chord Progression

Key of C starting with the E form.

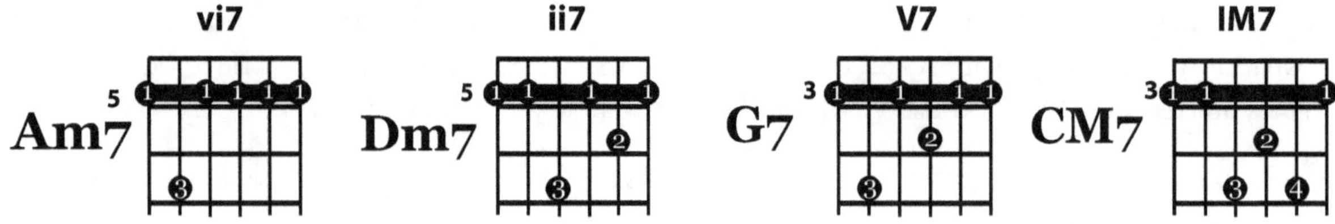

Key of G starting with the A form.

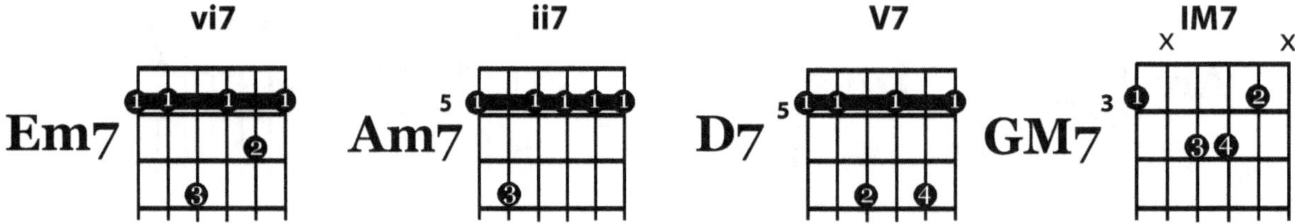

Exercise 17.15

Work out the chord progressions below using the A and E forms for the key of C and the Key of G. If there are two chords per measure play the first chord on beat one and the second chord on beat three.

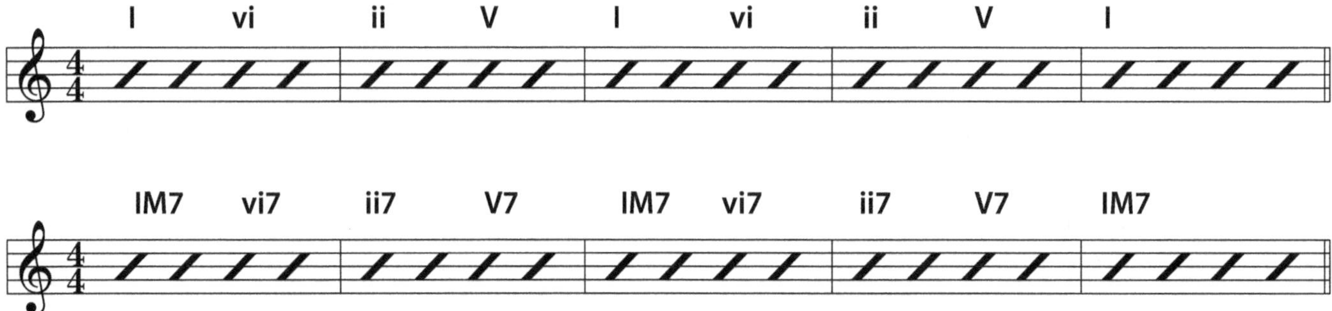

Exercise 17.16

Play the progressions above in the following keys:

key of:

D = Bm, Em, A, D or Bm7, Em7, A7, DM7

A = F♯m, Bm, E, A or F♯m7, Bm7, E7, AM7

E = C♯m, F♯m, B, E or C♯m7, F♯m7, B7, EM7

F = Dm, Gm, C, F or Dm7, Gm7, C7, FM7

B♭ = Gm, Cm, F, B♭ or Gm7, Cm7, F7, B♭M7

Once you've mastered these keys use the circle of fifths to complete the progressions in all keys.

Exercise 17.17

When the E and A chord forms feel comfortable explore the same progressions using other forms.

18 Harmonizing the C Scale Using Seventh Chords

So far we have written *harmonized major scales* in chapters 11 and 12, and have played seventh chords in all five forms in chapters 13 and 16. We can put the two together to *play a harmonized major scale*. We do this by using the five bar forms. Each scale will use only one bar form. This is a good way to begin training you ear to hear the chord relationships within one key.

Notice where the root is for each chord form. When played separately from the chord it is the major scale with all scale degrees on one string. Thinking of the whole and half steps in a major scale can help finger placement from one chord to the next.

It often becomes impractical and awkward to play the harmonized scale in a complete ascending pattern. Notice in the following examples, that the chords never move beyond 12th position and drop back down the neck when necessary to complete the scale.

C FORM

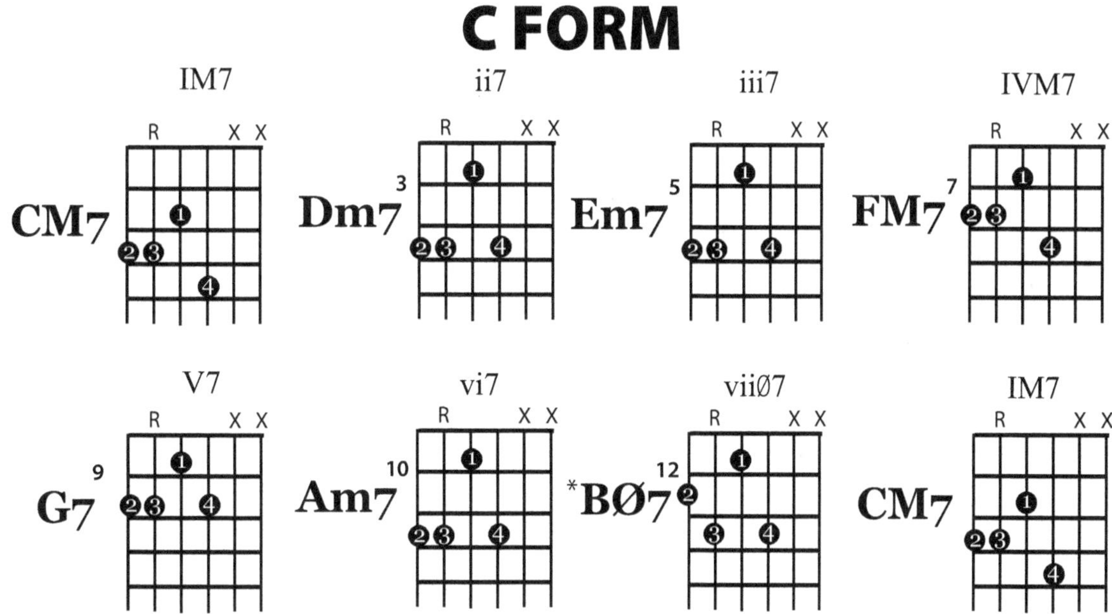

* Can be played in 12th or open position. (Open position omits the first finger).

A FORM

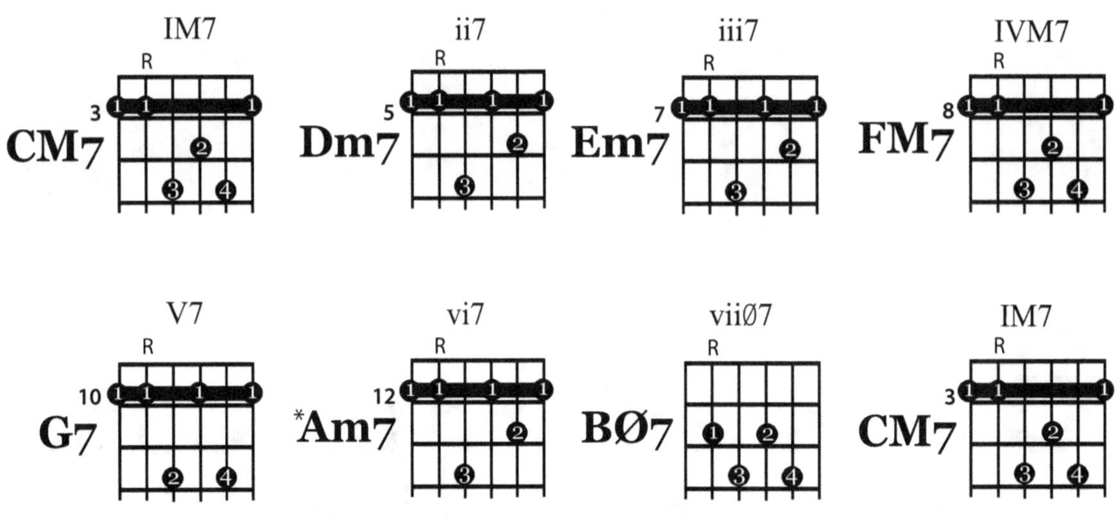

* Can be played in 12th or open position.

G FORM

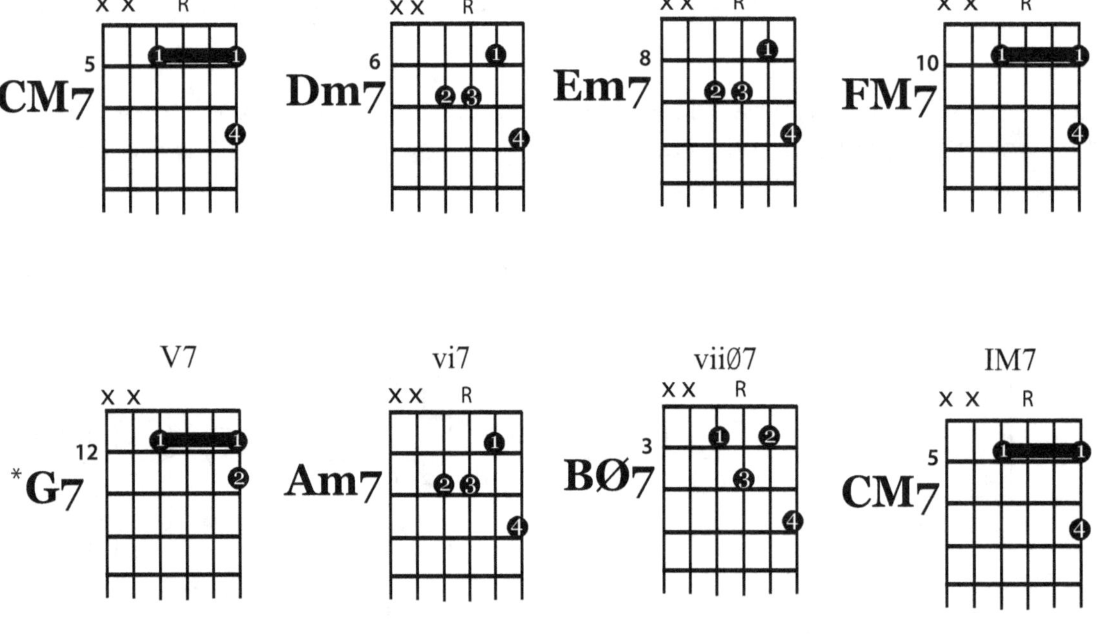

* Can be played in 12th or open position.

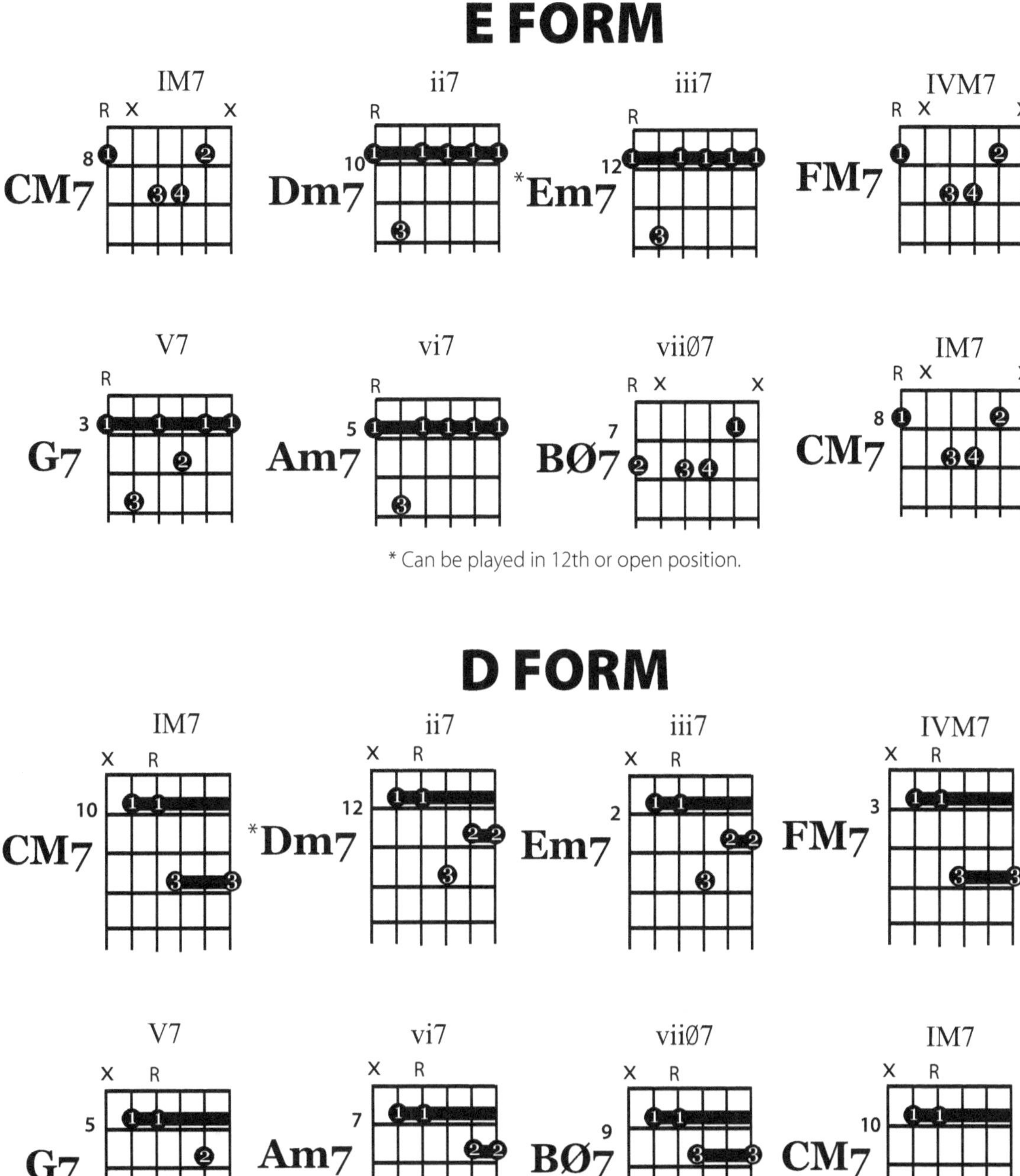

Exercise 18.1

Play and memorize the harmonized scales using all five forms. Be sure to learn them in every key.

Half Diminished Chords

As we learned in chapter 12 half diminished chords are built on the seventh scale degree of the major scale. The chord symbol can appear one of two ways. The symbol ø7 or m7♭5 can be used. In either case, the chords sound alike.

The two different symbols come from two different ways of figuring the chord:

Bø7 or Bm7♭5

ø7 = dimished triad + minor 7

Bø7 =	B	D	F	A
	1	3	5	7

m7♭5 = minor 7 triad with a flatted (lowered 5th)

Bm7♭5 =	B	D	F	A
	1	♭3	♭5	♭7

You will find the "m7♭5" symbol used abundantly in Jazz. The "♭" should not be taken literally; meaning the note is not always a flat. Rather it means the scale degree is *lowered* by a half step.

Ø7/m7♭5 Chord Forms

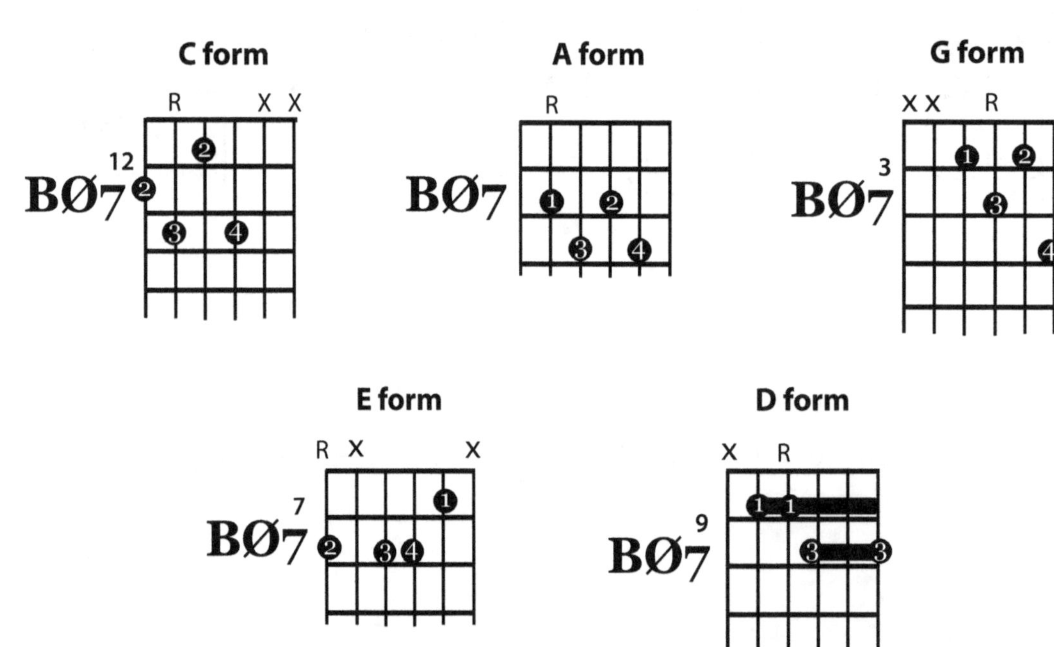

19 Other Common Chord Symbols

In addition to the sevenths, there are a variety of other symbols that can follow triads. In this chapter we won't attempt to cover them all but we'll talk about some of the more common ones you may encounter.

Slash Chords

Slash chords are written like this: **C/B or Am/G.** These chords cause a great deal of confusion because it appears that two different chords should be played at the same time; however, that is not the case. The first letter before the slash refers to the ***chord*** to be played. The Letter after the slash indicates the ***note*** to be played in the lowest voice of the chord (the bass part or root).

C/B then is a C chord with a B note in the bass. **Am/G** is an A minor chord with a G note in the bass as shown below. Depending on the chord and bass note some re-fingering might need to take place like in the **C/B** example.

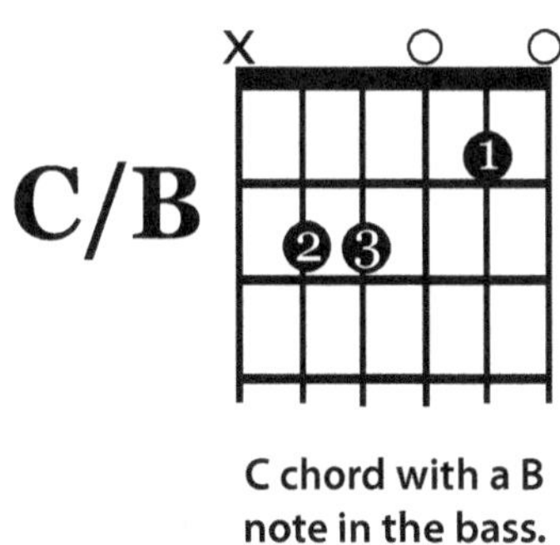

C chord with a B note in the bass.

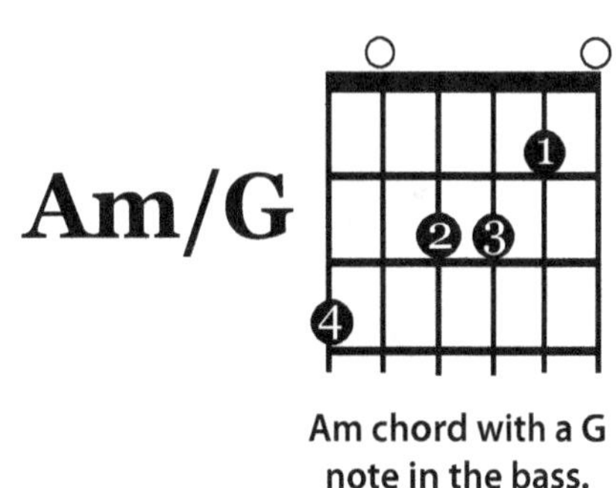

Am chord with a G note in the bass.

Slash chords help us to understand what is happening in the bass voice. Often these chords help transition from one chord to the next as shown in our example below. Here we see the chords **C, C/B**, and **Am**. Our bass voice descends down the scale from **C** to **B**, and lands on **A** when the Am chord is played.

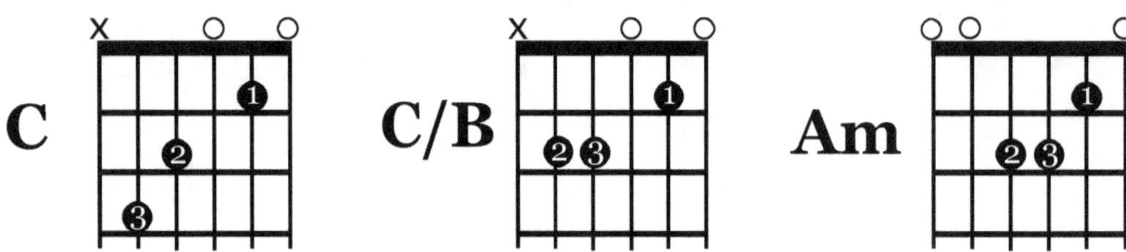

SUS Chords

Sus is an abbreviation for ***suspended***. What is 'suspended' in this type of chord is the third. It is replaced by the fourth note above the root of the chord. For instance if we see the chord **Dsus** or **Dsus4** the chord is spelled D, F♯, A. The fourth note above the root D is G. G replaces F♯ in the chord suspending or delaying the third of the chord. Often, but not always the 'sus' chord will resolve to the basic triad. In other words, **Dsus4** will be followed by a **D** chord.

Below are some common sus chord fingerings followed by the chord to which it often resolves.

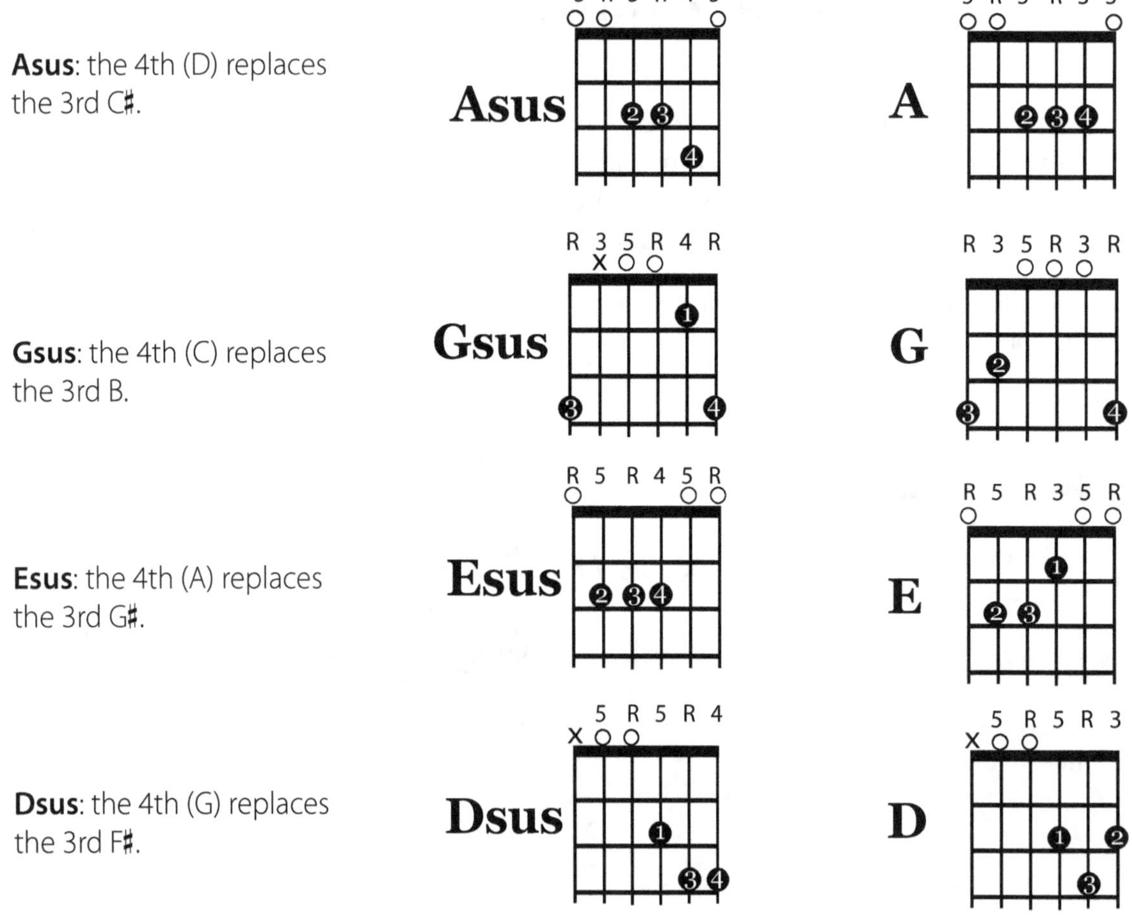

Add 9 or 2 Chords

The **add 9** or **2** after a chord symbol means just what it says. Add the 9th or the 2nd pitch above the root note of the triad to the triad. The 9 and the 2 are really the same pitch. For instance if we saw a C add 9 or C2 chord either way we would get the answer D. If C is 1, D would have to be 2. If C is an octave higher it would be 8 so D one octave higher would be 9. Either way, a C add 9 or C2 chord is a C triad with a D added.

Below are some common add 9 or 2 chords. To keep things simple I have opted to name these add 9 instead of listing both names.

For comparison, the basic chord form is shown to the right of the add 9 chords.

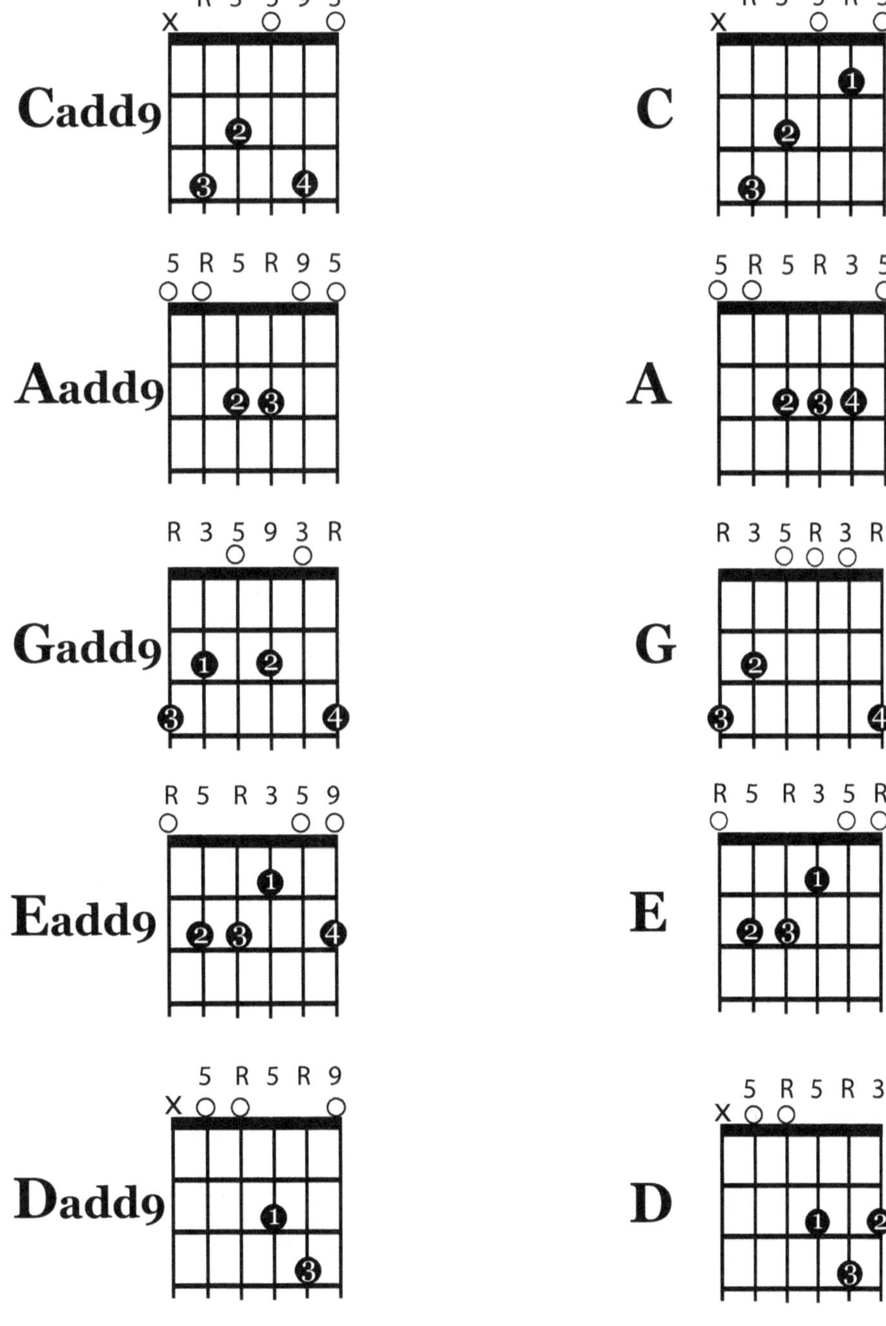

9 Chords

A chord followed by the number 9 is *different* than the add 9 chord. The 9 in this case is added to a chord that contains a minor seventh (m7). For comparison the basic 7th chord form is shown to the right of the 9 chords.

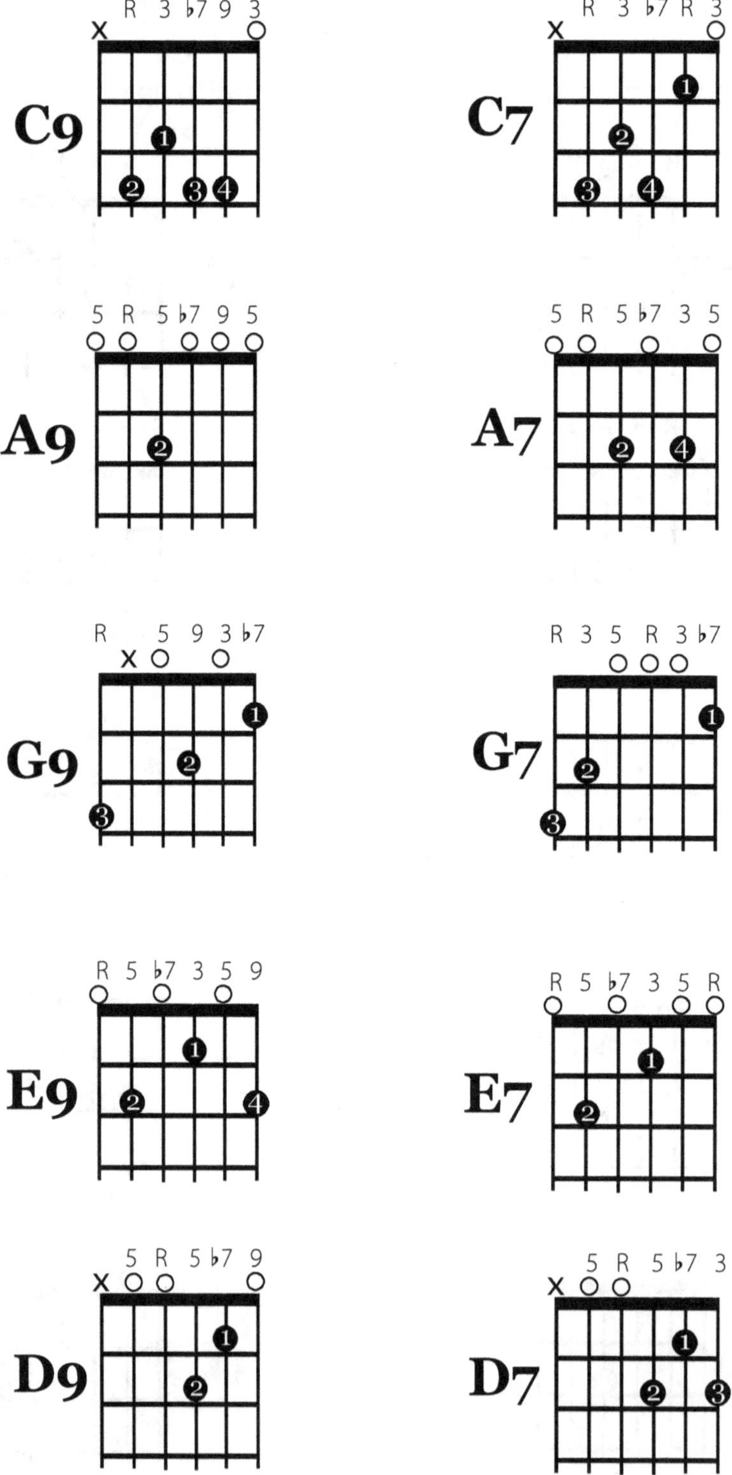

5 Chords

A chord followed by the number 5 means to omit the 3rd of the chord. For instance **A5** would have the chord members **A** (root) and **E** (fifth) omitting the third **C♯**. These are also referred as ***power chords***. As discussed in Chapter 17 under *Blues Progressions*, this is easily accomplished with the A and E forms.

The root and fifth are shown in black. The rest of the chord is grayed out.

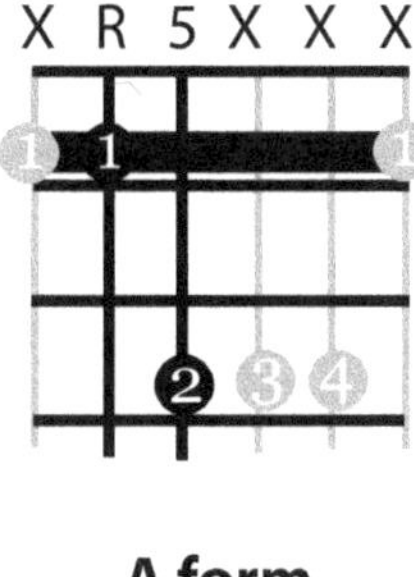

A form

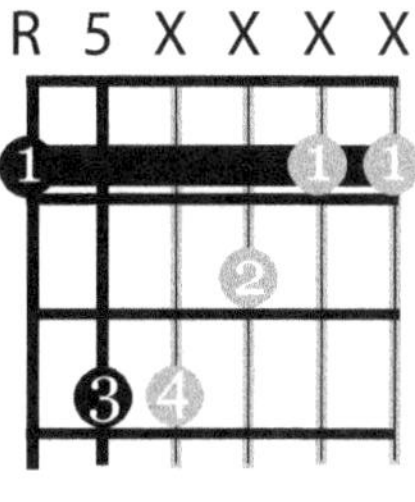

A form

Diminished Chords

A diminished chord has a 'o' symbol after the chord or sometimes the abbreviation 'dim' will follow: **A°**, **Adim**. Diminished chords are built from minor thirds. There is a minor third between the root and 3rd, 3rd and 5th and 5th and 7th.

B°7 triad

Below are two common fingerings for the diminished chord. They use all fretted notes so they are moveable. It isn't necessary that the '7' be included in the name. You will see it written both with and without it; however, it will always be included in the fingering.

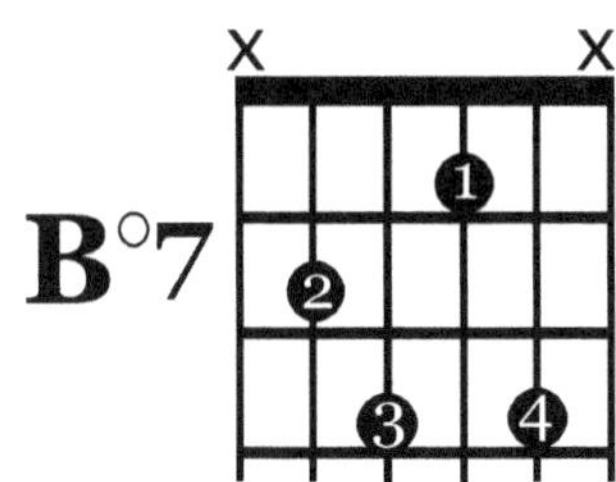

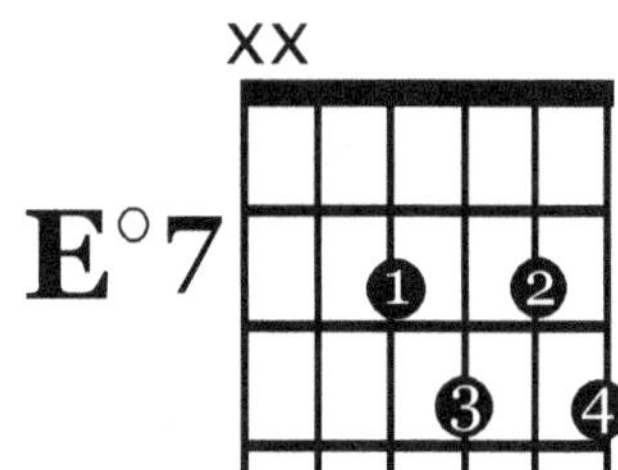

*The cool thing about a diminished chord is that any chord member can become the root name. For example the **B°7** chord could also be called **F°7, A♭°7 , or D°7**! This is possible because the chord is built entirely of m3's. How the chord is functioning will dictate the chord name.

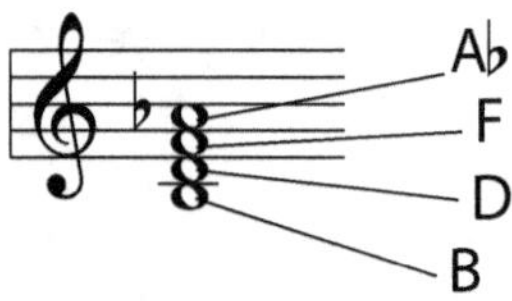

B°7 could also be named D°7, F°7, or A♭°7.

Glossary Of Terms

A=440 Hz - Musically, the pitch A above middle C on the piano. This pitch is also found in several places on the guitar, one being on the first string, fifth fret. Scientifically, 440 stands for 440 cycles per second at which a sound wave vibrates. Hz is the abbreviation for (Heinrich) Hertz, the physicist that classified the sound waves. (p. 16)

accidental - See chromatic sign. (p. 71)

acoustic guitar - A non electric guitar that uses steel strings. This guitar is also referred to as the steel string guitar. The pick is used as well as the finger-style approach. Country, folk, and folk-rock music are often played on this instrument. These guitars come in a variety of body styles including the popular dreadnought shape. (p. 5-7)

action - The distance the strings are elevated off of the neck of the guitar. A "low action" means the strings are as close to the neck as possible without causing the strings to buzz against the frets. This is preferred by many players because the strings are easy to depress. (p. 9)

anacrusis - See pickup notes. (p. 33)

barre chord - A chord that uses the first finger of the left hand to bar across one fret enabling the first finger to play several strings at one time. Also, bar or cegilla. (p. 53, 113)

barre forms - Bar chords that model the open C, A, G, E, and D chords. (p. 113)

bar lines - Lines that run perpendicular to the staff dividing the staff into bars or measures. (p. 20)

BCBC - An abbreviation for the right hand bass, chord, bass, chord pattern. (p. 60)

chord diagram - A diagram of the guitar neck that shows where the left-hand fingers are to be placed when forming a chord. (p. 23)

chromatic scale - All twelve pitches contained within an octave and played consecutively. The scale is built in half steps. A chromatic scale can be built from any pitch. (p. 72)

chromatic sign - A sharp (♯), flat (♭), or natural (♮) symbol placed to the left of a note, that raises or lowers the pitch of that note by one half step. Also called accidentals. (p. 71)

circle of fifths - An arrangement of the keys so that there are five alphabetical letters from one key to the next, up or back. As they move in order, the key signatures will increase or decrease by one sharp or flat. (p. 71)

classical guitar - An acoustic guitar that uses nylon strings. This guitar is traditionally used for fingerstyle playing. Classical music, and jazz and pop arrangements for finger-style guitar are often played on this instrument. Traditionally, the body style is a standard waisted, figure-eight shape without a cutaway as shown in chapter two. (p. 5, 6)

common finger - Left-hand finger(s) that remain on the same string and in the same fret when moving from one chord to another. (p. 34)

common move - Left-hand finger(s) that remain in the same fret but change strings when moving from one chord to another. (p. 34)

common time - Same as 4/4 time. (p. 21)

diminished triad - A three note chord consisting of a minor third between the root and third, and a minor third between the third and fifth. (p. 98) Chord diagram (p. 154)

dissonance - Sounds that create tension in music. (p. 102)

double bar lines - Two bar lines side by side that mark the end of a section and the beginning of another. (p. 20)

electric guitar - See solid body electric.

ending bar line - Two bar lines placed side by side, one thin and one thick, that mark the end of a musical composition. (p. 20)

enharmonic - Pitches that sound the same but have two different names, like F♯ and G♭. (p. 72)

finger-picking - Using the thumb (**p**) and first three fingers (**i**, **m**, and **a**) in the right hand to pluck the strings. (p. 12)

finger-style - see finger-picking.

flat-pick - see pick.

footstool - A small collapsible stool used to elevate the left leg when in the sitting position. (p. 4, 10)

G clef - see treble clef.

guide accidentals - Accidentals shown in parenthesis. They are used as a reminders that the note has already been altered. (p. 96)

half diminished seven chord - A diminished triad with a minor seventh. (p. 100, 148)

half step - The smallest distance from one pitch to the next immediate pitch up or down. (p. 79)

harmonic - A high, bell like pitch that is created by touching the string over a fret while plucking with the right-hand. The odd number frets through, and including fret twelve, produce natural harmonics. (p. 16)

harmonic minor scale - A minor scale that uses same notes as the natural minor scale except the seventh note is raised one half step. (p. 85)

harmonize - To add to pitches to an existing melody creating harmony. To harmonize the major scale means to add pitches three, five, and so on to the existing scale degrees. (p. 96)

interval - The distance from one pitch to another pitch. (p. 93)

introduction - The beginning bars of music before the melody or main theme begins. (p. 32)

key signature - The sharps or flats found at the beginning of the staff after the clef sign that indicates in what key the piece is to be played. (p. 75, 76)

lead sheet - A single staff of music that contains the melody with the chord symbols written above. (p. 32)

ledger lines - Small lines that are added above or below the staff to notate pitches that are not included on the staff. (p. 18)

luthier - A person who builds guitars. (p. 9)

major scale - Seven different pitches that move alphabetically and follow the pattern of whole step, whole step, half step, whole step, whole step, whole step, half step (W, W, H, W, W, W, H). A major scale can be built on any of the twelve pitches. (p. 73)

major seven - An interval containing five and a half steps. For example the distance from C to B. (p. 93, 94)

major triad - A three note chord consisting of a major third between the root and third, and a minor third between the third and fifth. (p. 97)

measures - The space between two bar lines that contain the number of beats designated by the time signature. (p. 28)

meter signature - Two numbers found at the beginning of a piece. One is above the other. The top number indicates the number of beats per measure, the bottom number indicates the type of note that is worth one beat or count. This is also known as a time signature. (p. 28)

metronome - A device that clicks a steady beat at different speeds. (p. 27)

minor seven - An interval containing five whole steps. For example the distance from C to B♭. (p. 93, 94)

minor triad - A three note chord consisting of a minor third between the root and third, and a major third between the third and fifth. (p. 97)

natural minor scale - The minor scale that follows the whole step half step pattern of whole step, half step, whole step, whole step, half step, whole step, whole step (W, H, W, W, H, W, W). The natural minor is built from the sixth scale degree of the relative major scale. (p. 84)

notes - Symbols that are placed on a staff to indicate pitch and duration. (p. 17)

octave - An interval containing six whole steps. For example from the note C to the next C note up or down is an octave. (p. 93, 94)

pick -A flat triangle-shaped device held between the index finger and thumb in the right-hand used to strike the strings. It is usually made out of hard plastic and comes in a variety of thicknesses. This is also referred to as the pick or plectrum. (p. 12)

pickup notes - One or more notes found before the first complete measure of a piece. Also called anacrusis. (p. 33)

pitch - The relative highness or lowness of a sound. (p. 17)

planted stroke - see prepared stroke (p. 13)

plectrum - see flat-pick.

prepared stroke - Placing the right-hand finger on the string before it is time to pluck that string. This stroke is also called the planted stroke. (p. 13)

primary chords - I, IV, and V chords in every major and minor key. The basic chords found in most musical compositions in the Western hemisphere. (p. 25)

relative minor - The minor key that shares the same key signature with its relative major key. The relative minor key is always a major sixth above or a minor third below the root of the major key. (p. 83)

repeat signs - Symbols found at the end and/or beginning of a section that indicate the section to be played again. (p. 20)

rest - Symbols that mark time but indicate silence instead of sound. (p. 19)

scale degree - Any note that is a member of a scale. If a note is the third note in a scale, then it is called the third scale degree. (p. 78)

seventh chords - Chords that include the seventh note above the root creating a four note chord. These chords consist of the root (1), 3, 5, and 7. (p. 99)

solid body electric guitar - An electric guitar made out of a solid piece of wood that needs amplification for sound. The pick is used primarily on this instrument. Country, rock, and heavy metal music are often played on this instrument. These guitars come in a variety of shapes. The Fender Stratocaster is among the most popular body styles. (p. 5, 8)

staff - A system of five lines and four spaces on which notes are placed. (p. 17)

tablature, TAB - A diagram of the guitar strings used for writing out right or left hand patterns. The sixth string is the lowest line, the first string is the highest. When writing for the right hand the letters p, i, m, and a are used. When writing for the left hand, numbers are used to indicate which fret to play. The notes above the letters or numbers indicate the rhythms to be played. (p. 59)

tempo - The speed or pace of the music. (p. 27)

time signature - See meter signature. (p. 21)

transpose - To rewrite a piece of music in a key that is different from the original key. (p. 81)

treble clef - The symbol found at the beginning of the staff that names the lines and spaces of the staff. The scroll around the second line indicates the pitch G. Also known as the G clef. (p. 18)

triad -A three note chord consisting of a root, third, and fifth. (p. 95)

turnaround - A chord progression that links the end of a piece back to the beginning. A common turnaround is the ii, V, I. (p. 141)

value - The duration of a note. (p. 17, 19)

whole step - Two half steps or a major second. (p. 73)

Appendix 1

Right Hand Patterns

Patterns in 4/4

1)

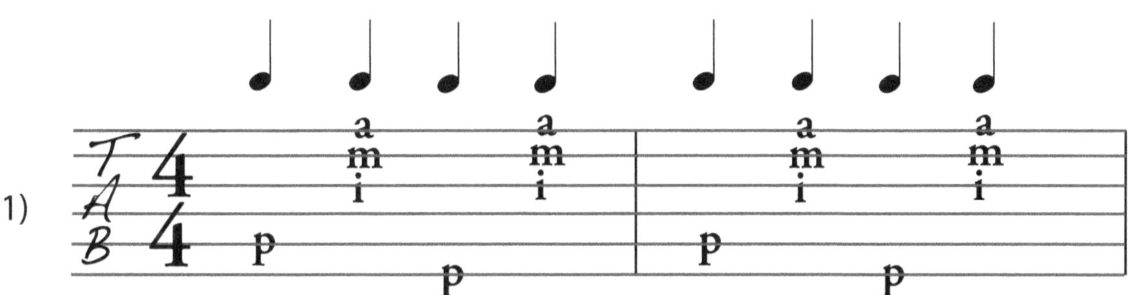

2)

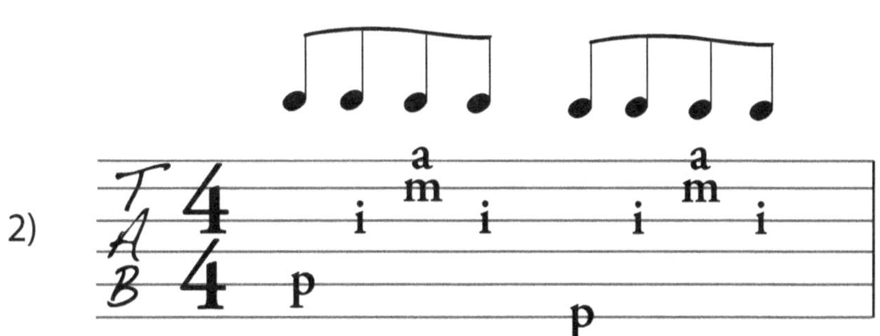

3)
T A B
4 4
a a
m m
i i i i
p p

4)
T A B
4 4
a a a a
m m
i i
p p

5)
T A B
4 4
a a
m m
i i
p p

6)
T A B
4 4
a
m m
i i i
p p

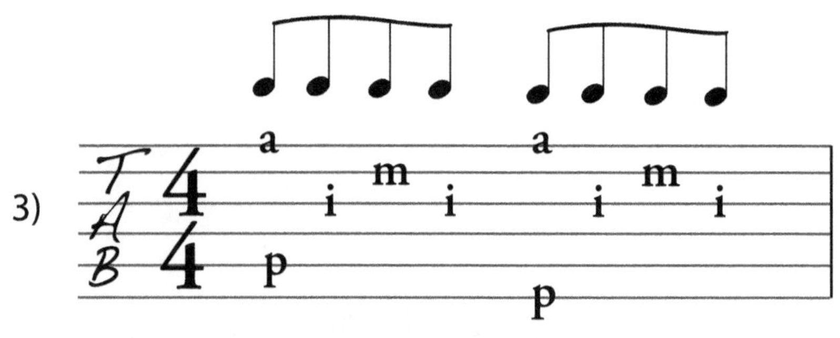

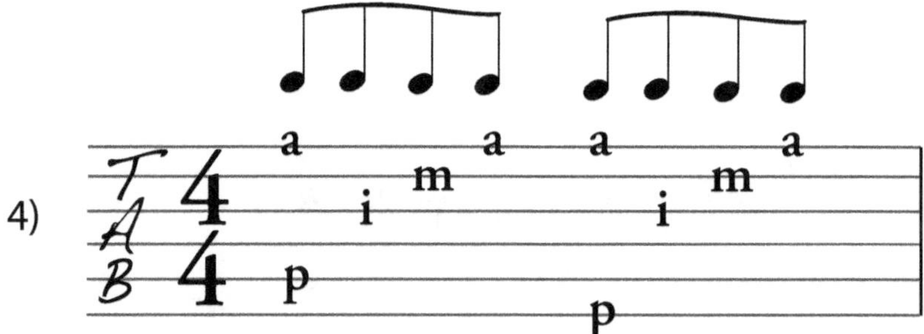

Patterns in 3/4

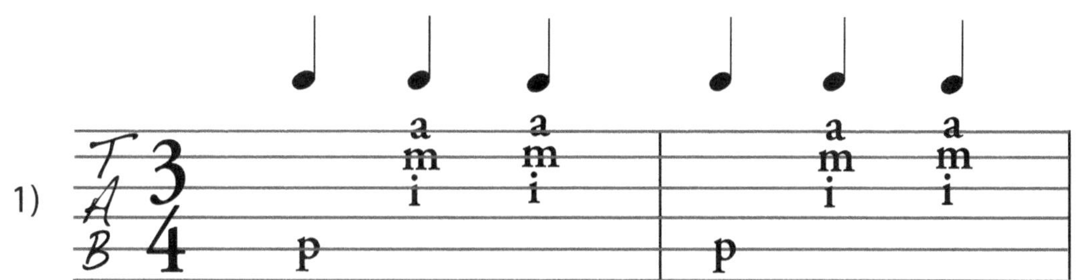

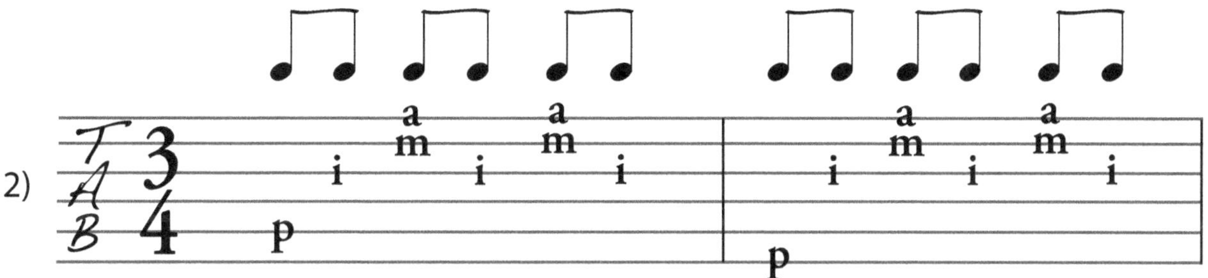

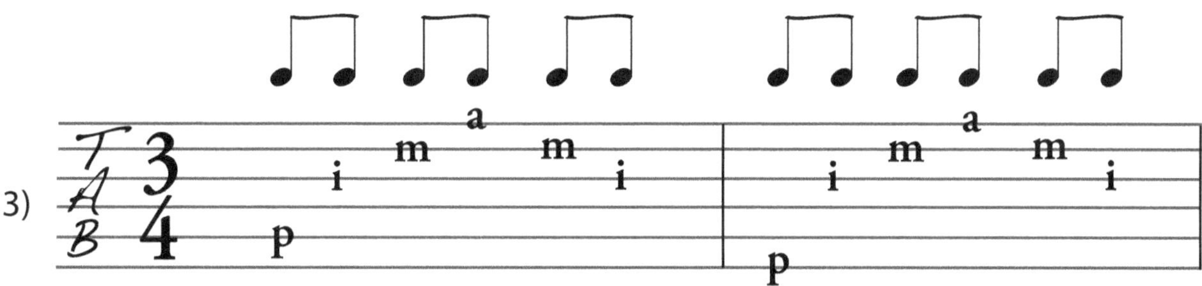

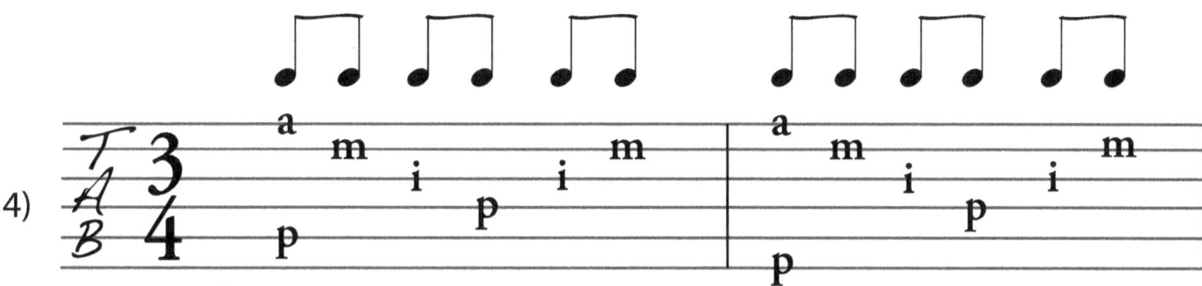

Appendix 2

Quick Chord Reference

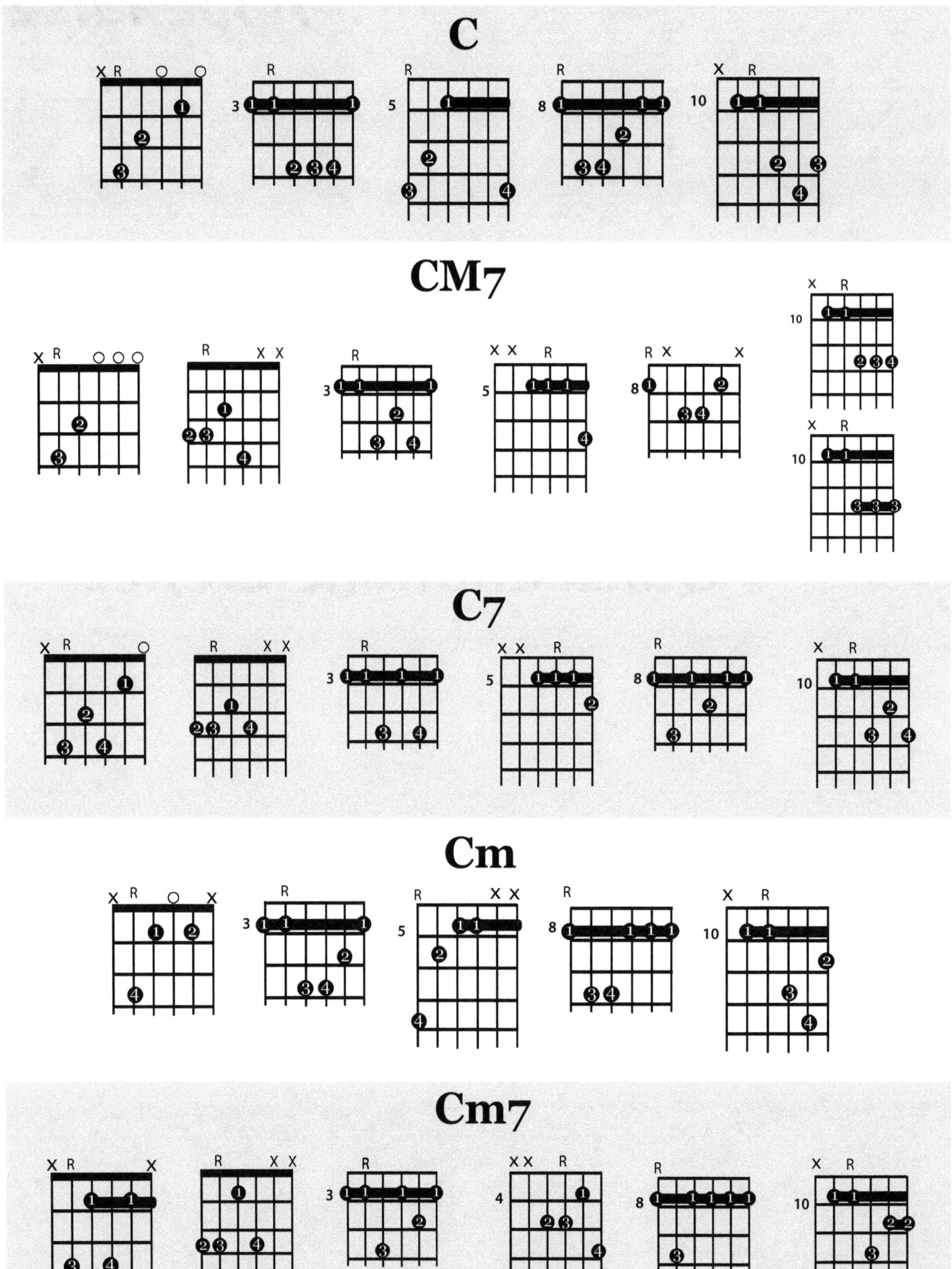
C
CM7
C7
Cm
Cm7

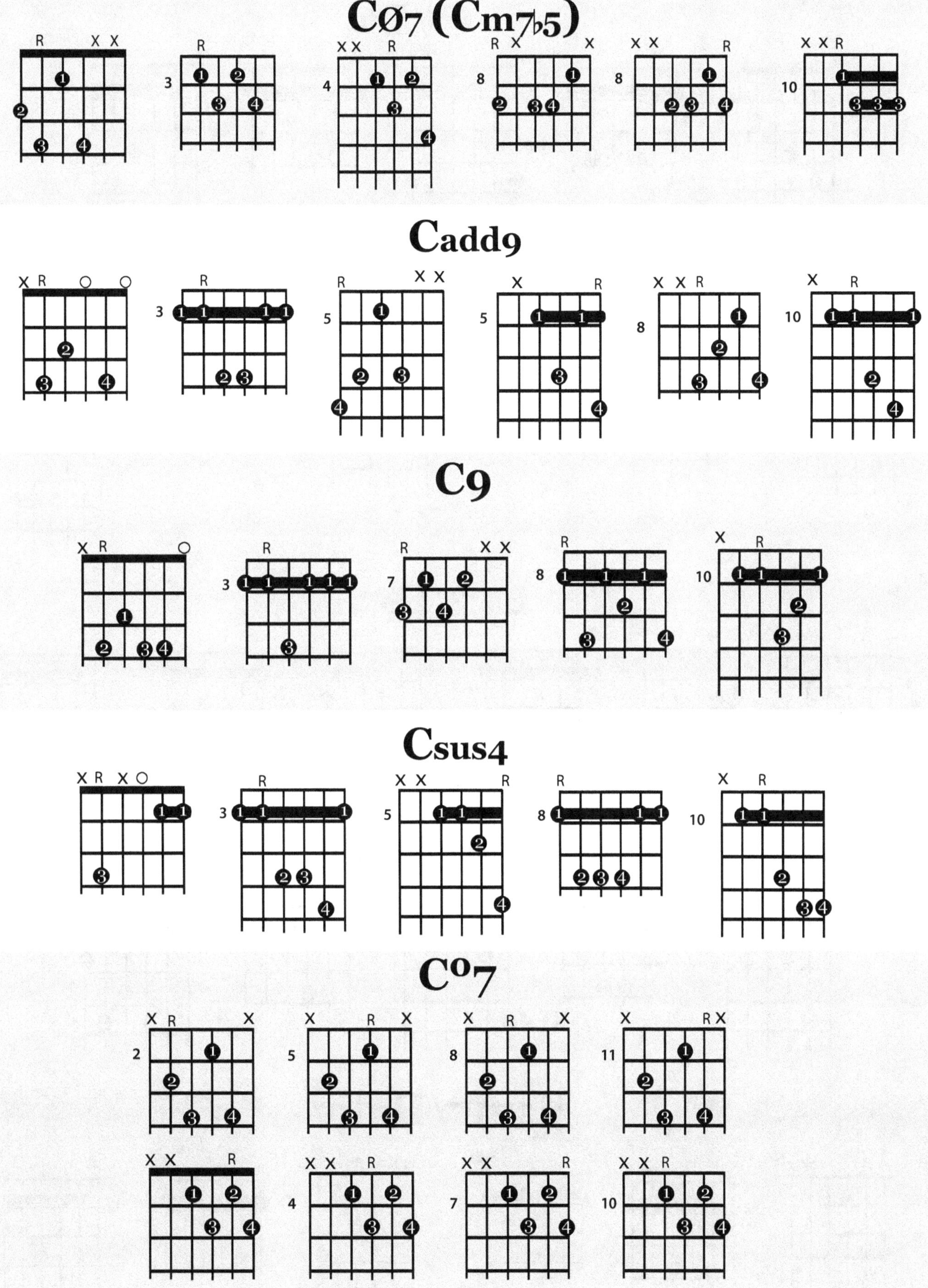
CØ7 (Cm7♭5)
Cadd9
C9
Csus4
Co7

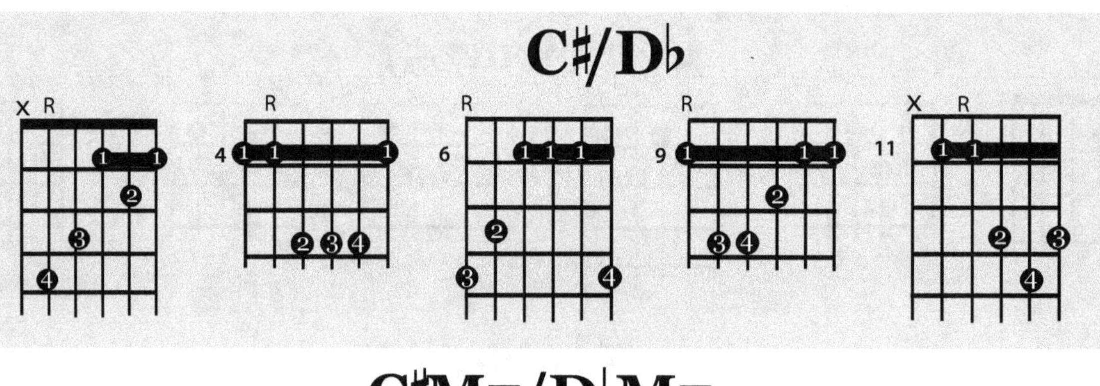

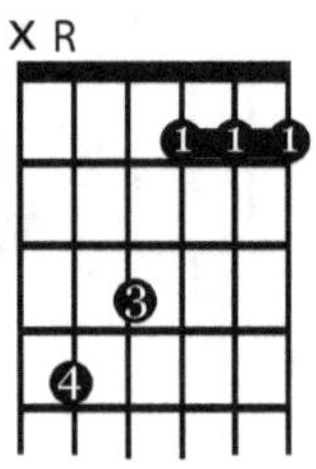
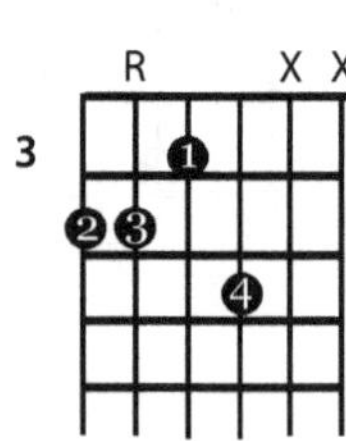
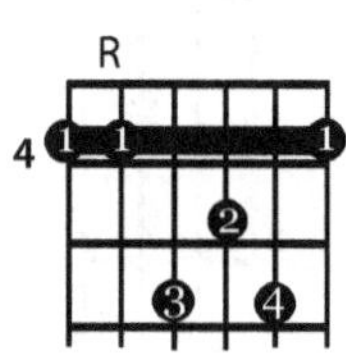
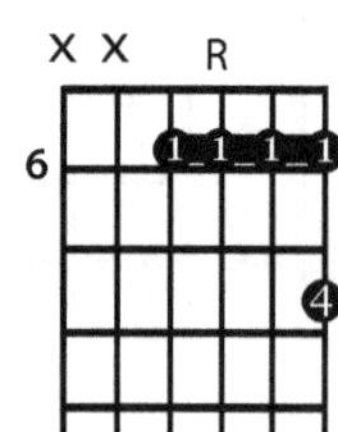
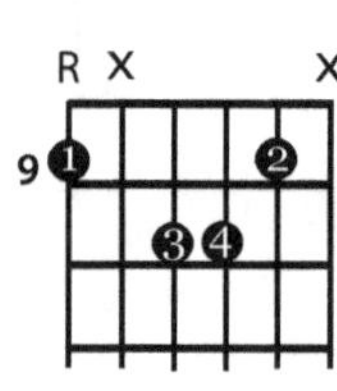
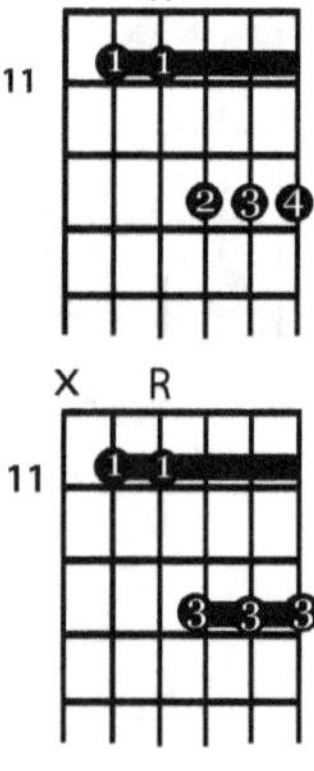

C♯7/D♭7

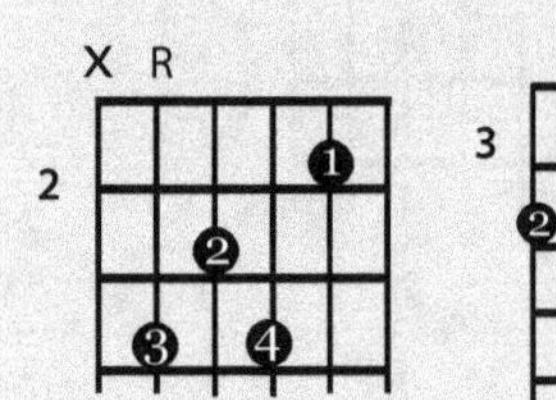
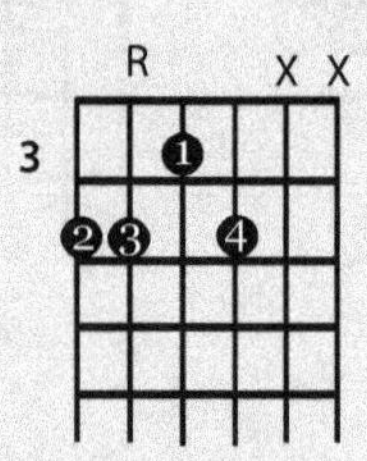
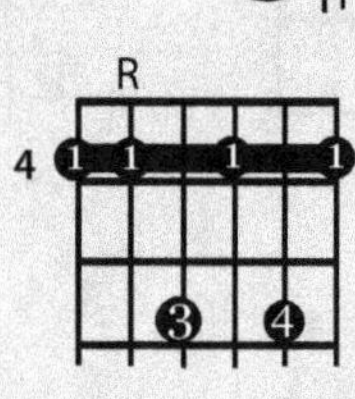
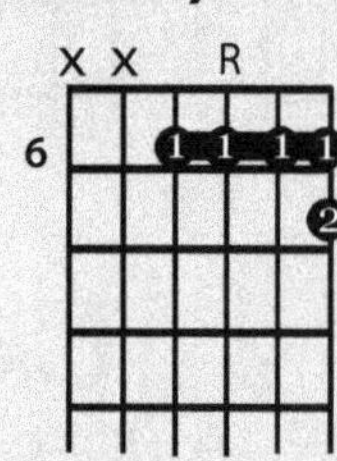
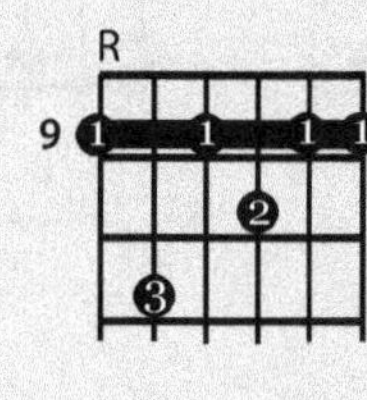
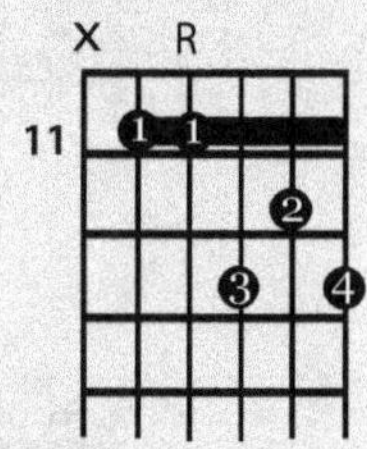

C♯m/D♭m

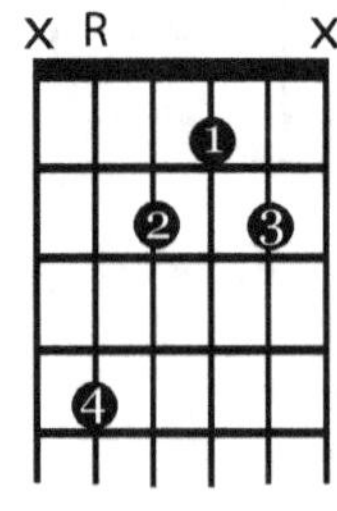
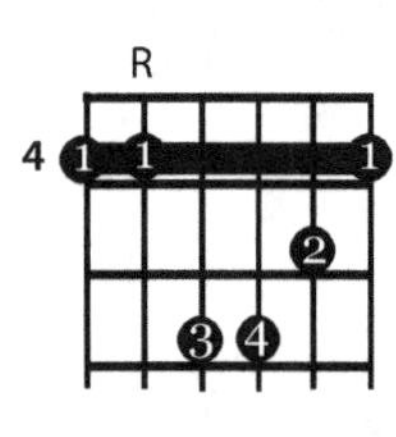
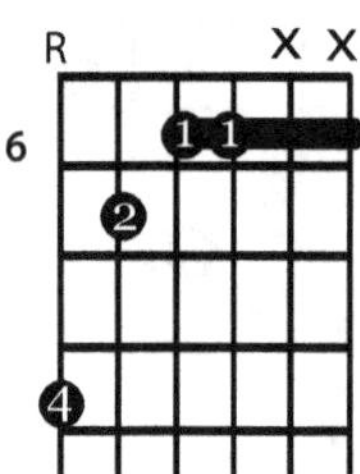
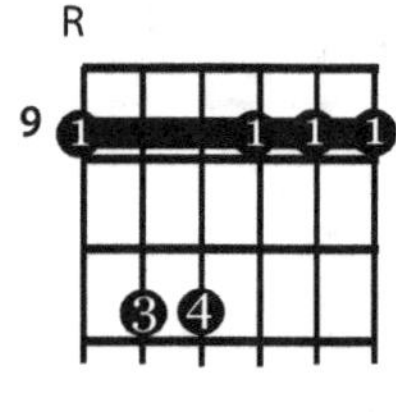
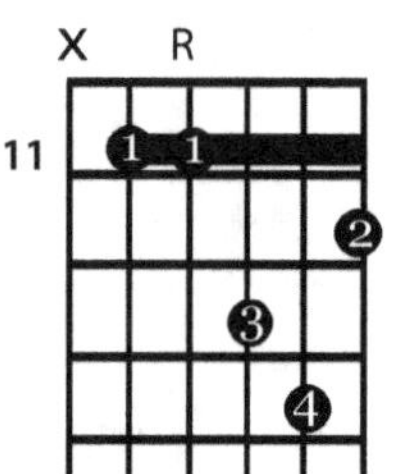

C♯m7/D♭m7

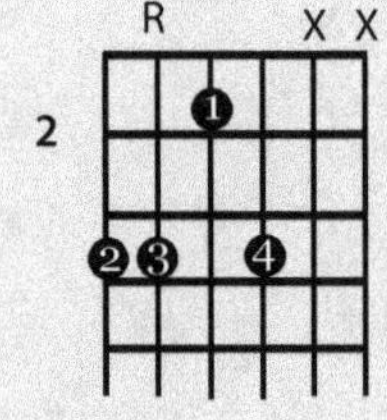
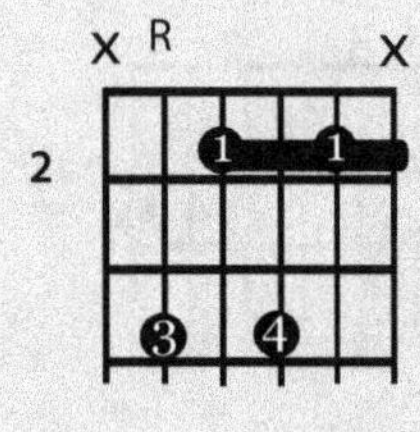
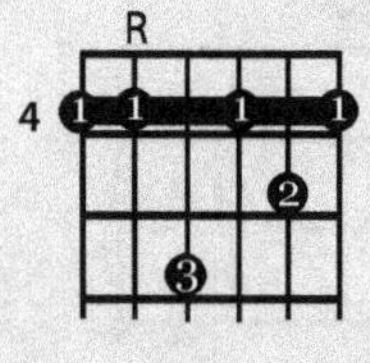
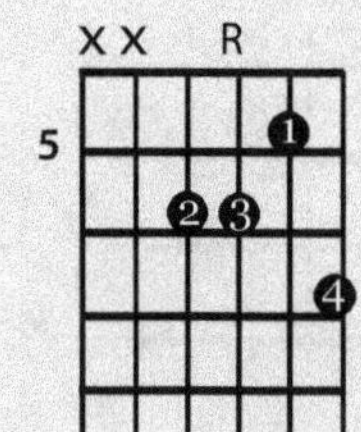
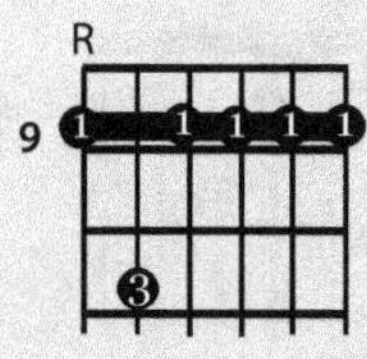
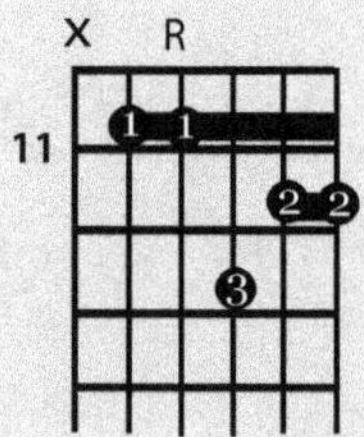

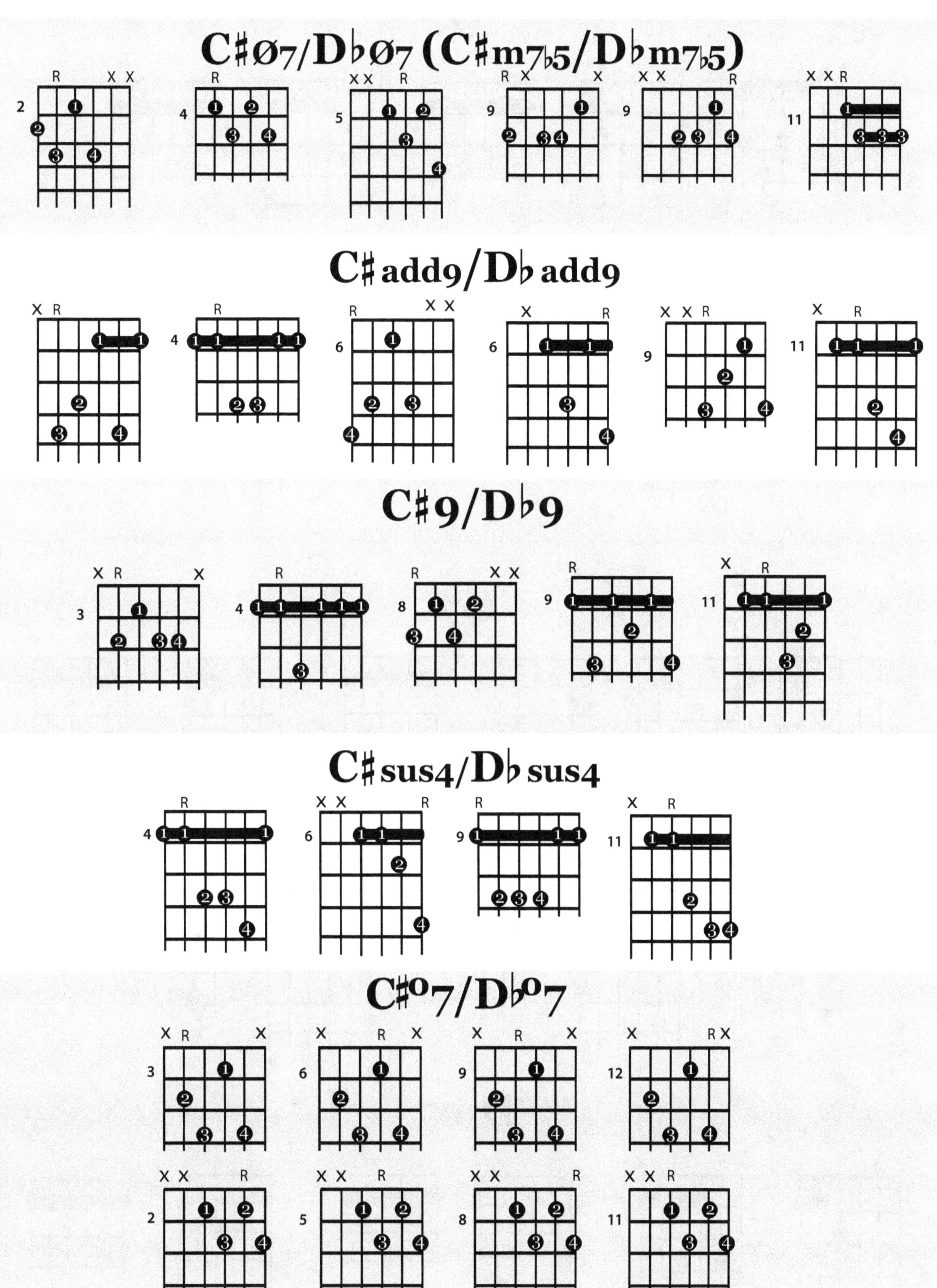
C♯ø7/D♭ø7 (C♯m7♭5/D♭m7♭5)
C♯add9/D♭add9
C♯9/D♭9
C♯sus4/D♭sus4
C♯°7/D♭°7

D

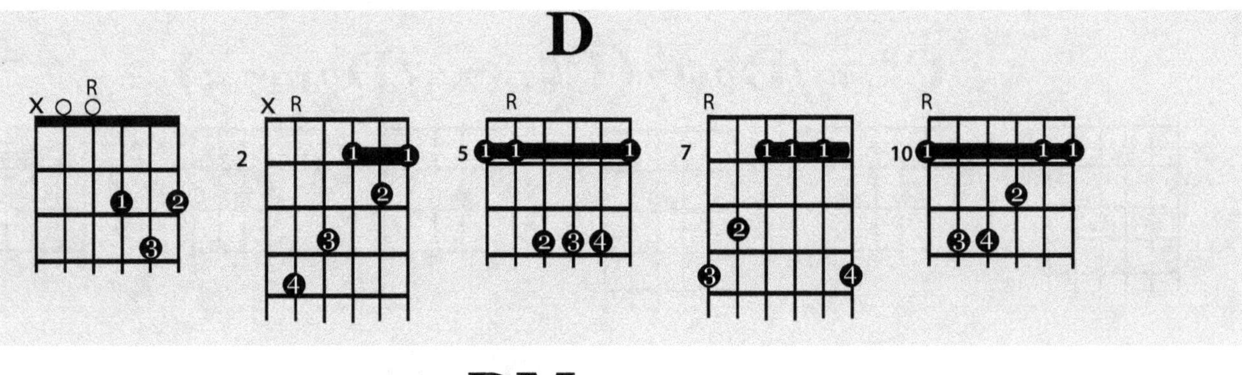

DM7

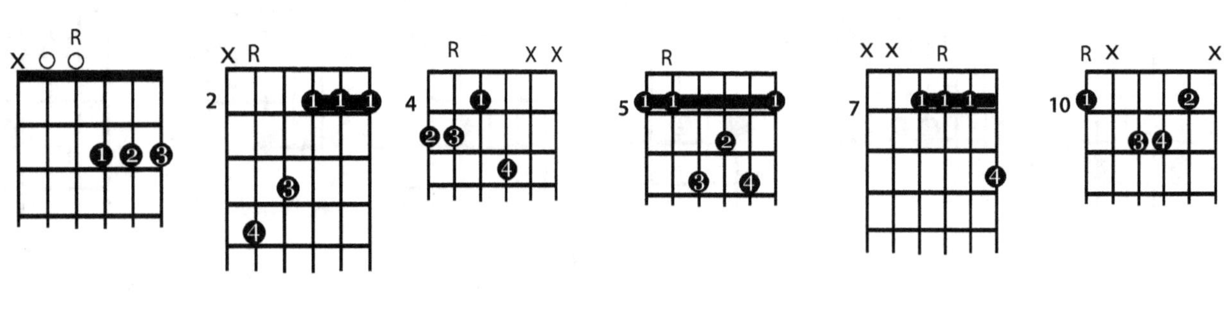

D7

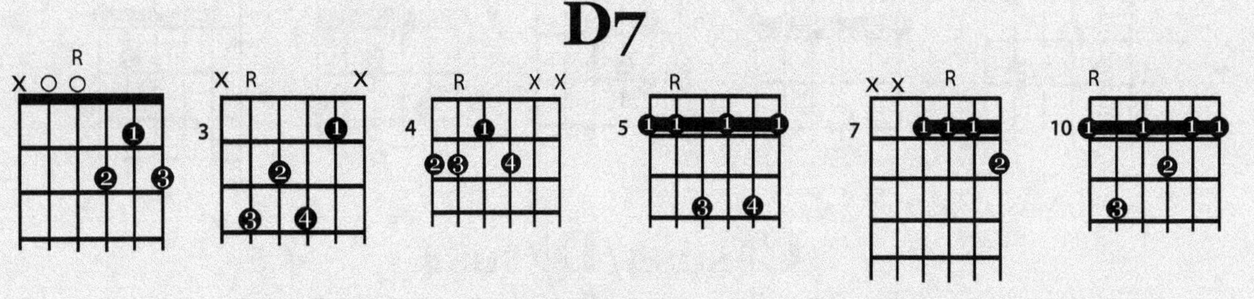

Dm

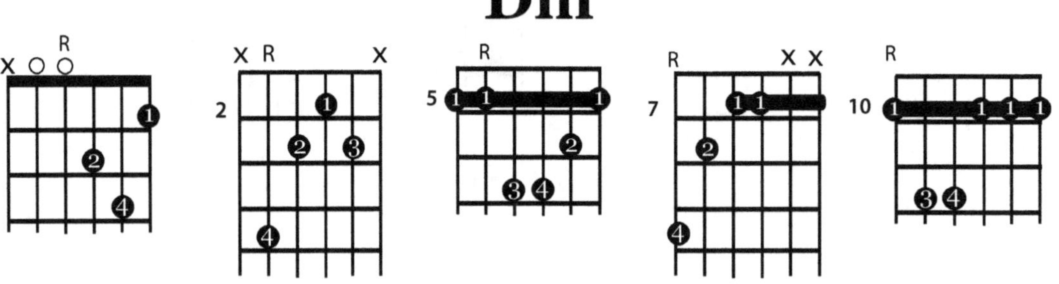

Dm7

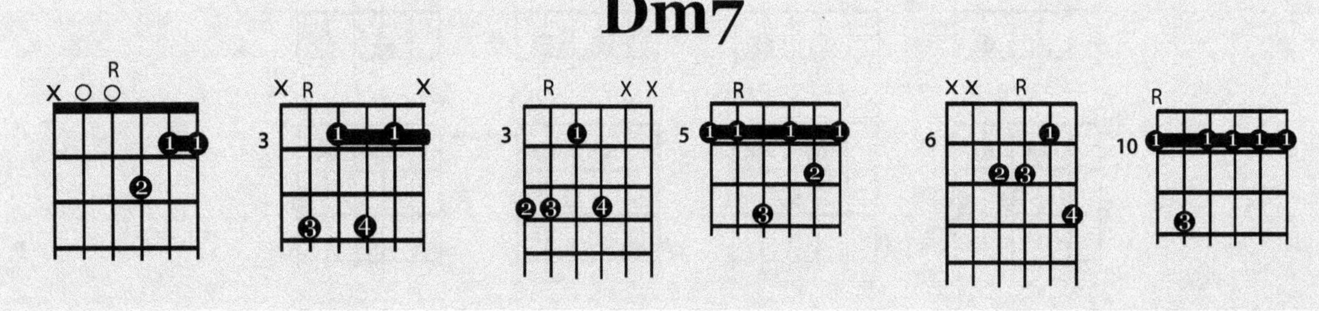

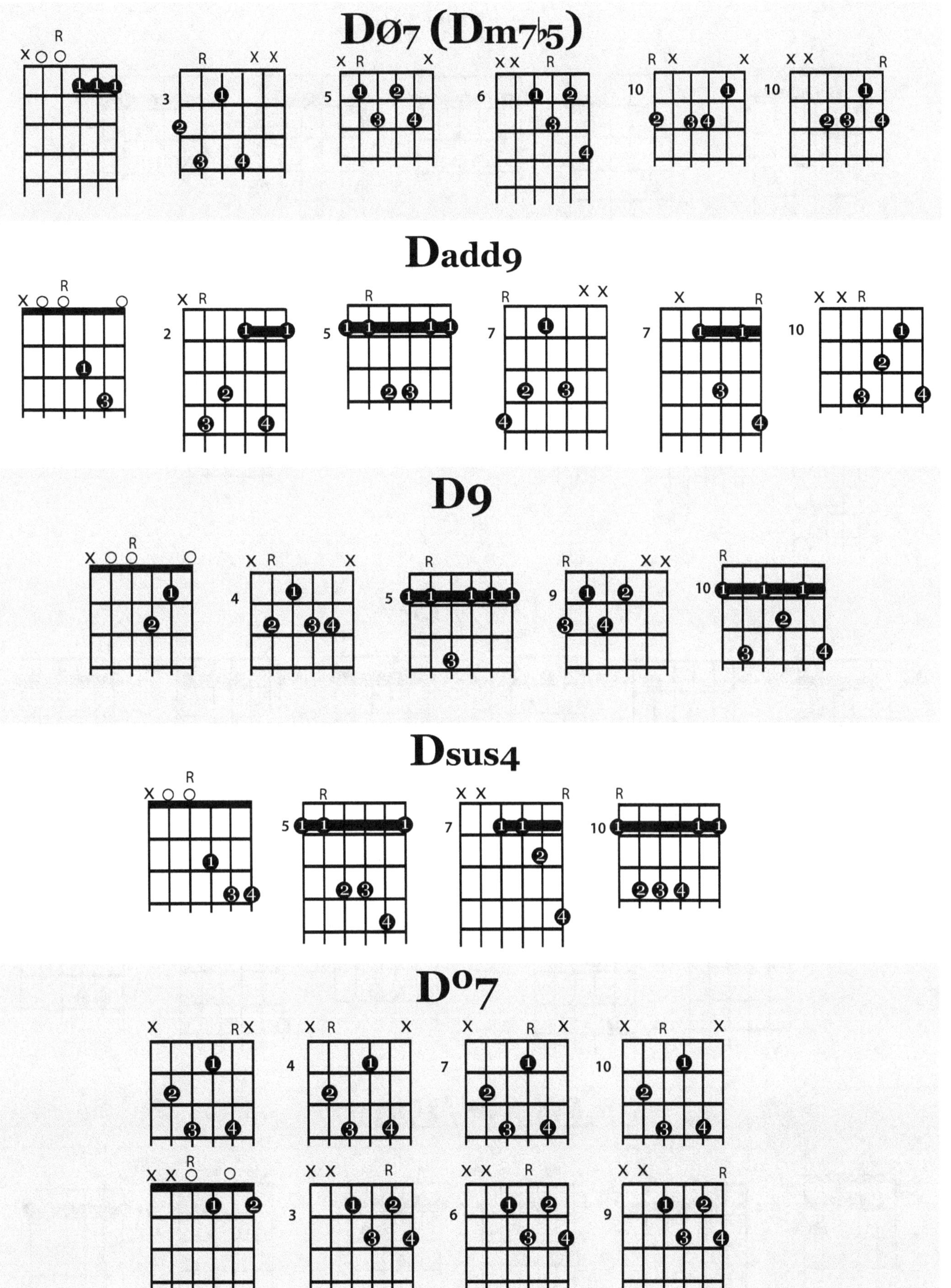
DØ7 (Dm7♭5)
Dadd9
D9
Dsus4
Dº7

D♯/E♭

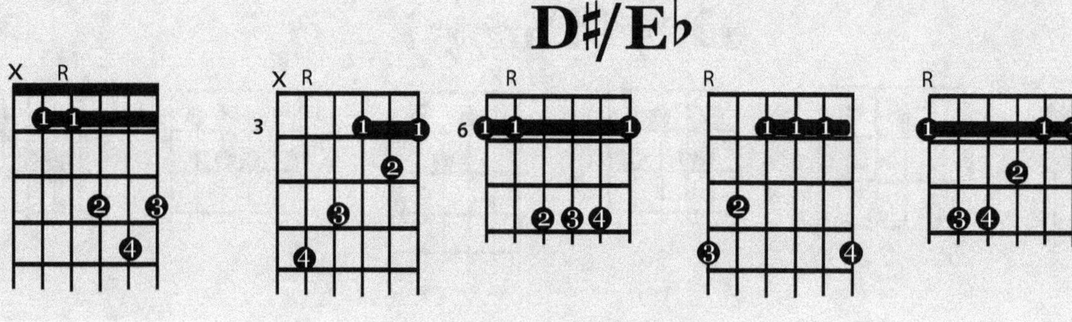

D♯M7/E♭M7

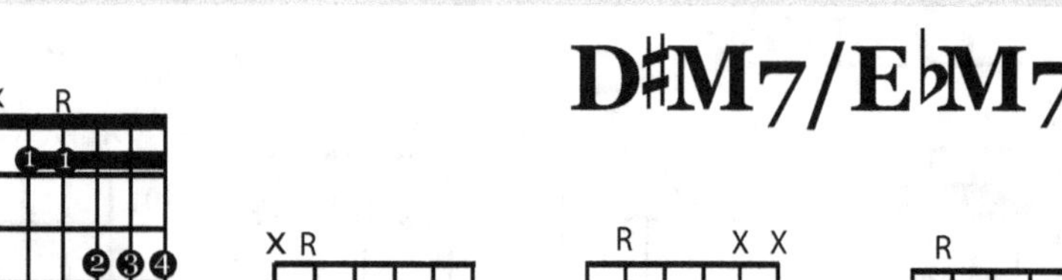

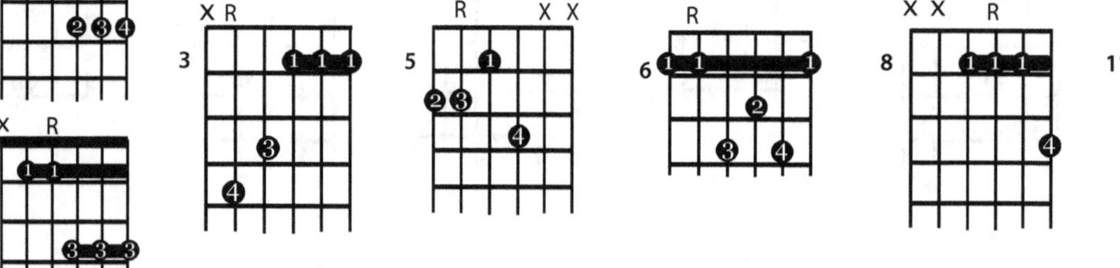

D♯7/E♭7

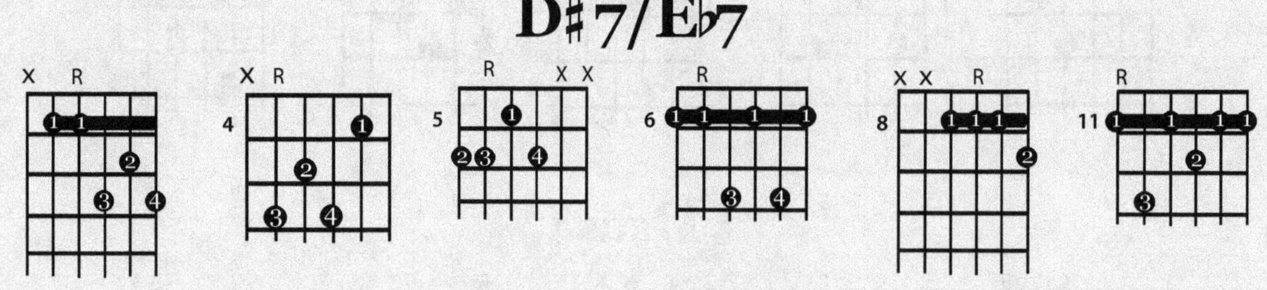

D♯m/E♭m

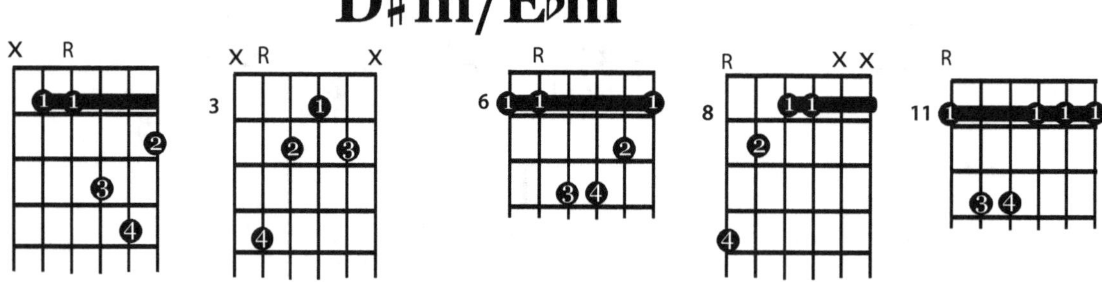

D♯m7/E♭m7

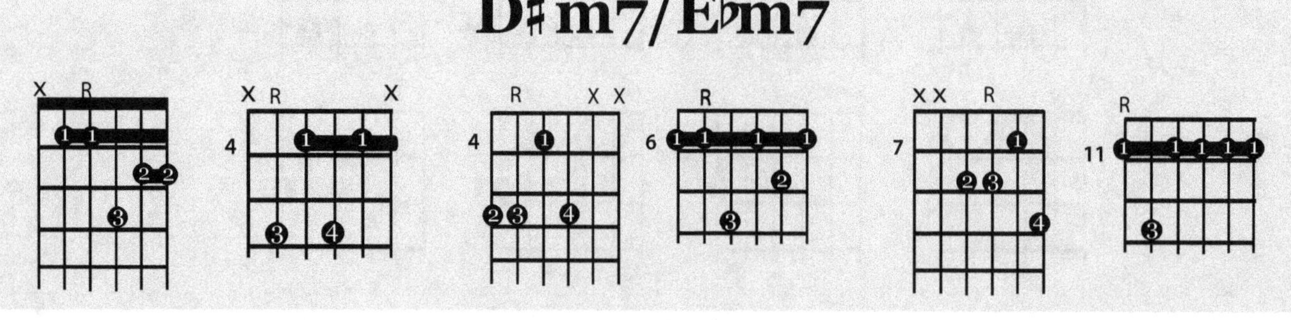

D♯ø7/E♭ø7 (D♯m7♭5/E♭m7♭5)

D♯add9/E♭add9

D♯9/E♭9

D♯sus4/E♭sus4

D♯°7/E♭°7

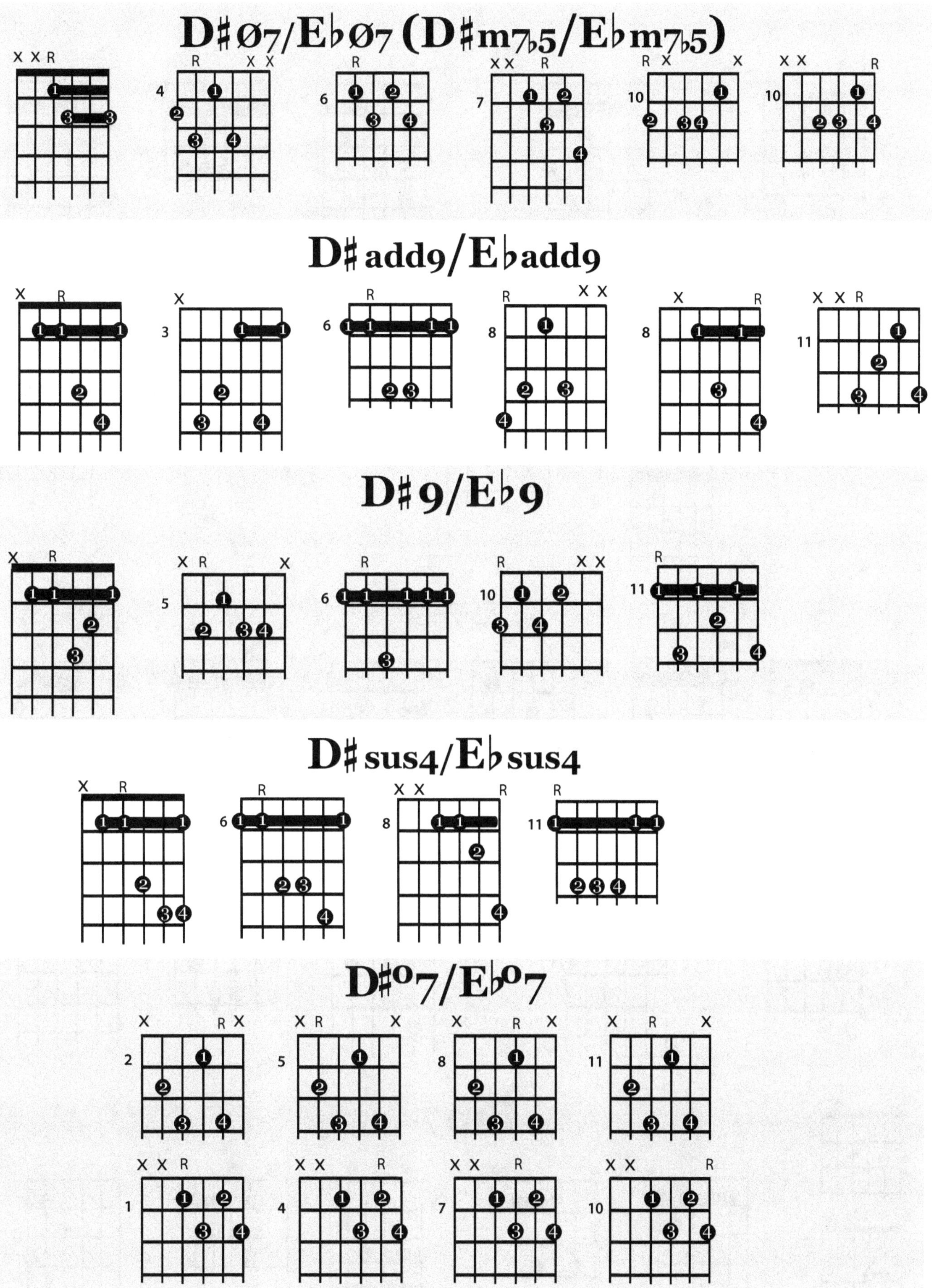

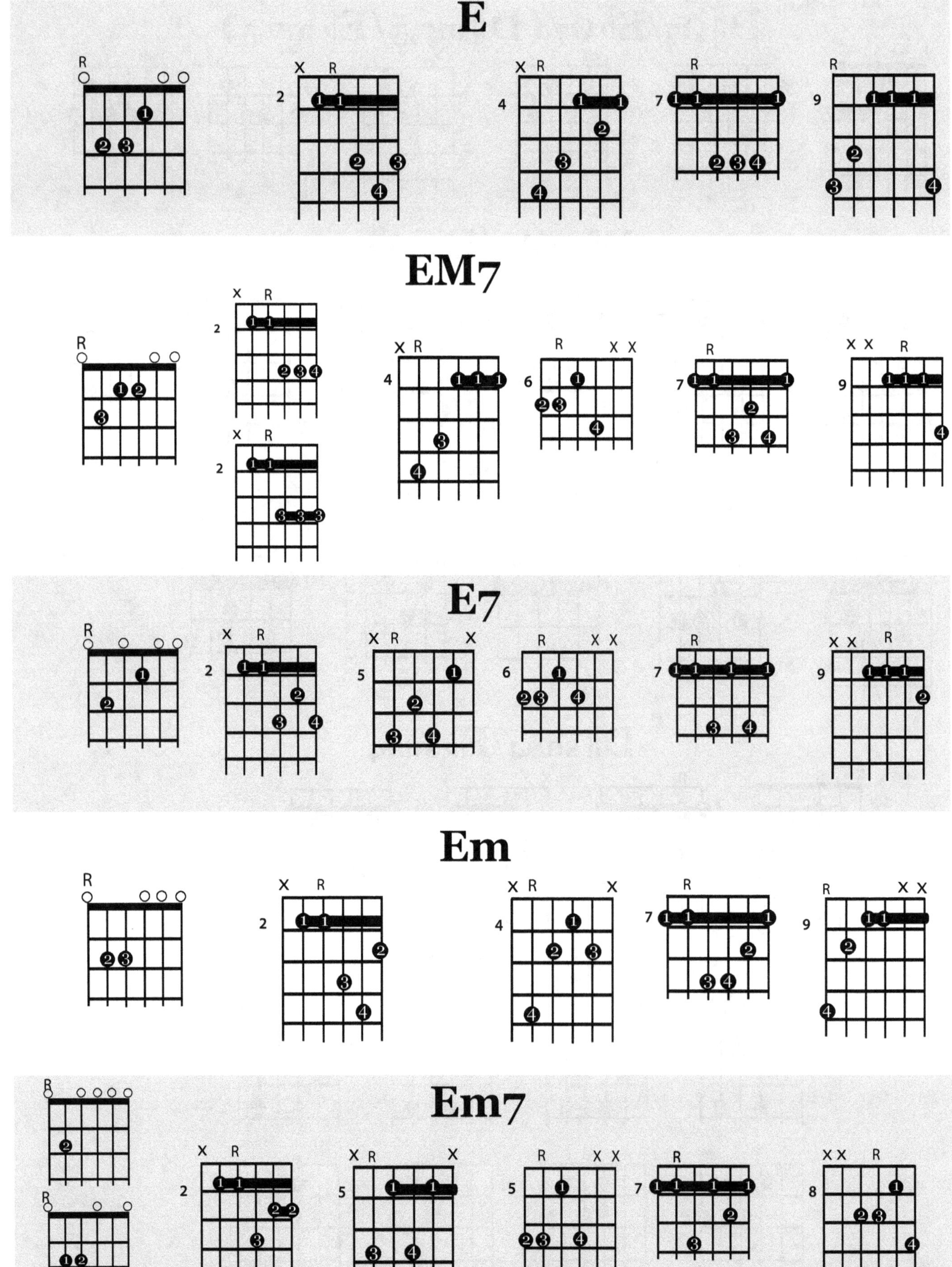
E
EM7
E7
Em
Em7

EØ7 (Em7♭5)

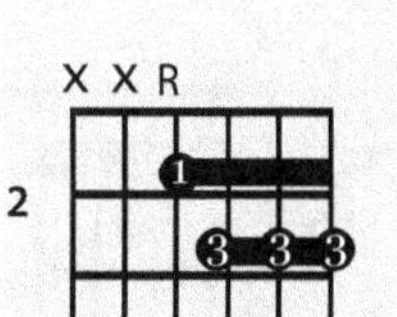

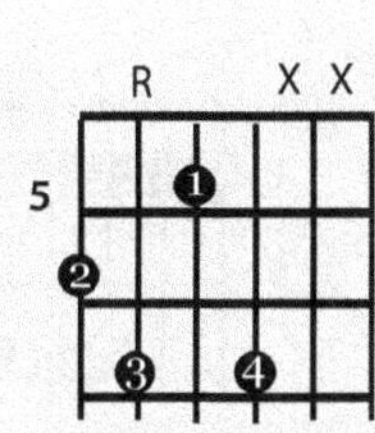

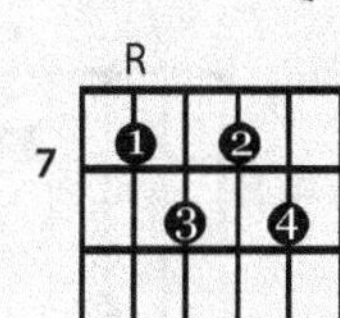

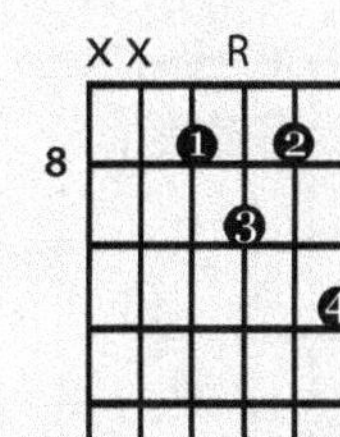

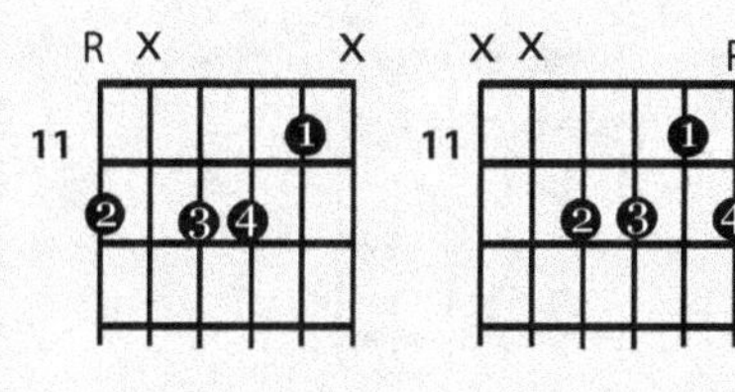

Eadd9

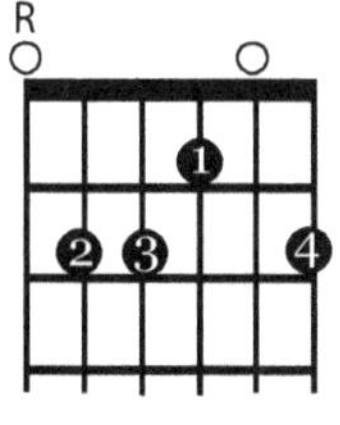

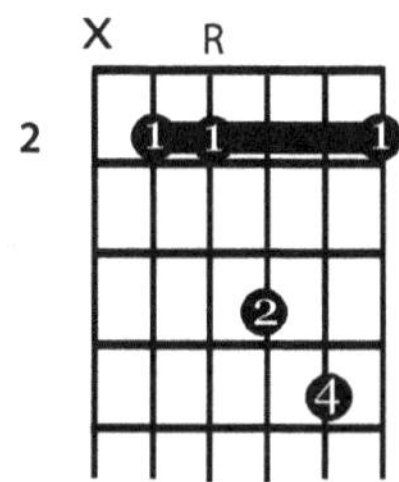

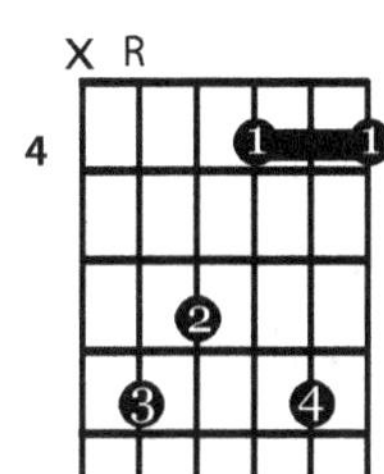

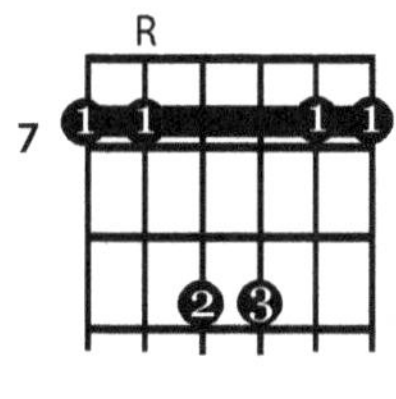

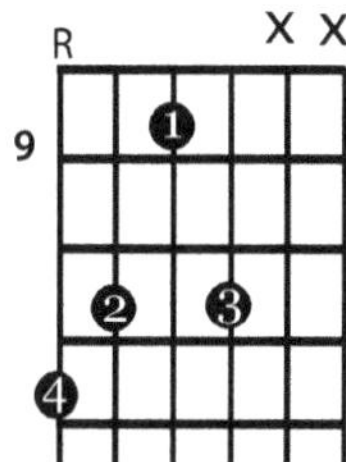

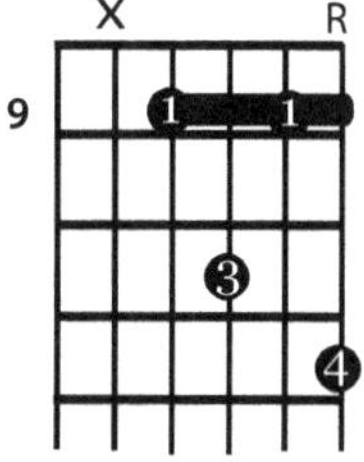

E9

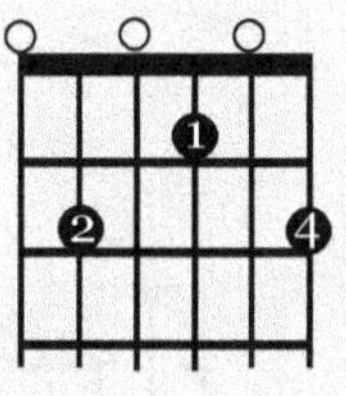
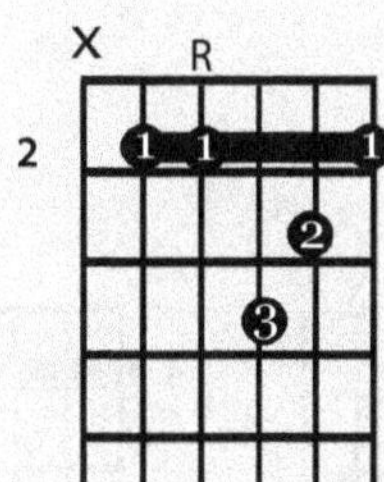

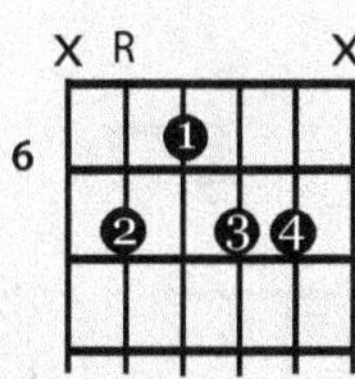

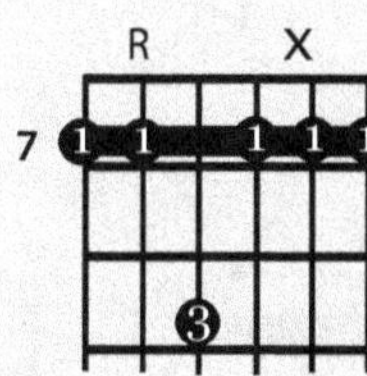

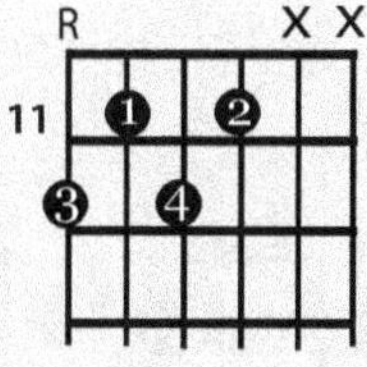

Esus4

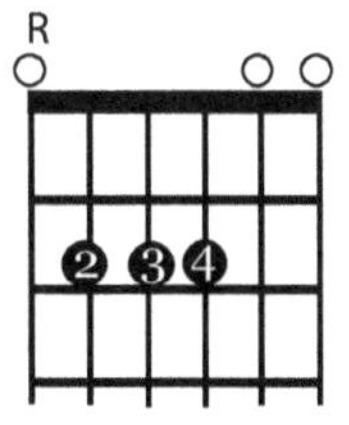

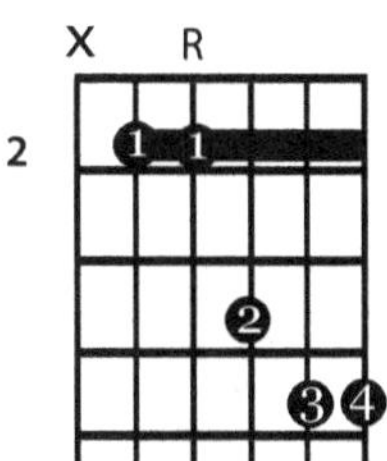

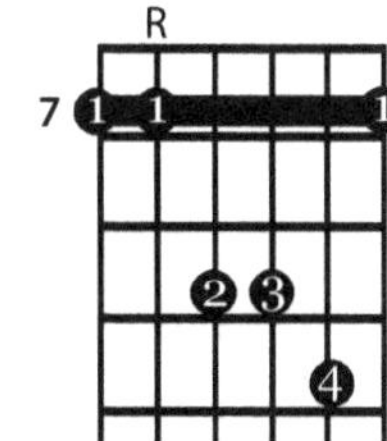

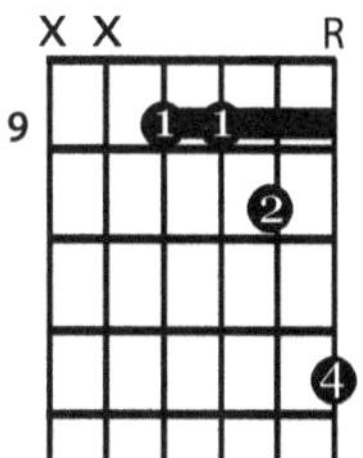

E°7

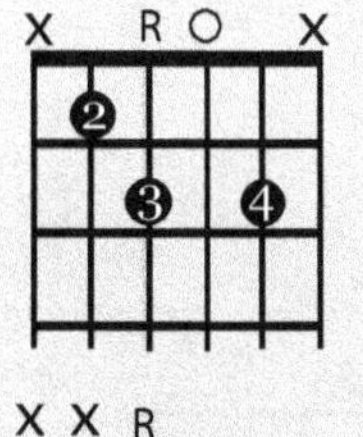

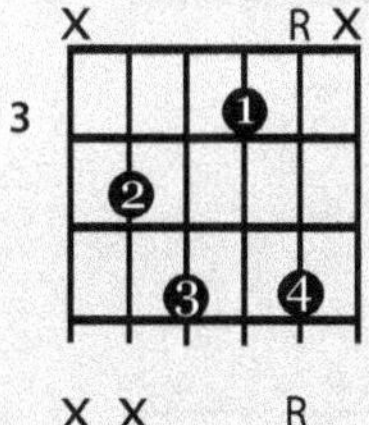

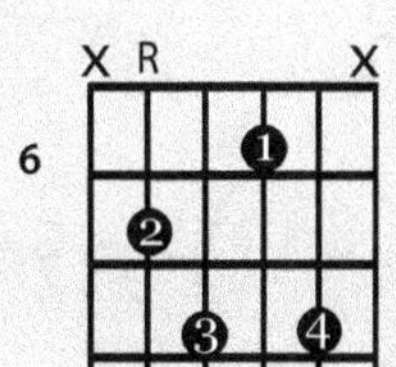

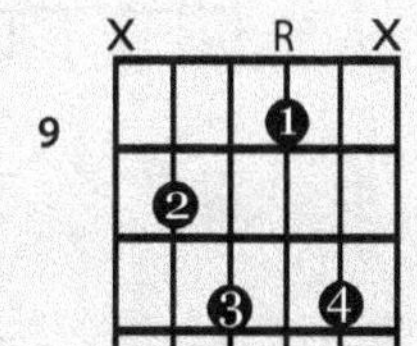

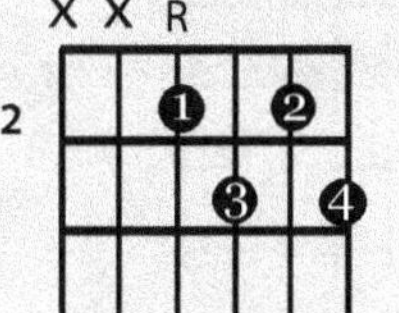

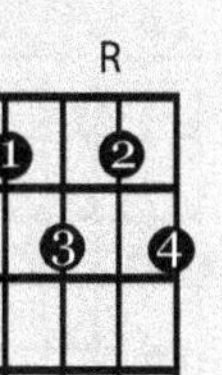

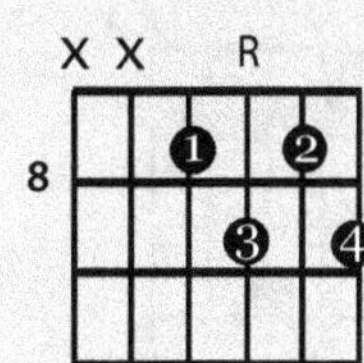

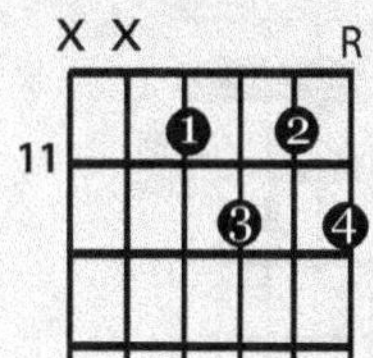

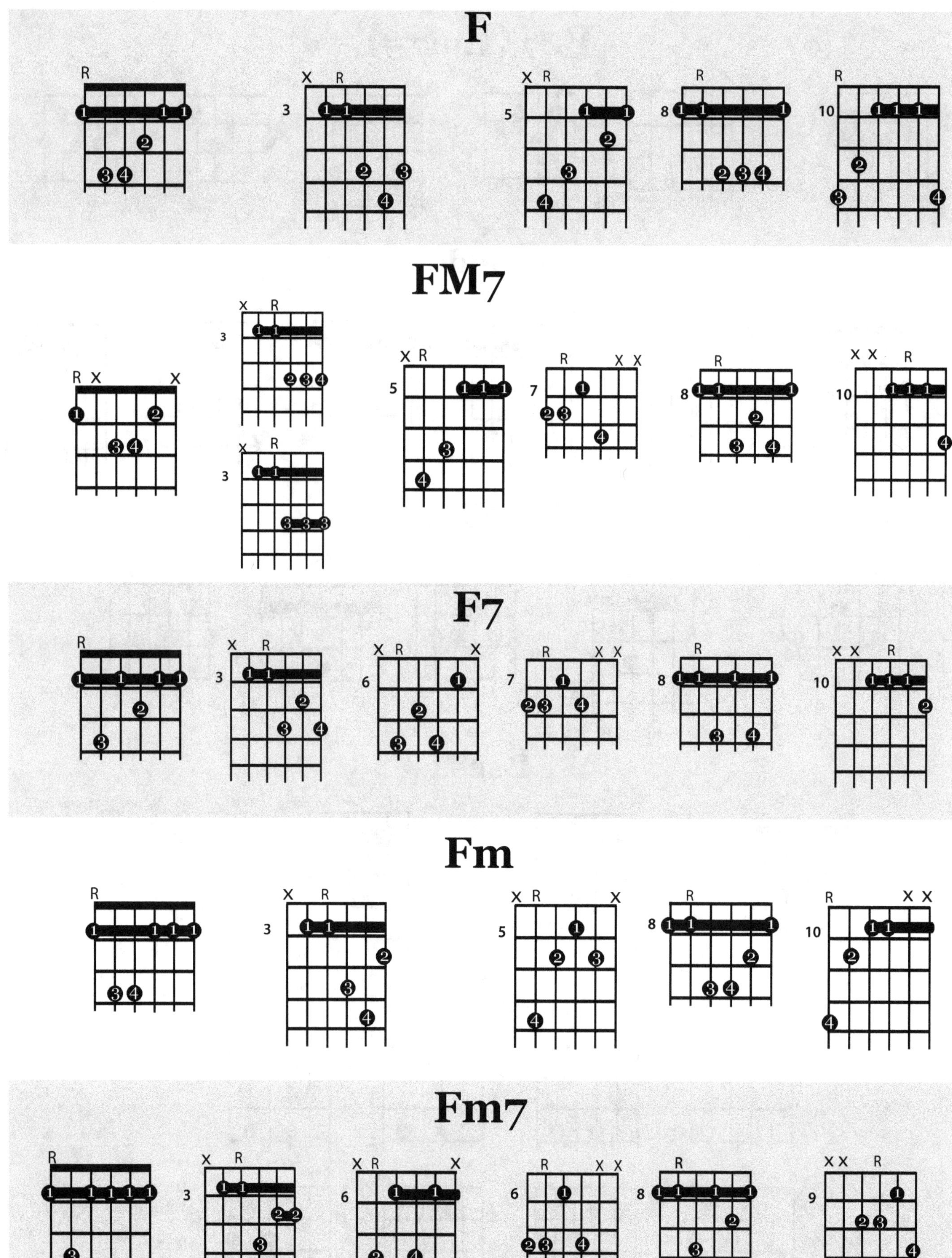
F
FM7
F7
Fm
Fm7

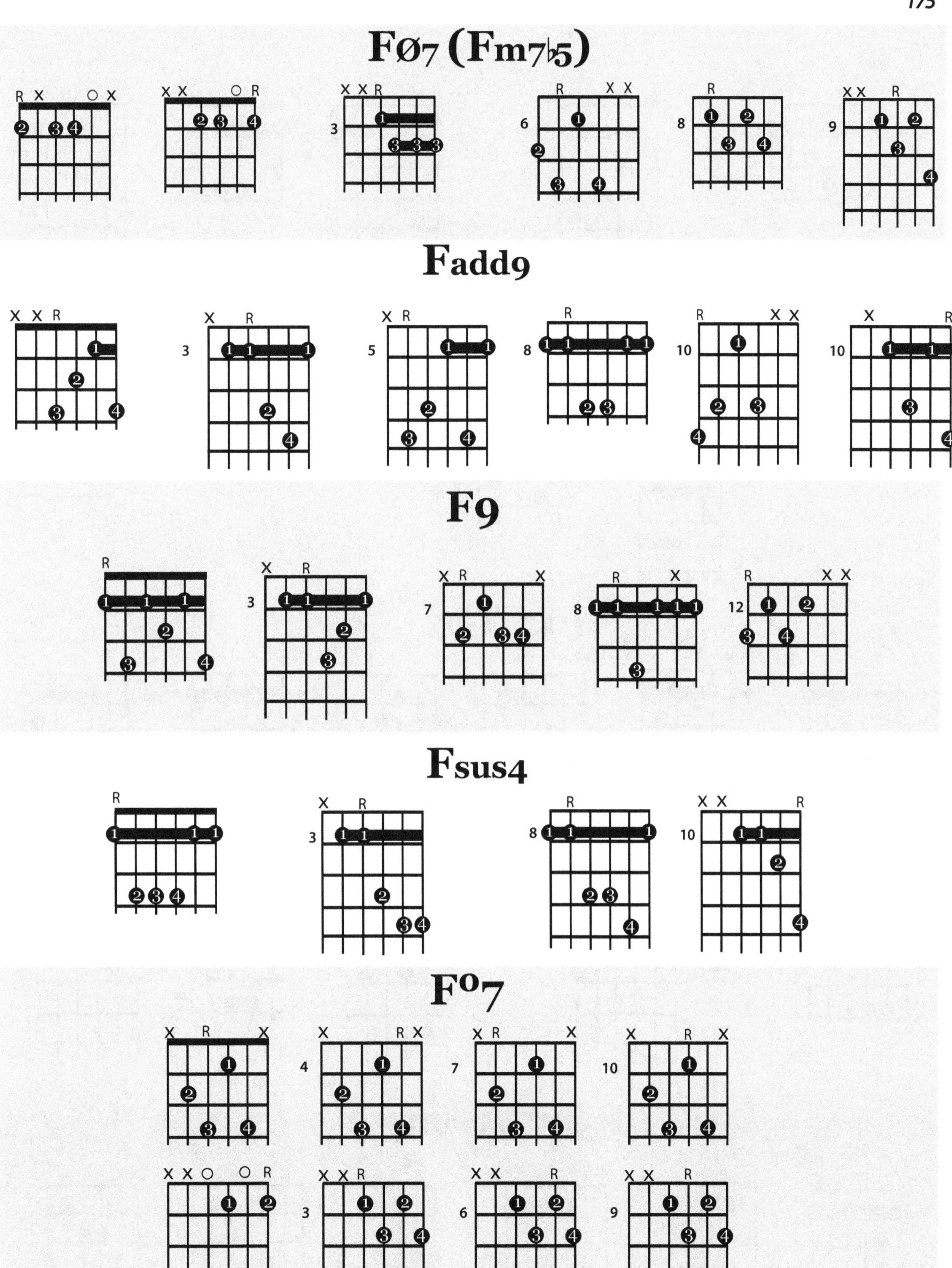
FØ7 (Fm7♭5)
Fadd9
F9
Fsus4
Fo7

F♯/G♭

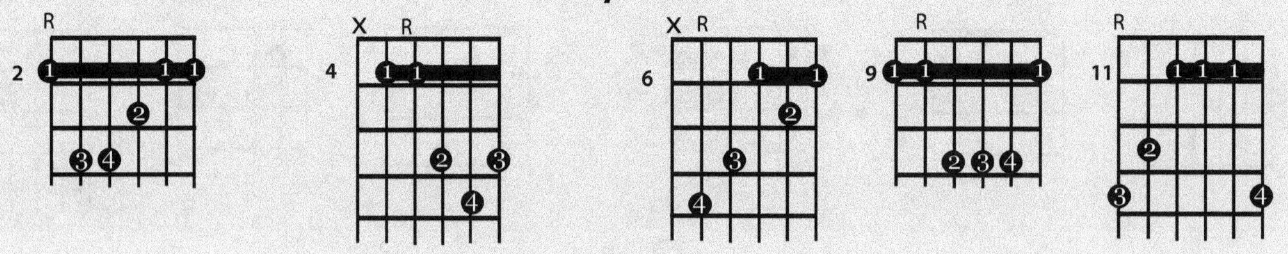

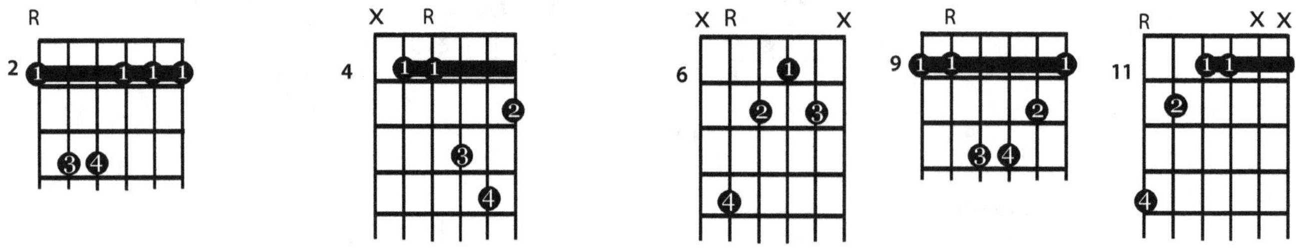

F♯M7/G♭M7

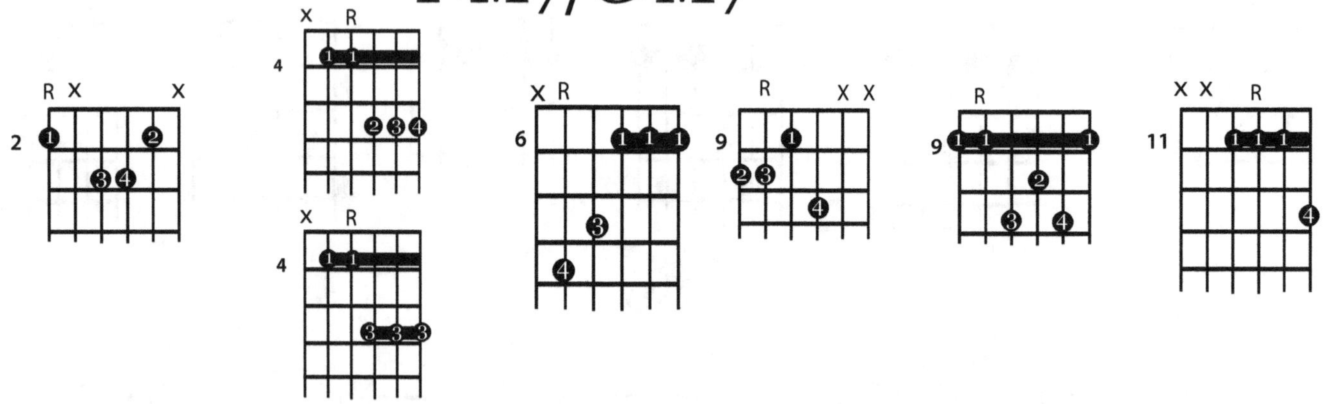

F♯7/G♭7

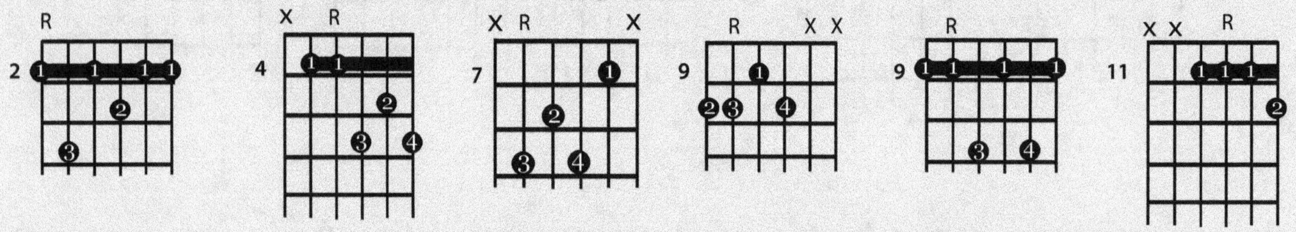

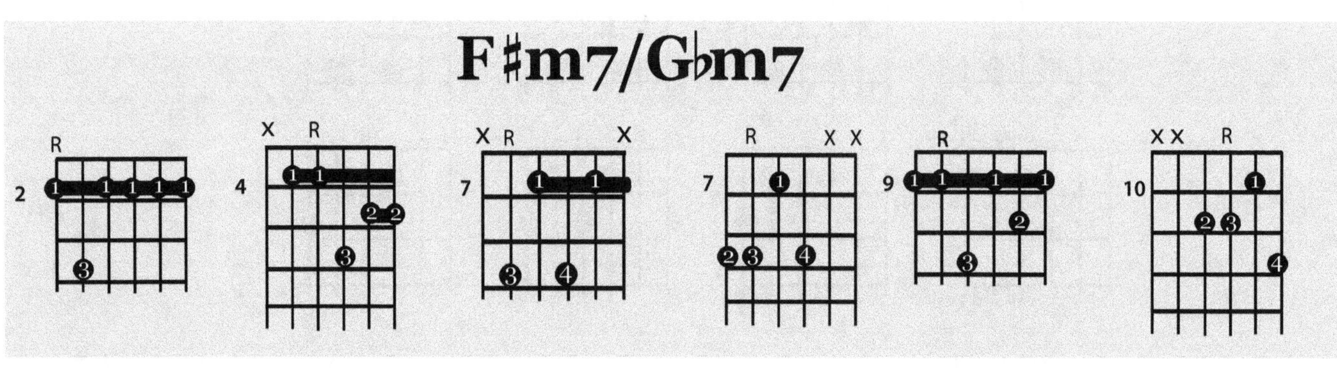

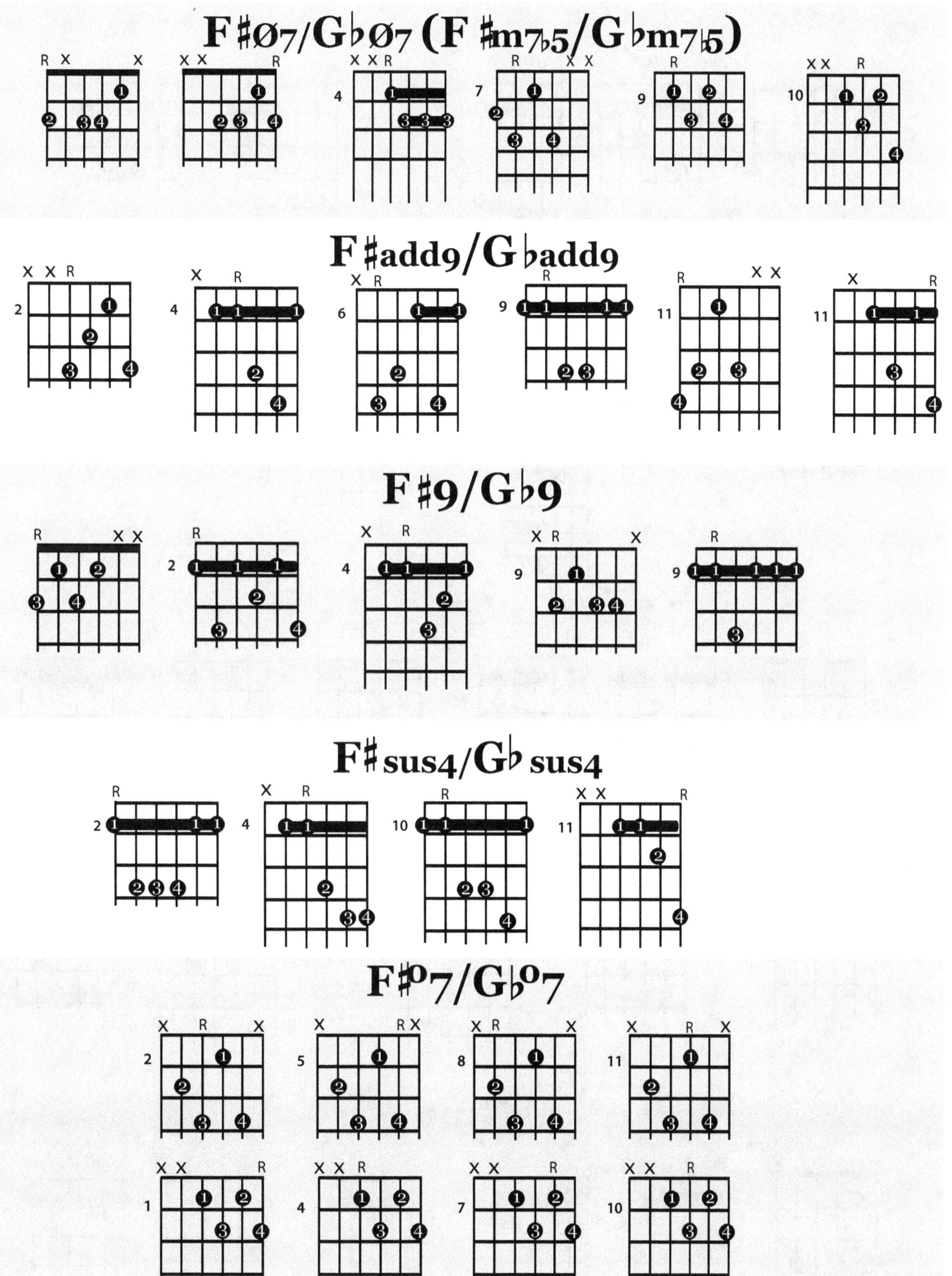
F♯ø7/G♭ø7 (F♯m7♭5/G♭m7♭5)
F♯add9/G♭add9
F♯9/G♭9
F♯sus4/G♭sus4
F♯°7/G♭°7

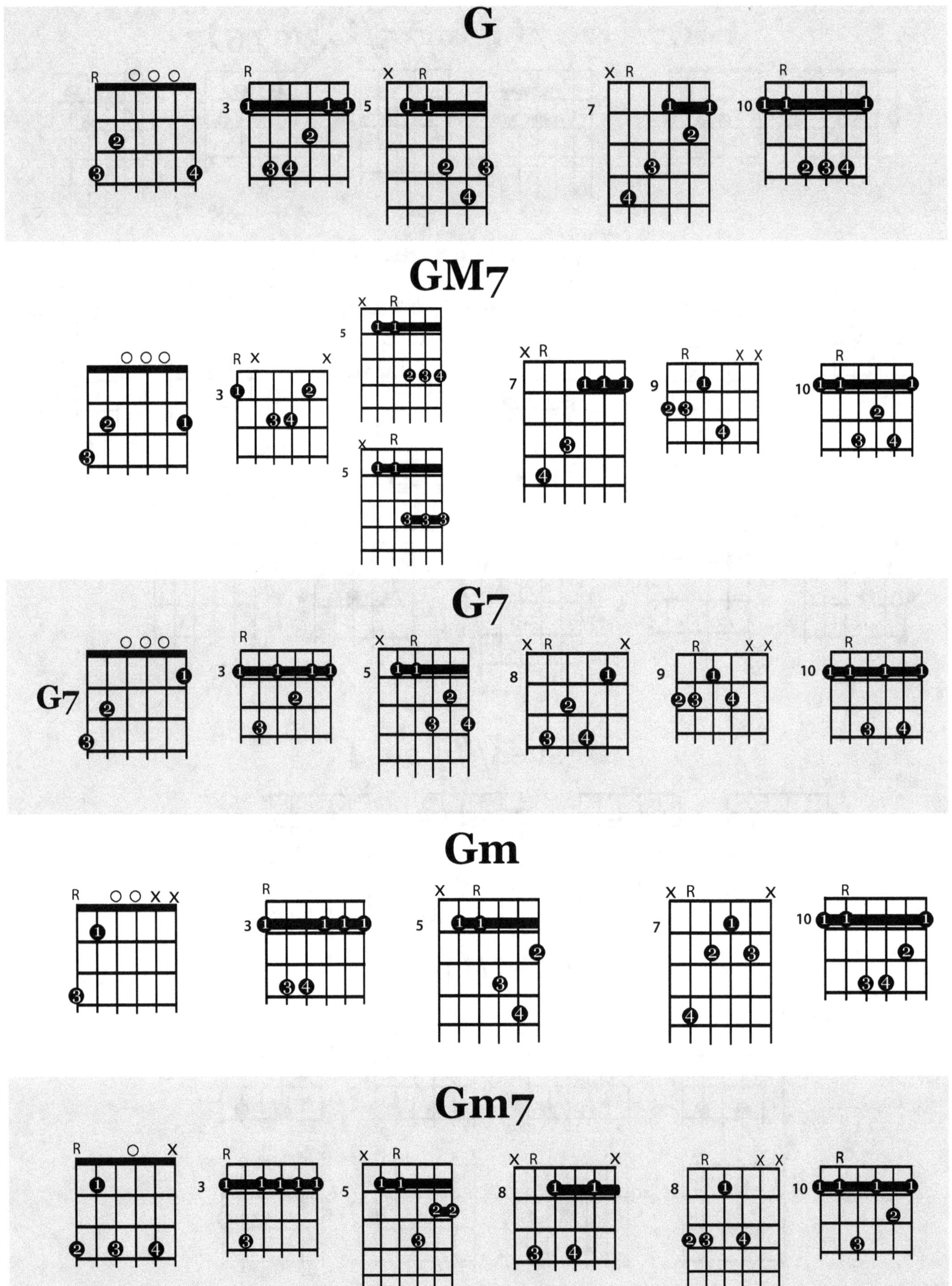
G
GM7
G7
Gm
Gm7

GØ7 (Gm7♭5)

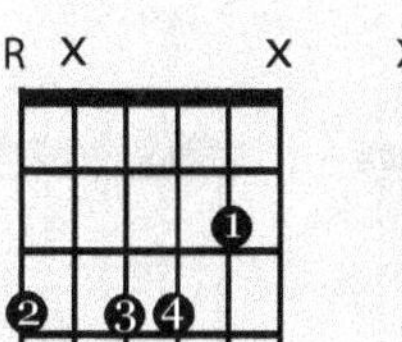
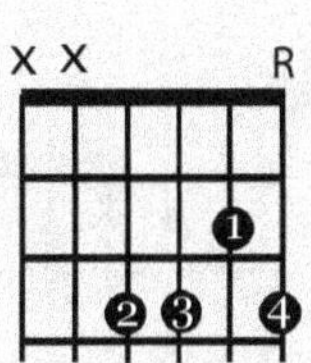
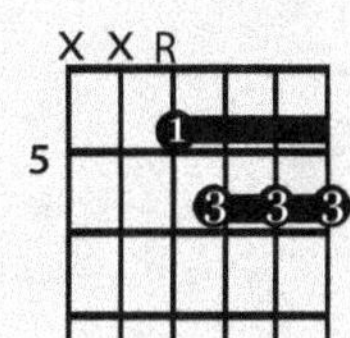
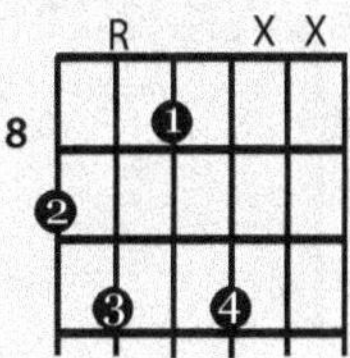
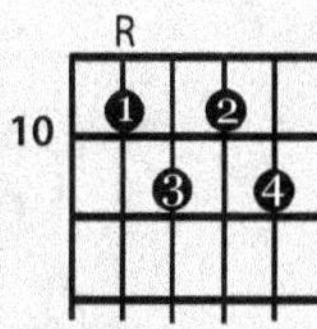
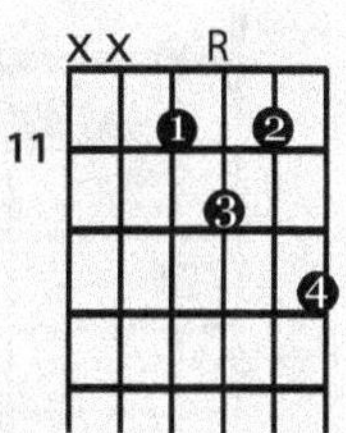

Gadd9

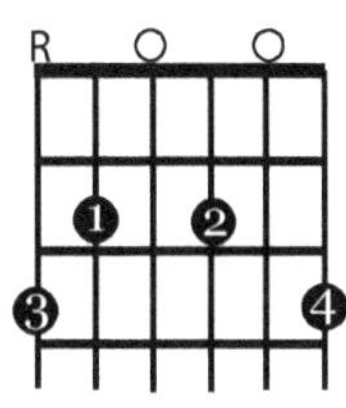
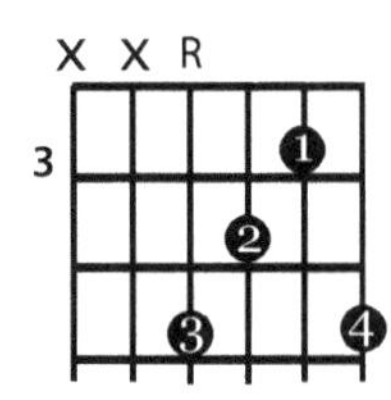
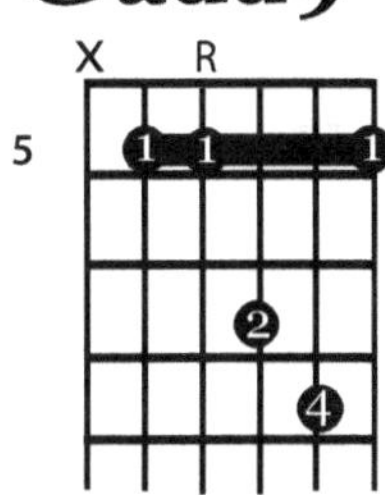
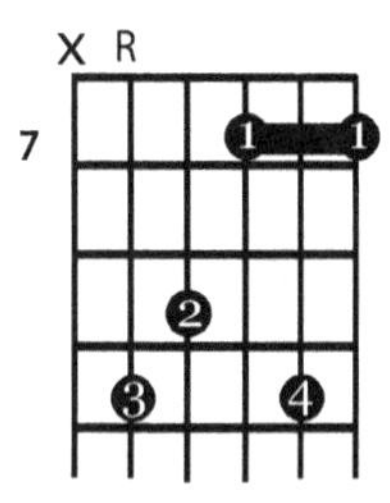
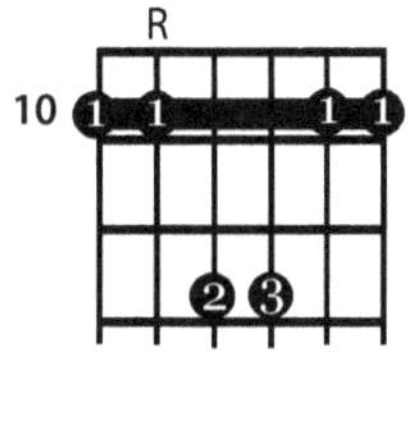

G9

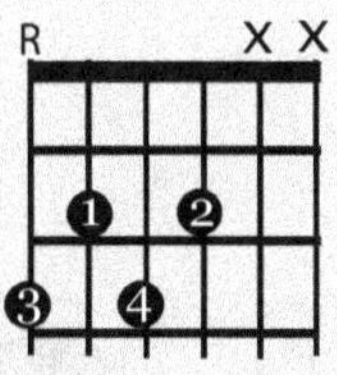
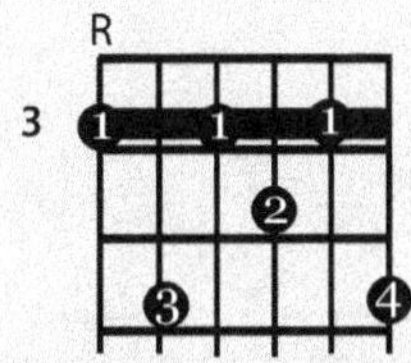
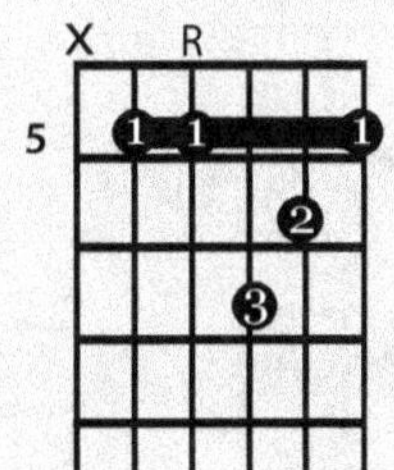
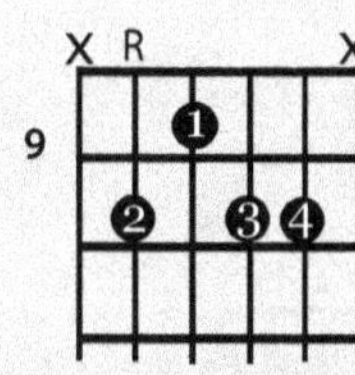
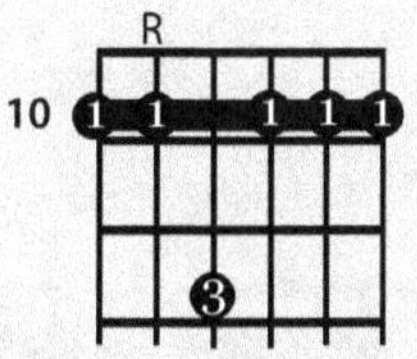

Gsus4

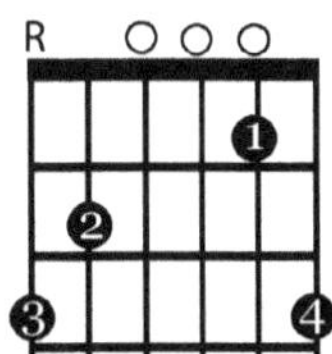
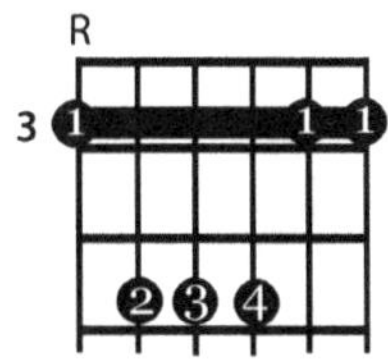
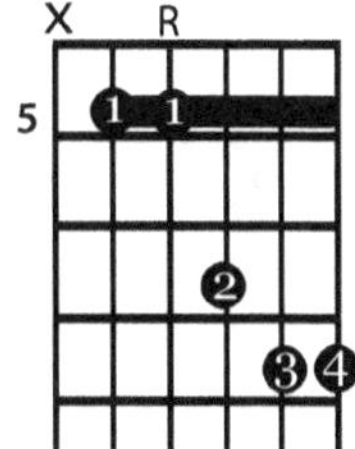
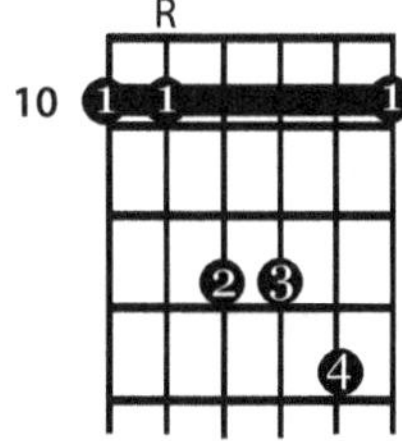

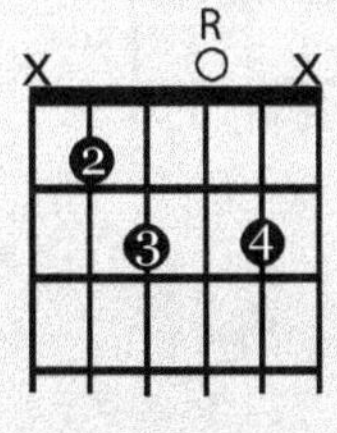
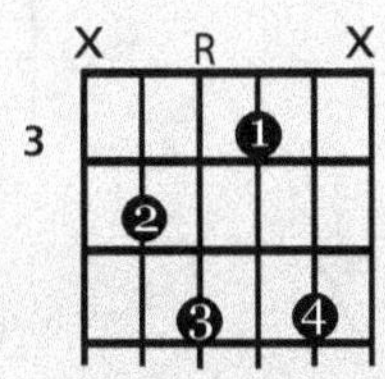
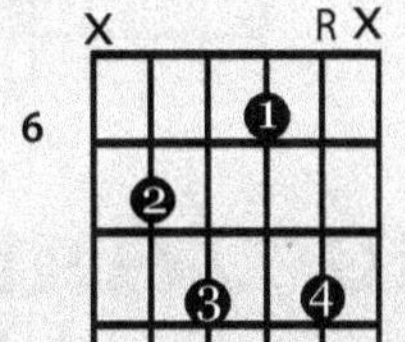
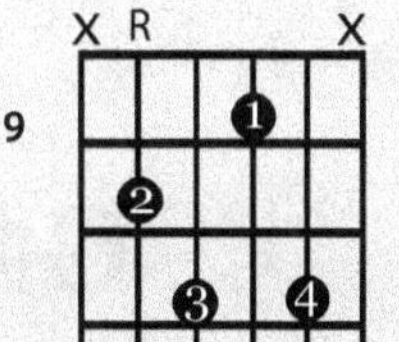
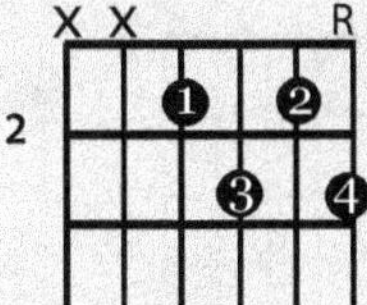
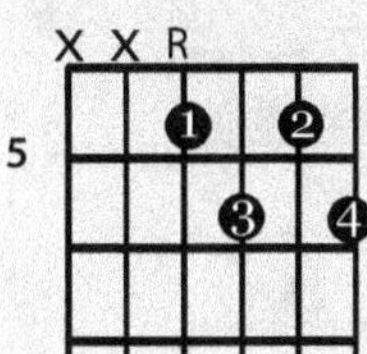
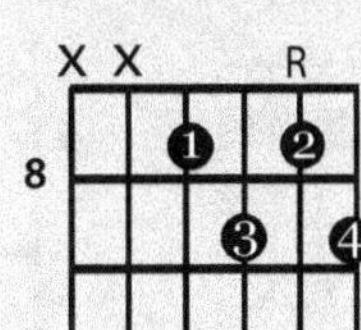
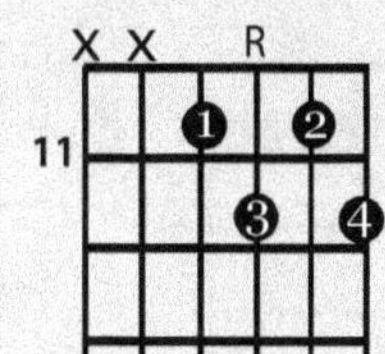

G♯/A♭

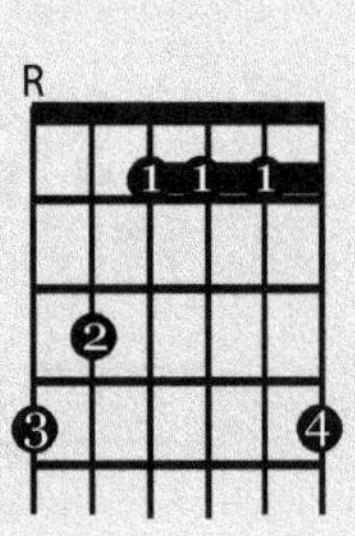
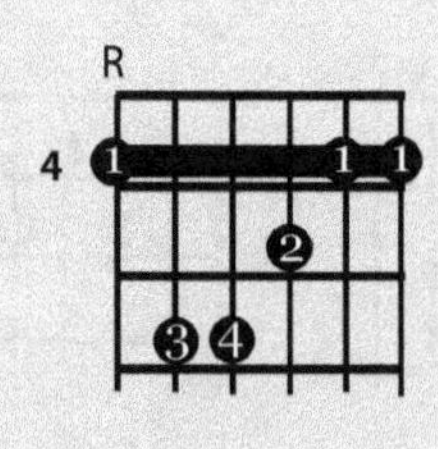
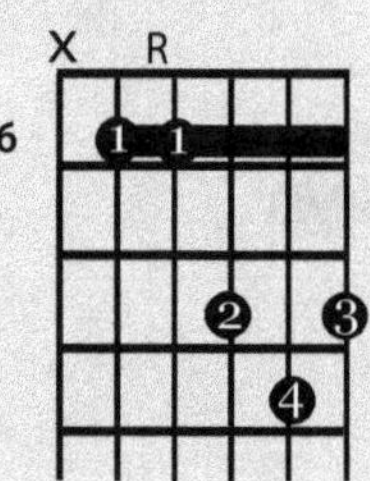
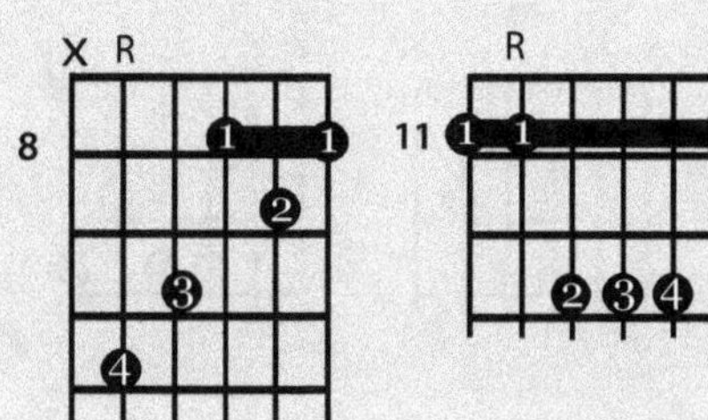

G♯M7/A♭M7

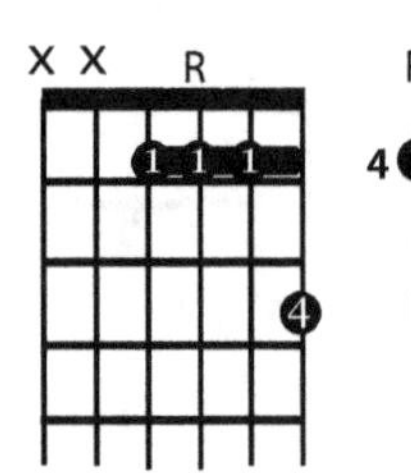
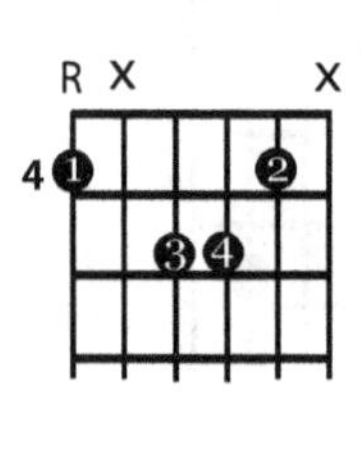
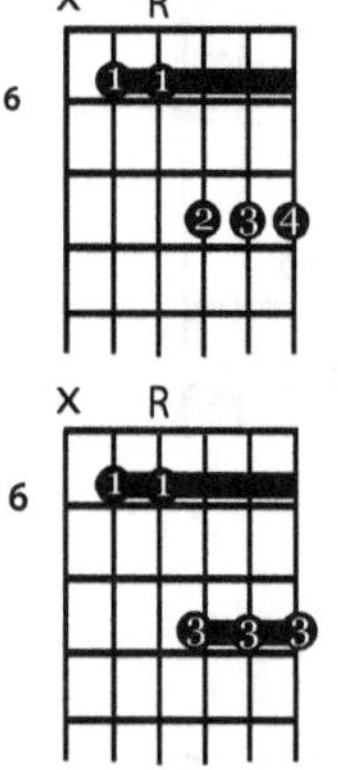
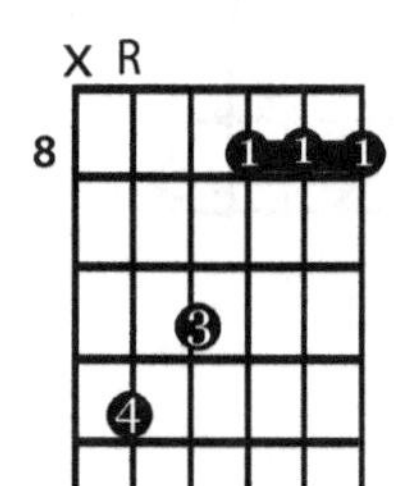
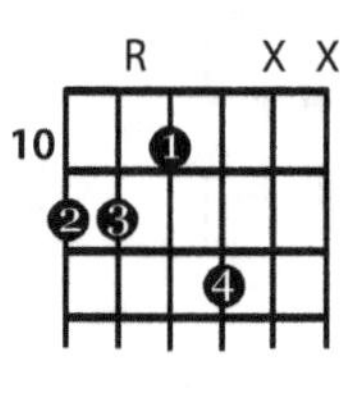
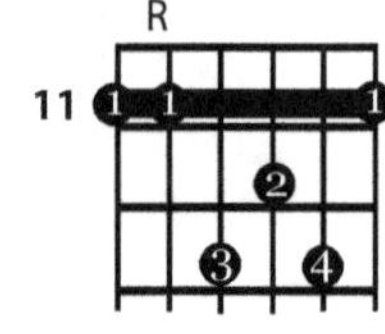

G♯ 7/A♭7

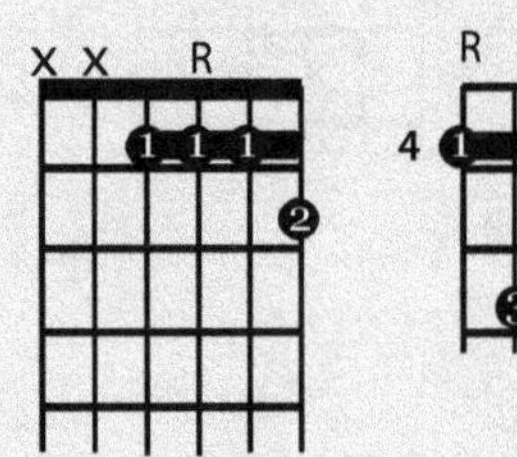
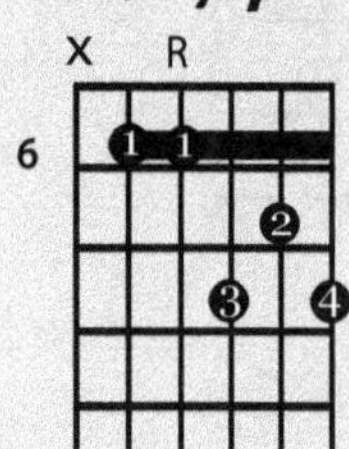
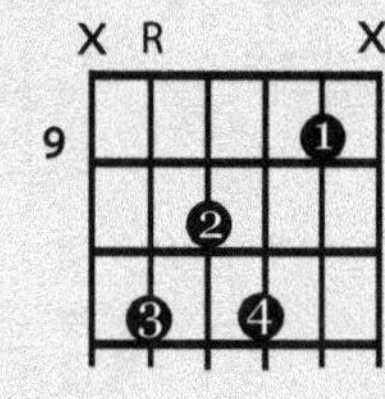
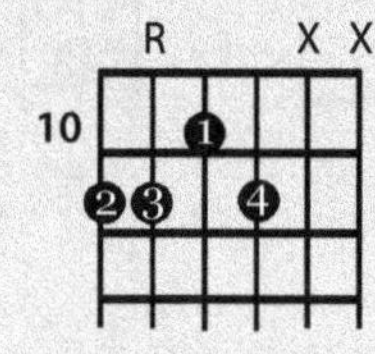
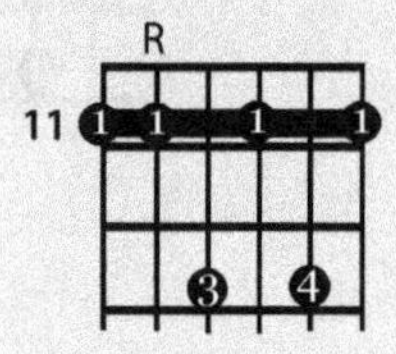

G♯ m/A♭m

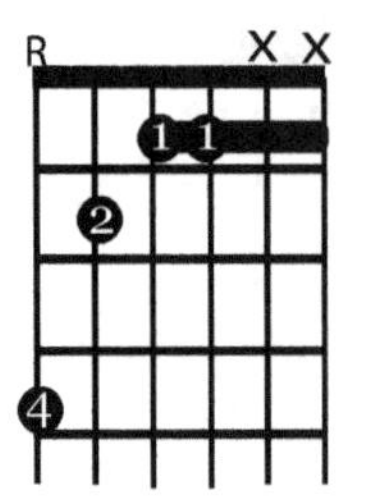
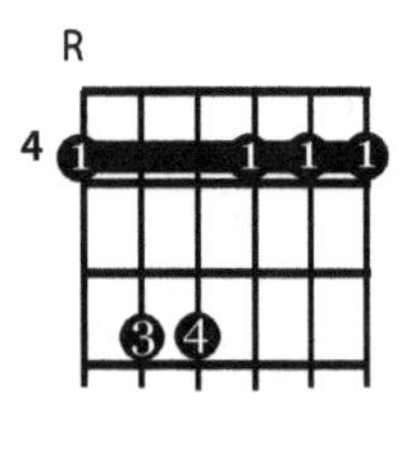
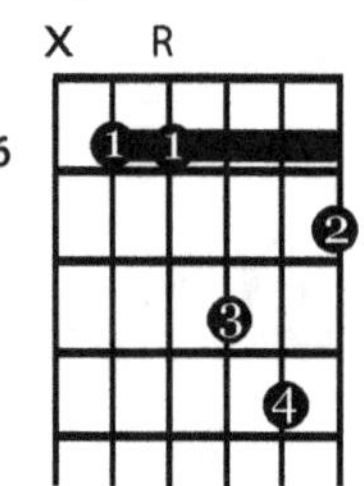
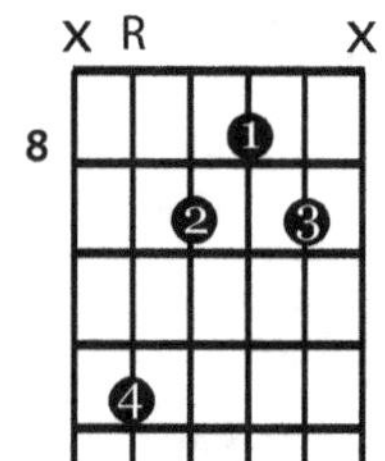
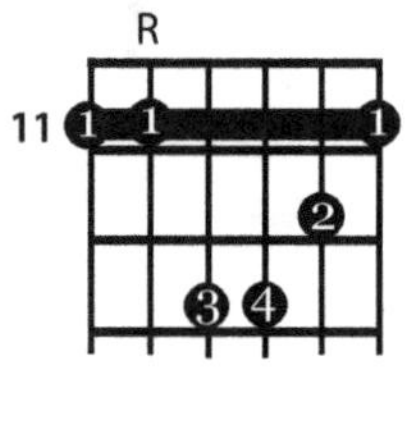

G♯m7/A♭m7

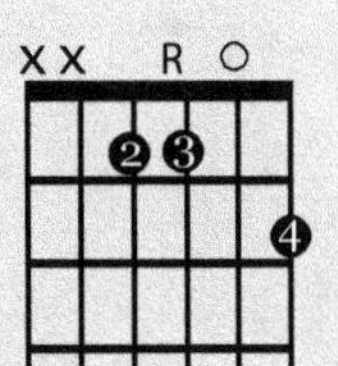
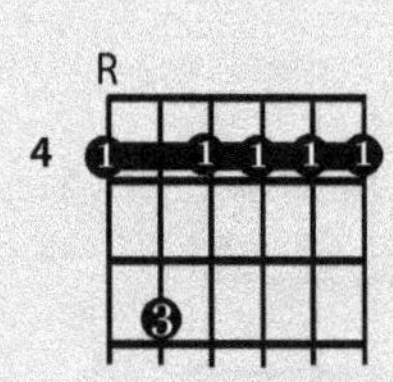
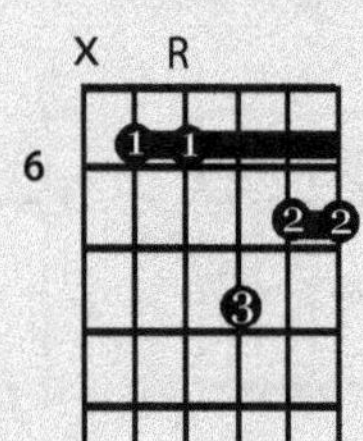
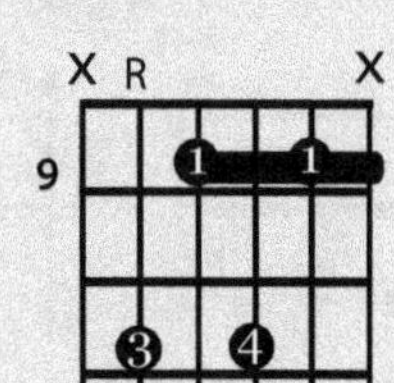
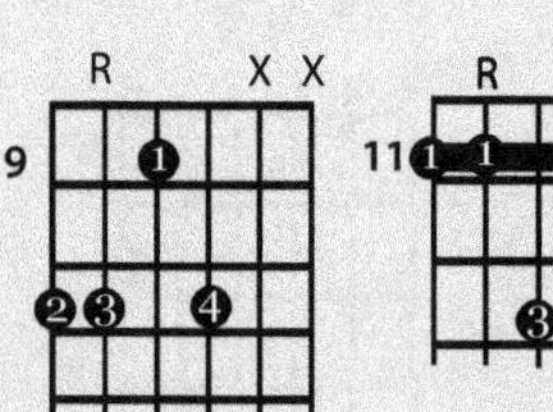

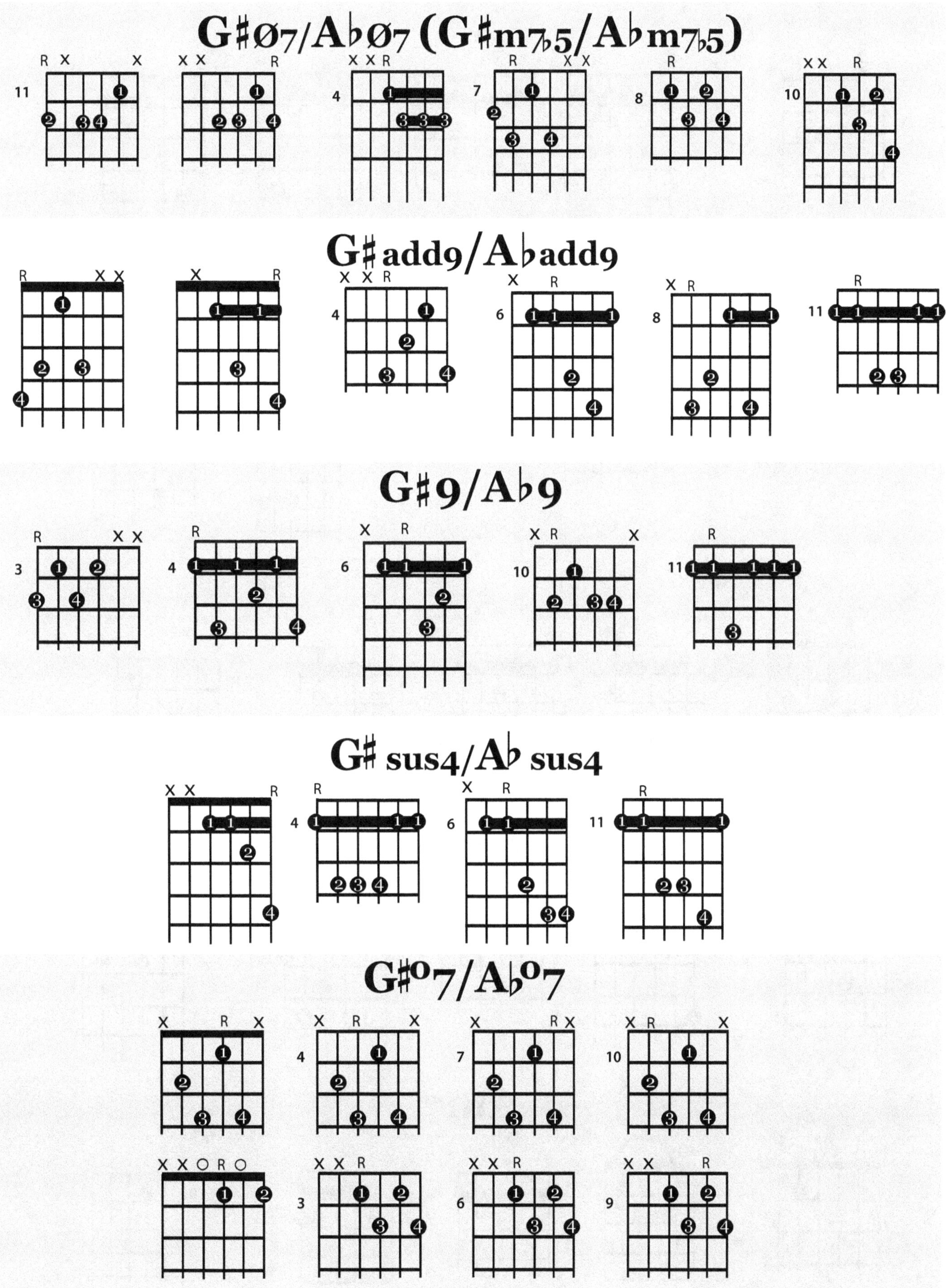
G♯ø7/A♭ø7 (G♯m7♭5/A♭m7♭5)
G♯add9/A♭add9
G♯9/A♭9
G♯ sus4/A♭ sus4
G♯o7/A♭o7

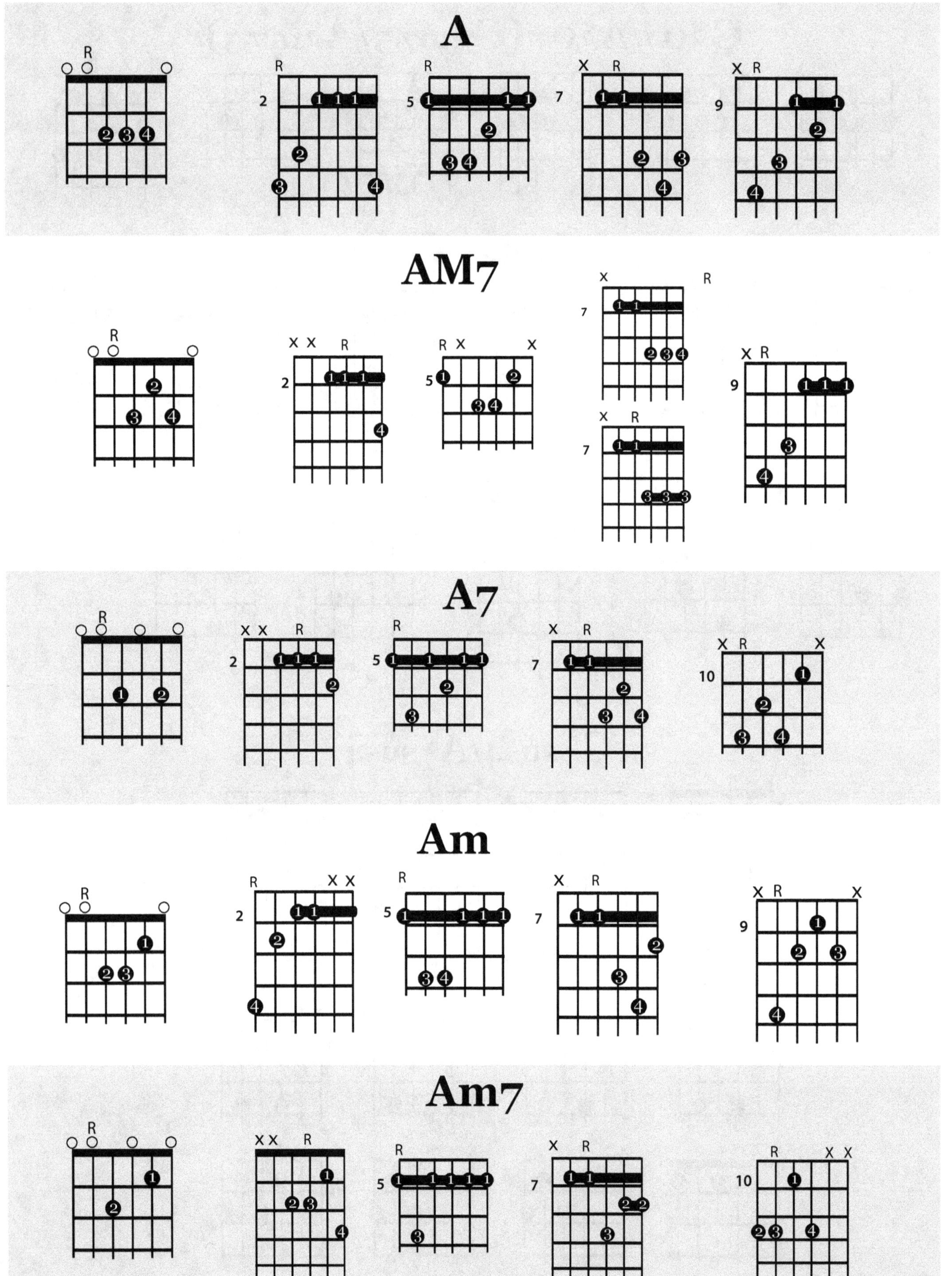
A
AM7
A7
Am
Am7

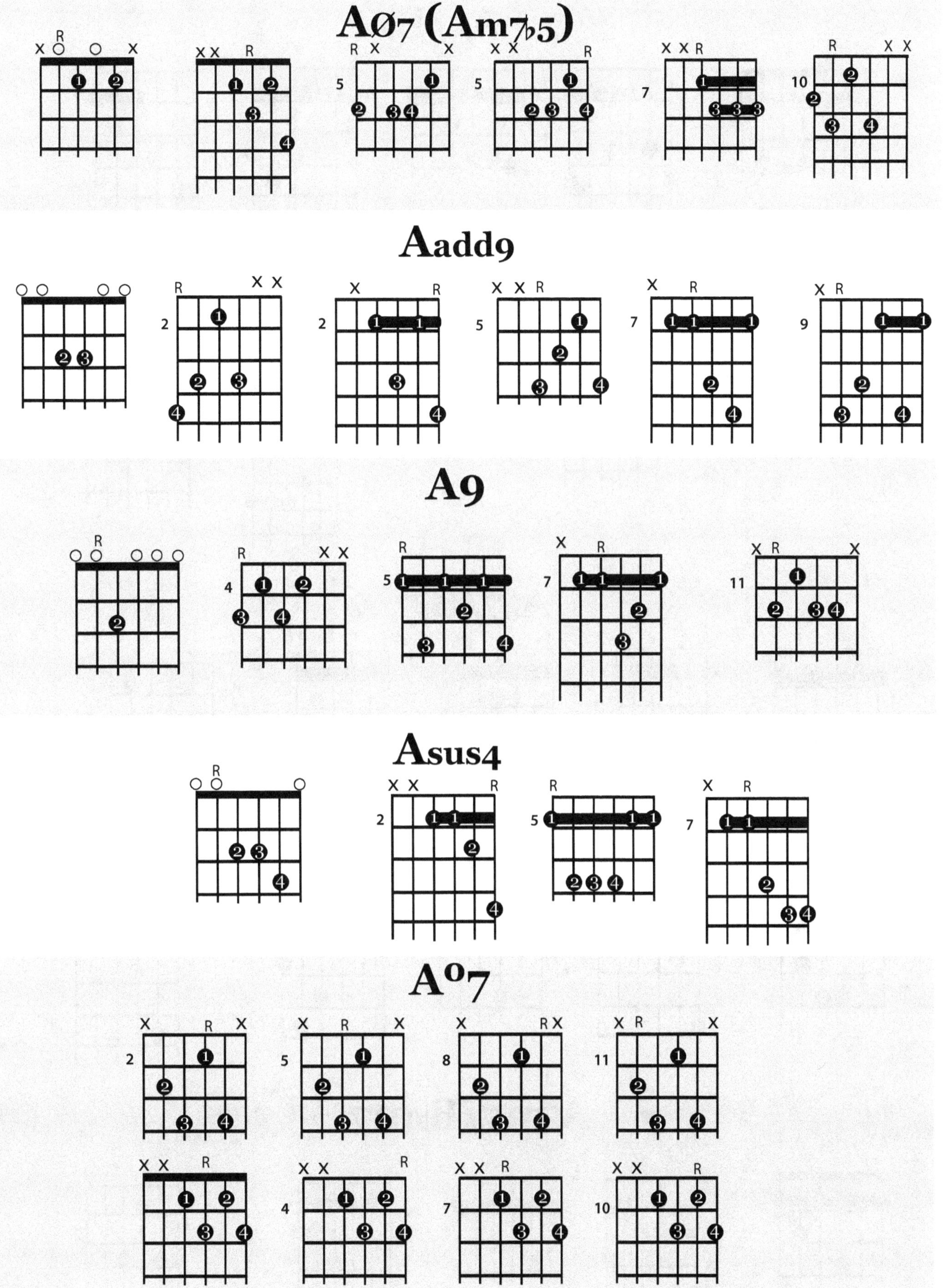
Aø7 (Am7♭5)
Aadd9
A9
Asus4
A°7

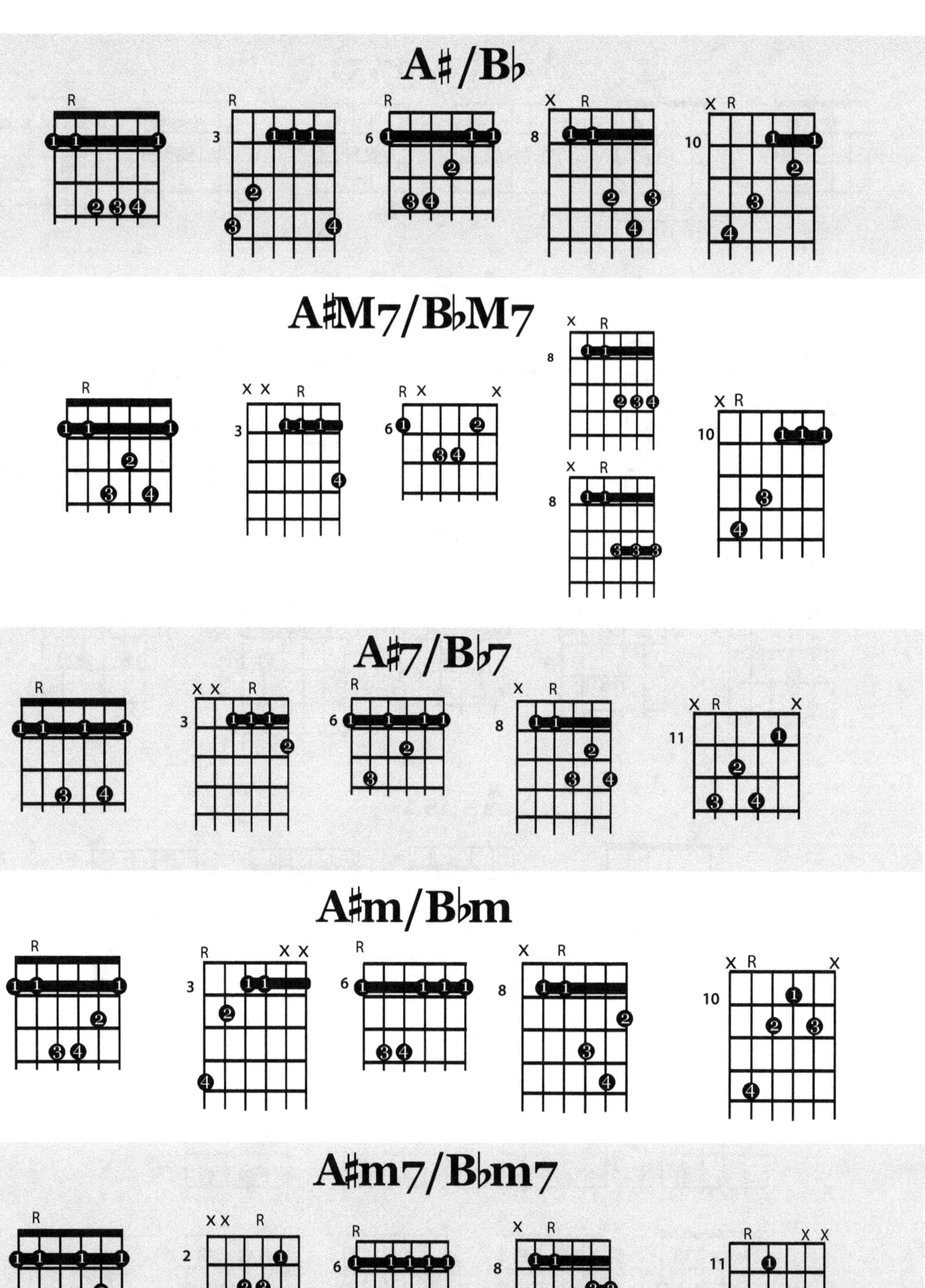
A♯/B♭
A♯M7/B♭M7
A♯7/B♭7
A♯m/B♭m
A♯m7/B♭m7

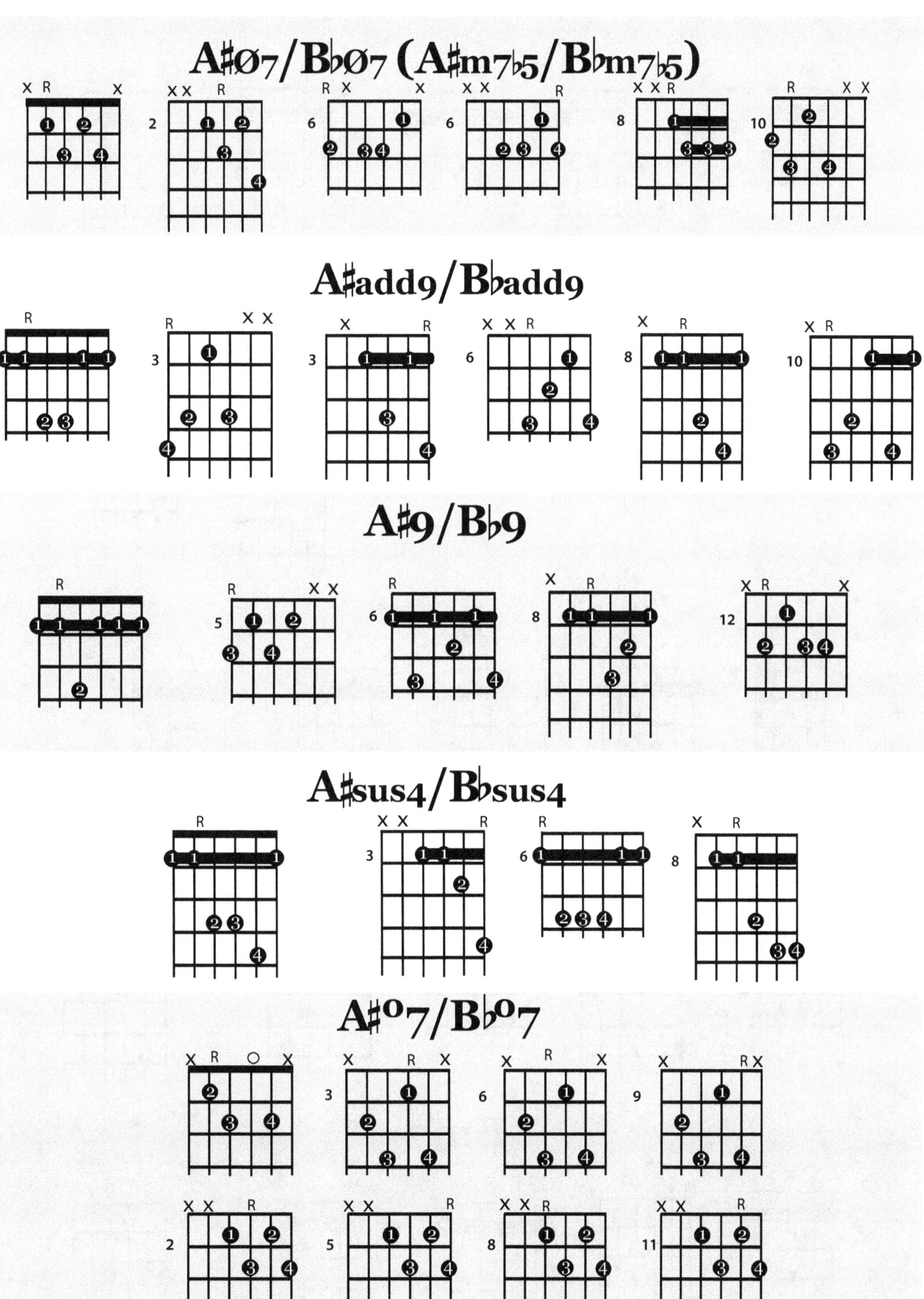
A♯ø7/B♭ø7 (A♯m7♭5/B♭m7♭5)
A♯add9/B♭add9
A♯9/B♭9
A♯sus4/B♭sus4
A♯°7/B♭°7

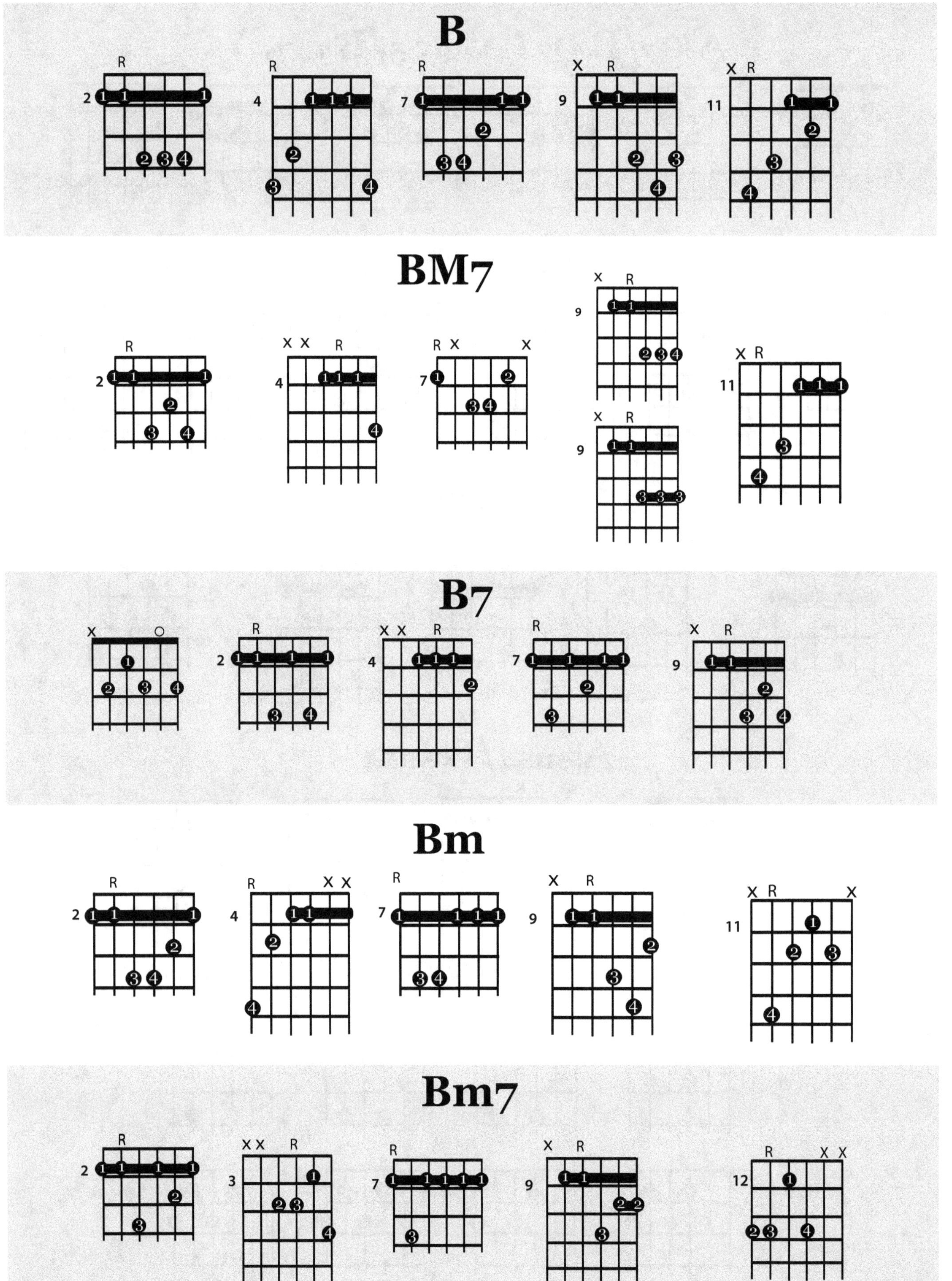
B
BM7
B7
Bm
Bm7

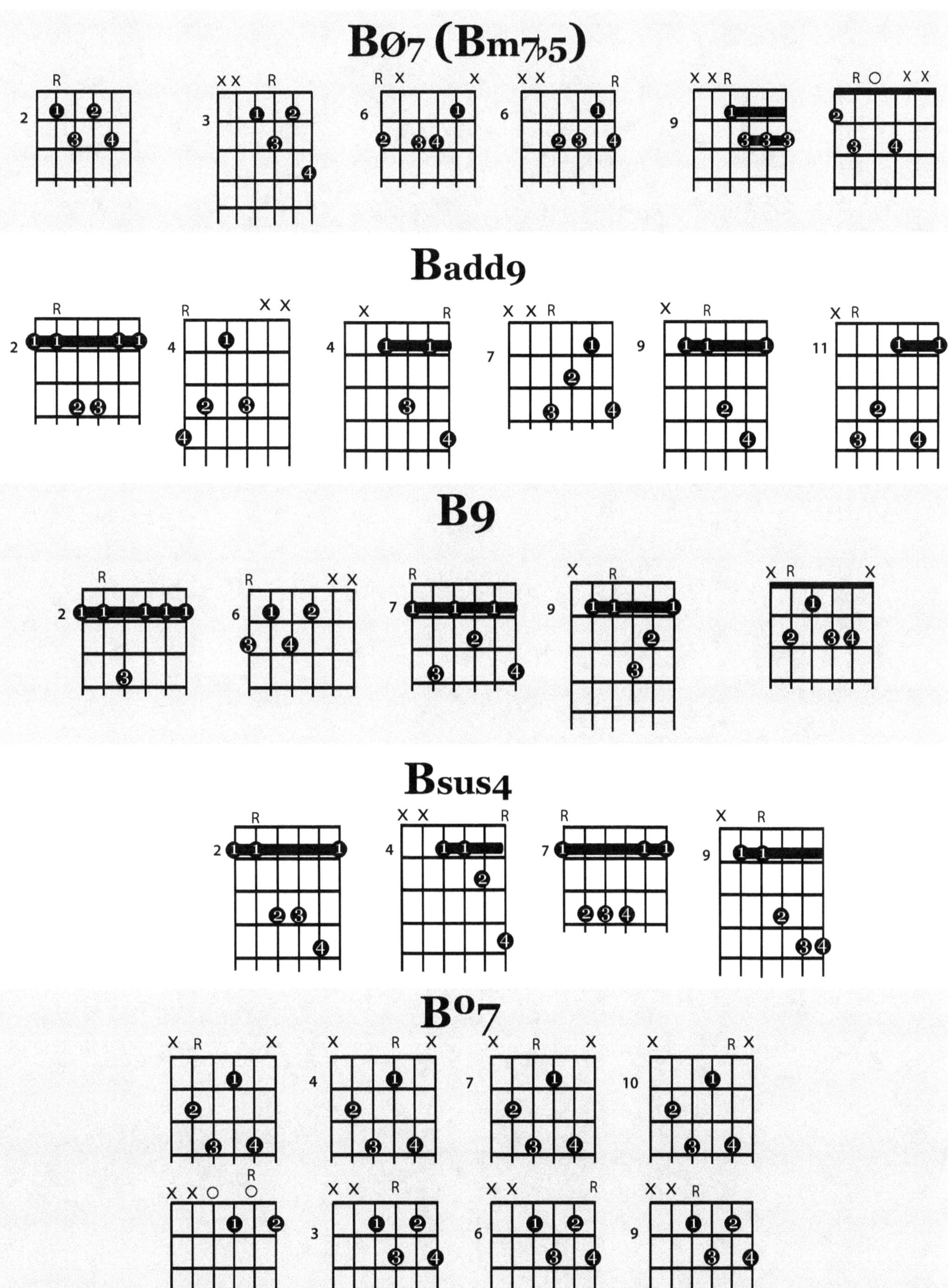
BØ7 (Bm7♭5)
Badd9
B9
Bsus4
B°7

www.ingramcontent.com/pod-product-compliance
Lightning Source LLC
LaVergne TN
LVHW061244100826
845148LV00008B/1018
* 9 7 8 0 9 6 5 2 9 9 9 0 9 *